T0223400

Communications
in Computer and Information Science 256

Tai-hoon Kim   Hojjat Adeli
Adrian Stoica   Byeong-Ho Kang (Eds.)

Control and Automation, and Energy System Engineering

International Conferences, CA and CES^3 2011
Held as Part of the Future Generation
Information Technology Conference, FGIT 2011
in Conjunction with GDC 2011
Jeju Island, Korea, December 8-10, 2011
Proceedings

 Springer

Volume Editors

Tai-hoon Kim
Hannam University, Daejeon, Korea
E-mail: taihoonn@empas.com

Hojjat Adeli
The Ohio State University, Columbus, OH, USA
E-mail: adeli.1@osu.edu

Adrian Stoica
Jet Propulsion Laboratory, Pasadena, CA, USA
E-mail: adrian.stoica@jpl.nasa.gov

Byeong-Ho Kang
University of Tasmania, Hobart, TAS, Australia
E-mail: byeong.kang@utas.edu.au

ISSN 1865-0929   e-ISSN 1865-0937
ISBN 978-3-642-26009-4   e-ISBN 978-3-642-26010-0
DOI 10.1007/978-3-642-26010-0
Springer Heidelberg Dordrecht London New York

Library of Congress Control Number: Applied for

CR Subject Classification (1998): C.2, H.4, D.2, I.2, F.2, F.1

Typesetting: Camera-ready by author, data conversion by Scientific Publishing Services, Chennai, India

Printed on acid-free paper

Springer is part of Springer Science+Business Media (www.springer.com)

Foreword

Control and Automation (CA), Circuits, Control, Communication, Electricity, Electronics, Energy, System, Signal and Simulation are areas that attract many professionals from academia and industry for research and development. The goal of the CA and CES^3 conferences is to bring together researchers from academia and industry as well as practitioners to share ideas, problems and solutions relating to the multifaceted aspects of this subject area.

We would like to express our gratitude to all of the authors of submitted papers and to all attendees for their contributions and participation.

We acknowledge the great effort of all the Chairs and the members of Advisory Boards and Program Committees of the above-listed event. Special thanks go to SERSC (Science and Engineering Research Support Society) for supporting this conference.

We are grateful in particular to the speakers who kindly accepted our invitation and, in this way, helped to meet the objectives of the conference.

December 2011   Chairs of CA 2011 and CES^3 2011

Preface

We would like to welcome you to the proceedings of the 2011 International Conference on Control and Automation (CA 2011) and Circuits, Control, Communication, Electricity, Electronics, Energy, System, Signal and Simulation (CES^3) – the partnering events of the Third International Mega-Conference on Future-Generation Information Technology (FGIT 2011) held during December 8–10, 2011, at Jeju Grand Hotel, Jeju Island, Korea.

CA 2011 focused on various aspects of advances in control and automation, while CES^3 focused on various aspects of advances in circuits, control, communication, electricity, electronics, energy, systems, signals and simulation. They provided a chance for academic and industry professionals to discuss recent progress in the related areas. We expect that the conferences and their publications will be a trigger for further related research and technology improvements in this important subject.

We would like to acknowledge the great effort of the CA 2011 and CES^3 2011 Chairs, Committees, Special Session Organizers, as well as all the organizations and individuals who supported the idea of publishing this volume of proceedings, including the SERSC and Springer.

We are grateful to the following keynote, plenary and tutorial speakers who kindly accepted our invitation: Hsiao-Hwa Chen (National Cheng Kung University, Taiwan), Hamid R. Arabnia (University of Georgia, USA), Sabah Mohammed (Lakehead University, Canada), Ruay-Shiung Chang (National Dong Hwa University, Taiwan), Lei Li (Hosei University, Japan), Tadashi Dohi (Hiroshima University, Japan), Carlos Ramos (Polytechnic of Porto, Portugal), Marcin Szczuka (The University of Warsaw, Poland), Gerald Schaefer (Loughborough University, UK), Jinan Fiaidhi (Lakehead University, Canada) and Peter L. Stanchev (Kettering University, USA), Shusaku Tsumoto (Shimane University, Japan), Jemal H. Abawajy (Deakin University, Australia).

We would like to express our gratitude to all of the authors and reviewers of submitted papers and to all attendees for their contributions and participation, and for believing in the need to continue this undertaking in the future.

Last but not the least, we give special thanks to Ronnie D. Caytiles and Yvette E. Gelogo of the graduate school of Hannam University, who contributed to the editing process of this volume with great passion.

This work was supported by the Korean Federation of Science and Technology Societies Grant funded by the Korean Government.

December 2011

Tai-hoon Kim
Hojjat Adeli
Adrian Stoica
Byeong-Ho Kang

Organization

Honorary Chair

Hojjat Adeli   Ohio State University, USA

General Chair

Adrian Stoica   NASA Jet Propulsion Laboratory, USA

Program Chairs

Byeong-Ho Kang   University of Tasmania, Australia
Tai-hoon Kim   GVSA and University of Tasmania, Australia

Publicity Chair

Aboul Ella Hassanien   Cairo University, Egypt

Publication Chair

Yongho Choi   Jungwon University, Korea

Program Committee

Albert Cheng
Alessandro Casavola
Barry Lennox
Bernard Grabot
Choonsuk Oh
Christian Schmid
Chun-Yi Su
DaeEun Kim
DongWon Kim
Feng-Li Lian
Guang-Ren Duan
Guoping Liu
Guo-Ying Gu

Gwi-Tae Park
Hideyuki Sawada
Hojjat Adeli
Hong Wang
Jong H. Park
Jong-Wook Kim
Jurek Sasiadek
Jus Kocijan
Kwan-Ho You
Kwon Soon Lee
Makoto Itoh
Manuel Haro Casado
Mitsuji Sampei

Myotaeg Lim
Peter Simon Sapaty
Pierre Borne
Pieter J. Mosterman
S.C. Kim
Soochan Kim
Thomas Parisini
Zhong-Ping Jiang
Zuwairie Ibrahim
Ronnie D. Caytiles
Yvette E. Gelogo

Special Session Organizers

Hak-Man Kim
Hae Young Lee

Table of Contents

Fuzzy Logic System Based Obstacle Avoidance
for a Mobile Robot

Sheng Jin and Byung-Jae Choi

School of Electronic Engineering,
Daegu University,
Jillyang Gyeongsan-city Gyeongbuk, Korea
jinshengqq@hotmail.com, bjchoi@daegu.ac.kr

Abstract. In this paper we present an obstacle avoidance control algorithm for mobile robot based on SFLC (simple fuzzy logic controller). With efficient fuzzy logic look-up table to replace the traditional complicated operation. This method has better performance than traditional methods in efficiency. The SFLC output of even a wheel to control direction and speed of obstacle avoidance. Set a number of obstacles on the path in the simulation. And let the robot automatically to the target. Experiments show that the robot has a good obstacle avoidance path and efficiency.

Keywords: fuzzy control; intelligent obstacle avoidance; mobile robot.

1   Introduction

Intelligent mobile robot is a robot working in a complex environment with the capabilities of self-planning, self-organizing and self-adapting. The core problem of its study is how to navigate and avoid obstacles. To achieve automatic control of robot's walking, first of all, it's necessary to fully perceive the surrounding environment information, and then convert it to control information in order to make sure that the robot can bypass all the obstacles safely during the move.

Obstacle avoidance control algorithms commonly used include: artificial potential field method, fuzzy logic, neural-network control and self-adaptive control, etc. Fuzzy logic method combines the robustness possessed by fuzzy control with the "perception - action" behavior based on physiology, which puts forward a more effective solution for mobile robots' navigation and obstacle avoidance in complex environments. Compared with the traditional control method, fuzzy control has more distinct advantage, better control capacity and robustness than PID does.

2   Architecture of Mobile Robot System

The used robot is a full autonomous wheeled robot intended for indoor environment. It has two identical parallel, wheels which are controlled by two independent DC gear motors. Also it assumed that each wheel is perpendicular to the ground and the contact between the wheels and the ground is pure rolling and non-slipping.

T.-h. Kim et al. (Eds.): CA/CES³ 2011, CCIS 256, pp. 1–6, 2011.
© Springer-Verlag Berlin Heidelberg 2011

The velocity of the center of mass of the robot is orthogonal to the wheels' axis - L. The center of mass of the mobile robot (x, y) is located in the middle of the axis connecting the wheels (L), likes in Fig. 1.

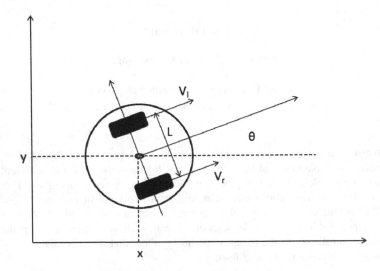

Fig. 1. Kinematics model of the robot

This robot type is relatively easy to model and build. The angular velocities (l and r) of the two wheels are independently controlled. The relationship between angular velocity and linear velocity:

$$V_L = r\,\omega_L, \quad V_R = r\,\omega_R$$

$$\omega = \frac{V_R - V_L}{L} = r\,\frac{\omega_R - \omega_L}{L}$$

$$v = \frac{V_R + V_L}{2} = r\,\frac{\omega_R + \omega_L}{2}$$

The sensors are mounted on the front platform at 60° one each other from the central axis, like in Fig. 2.

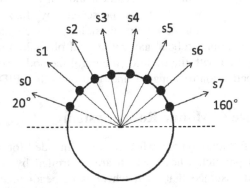

Fig. 2. Robotic perception system model

3   Fuzzy Controller Design

Fuzzy control system was born as the achievement of the rule-based expert system combined with traditional control, fuzzy set theory and control theory. It uses fuzzy controller (FC) to replace the traditional controller C, which is the main difference from the traditional control system. The basic block diagram of fuzzy control system is shown as Figure 3.

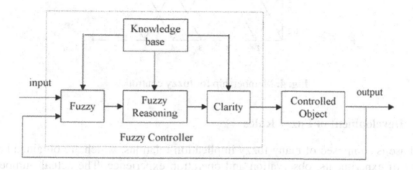

Fig. 3. Composition diagram of fuzzy controller

3.1   Determination of Input Variables and Output Variables

The fuzzy obstacle avoidance strategy adopted here is to make a compromise between the target reaching behavior and the obstacle avoidance behavior. The inputs to the fuzzy reasoning are the robot rotation angle (between robot orientation and robot target orientation) and the distances measured from obstacle to the orientation of sensors. The outputs are angular velocities of the two wheels.

3.2   Fuzzification

In this research the domain of distances dl, df and dr is constructed adopting linearization method after many tests. Linguistic variables such as "NB", "NM", "NS", "ZO", "PS", "PM" and "PB" are taken for seven-membership function. Figure 4(a) shows the membership function of distance. Similarly, the domain of robot target orientation angle θ is constructed with {NB, NM, NS, ZO, PS, PM, PB} and the membership function is shown in Figure 4(b). The domain of angular velocities of the two wheels is constructed with {SB, SM, SS, NO, FS, FM, FB} (SB signify "slow big", SM signify "slow middle", SS indicates "slow small", NO in token of "normal", FS signify "fast small", FM signify "fast middle" and FB signify "fast big") and the membership function is shown in Figure 4(c).

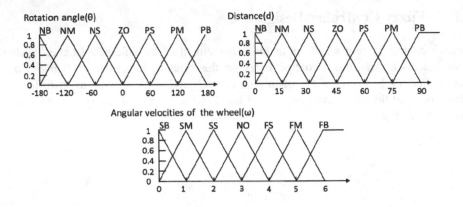

Fig. 4. Membership for fuzzy controller

3.3   Development of Fuzzy Rules

Rule base is composed of many fuzzy implication relations, which are obtained based on lots of experiments, observation and operation experience. The actual number of fuzzy rules should be taken depends on many factors, and the general principle is that on the premise of completeness, try to take less number of rules to simplify the design and implementation of fuzzy controller. The rule of fuzzy controller(SFLC) is shown as Figure 5.

$$D = \frac{\theta + \lambda d}{\sqrt{1+\lambda^2}}$$

D	NB	NM	NS	ZO	PS	PM	PB
u	FB	FM	FS	NO	SS	SM	SB

Fig. 5. Rule table for SFLC

3.4   Defuzzification

In the defuzzification process, the fuzzy quantity in fuzzy reasoning is converted into the accurate value needed in the actual control. Generally, there are several common methods: maximum membership grade, median clustering, average maximum membership grade and center of gravity, etc. This paper uses the center of gravity (COG).

$$\text{COG:} \qquad u^* = \frac{\int_u u \cdot C(u) du}{\int_u C(u) du}$$

4   Simulation and Experiment

In order to verify the validity and reliability of the proposed theory, this paper simulates the path planning. Firstly, write the simulation program, and then design the environment for the robot in Matlab R2010a. (0, 0) is starting point, (25, 25) is the destination. Set several obstacles in the path. The path planned during the simulation is shown as Figure 6, from which it can be seen that the robot avoided obstacles as it approached the obstacle, while it's in security zone, the robot planed a path similar to a straight line, turning to the target point. We can see that the robot can avoid the obstacle safely and reach the target point successfully and the Path is shorter than [9].

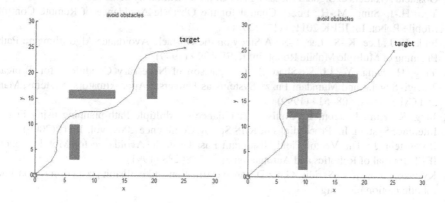

Fig. 6. Obstacle avoidance path

	Path(m)	Time(s)
Simulation1	41.5	55.6
Simulation2	43.8	59.7

Fig. 7. Path and time

5   Conclusion

In this paper, a fuzzy logic control system is developed for intelligent avoidance obstacle of mobile robot. The inputs to the fuzzy controller are: the angle between robot heading and robot target orientation and the distance between obstacle and robot. We proposed the SFLC(single-input fuzzy logic controller) method for energy-saving. Simulation results have demonstrated that the proposed fuzzy control system is low consumption and safe for the robot obstacle avoidance with optimal path.

References

1. Lee, C.C.: Fuzzy logic in control systems: Fuzzy logic controller—Part I & II. IEEE Trans. Syst., Man, Cybern. 20(2), 404–435 (1990)
2. Mamdani, E.H., Baaklini, N.: Prescriptive method for deriving control policy in a fuzzy-logic controller. Digital Object Identifier (1975)
3. Khatib, O.: Real-Time Obstacle Avoidance for manipulator and Mobile Robots. The International Journal of Robotic Research, 90–98 (1986)
4. Kim, D.-H., Oh, J.-H.: Globally asymptotically stable stracking control of mobile robots. In: Proc. of IEEE Int. Control Applications, pp. 1297–1301. IEEE Press, New York (1998)
5. Chae, M.-S., Jung, T.-Y., Kang, S.-B.: A Fuzzy Control of Autonomous Mobile Robot for Obstacle Avoidance. Signal Processing and Communication Systems (2005)
6. Yeo, H.-J., Sung, M.-H.: Fuzzy Control for the Obstacle Avoidance of Remote Control Mobile Robot. In: IEEK 2011, vol. 1 (2011)
7. Park, K.-J., Lee, K.-S., Lee, J.-S.: A Study on the Obstacle Avoidance Algorithm and Path Planning of Multiple Mobile Robot. In: KIEE 1999 (1999)
8. Ying, H., Ding, Y., Li, S., Shao, S.: Comparison of Necessary Conditions for Typical Takagi–Sugeno and Mamdani Fuzzy Systems as Universal Approximators. Systems, Man and Cybernetics, 508–514 (1999)
9. Jung, K., Kim, J., Jeon, T.: Collision Avoidance of Multiple Path-planning using Fuzzy Inference System. In: Proceedings of KIIS Spring Conference 2009, vol. 19(1) (2009)
10. Borenstein, J.: The Vector Field Histogram Fast Obstacle Avoidance for Mobile Robot. IEEE Journal of Robotics and Automation 7(3), 278–288 (1991)
11. Kyriakopoulos, K.J., Saridis, G.N.: Distance estimation and collision prediction for on-line robotic motion planning

Solving the Generalized Steiner Problem in Edge-Survivable Networks

Pablo Sartor and Franco Robledo

Instituto de Computación, Facultad de Ingeniería, Universidad de la República,
Julio Herrera y Reissig 565, Montevideo, Uruguay. CP 11.300
{psartor,frobledo}@fing.edu.uy
http://www.fing.edu.uy

Abstract. The Generalized Steiner Problem with Edge-Connectivity constraints (GSP-EC) consists of computing the minimal cost subnetwork of a given feasible network where some pairs of nodes must satisfy edge-connectivity requirements. It can be applied in the design of communications networks where connection lines can fail and is known to be an NP-Complete problem. In this paper we introduce an algorithm based on GRASP (Greedy Randomized Adaptive Search Procedure), a combinatorial optimization metaheuristic that has proven to be very effective for such problems. Promising results are obtained when testing the algorithm over a set of heterogeneous network topologies and connectivity requirements; in all cases with known optimal cost, optimal or near-optimal solutions are found.

Keywords: Network Design, Edge-Connectivity, Survivability, Steiner Problems, Metaheuristics, GRASP.

1 Introduction

The design of communication networks often involves two antagonistic goals. On one hand the resulting design must have the lowest possible cost; on the other hand, certain survability requirements must be met, i.e. the network must be capable to resist failures of some of its components. One way to do it is by specifying a connectivity level (a positive integer) and constraining the design process to only consider topologies that have at least that amount of disjoint paths (either edge or node disjoint) between each pair of nodes. In the most general case, the connectivity level can be fixed independently for each pair of nodes (heterogeneous connectivity requirements), some of them having even no requirement at all. This problem is known as Generalized Steiner Problem (GSP) [10] and it is an NP-Complete problem [18]. Some references on the GSP and related problems can be found in are [1], [2], [3], [4], [6], [11], [12], [19], [20] most of them using polyhedral approaches and addressing particular cases (specific types of topology and or connectivity levels). Topologies verifying edge-disjoint path connectivity constraints ensure that the network can survive failures in the connection lines; while node-disjoint path constraints ensure that the network can survive failures both in switch sites as well as in connection lines.

T.-h. Kim et al. (Eds.): CA/CES³ 2011, CCIS 256, pp. 7–16, 2011.

Finding a minimal cost subnetwork satisfying edge-connectivity requirements is modeled as a GSP edge-connected (GSP-EC) problem; whereas the corresponding problem involving node-connectivity requirements is known as the GSP-NC (node-connected) problem. The remainder of this paper is organized as follows. Notation, auxiliary definitions and formal definition of the GSP-EC are introduced in Section II. The GRASP metaheuristic and the particular implementation that we propose for the GSP-EC are presented in Section III. Experimental results obtained when applying the algorithms on a test set of GSP-EC instances with up to one hundred nodes and four hundred edges are presented in Section IV. Finally conclusions are presented in Section V.

2   Problem Formalization

We use the following notation to formalize the GSP-EC. $G = (V, E, C)$: simple undirected graph with weighted edges. V: nodes of G. E: edges of G. C : $E \rightarrow \mathbb{R}^+$: edge weights. $T \subseteq V$: terminal nodes (the ones for which connectivity requirements exist). $R : R \in \mathbb{Z}^{|T| \times |T|}$: symmetrical integer matrix of connectivity requirements; $r_{ij} = r_{ji} \geq 0, \forall i, j \in T; r_{ii} = 0, \forall i \in T$. The set V models existing sites among which a certain set E of feasible links could be deployed, being the cost of including a certain link in the solution given by the matrix C. The set T models those sites for which at least one connectivity requirement involving other site has to be met; these requirements are specified using the matrix R. Nodes in the set $V \setminus T$ (known as "Steiner nodes") model sites that can potentially be used but for which no requirements exist. Using this notation the GSP-EC can be defined as follows. **GSP-EC**: Given the graph G with edge weights C, the terminals set T and the connectivity requirements matrix R, the objective is to find a minimum cost subgraph $G_T = (V, E_T, C)$ of G where every pair of terminals i, j is connected by r_{ij} edge-disjoint paths.

3   The GRASP Metaheuristic

GRASP (Greedy Randomized Adaptive Search Procedure) is a metaheuristic that proved to perform very well for a variety of combinatorial optimization problems. A GRASP is an iterative "multistart local optimization" procedure which performs two consecutive phases during each iteration: **Construction Phase**: it builds a feasible solution that chooses (following some randomized criteria) which elements to add from a list of candidates defined with some greedy approach; **Local Search Phase**: it explores the neigborhood of the feasible solution delivered by the Construction Phase, moving consecutively to lower cost solutions until a local optimum is reached. Typical parameters are the size of the list of candidates, the amount of iterations to run *MaxIter* and a seed for random number generation. After having run *MaxIter* iterations the procedure returns the best solution found. Details about this metaheuristic can be found in [21], [13]. In the next sections we introduce algorithms for implementing the Construction and Local Search Phases, as well as the main GSP algorithm invoking both phases to solve the GSP-EC.

3.1   Construction Phase Algorithm

The algorithm, shown in Figure 1, is an improvement for the edge-connected case over the one found in [14]. It proceeds by building a graph which satisfies the requirements of the matrix R; it starts with an edgeless graph and in each iteration one new path is added to the solution G_{sol} under construction. The matrix $M = (m_{ij})_{i,j \in T}$ records the amount of connection requirements not yet satisfied in G_{sol} between the terminal nodes i and j; the sets P_{ij} record the r_{ij} disjoint paths found for connecting the nodes i, j; and an auxiliary matrix $A = \{A_{ij}\}$ records how many times it was impossible to find one more path between two terminal nodes i, j whose requirements r_{ij} were not yet covered. An improvement over the one in [14] is that by altering the costs in line 2 we ensure the existence of a non-zero probability of building an optimal solution regardless of what the problem instance is. We have proven that a sufficient condition is that all edges have their costs altered independently with any probability distribution assigning non-zero probabilities to any open subinterval of $(0, +\infty)$. A complete proof can be found in an extended version of this paper ([16]) as well as examples of instances (even trivial ones) for which this is not accomplished by previous algorithms. Moreover, by altering costs our proposed algorithm proceeds by just computing the shortest path in its main loop, instead of computing a set of "simultaneously disjoint shortest paths" and then randomly choosing one (as in previous algorithms), thus involving less computing.

3.2   Local Search Phase Algorithms

The local search phase starts with a feasible solution obtained from the construction phase and proceeds by consecutively moving to neighbour solutions which reduce the cost of the solution graph until it reaches a local optimum. Any local search algorithm needs a precise definition of the neighbourhood concept; we propose two different ones, which we chain inside our suggested LocalSearchPhase algorithm. They are defined in terms of a structural decomposition of graphs based on the following components. Given a GSP-EC instance and a feasible solution G_{sol}, we define a **key-node** as a non-terminal node with degree at least three in G_{sol}; a **key-path** as a path in G_{sol} such that all intermediate nodes are non-terminal with degree two in G_{sol} and whose endpoints are either terminal nodes or key-nodes; and given a GSP-EC instance, a feasible solution G_{sol} and any node v of G_{sol}, we define as the **key-star** associated to v the subgraph of G_{sol} obtained through the union of all key-paths with v as an endpoint.

Path-Based Local Search Neighbourhood. Our first neighbourhood is based on the replacement of any key-path k by another key-path with the same endpoints, built with any edge from the feasible connections graph G (even some of G_{sol}), provided no connectivity levels are lost when reusing edges. Let k be a key-path of a certain solution G_{sol} and P a set of paths which "certificates" its feasibility (as the one returned by ConstPhase). We will denote by $J_k(G_{sol})$ the set of paths $\{p \in P : k \subseteq p\}$. These are the paths which contain the key-path k. We will also denote by $\chi_k(G_{sol})$ the edge set

Procedure ConstPhase(G, C, T, R)

1: $G_{sol} \leftarrow (T, \emptyset); m_{ij} \leftarrow r_{ij} \forall i, j \in T; P_{ij} \leftarrow \emptyset \forall i, j \in T; A_{ij} \leftarrow 0 \forall i, j \in T$
2: $C \leftarrow$alter-costs(C)
3: **while** $\exists m_{ij} > 0 : A_{ij} <$MAX_ATTEMPT **do**
4:     let i, j be any two terminals with $m_{ij} > 0$
5:     $G' \leftarrow G \setminus P_{ij}$
6:     let $C' = (c'_{uv}) : c'_{uv} \leftarrow$ [0 if $(u, v) \in G_{sol}; c_{uv}$ otherwise]
7:     $p \leftarrow$ shortest-path(G', C', i, j)
8:     **if** $\not\exists p$ **then**
9:         $A_{ij} \leftarrow A_{ij} + 1; P_{ij} \leftarrow \emptyset; m_{ij} \leftarrow r_{ij}$
10:     **else**
11:         $G_{sol} \leftarrow G_{sol} \cup \{p\}$
12:         $P_{ij} \leftarrow P_{ij} \cup \{p\}; m_{ij} \leftarrow m_{ij} - 1$
13:         $[P, M] \leftarrow$ general-update-matrix(G_{sol}, P, M, p, i, j)
14:     **end if**
15: **end while**
16: **return** G_{sol}, P

Fig. 1. ConstPhase pseudo-code

$$\chi_k(G_{sol}) = \bigcup_{q=i...j \in J_k(G_{sol})} E(P_{ij} \setminus q) \qquad (1)$$

where $i...j$ stands for a path with extremes i and j. These are the edges that, if used to replace the key-path k in P (obtaining a path set P'), would turn to be shared by some paths from G_{sol} with the same endpoints, thus invalidating the resulting set P' as a feasibility certificate. We can now define our first neighbourhood.

Definition 1. Neighbourhood1: *Given a GSP-EC instance and a feasible solution G_{sol}, it is the set of all graphs obtained by replacing any key-path k of G_{sol} by another path p such that $cost(p) < cost(k)$ and the edges of p are chosen from the set $E \setminus \chi_k(G_{sol})$ and/or k. (Recall that E represents the feasible edges between nodes).*

Based on these definitions we built the path-based local search algorithm LocalSearchPhase1 shown in Figure 2. After computing the decomposition in key-nodes and key-paths of the set S, loop 3-20 looks for succesive cost improvements until no more can be done. The iterations proceed by analyzing each key-path k, trying to find a suitable replacement with lower cost for it. Line 6 computes the edge set $E(k) \cup (E \setminus \chi_k(S))$, where edges are to be chosen from to build the replacing key-path. This set is such that, as seen above, ensures no loss of connectivity levels in the new solution obtained, while allowing the reuse of edges already present in the current solution S. Line 7 computes a new cost matrix C' where the cost of all edges of $S \setminus k$ are zeroed (reusing them will add no extra cost). Line 8 computes the path with lower cost according to the matrix C'

over the subgraph computed in line 6. Line 9 verifies if the adoption of the new key-path implies a cost reduction. If so, it is acknowledged by the flag *improve* and k is replaced in all paths of S which included k. Care is taken to remove cycles and recompute the k-decomposition if a certain node happens to have a degree greater than two after the replacement (lines 12-14); if the latter does not happen, line 16 simply updates the k-decomposition by replacing the key-path (and a full new k-decomposition is avoided). After exiting the main loop, line 21 returns a feasible solution whose cost can no more be reduced by moving to neighbour solutions.

Procedure LocalSearchPhase1(G, C, T, S)

```
 1: improve ← TRUE
 2: κ ← k-decompose(S)
 3: while improve do
 4:    improve ← FALSE
 5:    for all kpath k ∈ κ with endpoints u, v do
 6:       G' ← the subgraph induced from G by E(k) ∪ (E \ χ_k(S))
 7:       C' ← (c'_{ij})/c'_{ij} = 0 if (i, j) ∈ S \ k; c'_{ij} = c_{ij} otherwise
 8:       k' ← shortest-path(G', C', u, v)
 9:       if cost(k', C') < cost(k, C') then
10:          improve ← TRUE
11:          update S : ∀p ∈ J_k(S)(p ← (p \ k) ∪ k')
12:          if ∃z ∈ V(k'), z ∉ {u, v}, degree(z) ≥ 3 in S then
13:             remove-cycles(J_k(S))
14:             κ ← k-decompose(S)
15:          else
16:             κ ← κ \ {k} ∪ {k'}
17:          end if
18:       end if
19:    end for
20: end while
21: return S
```

Fig. 2. LocalSearchPhase1 pseudo-code

Key-Star-Based Local Search Neighbourhood.

Our second neighbourhood is based on the replacement of key-stars, which frequently allow to improve feasible solutions that are locally optimal when only considering Neighbourhood1. In the case of the GSP-NC, as no node sharing is allowed among disjoint paths, all key-stars are trees (named *key-trees*); a key-tree replacement neighbourhood for the GSP-NC can be found in [15], [14]. Due to the possibilty of sharing nodes among edge-disjoint paths, when working with GSP-EC problems, we have to work with key-stars, and unlike [15] we will allow the root node to be a terminal node in order to get a broader neighbourhood. In the GSP-NC any key-tree can be replaced by any tree with the same leaves with no loss of connectivity levels. In the GSP-EC, if the replacing structure is also a key-star the same holds true; but it does not for other general structures (non-star trees included). We propose an algorithm that given a key-star k, deterministically seeks for the lowest cost replacing key-star k' able to "repair" the paths from P broken when removing the edges of k. Let k be a key-star in a certain feasible solution G_{sol} and P a set of paths which "certificates" its feasibility (as the one returned by ConstPhase). For allowing as much reusing of edges as possible, we can extend our previous definition of $J_k(G_{sol})$ and $\chi_k(G_{sol})$ to consider key-stars k instead of key-paths; and thus we can define the key-star based neighbourhood as follows.

Definition 2. Neighbourhood2: *Given a GSP-EC instance and a feasible solution G_{sol}, it is the set of all graphs obtained by replacing any key-star k of G_{sol} by the lowest possible cost key-star k' such that k' preserves the same connectivity among the leaves of k and its terminal nodes, and the edges of k' are chosen from the set $E \setminus \chi_k(G_{sol})$ and/or k.*

We present the star-based local search algorithm LocalSearchPhase2 in Figure 3. It looks at the k-stars given by the k-decomposition of S, determining for each one the best key-star able to replace it, until an improvement is obtained. To do so the procedure BestKeyStar (shown in Figure 3) is used. Given a key-star k we denote by θ_k its root node; by ψ_k the set of its leaf nodes; and by $\hat{\delta}_{k,m}$ (being m the root node of k or one of its leaves) the highest amount of key-paths that join m in k with any other node that is root or leaf in k. The algorithm is based on the idea of building key-stars by employing the simult-shortest-paths algorithm (in our tests we used the one introduced in [5]). Lines 1-2 compute the subgraph of G obtained by removing the edges that could cause loss of connectivity level if reused; the altered cost matrix C' with cost zero for reused edges; and adds a virtual node w whose purpose is explained below. Lines 4-7 determine the set of leaf nodes that the key-star to build must have. Lines 8-10 connect each of the latter to w with an appropriate number of parallel zero-cost edges totalling $\delta_{G',w}$ (degree of w in G') edges. The loop 12-17 considers nodes of G that could be potencial roots z of the key-star to be found, and then builds the lowest-cost one with root node z through the application of the already mentioned simult-shortest-path algorithm on the graph G' in line 13; $\delta_{G',w}$ edge-disjoint paths connecting z and w are requested. If found (lines 14-16) and with lower cost than k then the new key-star and its associated cost are recorded as the best ones so far found. After having considered all possible root nodes, line 18 returns both the best key-star and its cost according to C'. The process is depicted in Figure 4, where a key-star connecting the nodes t, u, v is replaced by another one with root node z.

3.3   GRASP Algorithm Description

Finally we can put together the pieces building a GRASP algorithm to solve the GSP-EC, using a compund local search phase that will operate by applying

Procedure LocalSearchPhase2
(G, C, T, S)

1: $improve \leftarrow$ TRUE
2: $\kappa \leftarrow$ k-decompose(S)
3: **while** $improve$ **do**
4:    $improve \leftarrow$ FALSE
5:    **for all** kstar $k \in \kappa$ **do**
6:       $[k', nCost] \leftarrow$
      BestKeyStar(G, C, T, S, k)
7:       **if** $nCost < cost(k, C)$ **then**
8:          $improve \leftarrow$ TRUE
9:          replace k by k' in all paths
         from S
10:        $\kappa \leftarrow$ k-decompose(S)
11:        **abort for all**
12:       **end if**
13:    **end for**
14: **end while**
15: **return** S

Procedure BestKeyStar(G, C, T, S, k)

1: $G' \leftarrow$ the subgraph induced from G by
   $E(k) \cup (E \setminus \chi_k(S))$
2: $C' \leftarrow (c'_{ij})/c'_{ij} = 0$ if $(i, j) \in S \setminus$
   $k; c'_{ij} = c_{ij}$ otherwise
3: add a "virtual node" w to G'
4: $\Omega \leftarrow \psi_k$
5: **if** $\theta_k \in T$ **then**
6:    $\Omega \leftarrow \Omega \cup \{\theta_k\}$
7: **end if**
8: **for all** $m \in \Omega$ **do**
9:    add $\hat{\delta}_{k,m}$ parallel edges (w, m) to G'
   with cost 0
10: **end for**
11: $c_{min} \leftarrow 0; k_{min} \leftarrow k$
12: **for all** $z \in V(G)$ **do**
13:    $k' \leftarrow$ simult-shortest-paths$(G', \delta_{G',w}, z, w)$
14:    **if** k' has $\delta_{G,w}$ paths $\wedge$ $cost(k', C') <$
   c_{min} **then**
15:       $c_{min} \leftarrow cost(k', C'); k_{min} \leftarrow k'$
16:    **end if**
17: **end for**
18: **return** $[k_{min}, c_{min}]$

Fig. 3. LocalSearchPhase2 pseudo-code

key-path movements until no further improvements are possible followed by a (single) key-star replacement, and so on. The cycle is repeated until no further improvements are found with none of both movements. Pseduo-code for the algorithm can be found in [16].

4 Performance Tests

This section presents the results obtained after testing our algorithms with twenty-one test cases. The algorithms were implemented in C/C++ and tested on a 2 GB RAM, Intel Core 2 Duo, 2.0 GHz machine running Microsoft Windows Vista. All instances were run with the parameter $MaxIters$ set to 100. To our best knowledge, no library containing benchmark instances related to the GSP-NC nor GSP-EC exists; we have built a set of twenty-one test cases that are based in cases found in the following public libraries: **Steinlib** [7]: instances of the Steiner problem; in many cases the optimal solution is known, in others the best solution known is available; **Tsplib** [8]: instances of diverse graph theory

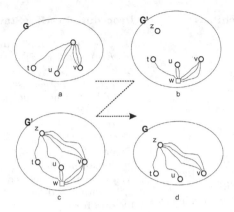

Fig. 4. Computing the best key-star

related problems, including a "Traveling Salesman Problem" section. The main characteristics of the twenty-one test cases are shown in Table 1. For each case we show the amount of nodes (V), feasible edges (E), terminal nodes (T) and Steiner (non terminal) nodes (St). We also show the level of edge-connectivity requirements *Redund.* (one, two, three or mixed) and the optimal costs *Opt* when available. Details about the twenty-one instances can be found in [16]; as well as source data and best solutions found in [17]. Computational results of the tests can be found in Table 1 under the following columns. *Reqs*: total amount of terminal-to-terminal disjoint paths found in the best solution (which, if the feasible connections network is compatible with all the requirements given by R, should amount $\sum_{i,j} r_{ij}/2$; *t(ms)*: average running time (in ms) per iteration; *Cost*: cost of the best solution found; *LSI*: "local search improvement", the percentage of cost improvement achieved by the local search phase when compared to the cost of the solution delivered by the construction phase, for the best solution found. In all cases with connectivity requirements equal to one (1-EC) for all pairs of terminals (for which the optimal costs are known) every best solution found is optimal, with the exception of the case hc-6p-r1 (found cost 4033 being the optimal cost 4003). Note also that the average cost improvement over the solution delivered by ConstPhase (LSI) amounts to 6.7% (when computed only for the best solutions found). All solutions found are edge-minimal regarding feasibility (no edge can be supressed without losing required connectivity levels); and in all cases the maximum possible number of requirements are satisfied (i.e. for all pairs of terminals i, j, whether their requirement r_{ij} was satisfied or f_{ij} disjoint paths were found being f_{ij} the maximum achievable amount of disjoint paths joining i and j given by the topology of the feasible connections graph G).

Table 1. Test Cases and Numerical Results

Case	V	E	T	St	Redund.	Opt	Reqs.	t(ms)	Cost	%LSI
b01-r1	50	63	9	41	1-EC	82	36	77	82	3.0
b01-r2	50	63	9	41	2-EC	NA	42	80	98	3.4
b03-r1	50	63	25	25	1-EC	138	300	2611	138	10.6
b03-r2	50	63	25	25	2-EC	NA	378	3108	188	4.1
b05-r1	50	100	13	37	1-EC	61	78	298	61	9.2
b05-r2	50	100	13	37	2-EC	NA	144	1389	120	5.2
b11-r1	75	150	19	56	1-EC	88	171	1477	88	13.8
b11-r2	75	150	19	56	2-EC	NA	324	4901	180	3.4
b17-r1	100	200	25	75	1-EC	131	300	6214	131	10.2
b17-r2	100	200	25	75	2-EC	NA	531	15143	244	3.0
cc3-4p-r1	64	288	8	56	1-EC	2338	28	388	2338	10.0
cc3-4p-r3	64	288	8	56	3-EC	NA	84	2221	5991	4.6
cc6-2p-r1	64	192	12	52	1-EC	3271	66	2971	3271	2.4
cc6-2p-r2	64	192	12	52	2-EC	NA	132	4801	5962	10.2
cc6-2p-r123	64	192	12	52	1,2,3-EC	NA	140	6317	8422	9.8
hc-6p-r1	64	192	32	32	1-EC	4003	496	25314	4033	6.8
hc-6p-r2	64	192	32	32	2-EC	NA	992	28442	6652	3.5
hc-6p-r123	64	192	32	32	1,2,3-EC	NA	957	26551	7930	5.2
bayg29-r2	29	406	11	18	2-EC	NA	110	975	6856.88	4.6
bayg29-r3	29	406	11	18	3-EC	NA	165	2413	11722	4.2
att48-r2	48	300	10	38	2-EC	NA	90	1313	23214	13.0
Averages							265	6524	-	6.7

5 Conclusion

The algorithm GRASP_GSP was shown to find good quality solutions to the
GSP-EC when applied to a series of heterogeneous test cases with up to 100
nodes and up to 406 edges. It was also shown to guarantee for all instances a
non-zero probability of finding an optimal solution avoiding local optima traps
(see [16]). For all cases with known optimal cost the algorithm was able to find
solutions with costs no more than 0,74% higher than the optimal cost. Significant
cost reductions are achieved after applying the local search phase over the greedy
solutions built by the construction phase. Execution times were comparable to
the ones of previous similar works like [15] for the node-connected version of the
GSP.

References

1. Agrawal, A., Klein, P., Ravi, R.: When trees collide: An approximation algorithm for the generalized steiner problem on networks. SIAM Journal on Computing 24(3), 440–456 (1995)

2. Baïou, M., Mahjoub, A.R.: Steiner 2-edge connected subgraph polytope on series-parallel graphs. SIAM Journal on Discrete Mathematics 10(1), 505–514 (1997)
3. Baïou, M.: Le problème du sous-graphe Steiner 2-arête connexe: Approche polyédrale. PhD thesis, Université de Rennes I, Rennes, France (1996)
4. Baïou, M.: On the dominant of the Steiner 2-edge connected subgraph polytope. Discrete Applied Mathematics 112(1-3), 3–10 (2001)
5. Bhandari, R.: Optimal physical diversity algorithms and survivable networks. In: Proceedings of the Second IEEE Symposium on Computers and Communications, pp. 433–441 (July 1997)
6. Coullard, C.R., Rais, A., Wagner, D.K., Rardin, R.L.: Linear-time algorithms for the 2-Connected Steiner Subgraph Problem on Special Classes of Graphs. Networks 23(1), 195–206 (1993)
7. Koch, T.: Konrad-Zuse-Zentrum fr Informationstechnik Berlin. Steinlib test data library, http://steinlib.zib.de/steinlib.php
8. Ruprecht-Karls-Universitat Heidelberg. Tsplib network optimization problems library, http://comopt.ifi.uni-heidelberg.de/software/TSPLIB95
9. Kerivin, H., Mahjoub, A.: Design of Survivable Networks: A survey. Networks 46(1), 1–21 (2005)
10. Krarup, J.: The generalized steiner problem. Technical report, DIKU, University of Copenhagen (1979)
11. Mahjoub, A.R., Pesneau, P.: On the Steiner 2-edge connected subgraph polytope. RAIRO Operations Research 42(1), 259–283 (2008)
12. Monma, C.L., Munson, B.S., Pulleyblank, W.R.: Minimum-weight two connected spanning networks. Mathematical Programming 46(1), 153–171 (1990)
13. Resende, M.G.C., Ribeiro, C.C.: Greedy randomized adaptive search procedures. In: Glover, F., Kochenberger, G. (eds.) Handbook of Metaheuristics, pp. 219–249. Kluwer Academic Publishers (2003)
14. Robledo, F., Canale, E.: Designing backbone networks using the generalized steiner problem. In: 7th International Workshop on Design of Reliable Communication Networks, DRCN 2009, vol. 1, pp. 327–334 (October 2009)
15. Robledo, F.: GRASP heuristics for Wide Area Network design. PhD thesis, IRISA, Université de Rennes I, Rennes, France (February 2005)
16. Sartor, P.: Technical Report RT 11-09, Universidad de la República, Montevideo, Uruguay (2011),
http://www.fing.edu.uy/inco/pedeciba/bibliote/reptec/TR1109.pdf
17. Universidad de Montevideo. GSP-EC test set with best results found,
http://www2.um.edu.uy/psartor/grasp-gsp-ec.zip
18. Winter, P.: Steiner problem in networks: a survey. Networks 17(2), 129–167 (1987)
19. Stoer, M.: Design of survivable networks. Lecture Notes in Mathematics, vol. 1531. Springer, Heidelberg (1992)
20. Kerivin, H., Mahjoub, R.: Design of survivable networks: A survey. Networks 46(1), 1–21 (2005)
21. Feo, T.A., Resende, M.G.C.: Greedy Randomized Adaptive Search Procedures. Journal of Global Optimization 6, 109–133 (1995)

A Note on Practically Output Tracking Control of Nonlinear Systems That May Not Be Linearizable at the Origin

Keylan Alimhan[1] and Naohisa Otsuka[2]

[1] School of Science and Engineering, Tokyo Denki University,
Hatoyama-Machi, Hiki-Gun, Saitama 350-0394, Japan
keylan@live.jp
[2] Division of Science, School of Science and Engineering,
Tokyo Denki University,
Hatoyama-Machi, Hiki-Gun, Saitama 350-0394, Japan
otsuka@mail.dendai.ac.jp

Abstract. This paper studies a globally practical output tracking control of nonlinear systems in the strict-feedback form, whose chained integrator part has the power of positive odd rational numbers. Since the power is not restricted to be larger than or equal to one, the linearization of the system at the origin may fail. Nevertheless, it is proved that, under mild assumptions, globally practical output-tracking is achievable by continuous (possibly non differentiable) state feedback.

Keywords: Nonlinear Systems, Practical Output Tracking , Continuous State Feedback.

1 Introduction

Output tracking control is one of the most important problems in control theory, and lots of efforts have been made to this problems during the last decades. With the help of the nonlinear output regulator theory [1],[2] and the method of adding a power integrator [3]-[5], series of research results have been obtained [6]-[8].

This paper deals with the practical output tracking problem with a state feedback for a class of nonlinear systems having the following form:

$$\dot{z}_i = z_{i+1}^{p_i} + \phi_i(z_1,....z_i), \quad i = 1,...,n-1,$$
$$\dot{z}_n = u^{p_n} + \phi_n(z_1,....z_{n-1}, z_n), \qquad (1)$$
$$y = z_1,$$

where $z = (z_1,...,z_n)^T \in R^n$ and $u \in R$ are the system states and the control input, respectively, $\phi_i(z_1,...,z_i)$, $i = 1, ..., n$ are C^1- functions vanishing at the origin and $p_i \in R_{odd} := \{q \in R : q$ are rational numbers whose numerators and denominators are all positive odd integers$\}$ for $i = 1,...,n$ (also call such p_i a positive odd rational number in [9]).

T.-h. Kim et al. (Eds.): CA/CES³ 2011, CCIS 256, pp. 17–25, 2011.

Remark 1. A function $f : R^n \rightarrow R$ is said to be C^k-function, if its partial derivatives exist and are continuous up to order k, $1 \leq k < \infty$. A C^0-function means it is continuous. A C^∞-function means it is *smooth*, that is, it has continuous partial derivatives of any order.

Here, we first give a precise definition of our practical output tracking problem.

The global practical output tracking problem. Consider the system (1) and assume that the reference signal $y_r(t)$ is a time-varying C^1-bounded function on $[0, \infty)$. Then, the global practical output tracking problem by a state controller is defined as follows: For any given positive real number ε, design a continuous controller having the following structure

$$u = u(z, y_r(t)), \tag{2}$$

such that

(i) all the states of the closed-loop system (1) and (2) are well-defined on $[0, +\infty)$ and globally bounded;

(ii) the global practical output tracking is achieved, that is, for every $z(0) \in R^n$ there is a finite time $T := T_{(\varepsilon, z(0))} > 0$, such that the output $y(t)$ of the closed-loop system (1) with (2) satisfies

$$\left| y(t) - y_r(t) \right| = \left| z_1(t) - y_r(t) \right| < \varepsilon, \quad \forall t \geq T > 0. \tag{3}$$

The problems of global practical output tracking for system (1) were investigated in [6], [8], [10] and [11] for $p_i \geq 1, i = 1, \ldots, n$. However, if $p_i < 1$, then the system is not linearizable at each point $z \in R^n$ with $z_{i+1} = 0$ as well as at the origin, hence the design method in [6] does not work. Further the global stabilization problem of system (1) for $p_i < 1, i = 1, \ldots, n$, has been studied in [9]. However, to our best knowledge, this problem of global practical output tracking remains unclear and largely open. The objective of this paper is to prove that the global practical output tracking problem is also solvable under the same conditions of [9] without imposing any extra growth condition.

2   Main Result

In this section, we state our main result.

Theorem 1 (*Main result*). Suppose that, for the system (1), $p_i \in R_{odd}, i = 1, \ldots, n$. If there exist $\mu_i \in R_{odd}, i = 0, 1, \ldots, n$ such that

$$\mu_i \geq 1, \quad i = 0, 1, \ldots, n, \tag{4}$$

$$\frac{p_1}{\mu_1} \leq \frac{1}{\mu_0}, \quad \frac{p_2}{\mu_2} \leq \min\left\{ \frac{1}{\mu_0}, \frac{1}{\mu_1} \right\}, \ldots, \frac{p_n}{\mu_n} \leq \min\left\{ \frac{1}{\mu_0}, \frac{1}{\mu_1}, \ldots, \frac{1}{\mu_{n-1}} \right\} \tag{5}$$

$$\text{and} \quad 0 \leq \frac{1}{\mu_0} - \frac{p_1}{\mu_1} \leq \frac{1}{\mu_1} - \frac{p_2}{\mu_2} \leq \ldots \leq \frac{1}{\mu_{n-1}} - \frac{p_n}{\mu_n}, \tag{6}$$

then, the global practical output tracking problem is solvable by a C^0 state-feedback controller of the form (2).

Remark 2. If the (4)-(6) hold with all $\mu_i = 1$, $i = 0,1, ..., n$, then the feedback controller $u = u(z, y_r(t))$ is smooth.

3   Proof of the Main Result

In order to prove Theorem1, we first present several technical Lemmas borrowed from [4], [6], [10] and [11], which will play an important role in our later controller design.

Lemma 1[6]. For any positive real numbers x, y and $m \geq 1$, the following inequalities holds:

$$x \leq y + (x/m)^m ((m-1)/y)^{m-1}.$$

Lemma 2[4]. For all $x, y \in R$ and a constant $p \geq 1$ the following inequalities hold:

(i) $|x+y|^p \leq 2^{p-1} |x^p + y^p|$.

(ii) $(|x|+|y|)^{1/p} \leq |x|^{1/p} + |y|^{1/p} \leq 2^{(p-1)/p} (|x|+|y|)^{1/p}$

and further if $p \in R_{odd}^{\geq 1} = \{ q \in R : q \geq 1 \text{ and } q \text{ is a ratio of odd integers} \}$ then

$|x-y|^p \leq 2^{p-1} |x^p - y^p|$ and $|x^{1/p} - y^{1/p}| \leq 2^{(p-1)/p} |x-y|^{1/p}$.

Lemma 3[10]. For any positive real numbers c, d and any $x, y \in R$, there exists a real-valued function $\gamma(x, y) > 0$ such that the following inequality holds:

$$|x|^c |y|^d \leq \frac{c}{c+d} \gamma(x, y) |x|^{c+d} + \frac{d}{c+d} (\gamma(x, y))^{-c/d} |y|^{c+d}.$$

Lemma 4[11]. Let $x_1, \cdots, x_n$ and p be positive real numbers. Then, the following inequality holds:

$$(x_1 + \cdots + x_n)^p \leq \max(n^{p-1}, 1) \cdot (x_1^p + \cdots + x_n^p).$$

Lemma 5[10]. Let $f : [a, b] \to R$ be a monotone continuous function with $f(a) = 0$. Then the following inequality holds:

$$\left| \int_a^b f(x)dx \right| \leq |f(b)| \cdot |b-a|.$$

Lemma 6[4]. Let $\phi_i : R^i \to R$ $(i = 1, \ldots, n)$ be C^1 functions with $\phi_i(0) = 0$. Then, there exist smooth nonnegative functions $\gamma_i(x_1, \ldots, x_i)$ such that

$$|\phi_i(x_1, \ldots, x_i)| \leq (|x_1| + \cdots + |x_i|) \cdot \gamma_i(x_1, \ldots, x_i).$$

Proof of Theorem1: With those $\mu_i \in R_{odd}$, $i = 0,1, \ldots, n$ selected from the conditions of the Theorem 1, we choose $v_i \geq 1$, $i = 0,1, \ldots, n-1$, satisfying

$$v_0 + p_1/\mu_1 = v_1 + p_2/\mu_2 = \ldots = v_{n-1} + p_n/\mu_n. \tag{7}$$

Then, the proof will be done by induction.

Let $x_1 = z_1 - y_r$ and given $x_i = z_i$, $i = 2,\ldots,n$. Then, we have

$$
\begin{aligned}
\dot{x}_1 &= x_2^{p_1} + \phi_1(x_1 + y_r) - \dot{y}_r(t) \\
\dot{x}_2 &= x_3^{p_2} + \phi_2(x_1 + y_r, x_2) \\
&\vdots \\
\dot{x}_{n-1} &= x_n^{p_{n-1}} + \phi_{n-1}(x_1 + y_r, x_2, \ldots, x_{n-1}) \\
\dot{x}_n &= u^{p_n} + \phi_{n-1}(x_1 + y_r, x_2, \ldots, x_{n-1}, x_n) \\
y &= x_1 + y_r
\end{aligned} \tag{8}
$$

Step 1: We construct the Lyapunov function as

$$V_1(x_1) = \int_{x_1^*}^{x_1} \left(s^{\mu_0} - x_1^{*\mu_0} \right)^{v_0} ds,$$

where $x_1^* \equiv 0$ for convenience. Note that V_1 is C^1, positive definite and proper.

A direct calculation gives

$$\dot{V}_1(x_1) = \left(x_1^{\mu_0} \right)^{v_0} \left(x_2^{p_1} + \phi_1(x_1 + y_r) - \dot{y}_r(t) \right)$$

Since $y_r(t)$ and $\dot{y}_r(t)$ are bounded and by Lemma 6, it can be shown that there is a smooth functions $\overline{\gamma}_1(x_1)$ and $\kappa_1(x_1) = M\left(1 + \overline{\gamma}(x_1)\right)$ satisfying

$$\dot{V}_1(x_1) \leq \left(x_1^{\mu_0} \right)^{v_0} \left(x_2^{p_1} - x_2^{*p_1} \right) + \left(x_1^{\mu_0} \right)^{v_0} x_2^{*p_1} + |x_1|^{\mu_0 v_0} |x_1| \overline{\gamma}_1(x_1) + |x_1|^{\mu_0 v_0} \kappa_1(x_1).$$

Since $\mu_0 p_1/\mu_1 \leq 1$ by (5), we have

$$|x_1| \leq |x_1|^{\mu_0 p_1/\mu_1} \left(1 + |x_1|^{s - \mu_0 p_1/\mu_1} \right), \quad s \geq 1.$$

Then, by taking a smooth function $\tilde{\gamma}(x_1)$ such that

$$\left(1 + |x_1|^{s - \mu_0 p_1/\mu_1} \right) \overline{\gamma}_1(x_1) \leq \tilde{\gamma}_1(x_1)$$

we obtain

$$\dot{V}_1(x_1) \leq \left(x_1^{\mu_0} \right)^{v_0} \left(x_2^{p_1} - x_2^{*p_1} \right) + \left(x_1^{\mu_0} \right)^{v_0} x_2^{*p_1} + \left(x_1^{\mu_0} \right)^{v_0 + p_1/\mu_1} \tilde{\gamma}_1(x_1) + |x_1|^{\mu_0 v_0} \kappa_1(x_1), \tag{9}$$

where x_2^* is a virtual controller to be determined later.

Moreover, observe that for any real number $\delta > 0$, by Lemma1 (Let $x = |x_1^{\mu_0}|^{v_0} \kappa_1(x_1)$, $y = \delta^{v_0 + p_1/\mu_1}$ and $m = (v_0 + p_1/\mu_1)/v_0$)), there always exists a positive smooth function $\rho_1(x_1)$ such that

$$\left| x_1^{\mu_0} \right|^{v_0} \kappa_1(x_1) \leq \delta^{v_0 + p_1/\mu_1} + \left(x_1^{\mu_0} \right)^{v_0 + p_1/\mu_1} \rho_1(x_1), \tag{10}$$

where $\rho_1(x_1) \geq \left(\kappa_1(x_1)/1 + p_1/(\mu_1 v_0)\right)^{1+p_1/(\mu_1 v_0)} \cdot \left(p_1/\delta^{v_0 + p_1/\mu_1} \mu_1 v_0\right)^{p_1/\mu_1 v_0}$ is a smooth function.

Combining (9) with (10) results in

$$\dot{V}_1(x_1) \leq \left(x_1^{\mu_0}\right)^{v_0}\left(x_2^{p_1} - x_2^{*p_1}\right) + \left(x_1^{\mu_0}\right)^{v_0} x_2^{*p_1} + \left(x_1^{\mu_0}\right)^{v_0 + p_1/\mu_1}\left(\tilde{\gamma}_1(x_1) + \rho_1(x_1)\right) + \delta^{v_0 + p_1/\mu_1}.$$

If we take the virtual controller x_2^* as

$$x_2^{*p_1} = -\left(x_1^{\mu_0}\right)^{p_1/\mu_1}\left(n + \tilde{\gamma}_1(x_1) + \rho_1(x_1)\right) = -\left(x_1^{\mu_0}\right)^{p_1/\mu_1} \beta_1^{p_1/\mu_1}(x_1).$$

Then, it follows that

$$\dot{V}_1(x_1) \leq -n\left(x_1^{\mu_0}\right)^{v_0 + p_1/\mu_1} + \left(x_1^{\mu_0}\right)^{v_0}\left(x_2^{p_1} - x_2^{*p_1}\right) + \delta^{v_0 + p_1/\mu_1}.$$

Step 2: Define $\xi_1 = x_1^{\mu_0} - x_1^{*\mu_0}$, $\xi_2 = x_2^{\mu_1} - x_2^{*\mu_1}$.

We construct the Lyapunov function as

$$V_2(x_1, x_2) = V_1(x_1) + U_2(x_1, x_2) := V_1(x_1) + \int_{x_2^*}^{x_2}\left(s^{\mu_1} - x_2^{*\mu_1}\right)^{v_1} ds.$$

Note that V_2 is C^1, positive definite and proper function.

It is not difficult to prove the following inequality.

$$\dot{V}_2(x_1, x_2) \leq -(n-1)\xi_1^{v_0 + p_1/\mu_1} + \xi_2^{v_1}\left(x_3^{p_2} - x_3^{*p_2}\right) + \xi_2^{v_1} x_3^{*p_2}$$

$$+ \xi_2^{v_1 + p_2/\mu_2}\left(c_2 + \rho_2(x_1, x_2) + \hat{\lambda}_2(x_1, x_2) + \overline{\gamma}_2(x_1, x_2)\right) + \delta^{v_0 + p_1/\mu_1} + 2\delta^{v_1 + p_2/\mu_2}.$$

Therefore, by taking the virtual control x_3^* as

$$x_3^{*p_2} = -\xi_2^{p_2/\mu_2}\left\{(n-1) + \left(c_2 + \rho_2(x_1, x_2) + \hat{\lambda}_2(x_1, x_2) + \overline{\gamma}_2(x_1, x_2)\right)\right\}$$

$$=: -\xi_2^{p_2/\mu_2} \beta_2^{p_2/\mu_2}(x_1, x_2)$$

Then, we obtain

$$\dot{V}_2(x_1, x_2) \leq -(n-1)\left(\xi_1^{v_0 + p_1/\mu_1} + \xi_2^{v_1 + p_2/\mu_2}\right) + \xi_2^{v_1}\left(x_3^{p_2} - x_3^{*p_2}\right) + 2\sum_{i=1}^{2} \delta^{v_{i-1} + p_i/\mu_i}.$$

Step k: Suppose at the *k*-1 th step, there are a C^1, positive definite and proper Lyapunov function $V_{k-1}(x_1, \ldots, x_{k-1})$ and a set of C^0 virtual controllers $x_1^*, \cdots, x_k^*$ defined by

$$x_1^* = 0, \qquad\qquad\qquad \xi_1 = x_1^{\mu_0} - x_1^{*\mu_0}$$

$$x_2^{*\mu_1} = -\xi_1 \beta_1(x_1), \qquad\qquad \xi_2 = x_2^{\mu_1} - x_2^{*\mu_1}$$

$$\vdots \qquad\qquad\qquad\qquad \vdots$$

$$x_k^{*\mu_{k-1}} = -\xi_{k-1}\beta_{k-1}(x_1, x_2 \ldots, x_{k-1}), \qquad \xi_k = x_k^{\mu_{k-1}} - x_k^{*\mu_{k-1}},$$

where $\beta_i^{p_i/\mu_i}(x_1, x_2, \ldots, x_i)$, $1 \leq i \leq k-1$, are smooth positive functions such that

$$\dot{V}_{k-1}(x_1, x_2, \ldots, x_{k-1}) \leq -(n-k+2)\left(\xi_1^{v_0 + p_1/\mu_1} + \cdots + \xi_{k-1}^{v_{k-2} + p_{k-1}/\mu_{k-1}}\right)$$

$$+ \xi_{k-1}^{v_{k-2}}\left(x_k^{p_{k-1}} - x_k^{*p_{k-1}}\right) + 2\sum_{i=1}^{k-1} \delta^{v_{i-1} + p_i/\mu_i}. \tag{11}$$

We claim that (11) also holds at *Step* k. To prove this claim, consider the Lyapunov function

$$
\begin{aligned}
V_k\left(x_1, x_2, \ldots, x_k\right) &= V_{k-1}\left(x_1, x_2, \ldots, x_{k-1}\right) + U_k\left(x_1, x_2, \ldots, x_k\right) \\
&= V_{k-1}\left(x_1, x_2, \ldots, x_{k-1}\right) + \int_{x_k^*}^{x_k}\left(s^{\mu_{k-1}} - x_k^{*\mu_{k-1}}\right)^{\nu_{k-1}} ds
\end{aligned}
\tag{12}
$$

The function $V_k\left(x_1, x_2, \ldots, x_k\right)$ can be shown to be C^1, proper and positive definite with the following property: for $i = 1, \ldots, k-1$,

$$
\frac{\partial U_k}{\partial x_i} = -\int_{x_k^*}^{x_k} \nu_{k-1}\left(s^{\mu_{k-1}} - x_k^{*\mu_{k-1}}\right)^{\nu_{k-1}-1} ds \frac{\partial\left(x_k^{*\mu_{k-1}}\right)}{\partial x_i}, \quad \frac{\partial U_k}{\partial x_k} = \left(x^{\mu_{k-1}} - x_k^{*\mu_{k-1}}\right)^{\nu_{k-1}} = \xi_k^{\nu_{k-1}}
$$

and there is a known constant $N > 0$, such that

$$
U_k \geq N\left(x_k - x_k^*\right)^{\nu_{k-1}}.
\tag{13}
$$

Proofs of these properties proceed just in the same way as in the proofs for [4] and [5], where the set of positive odd integers is considered instead of our R_{odd}.

With these properties, we obtain

$$
\begin{aligned}
\dot{V}_k\left(x_1, x_2, \ldots, x_k\right) \leq &-(n-k+2)\sum_{i=1}^{k-1} \xi_i^{\nu_{i-1}+p_i/\mu_i} + \xi_{k-1}^{\nu_{k-2}}\left(x_k^{p_{k-1}} - x_k^{*p_{k-1}}\right) \\
&+ \xi_k^{\nu_{k-1}}\left(x_{k+1}^{p_k} + \phi_k\left(x_1 + y_r, x_2, \ldots, x_k\right)\right) + \sum_{i=1}^{k-1}\frac{\partial U_k}{\partial x_i}\dot{x}_i + 2\sum_{i=1}^{k-1}\delta^{\nu_{i-1}+p_i/\mu_i}.
\end{aligned}
$$

Similar to *Step* 1 and *Step* 2 and by Lemma 1-6, it is not difficult to prove the following

$$
\begin{aligned}
\dot{V}_k\left(x_1, x_2, \ldots, x_k\right) \leq &-(n-k+1)\sum_{i=1}^{k-1} \xi_i^{\nu_{i-1}+p_i/\mu_i} + \xi_k^{\nu_{k-1}}\left(x_{k+1}^{p_k} - x_{k+1}^{*p_k}\right) + \xi_k^{\nu_{k-1}} x_{k+1}^{*p_k} \\
&+ \xi_k^{\nu_{k-1}+p_k/\mu_k}\left(c_k + \tilde{\lambda}_k\left(x_1, x_2, \ldots, x_k\right) + \overline{\gamma}_k\left(x_1, x_2, \ldots, x_k\right)\right) + 2\sum_{i=1}^{k}\delta^{\nu_{i-1}+p_i/\mu_i}.
\end{aligned}
$$

Therefore, by taking the virtual control x_{k+1}^* as

$$
\begin{aligned}
x_{k+1}^{*p_k} &= -\xi_k^{p_k/\mu_k}\left\{(n-k+1) + \left(c_k + \tilde{\lambda}_k\left(x_1, x_2, \ldots, x_k\right) + \overline{\gamma}_k\left(x_1, x_2, \ldots, x_k\right)\right)\right\} \\
&=: -\xi_k^{p_k/\mu_k} \beta_k^{p_k/\mu_k}\left(x_1, x_2, \ldots, x_k\right).
\end{aligned}
$$

Then, we obtain

$$
\dot{V}_k\left(x_1, x_2, \ldots, x_k\right) \leq -(n-k+1)\sum_{i=1}^{k} \xi_i^{\nu_{i-1}+p_i/\mu_i} + \xi_k^{\nu_{k-1}}\left(x_{k+1}^{p_k} - x_{k+1}^{*p_k}\right) + 2\sum_{i=1}^{k}\delta^{\nu_{i-1}+p_i/\mu_i}
$$

which proves the inductive argument. Note again that x_{k+1}^* and $x_{k+1}^{*p_k}$ may not be C^1, but $x_{k+1}^{*\mu_k}$ is.

At the *n*th step, by applying the feedback control

$$
u^{p_n} = x_{n+1}^{*p_n} = -\xi_n^{p_n/\mu_n} \beta_n^{p_n/\mu_n}\left(x_1, x_2, \ldots, x_n\right)
\tag{14}
$$

with the C^1, proper and positive definite Lyapunov function $V_n\left(x_1, x_2 \ldots, x_n\right)$ constructed via the inductive procedure, we arrive at

$$\dot{V}_n\left(x_1, x_2, \ldots, x_n\right) \le -\sum_{i=1}^{n} \xi_i^{v_{i-1}+p_i/\mu_i} + 2\sum_{i=1}^{n} \delta^{v_{i-1}+p_i/\mu_i}.$$

Recall that $V\left(x_1, x_2, \ldots, x_n\right) = \sum_{k=1}^{n} U_k\left(x_1, x_2, \ldots, x_k\right)$, where U_k's are defined in (12). Since, for any $\tau > 0$, by Lemma 4,

$$V^{\tau}\left(x_1, x_2, \ldots, x_n\right) \le c\sum_{k=1}^{n} U_k^{\tau}\left(x_1, x_2, \ldots, x_k\right), \quad \forall\left(x_1, x_2, \ldots, x_n\right) \in R^n,$$

where $c := \max(1, n^{\tau-1})$. Moreover, we have

$$U_k\left(x_1, x_2, \ldots, x_k\right) = \left[\int_{x_k^*}^{x_k}\left(s^{\mu_{k-1}} - x_k^{*\mu_{k-1}}\right)^{v_{k-1}} ds\right] \le \left|x_k - x_k^*\right|\left|x_k^{\mu_{k-1}} - x_k^{*\mu_{k-1}}\right|^{v_{k-1}}$$

$$\le 2\left(\xi_k^{p_k/\mu_k + v_{k-1}}\right)^{(1/\mu_{k-1} + v_{k-1})/(p_k/\mu_k + v_{k-1})} = 2\left(\xi_k^{p_k/\mu_k + v_{k-1}}\right)^{\sigma},$$

where $\sigma = \left(1/\mu_{k-1} + v_{k-1}\right)/\left(p_k/\mu_k + v_{k-1}\right)$. Therefore,

$$\dot{V}_n\left(x_1, x_2, \ldots, x_n\right) \le -\frac{1}{2n^{\sigma-1}} V_n^{1/\sigma}\left(x_1, x_2, \ldots, x_n\right) + 2\sum_{i=1}^{n} \delta^{v_{i-1}+p_i/\mu_i}$$

$$= -\left(V_n\left(x_1, x_2, \ldots, x_n\right) \Big/ \left(2n^{\sigma-1}\right)^{\sigma}\right)^{1/\sigma} + 2\sum_{i=1}^{n} \delta^{v_{i-1}+p_i/\mu_i}.$$

It will be shown that all the states $x(t)$ of closed-loop system (8) and (14) are well-defined on $[0, +\infty)$ and globally bounded. First, introduce the following set

$$\Omega := \left\{x(t) \in R^n \,\middle|\, V_n(x) \ge \left(6n^{\sigma-1}\sum_{i=1}^{n} \delta^{v_{i-1}+p_i/\mu_i}\right)^{\sigma}\right\}, \tag{15}$$

and let $x(t)$ be the trajectory of (8) with an initial state $x(0)$. If $x(t) \in \Omega$, then it follows from (15) that

$$\dot{V}_n(x(t)) \le -\frac{1}{2n^{\sigma-1}} V_n^{1/\sigma}(x(t)) + 2\sum_{i=1}^{n} \delta^{v_{i-1}+p_i/\mu_i} \le -\sum_{i=1}^{n} \delta^{v_{i-1}+p_i/\mu_i} < 0. \tag{16}$$

This implies that, as long as $x(t) \in \Omega$, $V_n(x(t))$ is strictly decreasing with time t, and hence $x(t)$ must enter the complement set $R^n - \Omega$ in a finite time $T \ge 0$ and stay there forever. Therefore, (16) leads to

$$V_n(x(t)) - V_n(x(0)) = \int_0^t \dot{V}_n(x(t))dt < 0, \quad t \in [0, T)$$

$$V_n(x(t)) < \left(6n^{\sigma-1}\sum_{i=1}^{n} \delta^{v_{i-1}+p_i/\mu_i}\right)^{\sigma}, \quad t \in [T, \infty) \tag{17}$$

which shows $V_n \in L^{\infty}$, and so do x_1 and U_k.

By $z_1 = x_1 + y_r$ and $y_r \in L^{\infty}$, we conclude $z_1 \in L^{\infty}$ as well. Noting

$$x_2^{*p_1} = -\left(x_1^{\mu_0}\right)^{p_1/\mu_1}\left(n + \rho_1(x_1)\right) = -\left(x_1^{\mu_0}\right)^{p_1/\mu_1} \beta_1^{p_1/\mu_1}(x_1)$$

and $\rho_1(x_1)$ is smooth function of x_1, we have $x_2^{*p_1} \in L^\infty$. By $U_2 \in L^\infty$ and (13), $(x_2 - x_2^*) \in L^\infty$ and $x_2 \in L^\infty$. Inductively, we can prove $x_i \in L^\infty$, $i = 3, 4, \cdots, n$ and so do $x(t)$.

Thus, all the solutions $x(t)$ of the closed-loop system (8) and (14) are well-defined and globally bounded on $[0, +\infty)$.

Next, it will be shown that

$$|y(t) - y_r(t)| = |z_1(t) - y_r(t)| < \varepsilon, \quad \forall t \ge T > 0. \tag{18}$$

This is easily shown from (13), (17) and by tuning the parameter δ as follows:

$$|y(t) - y_r(t)| = |x_1(t)| \le V_n(x(t)) \le \left(6n^{\sigma-1} \sum_{i=1}^{n} \delta^{v_{i-1} + p_i/\mu_i} \right)^\sigma < \varepsilon.$$

Therefore, for any $\varepsilon > 0$, there is $\delta(\varepsilon) > 0$ such that (18) is satisfied. This completes the proof of Theorem 1.

4   Conclusions

In this paper, we have developed a systematic approach to construct a continuous practical output tracking controller for nonlinear systems in the strict feedback form, whose chained integrator part has the power of positive odd rational numbers. Such a controller guarantees that the states of the closed-loop system are globally bounded, while the tracking error can be bounded by any given positive number after a finite time.

Acknowledgments. This work was supported in part by the Japanese Ministry of Education, Science and Culture under the Grant-Aid of General Scientific Research C-22560453.

References

1. Isidori, A., Byrnes, C.I.: Output regulation of nonlinear system. IEEE Transactions on Automatic Control 35, 31–140 (1990)
2. Byrnes, C.I., Psicoli, F.D., Isidori, A.: Output Regulation of Uncertain Nonlinear Systems. Birkhäuser, Boston (1997)
3. Lin, W., Qian, C.J.: Adding one power integrator: a tool for global stabilization of high-order lower-triangular systems. Systems and Control Letters 39, 339–351 (2000)
4. Qian, C.J., Lin, W.: Non-Lipschitz continuous stabilizers for nonlinear systems with uncontrollable unstable linearization. Systems and Control Letters 42, 185–200 (2001)
5. Qian, C.J., Lin, W.: A continuous feedback approach to global strong stabilization of nonlinear systems. IEEE Transactions on Automatic Control 46, 1061–1079 (2001)
6. Qian, C.J., Lin, W.: Practical output tracking of nonlinear systems with uncontrollable unstable linearization. IEEE Transactions on Automatic Control 47, 21–36 (2002)
7. Marconi, L., Isidori, A.: Mixed internal mod el-based and feedforward control for robust tracking in nonlinear systems. Automatica 36, 993–1000 (2000)

8. Lin, W., Pongvuthithum, R.: Adaptive output tracking of inherently nonlinear systems with nonlinear parameterization. IEEE Transactions on Automatic Control 48, 1737–1749 (2003)
9. Back, J., Cheong, S.G., Shim, H., Seo, J.H.: Nonsmooth feedback stabilizer for strict-feedback nonlinear systems that not be linearizable at the origin. Systems and Control Letters 56, 742–752 (2007)
10. Sun, Z.-Y., Liu, Y.-G.: Adaptive practical output tracking control for high-order nonlinear uncertain systems. Acta Automatica Sinica 34, 984–989 (2008)
11. Alimhan, K., Inaba, H.: Practical output tracking by smooth output compensator for uncertain nonlinear systems with unstabilisable and undetectable linearisation. International Journal of Modelling, Identification and Control 5, 1–13 (2008)

Analysis of Non-linear Adaptive Friction and Pitch Angle Control of Small-Scaled Wind Turbine System

Faramarz Asharif, Shiro Tamaki, Tsutomu Nagado,
Tomokazu Nagtata, and Mohammad Reza Asharif

Faculty of Engineering, University of the Ryukyus,
1 Senbaru, Nishihara, Okinawa 903-0213
faramarz@neo.ie.u-ryukyu.ac.jp

Abstract. The aim of this research is toanalyze the behavior of wind turbine system for passive and adaptive resistance non-linear control. In general, the wind turbine system is generating energy from the revolution of blades. The revolution of blades is depended on the velocity of wind. So, if we have strong wind then the revolution of blade is increased and in consequently more energy will generated. Therefore, usually the wind turbine systems are located in gale area in order to generate energy efficiency. However, there are limits of the revolution of blades or the angular velocity of blades. If the angular velocity exceeds the limit then wind turbine system may breakdown. Thus in this paper, in order to avoid the malfunction of wind turbine system, adaptive and passive non-linear control of resistance is considered. As consequences, the adaptive resistance has more stable and smooth angular velocity compare to passive resistance.

Keywords: Wind Turbine System, Adaptive Control, Non-linear Control, Angular velocity and pitch angle, Stall Control.

1 Introduction

In these days the wind turbine system has big role to the new generation of life. According to the journals the oil has maximum usage of 150 years. So, if we continue using oil, there would be serious problem. Therefore, the efficient energy is required from wind turbine system. The purpose of this research is to control the angular velocity of blades in the case of strong input wind to the turbine. In general, the wind turbine system is located in gale area in order to generate energy efficiency. However, in the case of storm the wind turbine must standstill the operation. Thus, no energy will generate. So, in order to avoid this wasteful time, we have considered the controlling the resistance of angular velocity and pitch angle of blade. By utilization of resistance and pitch angle of blade, the angular velocity of blade is controllable even in storm. So, in this paper two different schemes is proposed. The one is adaptive control of resistance and the other one is passive control of resistance. Also at the same time pitch angle of blade is controlled. The aim of using resistance is to decrease the angular velocity by friction between blades and axis of internal turbine of ring. Moreover, pitch angle is controller in order to decrease the angular velocity by friction which made by collision between wind and surface of blade. In next chapters, the detail dynamics and control method of wind turbine system and the comparison of adaptive and passive control of resistance are shown.

T.-h. Kim et al. (Eds.): CA/CES[3] 2011, CCIS 256, pp. 26–35, 2011.

2   Introduction to Small-Scaled Wind Turbine System

From old times, the utilization of small-sized wind turbine is widely used for pumping up and so on. In the spite of this, in these days the importation of electronic power generator of small scaled wind turbine is not volunteered. The important problem of small scaled wind turbine is the establishment of stall control against strong wind. As a result, there are many excessive rotations that may cause the damage accident. If this problem is solvable, then hereafter it will contribute large amount of energy. Thus, the innovation of small-sized wind turbine is very important part of the energy generation. In this research, the wind turbine system is considered to be located in gale area and by axis friction and pitch angle control the angular velocity of blade. The wind turbine rotates clockwise from the front perspective. In general, the blades of wind turbine descend 3 to 5 to the front and lays on the center axis with a slant of 2-4 degree. The axis is propped up by 2 springs which cross to the right angle of center axis. In this moment, pitch angle is optimized. As a matter of fact, when angular velocity reached to the stall control level, the angular velocity depends on spring factor. In this research by repeating experiments and numerical analysis, we consider the improvement of mechanism of spring installation inside turbine. The stall control mechanism is as follows. At first, in windless or calm, the attitude of blade is on axis. When wind turbine receive the strong wind to the area of swept by blade, the blades is strongly pushed to the backward. As a result the blades reach to stall angle and angular velocity is reduced. Secondly, when turbine receive strong wind, the centrifugal force will increase and with that force, the axis of blades shift to the central axis line and at the same time the slop angle become reverse pitch that reduce the angular velocity. These stall control dynamics are possible to realize by the movement of the blade to backward or forward and independently axis rotation. Finally the stall control is realized and angular velocity of blade is reduced and by this centrifugal force is vanished then the mechanism of blades, return to its origin position and it will start to rotate again. In other words, by passive control of installed spring to the blades, mechanism of stall control is realizable.

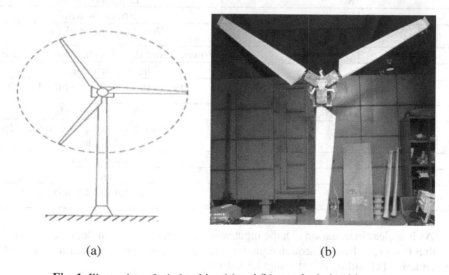

(a)   (b)

Fig. 1. Illustration of wind turbine (a) and (b) actual wind turbine

Dynamics of horizontal-axis wind turbine with pitch angle control is indicates as follows.

Dynamics of angular velocity

$$J_\omega \frac{d\omega(t)}{dt} = \frac{1}{2}C_T \rho AR \int_0^t V^2(t)e^{-(\tau-t)}d\tau\Theta(\theta) - \frac{1}{2}I_G\omega^2(t) - f_r\omega(t) \qquad (1)$$

Dynamics of pitch angle

$$J_b \frac{d^2\theta(t)}{dt^2} = MR^2\omega^2(t)\theta(t) - L\theta(t)k - c\frac{d\theta(t)}{dt} \qquad (2)$$

which we have:

$$\Theta(\theta) = \frac{\tilde{\theta}(t)}{\theta_{max}} \text{ and } \tilde{\theta}(t) = \theta_{max} - \theta(t).$$

Where, the parameters are indicates in the below table 1.

Table 1. Identification of parameters

J_ω	Inertia moment of blade
$\omega(t)$	Angular velocity
C_T	Torque factor
ρ	Density of atmosphere
A	Area swept by blade
R	Length of blade
V(t)	Speed of wind
$\Theta(\theta)$	Wind turbine stall factor
I_G	Power Generation Inertia Moment Factor
f_r	The axis friction factor
J_b	Inertia moment of a plate of blade
M	Mass of a blade
L	The distance from spring to the edge of blade
k	Factor of spring
c	damper
θ_{max}	Initial values of pitch angle

As it is clear in equation (1), the input wind includes with input delay and convolute with a first order filter. Through equation (2) the wind turbine stall factor is feedcaked to equation (1) and by this the angular velocity is controlled.

3   Adaptive Control of Axis Friction

As we discussed previously, the resistance control is considered to avoid exceeding the angular velocity from the limitation. Therefore, by rewriting the equation (1) the dynamics of wind turbine system of angular velocity is can be indicates as follows that if angular velocity exceed the limit the adaptive friction $\gamma(\omega(t))$ works and decrease the velocity. Otherwise $\gamma(\omega(t))$ has no influence.

$$\gamma(\omega(t)) = 1 + e^{\omega(t)-\omega_{\lim it}} \tag{3}$$

Dynamics of angular velocity with adaptive friction

$$J_\omega \frac{d\omega(t)}{dt} = \frac{1}{2}C_T \rho AR \int_0^t V^2(t)e^{-(\tau-t)}d\tau\Theta(\theta) - \frac{1}{2}I_G\omega^2(t) - f_r\gamma(\omega(t))\omega(t) \tag{4}$$

Also in order to have better performances, pitch angle control is required. Therefore, first we linearize the equation (2). Then we have:
   Here, we fix the angular velocity. Then we have:

Dynamics of pitch angle

$$J_b \frac{d^2\theta(t)}{dt^2} = MR^2\omega^2\theta(t) - \alpha L\theta(t)k - c\frac{d\theta(t)}{dt} \tag{5}$$

The Laplace transform of above equation is:

Laplace transform

$$J_b(s^2\theta(s) - s\theta(0) - \dot\theta(0)) = (MR^2\omega^2 - \alpha Lk)\theta(s) + c(s\theta(s) - \theta(0))$$

$$G_\theta(s) = \frac{(1-s)\theta(0)}{s^2 + \dfrac{c}{J_b}s + \dfrac{Lk\alpha - MR\omega^2}{J_b}} \tag{6}$$

$\dot\theta(0) = 0$ and $\theta(0) = \theta_{max}$. Here, if $\alpha = \dfrac{J_b + MR\omega^2}{Lk}$ and substitute to equation

(6), then we have: $G_\theta = \dfrac{(1-s)\theta(0)}{s^2 + \dfrac{c}{J_b}s + 1}$. According to final value theorem the steady

step response is: $\theta_{steady} = \theta(\infty) = \lim_{s\to 0} sG_\theta \dfrac{1}{s} = \theta(0)$

So, by choosing the $\alpha(\omega^2(t)) = \dfrac{J_b + MR\omega^2(t)}{Lk}$, the performance of turbine is improved.

4   Simulation and Analysis

In order to evaluate the adaptive and passive resistance control [1-5], we have simulated the non-linear model [6-7] of wind turbine system. The specification of simulation is shown as follows:

$$
\begin{cases}
J_\omega \dfrac{d\omega(t)}{dt} = \dfrac{1}{2} C_T \rho AR \int_0^t V^2(t) e^{-(\tau - t)} d\tau \Theta(\theta) - \dfrac{1}{2} I_G \omega^2(t) - f_r \gamma(\omega(t))\omega(t) \\[4mm]
J_b \dfrac{d^2\theta(t)}{dt^2} = MR^2 \omega^2 \theta(t) - \alpha L\theta(t)k - c\dfrac{d\theta(t)}{dt}
\end{cases}
$$

Where, $\gamma(\omega(t)) = 1 + e^{\omega(t) - \omega_{\lim it}}$ and $\alpha(\omega(t)) = \dfrac{J_b + MR\omega^2(t)}{Lk}$.

Table 2. Identification of parameters

Parameters	Values	Units
J_ω	16	$kg \cdot m^2$
$\omega(t)$	Variable	rad/s
C_T	0.2	$N \cdot m$
P	1.2	Kg/m^3
A	7.0686	m^2
R	1.5	m
V(t)	Reyleigh distribution	m/s
$\Theta(\theta)$	Variable	——
I_G	4.5185	$kg \cdot m^2$
f_r	0.001	$kg \cdot m^2$
J_b	8	$kg \cdot m^2$
M	14	kg
L	0.2	m
K	5000	N/m
c	100	$kg \cdot m^2$
θ_{max}	0.0873	rad
ω_{limit}	reference	rad/s

Operation factor in fig.2 is indicates as below:

$$
f(\omega) = 1 + e^{\omega(t) - (\omega_{ref} - 12)}, \quad z(\theta) = \frac{\theta_{max} - \theta(t)}{\theta_{max}}, \quad g(\omega) = \frac{J_b + MR\omega^2}{Lk}
$$

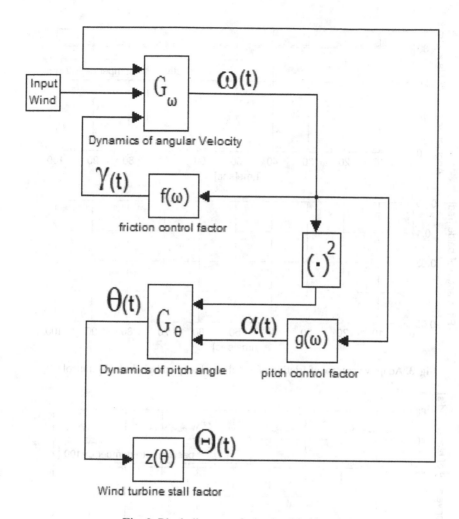

Fig. 2. Block diagram of adaptive friction control

Above block diagram shows the adaptive friction control and performance control of wind turbine. As it is shown, the friction control factor and pitch control factor are controlled by observing the angular velocity of blade. Finally the wind turbine stall factor is feedbacked to dynamics of angular velocity of blade. By this circulation angular velocity is controlled. In results we will see the behavior of angular velocity and pitch angle of blade for passive control and adaptive control. Here, the reference angular velocity is set to 30 [rad/s]. The input wind is Rayleigh distribution with average speed of 50[m/s] that in ordinary case wind turbine must stop running. The simulation process is to observe the angular velocity of blade and pitch angle of blade for passive and adaptive control of friction in two cases, one for pitch angle with damper and without damper. Finally compare the results of adaptive and passive control and analysis the behavior and performance of wind turbine system.

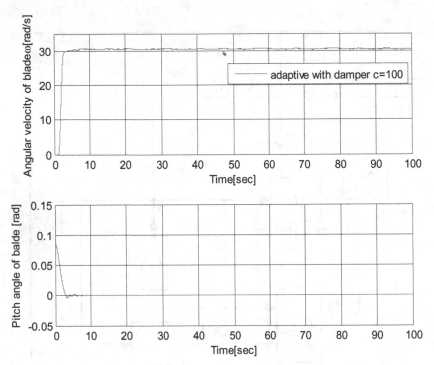

Fig. 3. Adaptive control of friction of angular velocity and pitch angle control

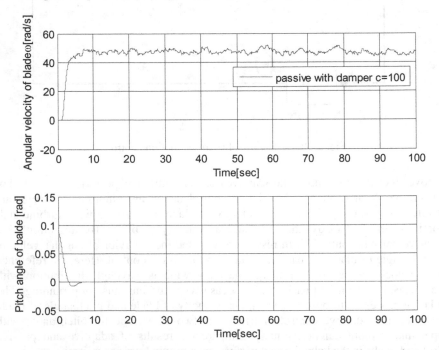

Fig. 4. Passive control of friction of angular velocity and pitch angle control

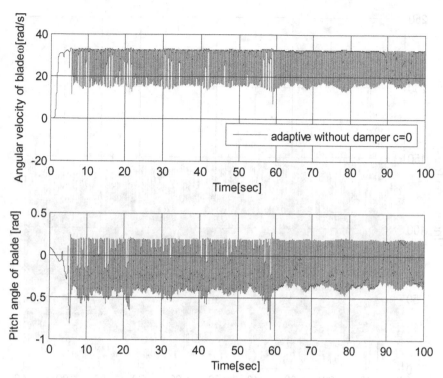

Fig. 5. Adaptive control of friction of angular velocity and pitch angle control without damper

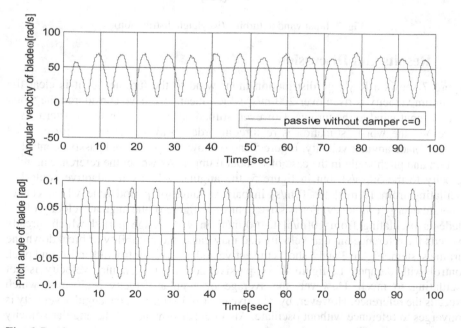

Fig. 6. Passive control of friction of angular velocity and pitch angle control without damper

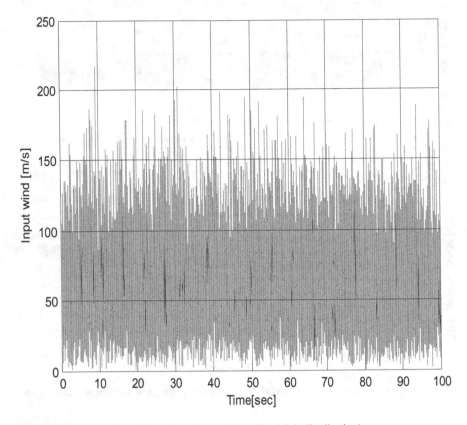

Fig. 7. Input wind to turbine (Reyleigh distribution)

5   Results and Discussion

Figure 7 shows a Reyleigh distribution input wind to the turbine. As it is clear the maximum velocity is risen over 200[m/s] which means we have considered the worst case of input wind to the turbine. However, sometimes it occurs in southeastern Asia. Therefore, the worst estimation is requiredin order to avoid the instability of wind turbines blade angular velocity. Figure 5 and 6 shows the active and passive control of friction and pitch angle in the case of without damper. As we set the reference angular velocity to the 30[m/s], but in figure 5, the angular velocity in adaptive control is oscillating from 19[m/s] to 30[m/s] in narrow range of period time which cannot generate energy efficiency. For passive control in figure 6, the angular velocity of the blade is oscillating from 10[m/s] to 60[m/s] in wide range period which already exceeds the reference angular velocity and may cause the instability or breakdown the turbine system. Figure 3 and 4 shows the active and passive control of friction and pitch control with damper. In figure 4 for passive control, the angular velocity is not oscillating so much. However, the average of angular velocity is 50[m/s] which exceeds the reference. However, by adaptive control in figure 3, the angular velocity is converges to reference without oscillate. Also the performance of the angular velocity is quite better than the passive control.

6   Conclusion

In this research, we aim to avoid the excess of wind turbines angular velocity using axis friction and pitch angle. As a result, the passive control with and without damper, it was the most inefficient and unstable scheme. Therefore, utilization of passive control in angular velocity control is not suitable perspective from efficiency energy generation and stability. For adaptive control without damper, the angular velocity is oscillating under the reference signal, so the stability of system is guaranteed. However, the performance of system is not quite good, therefore cannot anticipateaefficient energy generation. However, for adaptive control with damper, the angular velocity, it converges to reference signal without oscillating or overshoots. Therefore, the stability of system is guaranteed and the performance is controlled well by damper. Thus the most efficient and stable scheme of angular velocity control is utilization of adaptive control with damper in pitch angle of blade. However, there is some problem that the realization of adaptive control is quite hard part of the research due to the mechanical system tools. Therefore for future works we are going to design a semi-adaptive control for system in order to realize in actual system. Also the most important issue is consideration of time-delay. In this research we considered only input delay. However, in actual system, time-delay exists not only in the input part but also in the feedback part of system. Thus, the consideration of existence of time-delay element is required in order to design controller.

Acknowledgment. This work was supported by Grant-in-Aid for Scientific Research (C22560837). We wish to express our gratitude of this grant.

References

[1] Dorf, R.C., Bishop, R.H.: Modern Control System. Prentice Hall (2002)
[2] Pedrycz, W.: Robust Control Design an Optimal Control Approach. Wiley (2007)
[3] Franklin, G.F., Powell, J.D., Workman, M.: Digital Control of Dynamic System. Addison–Wesley (1997)
[4] Balas, G.J., Doyle, J.C., Glover, K., Packard, A., Smith, R.: Robust Control Toolbox TM 3 User's Guide. The Math Works
[5] Skogestad, S., Postlethwaite, I.: Multi Variable Feedback Control Analysis and Design. John Wiley & Sons (1996)
[6] Krstic, M., Kanellakopoulos, I., Kokotovic, P.: Nonlinear and Adaptive Control Design. John Wiley & Sons, Inc. (1995)
[7] Isidori, A.: Nonlinear Control System. Springer, Heidelberg (1995)
[8] Muljadi, E., Butterfield, C.P.: Pitch-controlled variable-speed wind turbine generation. IEEE Transaction on Industry Applications (2001)

A High Accuracy Method for Rapid Measurement of Resulted Code Pattern Radial Runout of Rotary Optical Encoder Disc

Ali Asfia[*] and Jafar Rezaei

Mechanical Engineering Department, Shahid Rajaei Teacher Training University
ali_asfia118@yahoo.com, A.Asfia@srttu.edu

Abstract. Optical rotary encoders are generally known as rotational angle measuring devices with high accuracy, resolution and reliability. One of important sources of error in these encoders is their disc code pattern radial runout. Usually, for high accuracy measurements in the range of ±1 arc sec to ±5 arc sec, the code pattern radial runout resulting from bearing or during installation must be significantly less than 1μm. In this paper, an instrument is purposed for installation of encoded disc that can rapidly measure radial runout of code pattern both during installation and after temporary installation of encoded disc with high accuracy and reliability. Systematic characteristics of this instrument are proven through mathematical equations. Accuracy of determination equations of this measuring method in various setup are evaluated and by analyzing its results, performance characteristics of the proposed instrument are extracted. The purposed instrument can communicate data with a PC, so avoids need to microscope as used in conventional assembly of encoder disc method and also may be used for automatic assemble or monitoring of assembly process of encoded disc.

Keywords: Rotary encoder, assembly of encoder disc, rotary encoder accuracy, runout, accuracy of determination.

1   Introduction

For improvement of positioning accuracy in processes performed by machine tools, an instrument is required to measure rotational angle with high resolution and reliability. Optical rotary encoders are generally known as rotational angle measurement devices with high accuracy, resolution and reliability [8, 12, 13].

Figure 1 shows the structure of a conventional optical rotary encoder that contains an encoded disc on which a radial code pattern is constructed. The encoded disc is mounted on encoder rotor to which load shaft is coupled. There is also one stationary mask on the encoder stator. It contains a section of encoded disc code pattern. A light source provides the necessary light beam that passes through the disc and stationary

---

[*] Corresponding author.

T.-h. Kim et al. (Eds.): CA/CES[3] 2011, CCIS 256, pp. 36–49, 2011.

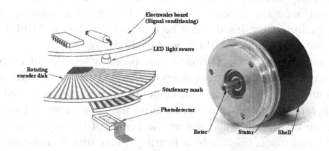

Fig. 1. Structure of a common optical rotary encode

mask code patterns and then is received by many photodetectors. During the rotation of encoded disc, intensity of light beam received by detectors is varied and detectors generate corresponding electric signals. Next signals are processed for counting.

Accuracy of rotary encoder is defined as positional deviation on single revolution of encoder shaft and single signal period [4, 6]. Positional deviation on single revolution encoder shaft is influenced by code pattern radial runout of encoded disc and directed deviation of radial code pattern [4, 6, 10, 16]. Positional deviation on single signal period is due to the quality of code pattern scanning, variations of code pattern line spacing, local code pattern flaws and encoded disc medium [4, 6, 10, 12]. Both types of positional deviation have inherent effect on drivers characteristics. Such influence is very powerful, especially on the drivers with digital velocity control [2, 4, 8].

Two basic methods for velocity measurement of motors are: Counting the encoder pulses in a given time which is named frequency meter, or measurement of the width of one pulse which is named periodimeter [2, 8, 13]. Second method provides accurate measurement of velocity on low speed. Later method is more accurate than the first one and provides possibilities to use robust torque controller with no noise or vibration problems. However its accuracy would perfectly depend on encoder accuracy [8]. That encoder must provide signals with a good edge to edge accuracy [2, 8].

2   Error Sources of Code Pattern Radial Runout and Method to Reduce It

Code pattern radial runout error contains three components:

1-. Code pattern radial runout from deflection of encoder's shaft under external loads (force of weight or process). Effect of this runout component was avoided by using either flexible coupling between the encoder shaft and the load shaft to which the rotor is attached or hollow shaft encoders (stator-coupled).
2-. Code pattern radial runout from radial runout of encoder bearings. To decrease this runout component, the bearings that are used on encoders must have high class of tolerances. The tolerance class illustrates two accuracy of bearing:

Dimensional accuracy which is important for assembling the bearing and functional accuracy which is important for machine rotating element. The lowest quality of bearing that can be used on encoders is ABEC4 and the best system is fabricated with ABEC7 or special bearing [6].

3-. Code pattern radial runout from inappropriate assembles of encoded disc on encoder rotor. For accurate assembles of encoded disc on encoder rotor, usually, optical microscope is used and the center of code pattern is moved to the center of shaft rotation, In this method, because the code pattern of encoded disc is located on own bearing and not on the center of bearings, therefore the code pattern radial runout resulted from bearings radial runout is avoided.

Generally, for high precision measuring in the range of ± 1" to ±5", resulted runout of the above three components must be significantly less than 1µm.

Figure 2 illustrates conventional method for mounting of encoded disc. In this method, first the encoder shaft is assembled on a flange via a set of bearings and then encoded disc is assembled on it's housing on the shaft and is temporarily tightened to the shaft by clips. By aligning the perimeter of the code pattern with an index mark, through eyepiece of a microscope, the disc is moved to a position that center of code pattern is located on the rotation axis. Finally the disc is joined to the shaft permanently by adhesive resin.

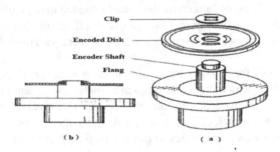

Fig. 2. Components for installing encoded disc

Because, encoded disc assembling process is performed visually, eye fatigue and operator error are matter. Also reticule scale resolution of the microscope is not usually less than 0.01 mm and it is so coarse to measure code pattern runout which is order of micrometers. Using microscope table (where toolmaker microscope is used) for measuring code pattern runout is time and labor intensive and inaccurate, so we need an accurate and quick instrument for measuring code pattern runout and installation of encoded disk.

3   Design of Purposed Instrument

In this paper an instrument is described for installing encoded disc that can measure runout of encoded disc easily and precisely during the installation or after temporary installation process. Figure 3 shows the assembly layout of this instrument that contains a base, a DC motor, an assembly fixture for installing encoded disc and C and D heads. To reduce the radial runout of encoder bearings by this instrument, the assembly fixture must be the encoder's stator.

Figure 4-a shows the XX view of figure 2. For clarity the C and D heads are eliminated. In this figure encoder's shaft (rotor) is assembled on a flange (stator) via a set of bearings (encoder's bearing) and encoded disc is tightened to the encoder shaft by clips. The rotor is rotated by an arrangement of belt and wheels. Figure 4-b shows the YY view of figure 2. In this figure the C head is shown in section view for illustration of its components. In this design, the heads operate according to geometric light principle; however if period of code pattern is less than 8µm, the heads have to operate according to diffraction and interference principles [1]. C and D heads are both identical in design and positioned symmetrically in respect to the axis of encoder shaft. They are used for scanning of code pattern during the installation process and generate analogue or digital signals. For adjustment of encoded disc this instrument is clamped to a toolmaker microscope table such as that shown in figure 5.

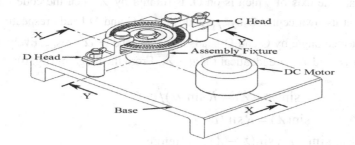

Fig. 3. Proposed instrument for installation of encoded disc

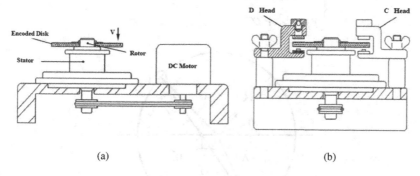

(a)   (b)

Fig. 4. (a) XX view from the instrument in figure 2, (b) YY view from the instrument in figure 2

Fig. 5. A toolmaker microscope for installation of encoded disc

Figure 6 shows the position of D and C heads relative to code pattern schematically. According to this figure, assume code pattern have runout e; if the encoder shaft, the axis of which is on Ó, is rotated by λ then the code pattern has rotated about its own center O by γ_1 and γ_2 for C and D heads respectively. Also error of detected angle by C and D heads are $-\alpha$ and $+\alpha'$ respectively. It can be proved that α and α' are identical for any λ. From the diagram (fig. 6):

$$\sin(\pi - \lambda) = R\sin(\alpha)/e \tag{1}$$

$$\sin(\lambda) = R\sin(\alpha')/e \tag{2}$$

We know that, $\sin(\lambda) = \sin(\pi - \lambda)$, Therefore:

$$\alpha = \alpha'$$

$$\therefore \begin{cases} \gamma_1 = \lambda - \alpha \\ \gamma_2 = \lambda + \alpha \end{cases} \tag{3}$$

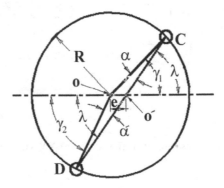

Fig. 6. Schematic of heads on code pattern

Primary signals that are generated by heads are sinusoidal and typical equations for those can be writhen as fallow [5, 11]:

$$V_1 = c_1 + a_1 \sin(Z\gamma_1) \text{ for C head} \tag{4}$$

$$V_2 = c_2 + a_2 \sin(Z\gamma_2 + \eta) \text{ for D head} \tag{5}$$

Where c = DC offset, a = AC amplitude, Z = number of lines in code pattern and η is phase shift of V_2 in relation to V_1 due to different position of heads on one pitch of code pattern (aren't located on identical position). Substituting γ_1 and γ_2 from equation 3 to equations 4 and 5, we have:

$$V_1 = c_1 + a_1 \sin(Z\lambda - Z\alpha) \tag{6}$$

$$V_2 = c_2 + a_2 \sin(Z\lambda + Z\alpha + \eta) \tag{7}$$

From relations 6 and 7, the total phase shift ϕ of two signals V_1 and V_2 are calculated as follow:

$$\phi = (Z\lambda + Z\alpha + \eta) - (Z\lambda - Z\alpha) = 2Z\alpha + \eta \tag{8}$$

In the above equation, the term $2Z\alpha$ is the error of angle velocity which is generated by radial runout of disc code pattern and varies periodically on one revolution of disc. This variation of phase angle between two signals V_1 and V_2 is called phase jitter and denoted as $\Delta\phi$.

Also α is derived from equation 1:

$$\alpha = \frac{e}{R}\sin(\lambda) \tag{9}$$

Where α is given in radians and maximizes on $\lambda = \pi/2$ and $\lambda = 3\pi/2$ as below:

$$\alpha_{max} = \pm\frac{e}{R} \tag{10}$$

According to equation 8, the phase jitter $\Delta\phi$ and maximum phase jitter $\Delta\phi_{max}$, is:

$$\Delta\phi = \left|\frac{2Ze}{R}\sin(\lambda)\right| \tag{11}$$

$$\Delta\phi_{max} = \frac{2Ze}{R} \tag{12}$$

Where $\Delta\phi$ is given in radians.

If we can measure $\Delta\phi_{max}$, therefore we can also calculate the radial runout of code pattern as below:

$$e = \frac{\Delta\phi_{max}R}{2Z} \tag{13}$$

4   Measurement of Phase Jitter

The most precise method for measurement of phase jitter is measurement of time variation between the same edges of both heads signals (Δt) and also measurement of time during one complete signal cycle (T) by a high frequency clock (Fig.7) and then calculation of $\Delta\phi_{max}$ by following equation:

$$\Delta\phi = \frac{\Delta t}{T} \cdot 2\pi$$

$$\therefore \Delta\phi_{max} = \frac{\Delta t_{max}}{T} \cdot 2\pi \tag{14}$$

By combining the equations 13 and 14, the code pattern radial runout can be determined as follow:

$$e = \frac{\Delta t_{max}}{T} \cdot S \tag{15}$$

Where, S is the mean width of code pattern lines in mm that is called line spacing and calculated as follow:

$$S = 2\pi R / 2z \tag{16}$$

Measured time T of one signal cycle contain error, due to the variation of angle velocity of the code pattern. This error is symmetric for signals V_1 and V_2. Then to avoid this error, the times T_1 and T_2 of one cycle of corresponding signals V_1 and V_2 must be simultaneously measured and then the time T is determined by arithmetic average of T_1 and T_2.

$$T = \frac{T_1 + T_2}{2} = \frac{60}{NZ} \tag{17}$$

Where N is rotation velocity of encoded disc in RPM.

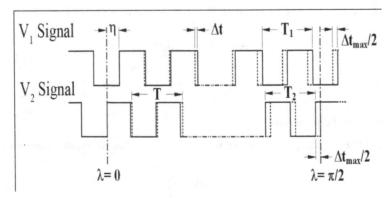

Fig. 7. Measurement of time Δt and T by digital signals of two heads

5   Accuracy of Determination Analysis

Using the equation 15 accuracy of determination in measurement of e may be calculated as following:

$$\sigma_e = e.\sqrt{\frac{\sigma_{\Delta t_{max}}^2}{\Delta t_{max}^2} + \frac{\sigma_T^2}{T^2} + \frac{\sigma_S^2}{S^2}} \tag{18}$$

Where σ_e is the accuracy of determination for e, $\sigma_{\Delta t_{max}}$ is the accuracy of determination for Δt_{max} and σ_T is the accuracy of determination for T. If we call F_c as the frequency for time measuring clock, $\sigma_{\Delta t_{max}}$ would equal $\pm 1/(2F_c)$ and σ_T equals $\pm 1/(2\sqrt{2}\,F_c)$. σ_S is the accuracy of determination of S and is related to the manufacturing process of encoder disc. As lithographic techniques are used in production of optical encoder discs, σ_S value depends on resist and lighting systems.

A typical value for σ_S would be about 30 nm [3]. As well if heads are misplaced on the code pattern in desired radius due to fabrication tolerances or thermal expansion of the designed instruments components, S would have systemic error. Fortunately the best optical sensor used in encoders is solar cell [1]. The area of this sensor for C and D heads can be selected to be bigger than code pattern line length, in which case measuring accuracy would be independent of the radial position of heads on the code pattern. As well for the fact that this optical sensor would receive the mean light intensity passing through much number of code pattern lines, S would be in practice the average width of much number of code pattern lines [9]. And σ_S would be $30/\sqrt{n_z}$ where n_z is the number of code pattern lines that the solar cell placed on simultaneously. However we consider the worst condition and suppose σ_S to be 30 nm.

As changing F_c we can change the values for σ_T and $\sigma_{\Delta t_{max}}$, e are divided in two Fixed and variable components. The variable component, $\Delta t_{max}/T$, is defined to be U, therefore we have:

$$e = U \cdot S \tag{19}$$

And σ_e would be:

$$\sigma_e = \sqrt{S^2 \sigma_U^2 + U^2 \sigma_S^2} \tag{20}$$

As well σ_U is equal to:

$$\sigma_U = \frac{e}{S} \cdot \sqrt{\frac{\sigma_{\Delta t_{max}}^2}{\Delta t_{max}^2} + \frac{\sigma_T^2}{T^2}} \tag{21}$$

Substituting the values for each parameter in equation 21 and after simplification of the equation we have:

$$\sigma_U = \frac{1}{2} \cdot \frac{ZN}{60F_c} \cdot \sqrt{1 + \frac{e^2}{2S^2}} \tag{22}$$

If $K = (ZN)/(60F_c)$, we have:

$$\sigma_U = \frac{1}{2}.K.\sqrt{1 + \frac{e^2}{2S^2}} \tag{23}$$

K value is the clock resolution in unit of one signal period of heads. Lowering the K value, we can decrease σ_u. The effect of K in reducing the variable component, $S\sigma_U$, and then σ_e is seen in fig.8. As seen in the figure, if K is lowered smaller than a certain value known as $K_{crit.}$, for the values of e bigger than $e_{crit.1}$, σ_e is reduced to $U\sigma_S$ and thereby for K values, smaller than $K_{crit.}$, based on a good approximation σ_e can be written as following.

$$\sigma_e = U\sigma_S = \frac{e}{S} \cdot \sigma_S \tag{24}$$

If permitted error in calculation of true σ_e is considered to be max 1%, $K_{crit.}$ May be calculated form the following equation:

$$K_{crit.} = 0.403 \cdot \frac{\sigma_S}{S} \tag{25}$$

As well $e_{crit.1}$ is calculated from the following equation.

$$e_{crit.1} = 3.51 \cdot \frac{KS^2}{\sigma_S} \tag{26}$$

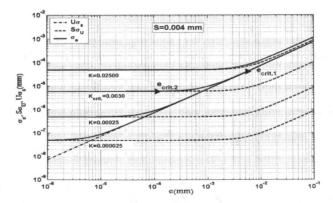

Fig. 8. Accuracy of determination (σ_e), fixed component of σ_e ($U\sigma_S$) and variable component of σ_e ($S\sigma_U$) versus radial turnout of code pattern (e) with different K values

For this section of accuracy of determination for e, as measuring accuracy can be improved up to $\pm(e/S)\sigma_S$ only, optimal K values may be calculated for any permitted radial runout e. In the same line if σ_e calculation error from the true value is considered to be 1%, optimum K value ($K_{opt.}$) may be calculated from the equation 27. We should expect 1% improvement in measuring accuracy if we use the recommended instrument with value very smaller than $K_{opt.}$.

$$K_{opt.} = 0.285 \cdot \frac{e\sigma_S}{S \cdot \sqrt{0.5e^2 + S^2}} \tag{27}$$

Fig.9 indicates $K_{opt.}$ and corresponding σ_e with a different S s. As shown in fig.9, increasing the e, $K_{opt.}$ can be maximum increased up to $K_{crit.}$. As well with determined value of e, $K_{opt.}$ would be smaller for bigger S s. Fortunately, today electronic technology has made it possible to use very small S s. However we should remember that there is minimum K value. If we call the lowest K value which can be selected by recommended instrument as $K_{min.}$, for any permitted radial runout error e, we can calculate the critical S according to equation 26 while for S values smaller than critical the measurement accuracy would be $\pm(e/S)\sigma_S$. But for S values bigger than that of critical S, measurement accuracy would be a function of $K_{min.}$. If this critical S is known a $S_{crit.1}$, then we have:

$$S_{crit.1} = 0.5 \cdot e \cdot \left[\sqrt{1 + \frac{1.3\sigma_S^2}{K_{min.}^2 e^2}} - 1 \right]^{\frac{1}{2}} \tag{28}$$

Considering fig.8, the second critical e can be obtained, for the bigger e of which, σ_e may be written with a good approximation as $\pm 0.5KS$. If the second critical e is known $e_{crit.2}$ and σ_e calculation error is considered to be 1% from its true value, $e_{crit.2}$ may be calculated as following:

$$e_{crit.2} = 0.071 \cdot \frac{KS^2}{\sigma_S} \tag{29}$$

In the same manner, with equation 30, $S_{crit.2}$ may be calculated for any permitted values of radial runout, in which for bigger S, possible error may be written as $\pm 0.5KS$ with a good approximation.

$$S_{crit.2} = 3.51 \cdot e \cdot \left[\sqrt{1 + \frac{1.3\sigma_S^2}{K_{min.}^2 e^2}} + 1 \right]^{\frac{1}{2}} \tag{30}$$

Accuracy of determination is calculated from equation 20 for the values of S between two critical S s. Fig.10 indicates the values of Ss versus σ_e, $S\sigma_U$ and $U\sigma_S$ with different values of $K_{min.}$. According to the figure there is an optimum S for each determined $K_{min.}$ for which σ_e is minimized. If we call optimum S as $S_{opt.}$, then we have:

$$S_{opt.} = \sqrt{\frac{2e\sigma_S}{K_{min.}}} \qquad `(31)$$

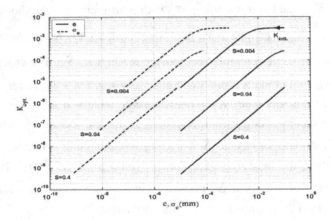

Fig. 9. $K_{opt.}$ and σ_e versus e, for different values of S

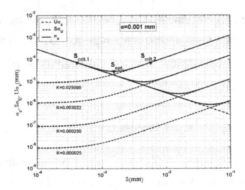

Fig. 10. Accuracy of determination σ_e, fixed component $U\sigma_S$ and variable component $S\sigma_U$ versus average code pattern line space S with different K values

Table 1 and 2 describe in brief different usage of recommended instrument for measuring radial runout of disc code pattern and installation of encoder disc.

Table 1. Specifications for recommended instrument for measuring code pattern's radial runout of an installed disc

e value	S value	Measuring accuracy	Adjusted K value	For accuracy improvement we should
All e quantities	All S values	$\pm\sqrt{S\sigma_U + U\sigma_S}$	$K > K_{crit.}$	Decrease K and σ_S
$e \geq e_{crit.1}$	All S values	$\pm(e/S)\sigma_S$	$K_{opt.}$ ↳ $K_{min.}$	Decrease σ_S
$e_{crit.2} < e <$	All S values	$\pm\sqrt{S\sigma_U + U\sigma_S}$	$K_{min.}$	Decrease σ_S and $K_{min.}$
$e \leq e_{crit.2}$	All S values	$\pm 0.5KS$	$K_{min.}$	Decrease $K_{min.}$

Table 2. Specifications of recommended instrument for installation of encoder disc

S value	e value	Measuring accuracy	Adjusted K value	For accuracy improvement we should
$S \leq S_{crit.1}$	All e values	$\pm(e/S)\sigma_S$	$K_{min.}$ or $K_{opt.}$	Decrease σ_S
$S_{crit.1} < S <$	All e values	$\pm\sqrt{S\sigma_U + U\sigma_S}$	$K_{min.}$	Decrease σ_S and $K_{min.}$
$S \geq S_{crit.2}$	All e values	$\pm 0.5KS$	$K_{min.}$	Decrease $K_{min.}$

If we use the recommended instrument according to table 1, the following inequality would prevail in measuring determined values of e for all S values

$$0.5KS < \sqrt{S\sigma_U + U\sigma_S} < (e/S)\sigma_S$$

So the best measuring accuracy for the code pattern runout is obtained when the inequality $e \leq e_{crit.2}$ applies. And if we use table 2 for installation of a disc with certain S, the inequality would always satisfies for all e quantities.

$$0.5KS > \sqrt{S\sigma_U + U\sigma_S} < (e/S)\sigma_S$$

So the best accuracy for installation of the disc is obtained when the inequality $S_{crit.1} < S < S_{crit.2}$. As well an fundamental index for instrument would be $K_{min.}$, so the instrument functionality would be higher for lower values of $K_{min.}$.

For the possibility of high speed measurement, we can measure code pattern radial runout repeatedly and then calculate its arithmetic average. Thereby we would have higher measuring accuracy which is expressed as $\pm \sigma_e / \sqrt{n}$ where n is the number of measurements.

6   Conclusion

One of the errors sources in optical rotary encoder measurement is their disc code pattern runout. A significant amount of the runout is due to runout of bearings and inappropriate installation process of encoded disc. Measuring the runout before permanent installation of encoded disc is significantly important in term of production costs, since correction of runout would be impossible after permanent installation. The runout can be quickly and accurately measured by recommended instrument during the process of installation or after temporary installation of the encoded disc. Operation of the instrument is described mathematically and performance characteristics of the instrument are indicated with analysis of measuring accuracy. Analyses indicate that the instrument can measure code pattern runout with high accuracy. By acquisition of two heads data by a PC and simulation of disc rotation and runout by software we require no microscope for installation of disc. The method may be used for automatic installation and monitoring of installation process of encoded disc.

References

1. Ernst, A.: Digital Linear and Angular Metrology. Verlag Modern Industrie AG & Co. (1990)
2. Madni, A.M., Wells, R.F.: An Advanced Steering Wheel Sensor, Industrial Technology (2000)

3. El-Kareh, B.: Fundamentals of Semiconductor Processing Technology. Kluwer Academic Publishers (1995)
4. Rainer Hagl, I.: Position Encoder Without Integral Bearing for Hollow Shafts. Heidenhainfo 5(2), 1–6 (1999)
5. Heidenhain GmbH, J.: Digital, Linear and Angular Metrology. Verlag moderne Industrie AG&Co. (1989)
6. Charkey, E.S.: Electromechanical Systems Component. John Wiley (1980)
7. FAG Rolling Bearings Standards programme (1992)
8. Briz, F., Cancelas, J.A., Diez, A.: Speed Measurement Using Rotary Encoders for High Performance ac Drives, pp. 538–542. IEEE (1994)
9. Galyer, G.F.W.: Metrology for Engineer. Caffell Publisher Ltd. (1980)
10. Heidenhain General Catalogue (1990)
11. Webster, J.G. (ed.): The measurement, Instrumentation, and sensors Handbook. CRC Press LLC, U.S. (1999)
12. Dumbrăvescu, N., Schiaua, S.: Possibilities to Increase The Resolution of Photoelectric Incremental Rorary Encoders. Materials Science in Semiconductor Processing 3, 557–561 (2000)
13. Bélanger, P.R.: Estimation of Angular Velocity and Acceleration from Shaft Encoder Measurement. In: Proceeding of the IEEE, International Conference on Robotics and Automation, Nice, France, pp. 585–592 (May 1992)
14. Korte, R.(President of Heidenhain): The Basics of Encoder, http://www.heidenhain.com
15. Orlosky, S., Avolio, G.: Basics of Rotary Optical Encoder. Control Engineering, 75–82 (1997)
16. Yo, I., Oku, H.: Deflection-Insensitive Optical Rotary Encoder, U.S. Patent #4,928,009

Design of Genetic Algorithm-Based Parking System for an Autonomous Vehicle

Xing Xiong and Byung-Jae Choi

School of Electronic Engineering, Daegu University
Jillyang, Gyeongsan, Gyeongbuk 712-714, Korea
GaleWing@gmail.com, bjchoi@daegu.ac.kr

Abstract. A Genetic Algorithm (GA) is a kind of search techniques used to find exact or approximate solutions to optimization and searching problems. This paper discusses the design of a genetic algorithm-based intelligent parking system. This is a search strategy based on the model of evolution to solve the problem of parking systems. A genetic algorithm for an optimal solution is used to find a series of optimal angles of the moving vehicle at a parking space autonomously. This algorithm makes the planning simpler and the movement more effective. At last we present some simulation results.

Keywords: Genetic Algorithm, Evolutionary Algorithm, Autonomous Vehicle, Parking System, Fitness.

1   Introduction

In recent years, autonomous parking problems have attracted a great deal of attention and more intelligent technologies are being applied to automobiles. Automatic parallel parking is an important capability for autonomous ground vehicles (AGVs). It allows the vehicles to be efficiently stored or placed when they are not in operation. It is even more important in military applications since it can be used to hide AGVs in the battlefield, for example between trees or in crevices or small buildings, hence preventing them from being detected or attacked. Several researchers studied path planning methods for the parallel parking control of AGVs, where the vehicles follow a designed sinusoidal path or a curve formed by two circular arcs ([1]-[3]).

There are many approaches suggested by researchers to solve the parking problem of autonomous vehicles in presence of static, based on soft computing. The basic method is to design a control algorithm that makes an automobile follow a reference trajectory via a tracking method. Soft computing consists of fuzzy logic, neural networks and evolutionary computation. There have been many attempts to use fuzzy logic for parking [1, 2]. Recently, it has been widespread using evolutionary computations which are robust, global and most straight forward to apply in situations where there is little or no prior knowledge about the problem to solve. GA and EA require no derivative information or formal initial estimates of the solution, and because they are stochastic in nature, they are capable of searching the global optimum.

A Genetic Algorithm is a kind of search techniques used to find exact or approximate solutions to optimization and searching problems. GAs is categorized as global search

T.-h. Kim et al. (Eds.): CA/CES³ 2011, CCIS 256, pp. 50–57, 2011.

heuristics. They are a particular class of Evolutionary Algorithms that use techniques inspired by evolutionary biology such as inheritance, mutation, selection, and crossover. GAs constructs a population of probable solutions and evolves it over the generations to find a better individual that is close to the optimal solution.

GAs are a part of evolutionary computing, which is a rapidly growing area of artificial intelligence. GAs searches the solution space of a function through the use of simulated evolution, i.e., the survival of the fittest strategy. In general, the fittest individuals of any population tend to reproduce and survive in the next generation, thus improving successive generations. As global optimization methods do not require gradient evaluation, GAs is applicable to solving a great range of optimization problems, including determination of the optimal combination of membership functions, and scaling factors reasoning rules ([4]-[8]).

In this paper our approach is based on the evolution programming principle: appropriate data structures and specialized "genetic" operators should do the job of taking care of constraints. The controlled process is the four-wheeled car. We assume that the wheels are fixed parallel to car body and allowed to roll or spin but have no side-slipping. The front wheels can turn to the left or right, however the left and right front wheels must be parallel.

This paper is organized as follows. In section 2, we introduce a way for a kinematic equation to move cars. We design the autonomous parking system based on genetic algorithms in Section 3. Computer simulation results are given to show the validity of the genetic control algorithm in Section 4. We discuss and conclude in Section 5.

2   Autonomous Vehicle and Moving Trajectories

The motion of an autonomous vehicle is firstly discussed [1]. The controlled process of the four-wheeled car is shown in Fig.1.

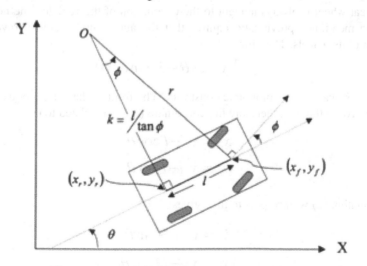

Fig. 1. Kinematic model of an autonomous vehicle

Considering the model shown on Fig.1, the rear wheel of the car are fixed parallel to car body and allowed to roll or spin but not slip. The front two wheels can turn to left or right, but the front wheels must be parallel. All the corresponding parameters of the autonomous vehicle depicted are defined in the Table 1.

Table 1. The GA-based Parking System Parameters

Parameter	Meaning
(x_r, y_r)	Position of the front wheel center
(x_f, y_f)	Position of the rear wheel center
Φ	Orientation of the steering-wheels with respect to the frame
θ	Angle between vehicle frame orientation and X-axis
l	Wheel-base of the mobile car
O	Center of curvature
r	Distance from point O to point
k	Curvature of the fifth-order polynomial
V	Velocity
pop_size	Population of chromosomes
p_{sz}	Probability of applying simple crossover
p_{ac}	Probability of applying arithmetical crossover
p_m	Probability of mutation
F	Total fitness of the population
p_i	Probability of a selection
q_i	Cumulative probability

The rear wheel is always tangent to the orientation of the vehicle. The no-slipping condition mentioned previously requires that the autonomous vehicle travels in the direction of its wheels. Therefore:

$$\dot{y}_r \cos\theta - \dot{x}_r \sin\theta = 0 \tag{1}$$

This is the so-called nonholonomic constraint. The front of the autonomous vehicle is fixed relative to the rear, therefore the coordinate (x_r, y_r) is related to (x_f, y_f):

$$x_r = x_f - l\cos\theta$$
$$y_r = y_f - l\sin\theta \tag{2}$$

Differentiating (2) with respect to time gives:

$$\dot{x}_r = \dot{x}_f + \dot{\theta}l\sin\theta$$
$$\dot{y}_r = \dot{y}_f - \dot{\theta}l\cos\theta \tag{3}$$

Substituting (3) into (1), we get:

$$\dot{x}_f \sin \theta - \dot{y}_f \cos \theta + \dot{\theta} l = 0$$

(4)

From Fig. 1, we have:

$$\dot{x}_f = V \cos(\theta + \phi)$$
$$\dot{y}_f = V \sin(\theta + \phi)$$

(5)

Substituting (5) into (4), we derive:

$$\dot{\theta} = V \frac{\sin \phi}{l}$$

(6)

The equations (5) and (6) are the kinematic equations of the autonomous vehicle with respect to the axle center of the front wheels. We rewrite them as:

$$\dot{x}_f = v \cos(\theta + \phi)$$
$$\dot{y}_f = v \sin(\theta + \phi)$$
$$\dot{\theta} = v \frac{\sin \phi}{l}$$

(7)

The equations in (7) are used to generate the next forward state position of the vehicle when the present states and control input are given. Following these equations describing the motion kinematics, we easily obtain the kinematic equations of the vehicle motion described by the position of the center of the front wheels (x_r, y_r).

3   Design of GA-Based Parking System

The central problem in applications of genetic algorithms is the constraints – few approaches to the constraint problem in genetic algorithms have previously been proposed. One of these uses penalty functions as an adjustment to the optimized objective function, other approaches use "decoders" or "repair" algorithms, which avoid building an illegal individual, or repair one, respectively. However, these approaches suffer from the disadvantage of being tailored to the specific problem and are not sufficiently broad to handle a variety of problems.

Our approach is based on the evolution programming principle: appropriate data structures and specialized "genetic" operators should do the job of taking care of constraints.

In GA, the fitness function plays the role of the environment, rating the potential solutions in terms of their fitness. The choice of a fitness function is usually very specific to the problem under consideration. The fitness function of a chromosome measures the objective cost function.

A path can be either feasible (collision free) or infeasible because the intermediate nodes can fall on any part of the parking area. The evaluation needs to be able to distinguish between the feasible and infeasible paths and tell the differences in the path qualities within either category. The evaluation function is [8]:

$$f(x) = \begin{cases} \dfrac{1}{y_{fr} - (x_{fr} * \tan\theta + y_e - x_e * \tan\theta)} & y_{fr} > x_{fr} * \tan\theta + y_e - x_e * \tan\theta \\ 0 & y_{fr} \le x_{fr} * \tan\theta + y_e - x_e * \tan\theta \end{cases} \quad (8)$$

The definition of individual fitness is according to the following rules:

1) If the generated path is not feasible (obstacle collision), its fitness is equal to zero.
2) If the generated path is feasible, its fitness is as follows:
   - If the vehicle and the obstacle have a common area, the higher the fitness.
   - The smaller the angle between the car and the goal-point, the higher the fitness.

In this section we present an evolution program GA-based system for this class of parking problems. The parking algorithm is based on the genetic algorithm and is summarized by:

Procedure GA-based Paring System
Begin
◆ *Generate initial solutions v*
◆ *Action*
    ★ *Compute the fitness for each chromosome in the current population using the fitness function*
    ★ *Update the best-so-far*
    ★ *Calculate the fitness value f(x) for each chromosome $v_i(i=1,...pop\_size)$*

$$F = \sum_{i=1}^{pop\_size} f_i(x)$$

    ★ *Find the total fitness of the population*
    ★ *Compute the probability of a selection p_i for each chromosome v_i*

$$p_i = \frac{f_i(x)}{F}$$

(i=1,...pop_size):
    ★ *Compute a cumulative probability q_i for each chromosome v_i*

$$q_i = \sum_{n=1}^{i} p_n$$

(i=1,...pop_size):
    ★ *Generate a random (float) number r from the range [0...1].*

★ *If $r<q_1$ then select the first chromosome v_i; otherwise select the ith chromosome v_i (i=1,2,...pop_size) such that $q_{i-1}<r\le=q_i$*

★ *Generate a random (float) number r from the range [0...1].*

★ *If $r<q_{ac}$ then select a given chromosome for arithmetical crossover.*

★ *Generate a random (float) number r from the range [0...1].*

★ *If $r<q_{sc}$ then select a given chromosome for single crossover.*

★ *Generate a random (float) number r from the range [0...1].*

★ *If $r<q_m$, the mutate the bit.*

★ *Generation = generation + 1.*

★ *End*

◆ *While (generation<maximum)*

◆ *End*

4   Simulation Results

The proposed algorithm has been tested using a MATLAB simulation environment. The autonomous vehicle simulation is given to demonstrate the effectiveness of the proposed scheme. Taking real life into account, the length of the garage is about 1.5 times longer than the car; the width of the garage is 1.5 to 2 times wider than the car.

In our simulation, the autonomous vehicle used in the simulation has the following dimensions: the CLMR length L=4m and the width W=2m. We assumed that the length of the garage is 5m and the width is 3.4m. We exploited the following situations to test the effectiveness of the proposed GA-based scheme. The CLMRs have a different initial location (x_f, y_f,) and orientation θ. The CLMRs all have the same end location (16, 0). The simulation results are shown in Figure. 2. The simulation time is also shown in the figure.

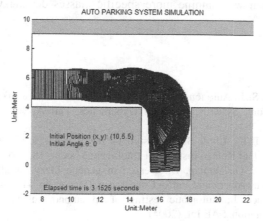

(a)   Start Posture (x_f, y_f, θ)= (10, 5.5, 0.0°)

Fig. 2. The simulation results of the long car parking

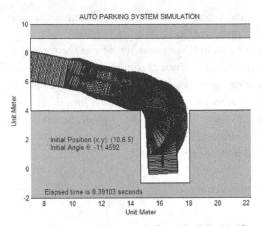

(b) Start Posture $(x_f, y_f, \theta) = (10, 6.5, -11.4°)$

Fig. 2. (*Continued*).

5   Conclusions

In this paper, we have presented the moving equations used in an autonomous car-like vehicle, designed its parking path using a genetic algorithm for optimal performance and a trajectory tracking controller. We incorporate problem-specific knowledge into our systems, using evolution programs. The GA-based parking system is a stronger method than the conventional parking system and can be applied to a function with only linear constraints. The advantage of the proposed method is that it yields an effective parking path and further extends the controlled workspace to a larger region. By the use of the GA, the performance of the parallel parking algorithm is tuned to behave well for both types of steering systems in tight parking spaces. We will prove the same results when we examine more specific classes dealing with the optimal control problem.

References

1. Li, T.-H.S., Chang, S.-J.: Autonomous fuzzy parking control of a car-like mobile robot. In: Proc. IEEE Int. Conf. Systems, Man and Cybernetics, Part A, vol. Aut3, pp. 415–465 (2003)
2. Hao, Y.-H., Kim, T.-K., Choi, B.-J.: Design of fuzzy logic based parking systems for intelligent vehicles. J. of Korean Institute of Intelligent Systems 18, 1–6 (2008)
3. Zhao, Y., Collins, E.-G., Dunlap, D.: Design of genetic fuzzy parallel parking control systems. In: Proc. The American Control Conference, Denver, pp. 4107–4112 (2003)
4. Bühler, O., Wegener, J.: Automatic testing of an autonomous parking system using evolutionary computation. SAE Int. (2004)
5. Zhang, H.-D., Dong, B.-H., Cen, Y.-W., Zheng, R.: Path planning algorithm for mobile robot based on path grids encoding novel mechanism. In: Int. Conference on Natural Computation, vol. 3 (2007)

6. Hu, X.-Z., Xie, C.-X.: Niche genetical agorithm for robot path planning. In: Int. Conference on Natural Computation, vol. 3 (2007)
7. Wan, T.-R., Chen, H., Earnshaw, R.: Real-time path planning for Navigation in unknown environment. In: Proc. Theory and Practice of Computer Graphics, vol. 3 (2003)
8. Geiger, B.-R., Horn, J.-F., Delullo, A.-M., Long, L.-N.: Optimal path planning of UAVs using direct collocation with nonlinear programming. In: AIAA GNC Conference, pp. 1–13 (2006)

A Model of Hierarchically Consistent Control of Nonlinear Dynamical Systems

Armen G. Bagdasaryan[1] and Tai-hoon Kim[2]

[1] Russian Academy of Sciences,
Trapeznikov Institute for Control Sciences,
Profsoyuznaya 65, 117997 Moscow, Russia
abagdasari@hotmail.com
[2] Department of Multimedia, Hannam University,
133 Ojeong-dong, Daedeok-gu, Daejeon, Korea
taihoonn@hnu.ac.kr

Abstract. Most of the real modern systems are complex, nonlinear, and large-scale. A natural approach for reducing the complexity of large scale systems places a hierarchical structure on the system architecture. In hierarchical control models, the notion of consistency is much important, as it ensures the implementation of high-level objectives by the lower level systems. In this work, we present a model for synthesis of hierarchically consistent control systems for complex nonlinear multidimensional and multicoupled dynamical systems, using invariant manifold theory.

Keywords: geometric control, nonlinear system, hierarchical consistency, dynamics, attractors, invariant manifolds, control system synthesis.

1 Introduction

Analysis and synthesis of control systems for complex multidimensional and multicoupled dynamic systems is accompanied by large amount of state coordinates. In this connection, in order to simplify and reduce the original system to a smaller dimension, methods for decomposition of complex and large-scale dynamical systems into simpler and independent subsystems are widely used. Among these methods, the principles of hierarchization of complex systems have received much attention, and various approaches to building hierarchical control systems have been developed greatly.

Typically, complexity is reduced by imposing a hierarchical structure on the system architecture. The main types of hierarchical structures are classified and described in [1]. In such a structure, systems of higher functionality reside at higher levels of the hierarchy and are therefore unaware of unnecessary lower-level details [2]. Fig. 1 shows a typical two-layer control hierarchy which is frequently used in the quite common planning and control hierarchical systems. Multilayered versions of Fig. 1 are used in many specific systems, from physical and engineering to social and economic, for example, multilevel control models were employed in [4]–[6] and in [7]–[11]. In this layered control paradigm, each

T.-h. Kim et al. (Eds.): CA/CES³ 2011, CCIS 256, pp. 58–64, 2011.
© Springer-Verlag Berlin Heidelberg 2011

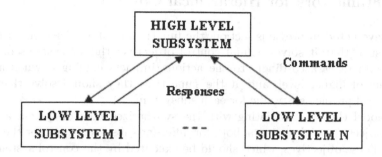

Fig. 1. Two-layer control hierarchy

layer has different objectives. In performing their tasks, the higher level uses a coarser system model than the lower level. One of the main challenges in hierarchical systems is the extraction of a hierarchy of models at various levels of abstraction which are compatible with the functionality and objectives of each layer [2].

In hierarchical control models, the notion of consistency is much important, as it ensures the implementation of high-level objectives by the lower level systems. In this work, a model for synthesis of hierarchically consistent control systems for complex nonlinear multidimensional and multicoupled dynamical systems is presented. The aim is to make a step toward translating the hierarchical models and concepts, presented in the paper [4], into the language of invariant manifold theory. Specifically, we are interested, for example, how hierarchical state, sequential-parallel state, aggregated state, coupled dynamics, etc., introduced for state transition diagrams, can be adequately described by means of invariant manifolds. The finite dimensional invariant manifold theory is not only very general, from the point of view of mathematical assumptions, but it is broadly applicable to a variety of specific systems arising in applications [12]–[18].

In our approach, a hierarchical system is understood as a set of interacting subsystems that organize separate hierarchical levels. On each level, the subsystems are described in the corresponding space of parameters and variables. Moreover, on each hierarchical level, the system has its local objectives – invariants, which are defined in the state space of the system. In such systems, a subsystem located at a higher level has a direct impact on the corresponding subsystems residing at lower level. This impact is performed by changing the objectives of subordinate subsystems. Although, the objectives and actions of subsystem of higher level are prioritized, and subsystems of lower level are obliged to obey them, the interaction between higher-level element and each of the lower-level elements is such that the efficiency of actions of one element depends on the actions of the other. Thus, the efficiency of the system as a whole depends not only on the top-down intervention, but also on the bottom-up response, that is, on the consistent behavior of all elements of the system.

2   A Framework for Hierarchical Control

As we have noted in previous section, the functioning of a subsystem of higher level is such that it solves a final control objective; the subsystems of lower level should react accordingly to the actions/impacts coming down from the subsystem of higher level, and at the same time they should solve their own local control problems, specific for each subsystem.

We model this by associating with the synthesized control system a set of control objectives G, invariants, both for different subsystems and for the whole system. These objectives, which should be executed by the control system, can be of different nature and depend on the concrete applied system.

The set of objectives G has a hierarchical structure; it is decomposed into subsets $\Sigma_j, j = \overline{1, N+1}$, consisting of the objectives of each of the subsystems, and

$$\bigcup_{j=1}^{N+1} \Sigma_j = G. \tag{1}$$

G_j is the set of objectives of j-th subsystem. For the set of objectives of the synthesized control system, we assume that $\bigcap_{j=1}^{N+1} \Sigma_j = \emptyset$. However, in case this condition does not hold, one has to define the priority rules and coordination procedures by means of certain formal scheme.

We assume that for the control system to ensure the implementation of objectives, it should produce a corresponding set of solutions Ξ. This set Ξ, analogously to (1), consists of subsets $\Delta_j, \overline{1, N+1}$, for which we suppose that

$$\bigcup_{j=1}^{N+1} \Delta_j = \Xi. \tag{2}$$

Therefore, the control system is designed such that each subset of objectives $\Sigma_j, j = \overline{1, N+1}$ is associated with corresponding subset of solutions $\Delta_j, \overline{1, N+1}$.

The dynamics of high-level control subsystem is described by the equation

$$S_h \quad : \quad \dot{\mathbf{x}}(t) = f\left[\mathbf{x}(t), \mathbf{u}(t), \mathbf{q}(t)\right], \tag{3}$$
$$\mathbf{y}(t) = h\left[\mathbf{x}(t), \mathbf{y}(t)\right],$$

where $\mathbf{x} \in \mathcal{X} \subset \mathbb{R}^n, \mathbf{u} \in \mathcal{U} \subset \mathbb{R}^m, \mathbf{y} \in \mathcal{Y} \subset \mathbb{R}^r, \mathbf{q} \in \mathcal{Q} \subset \mathbb{R}^d$; $\mathbf{x}(t), \mathbf{u}(t), \mathbf{y}(t)$, and $\mathbf{q}(t)$ represent, respectively, the state vector, the control vector, the output vector, and the perturbation vector.

The dynamics of each of the low-level subsystems is described by the equations

$$S_l \quad : \quad \dot{\mathbf{z}}(t) = g\left[\mathbf{z}(t), \mathbf{w}(t), \mathbf{v}(t)\right], \tag{4}$$
$$p = s\left[\mathbf{z}(t), \mathbf{w}(t)\right],$$

where $\mathbf{z} \in \mathcal{Z} \subset \mathbb{R}^k, \mathbf{w} \in \mathcal{W} \subset \mathbb{R}^\ell, \mathbf{v} \in \mathcal{V} \subset \mathbb{R}^\lambda$; $\mathbf{z}(t), \mathbf{w}(t), \mathbf{v}(t)$, and p represent, respectively, the state vector, the control vector, the perturbation vector, and the output variable of j-th subsystem; and $\dim \Sigma_j \leq \dim \mathcal{W}^{(j)}$. The neighbor levels are connected by the equation $\mathbf{x} = \mathbf{F}(\mathbf{p})$, where $\mathbf{p} = [p_1, p_2, ..., p_N]^T$.

The efficiency of the approach is justified by the following: first, the use of the correspondence "objectives–solutions" allows for natural dynamic decomposition of comlex nonlinear system into subsystems; second, each of the subsystems or a group of subsystems is immersed onto the intersection of the corresponding *local attractors*, invariant manifolds, related to the concrete subset of objectives $\Sigma_j, j = \overline{1, M}, M \leq N$, but the whole system is immersed into the *global attractor*, called *hierarchical state manifold*, which corresponds to the set of system objectives G (1); third, at a higher level of decision making one takes into account the behavior of the subsystems residing at the lower level, in the form of equations that describe the dynamics of these subsystems on local attractors – equations of "low-dimensional" dynamics. Another advantage is that this approach is applicable at any level of abstraction.

3   Design and Synthesis of Hierarchical Control System

Let us consider in more detail how the control system can be designed and synthesized with the use of the proposed in the previous section the general framework of hierarchical control model.

Let the behaviour of the control system of higher level is described by the vector differential equation:

$$S_{N+1}: \quad \dot{\mathbf{x}}(t) = \mathbf{A}(\mathbf{x})\mathbf{x} + \mathbf{B}(\mathbf{x})\mathbf{L} + \mathbf{H}(\mathbf{x}, \mathbf{f})\mathbf{f} \qquad (5)$$
$$\mathbf{y} = \mathbf{C}(\mathbf{x})\mathbf{x},$$

where $\mathbf{x} \in \mathbb{R}^n$ is the state vector of the control system of higher level, $\mathbf{y} \in \mathbb{R}^r$ is the output vector, $\mathbf{L} \in \mathbb{R}^N$ is the vector of control actions of the system of higher level, $\mathbf{f} \in \mathbb{R}^\theta$ is the perturbation vector; $\mathbf{A}(\mathbf{x}), \mathbf{B}(\mathbf{x}), \mathbf{C}(\mathbf{x})$, and $\mathbf{H}(\mathbf{x}, \mathbf{f})$ are the functional matrices of system state, input, output, and perturbation of dimensions $n \times n, n \times N, r \times n$, and $n \times \theta$, respectively.

The behaviour of the control subsystems of lower level is given by the following equations:

$$S_j: \quad \dot{\mathbf{z}}^{(j)}(t) = \mathbf{R}^{(j)}\left(\mathbf{z}^{(j)}\right)\mathbf{z}^{(j)} + \mathbf{P}^{(j)}\left(\mathbf{z}^{(j)}\right)\mathbf{u}^{(j)} + \mathbf{S}^{(j)}\mathbf{v}^{(j)}, \; j = \overline{1, N}, \quad (6)$$
$$Out_j = \mathbf{d}^{(j)}\left(\mathbf{z}^{(j)}\right)\mathbf{z}^{(j)},$$

where $\mathbf{z}^{(j)} \in \mathbb{R}^{\eta_j}$ is the state vector of j-th subsystem of lower level, Out_j is the output variable of j-th subsystem, $\mathbf{u}^{(j)} \in \mathbb{R}^{\mu_j}$ is the vector of control actions of j-th subsystem, $\mathbf{v}^{(j)} \in \mathbb{R}^{\sigma_j}$ is the perturbation vector acting on j-th subsystem of lower level, $\mathbf{R}^{(j)}\left(\mathbf{z}^{(j)}\right), \mathbf{P}^{(j)}\left(\mathbf{z}^{(j)}\right)$, and $\mathbf{S}^{(j)}$ are the matrices of dimensions $\eta_j \times \eta_j, \eta_j \times \mu_j$, and $\eta_j \times \sigma_j$, respectively; and $\mathbf{d}^{(j)}\left(\mathbf{z}^{(j)}\right)$ is the row matrix of the output.

The higher level and lower levels of hierarchical system are connected by the equation

$$L = \mathcal{F}(\mathbf{Out}) \tag{7}$$

where $\mathcal{F}$ is a functional and $\mathbf{Out} = [Out_1, Out_2, ..., Out_N]^T$.

The process of design of hierarchical structure of the control system is preceded by the synthesis of a set of local regulators of the subsystems of lower level. For this purpose, the subsets of objectives – invariants for subsystems of lower level, are defined. These subsets contain: (1) invariants that provide the implementation of the final control objective – global invariants, (2) invariants that determine the implementation of some relations/objectives – local invariants, by the subsystems $S_j, j = \overline{1, N}$ in the synthesized control system; besides, the dimension of the subset Σ_j can not exceed the dimension of control vector μ_j of the corresponding subsystem $S_j, j = \overline{1, N}$. Based on the subsets $\Sigma_j, j = \overline{1, N}$, we introduce a set of sequential-parallel invariant manifolds $\psi^{(j)} = 0$, which satisfy the vector functional differential equation

$$\dot{\psi}^{(j)}(t) + \Lambda^{(j)}\psi^{(j)} = 0, \tag{8}$$

where $\Lambda^{(j)}$ are matrices such that the solution $\psi^{(j)} = 0$ of the equation is asymptotically stable.

As soon as the points of trajectories of the subsystems $S_j, j = \overline{1, N}$ fall into the intersection of the corresponding set of invariant manifolds $\psi^{(j)} = 0$, the behavior of the subsystems is described by the equations of reduced dimensionality – equations of low-dimensional dynamics

$$S_j: \quad \dot{\hat{\mathbf{z}}}^{(j)}(t) = \hat{\mathbf{R}}^{(j)}\left(\hat{\mathbf{z}}^{(j)}, \phi^{(j)}\right)\hat{\mathbf{z}}^{(j)} + \hat{\mathbf{S}}^{(j)}\mathbf{v}^{(j)}, \; j = \overline{1, N}, \tag{9}$$

$$L_j = \mathbf{d}^{(j)}\left(\hat{\mathbf{z}}^{(j)}, \phi^{(j)}\right)\hat{\mathbf{z}}^{(j)},$$

where $\phi^{(j)}$ is an action for j-th subsystem.

The main distinction of this approach is that upon synthesizing the regulator of higher level, one takes into account the low-dimensional dynamics of subsystems of lower level. Therefore, using the equation (9) and the coupling equation (7), one can get the extended model of the subsystem of higher level

$$S_{N+1}: \quad \dot{\hat{\mathbf{x}}}(t) = \tilde{\mathbf{A}}(\hat{\mathbf{x}}, \phi)\hat{\mathbf{x}} + \mathbf{H}(\hat{\mathbf{x}}, \mathbf{f})\mathbf{f} \tag{10}$$

$$\mathbf{y} = \mathbf{C}(\mathbf{x})\mathbf{x},$$

where $\hat{\mathbf{x}}$ is the extended state vector of the subsystem of higher level.

The synthesis of coordinating regulator is accompanied by determination of the objectives subset of the subsystem of higher level (10). On the basis of this subset, one forms the set of sequential-parallel invariant manifolds $\psi^{(N+1)} = 0$ that satisfy the vector functional differential equation

$$\dot{\psi}^{(N+1)}(t) + \Lambda^{(N+1)}\psi^{(N+1)} = 0, \tag{11}$$

where $\Lambda^{(N+1)}$ are matrices such that the solution $\psi^{(N+1)} = 0$ of the equation is asymptotically stable.

Thus, as a result of the process of synthesis of hierarchical control system we find the set of equations of local regulators-executors

$$\mathbf{u}^{(j)} = \mathbf{u}^{(j)}\left(\mathbf{z}^{(j)}, \phi^{(j)}\right), j = \overline{1, N}. \tag{12}$$

These local regulators generate the collection of solution subsets $\Delta_j, j = \overline{1, N}$ and provide the implementation of the collection of objective subsets $\Sigma_j, j = \overline{1, N}$. Besides this, the coordinating regulator

$$\phi = \phi(\mathbf{x}). \tag{13}$$

is produced, which generates the solution subset Δ_{N+1} providing the implementation of the objective subset Σ_{N+1}.

The synthesized hierarchical control system (5), (6), (12), (13) provides the implementation of control objectives (or, solution of control problems) represented in the form of invariants set G. On the basis of invariants, the corresponding invariant manifolds of subsystems of higher level $\psi^{(N+1)} = 0$ and of lower levels $\psi^{(j)} = 0$ are constructed. By controlling by means of the local regulators (12), the points of trajectories of subsystems fall into the neighborhood of intersection of corresponding set of manifolds $\psi^{(j)} = 0$, which change under the actions of coordinating regulator of higher level (13). Thus, the up-down control methodology is realized. At the same time, if the system falls into the neighborhood of intersection of corresponding set of manifolds, then we immediately get the guaranteed and efficient implementation of control system objectives G. This also provides the asymptotic stability of synthesized hierarchical system in the admissible domain of changes of phase coordinates.

4   Conclusions

In this paper, we have proposed a technique for constructing hierarchically consistent control systems for solving complex control problems of nonlinear, multi-dimensional dynamical systems. This was achieved by applying the concepts of invariant manifold theory to hierarchical control of nonlinear dynamical systems. The approach is quite general to be applied to different kinds of control systems, and, in addition, it mathematically formalizes the concept of hierarchical and sequential/parallel inputs and states used in modern control system design.

Acknowledgments. This work was supported by the Security Engineering Research Center, granted by the Korea Ministry of Knowledge Economy.

References

1. Mesarovic, M.D.: Theory of Hierarchical, Multilevel, Systems. In: Mathematics in Science and Engineering, vol. 68. Academic Press, New York (1970)
2. Girard, A., Lafferriere, G., Sastry, S.: Hierarchically Consistent Control Systems. IEEE Trans. Automatic Control 45, 1144–1160 (2000)

3. Lollini, P., Bondavalli, A., Di Giandomenico, F.: A Modeling Methodology for Hierarchical Control System and its Application. J. Braz. Comp. Soc. 10, 57–69 (2005)
4. Bagdasaryan, A.: Discrete Dynamic Simulation Models and Technique for Complex Control Systems. Simulation Modelling Practice and Theory 19, 1061–1087 (2011)
5. Bagdasaryan, A., Kim, T.-H.: Dynamic Simulation and Synthesis Technique for Complex Control Systems. In: Ślęzak, D., Kim, T.-h., Stoica, A., Kang, B.-H. (eds.) CA 2009. CCIS, vol. 65, pp. 15–27. Springer, Heidelberg (2009)
6. Bagdasaryan, A.G.: Mathematical and Computer Tools of Discrete Dynamic Modeling and Analysis of Complex Systems in Control Loop. Int. J. Math. Models Methods Appl. Sci. 2, 82–95 (2008)
7. Mahmoud, M.S.: Multilevel Systems Control and Applications: A Survey. IEEE Transactions on System, Man, and Cybernetics 7(3), 125–143 (1978)
8. Park, J., Obeysekera, J., VanZee, R.: Multilayer Control Hierarchy for Water Management Decisions in Integrated Hydrologic Simulation Model. Journal of Water Resources Planning and Management 133(2), 117–125 (2007)
9. Singh, M.G., Hindi, K.: A Multilevel Multilayer Framework for Manufacturing Control. Journal of Intelligent and Robotic Systems 4, 75–93 (1991)
10. Tatjewski, P.: Advanced Control and On-line Process Optimization in Multilayer Structures. Annual Reviews in Control 32, 71–85 (2008)
11. Boskovic, J.D., Prasanth, R., Mehra, R.K.: A Multilayer Control Architecture for Unmanned Aerial Vehicles. In: Proc. of the American Control Conference, vol. 3, pp. 1825–1830 (2002)
12. Josić, K.: Invariant Manifolds and Synchronization of Coupled Dynamical Systems. Phys. Rev. Lett. 80, 3053–3056 (1998)
13. Kwong, C.P., Zheng, Y.-K.: Aggregation on Manifolds. Int. J. Systems Sci. 17(4), 581–589 (1986)
14. Liu, Y.: The Invariant Manifold Method and the Controllability of Nonlinear Control System. Appl. Math. Mech. 11(21), 1320–1330 (2010)
15. Karagiannis, D., Astolfi, A.: Non-linear and Adaptive Flight Control of Autonomous Aircraft Using Invariant Manifolds. J. Aerospace Engineering 224(4), 403–415 (2010)
16. Yu, X., Chen, G., Xia, Y., Song, Y., Cao, Z.: An Invariant-Manifold-Based Method for Chaos Control. IEEE Trans. Circuits and Systems 48(8), 930–937 (2001)
17. Tian, Y.-P., Yu, X.: Adaptive Control of Chaotic Dynamical Systems Using Invariant Manifold Approach. IEEE Trans. Circuits and Systems 47(10), 1537–1542 (2000)
18. Astolfi, A., Ortega, R.: Invariant Manifolds, Asymptotic Immersion and the (Adaptive) Stabilization of Nonlinear Systems. In: Zinober, A., Owens, D. (eds.) Nonlinear and Adaptive Control. LNCIS, vol. 281, pp. 1–20. Springer, Heidelberg (2003)
19. Zhong, H., Wonham, W.M.: On the Consistency of Hierarchical Supervision in Discrete-Event Systems. IEEE Trans. Automatic Control 35, 1125–1134 (1990)
20. Nijmeijer, H., van der Schaft, A.: Nonlinear Dynamical Control Systems. Springer, New York (1990)
21. Jurdjevic, V.: Geometric Control Theory. Cambridge University Press (1997)
22. Dubrovin, B.A., Fomenko, A.T., Novikov, S.P.: Modern Geometry. Springer, New York (1985)

RETRACTED CHAPTER: Characteristics Analysis of the Motor Block Lattice Resistor of a High Speed Train by Structure Improvement

Dae-Dong Lee[1], Jae-Myung Shim[2], and Dong-Seok Hyun[1]

[1] Department of Electrical Engineering, Hanyang University,
Seoul 133-791, Republic of Korea
ldd77@hanbat.ac.kr, dshyun@hanyang.ac.kr
[2] Department of Electrical Engineering, Hanbat National University,
Daejeon 305-719, Republic of Korea
jmshim@hanbat.ac.kr

Abstract. Dynamic braking, which is frequently used in high speed trains, is a function and device that provides braking force using the electricity that is generated from a traction electric motor, and also dissipates heat from the lattice resistor that converts the current from the traction electric motor into heat. The heat from the lattice resistor, which is located in the motor block of a high speed train, damages the resistor wires and induces cracks in the insulators that affect the dynamic choppers, traction inverters, and electric motors during dynamic braking, and makes it difficult to control driving during acceleration or deceleration. In this study, the motor block lattice resistor, which was recently suggested to compensate for these problems, was designed, and experiments were performed on heat analysis simulation and temperature increase. Further field tests were performed to verify the advantages of the motor block lattice resistor.

Keywords: Braking resistor, field test, high speed train, motor block lattice resistor, temperature increase test, total heat flux.

1   Introduction

Technologies of railway vehicles have been enhancing the overall capabilities to design and operate mass transportation systems such as general trains, subway trains, and light rail transit. Korea Train eXpress(KTX), which was recently introduced and operated, has 20 cars per train and currently has 46 trains running, 34 of which are domestically manufactured and the others, imported [1].

The power source of the train is 25kV, single-phase, 60Hz AC, and its traction and braking forces are 13,560 (kW) and 300 (KN), respectively. Its braking methods include regeneration braking, dynamic braking, and air braking. The motor block resistor, which is used in regeneration and dynamic braking, is called the lattice resistor.

The motor block is a key element of the performance enhancement and stability of a train. The electric braking circuit of a high speed train normally secures the braking force by controlling the braking chopper according to the amount of regenerated

---

This chapter has been retracted due to multiple publications. The erratum to this chapter is available at DOI: 10.1007/978-3-642-26010-0_48

T.-h. Kim et al. (Eds.): CA/CES³ 2011, CCIS 256, pp. 65–74, 2011.
© Springer-Verlag Berlin Heidelberg 2011

energy. In case of emergency braking or a dead section, however, when the current input to the motor block is above the limit, the circuit activates the dynamic braking, in which the excessive current is discharged as a form of heat through the lattice resistor. The heat from the lattice resistor, however, damages the resistor wires and induces cracks in the insulators that affect the dynamic choppers, inverters, and traction electric motors during dynamic braking, and make it difficult to control driving during acceleration or deceleration.

In this study, the motor block lattice resistor, which was recently suggested to compensate for these problems, was designed, and heat analysis simulation and temperature increase experiments were performed. The advantages of the motor block lattice resistor were verified through further field tests.

2   Motor Block Lattice Resistor

2.1   Structure of the Propulsion System of a High Speed Train

The parts of the motor block of a high speed train are shown in Fig. 1. The motor block has two thyristor converters, one smoothing reactor, two inverters, two three-phase synchronous motors, one chopper, and two Power Factor Correction (PFC) circuits for power factor control and harmonic wave reduction [2].

The main transformer converts the 25kV cable voltage into 1,800 V, and the two single-phase bridge rectifiers that are serially connected and make up a thyristor

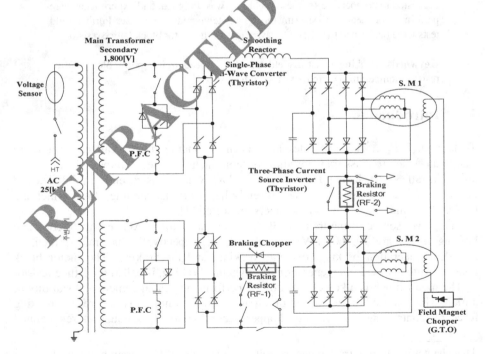

Fig. 1. Circuit of the propulsion control system of a high speed train

perform variable rectification of the transformer's second winding voltage according to the switching degree. The current of the rectified DC source is smoothened by the smoothing reactor and flows into the two traction electric motors, which are composed of two 1,130kW three-phase synchronous motors and two three-phase current-type inverters that control acceleration or deceleration and regeneration [3-5].

The inverter has a forced commutation mode and a natural commutation mode. In the forced commutation mode, the current is rectified by the capacitor and thyristor, and in the natural commutation mode, by the inter-phase voltage generated by the counter-electromotive force of a synchronous motor [6].

2.2   Structure and Role of the Motor Block Lattice Resistor

The motor block lattice resistor is installed at the direct-current link of the input unit of the high speed train's propulsion control system, as shown in Fig. 1. It is called a 'lattice resistor' because the resistors are arranged in the form of a lattice.

The lattice resistor is controlled by the separately excited inverter operation of a converter and composed of two circuits: one for securing the electric braking force in normal operations by controlling the braking chopper according to the amount of the regenerated energy, and the other for dissipating the generated electric energy from the synchronous motor in the case of a dead section, a cable voltage of over 25 kV, and a transformer malfunction.

One of the roles of the lattice resistor is to stabilize the direct end voltage through a chopper device and to perform dynamic braking in dead sections. This is why the lattice resistor is sometimes called a 'braking resistor.'

As seen in Fig. 1, the RF-1 lattice resistor is used to dissipate electric energy under dynamic braking, and RF-2 is used to adjust the cooling fan voltage to cool the resistor and the inside of the motor block.

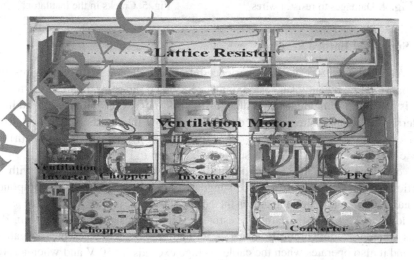

Fig. 2. Structure of the motor block

The lattice resistor, installed in the upper position of the motor block structure as seen in Fig. 2, is cooled by the fan motor located underneath, and the blown heat is discharged through high speed train hood, which is installed on top of the high speed train, as seen in Fig. 3. The damages to the resistor wires due to the heat, as seen in Fig. 4, and the cracks in the insulators, as seen in Fig. 5, affect dynamic braking.

Fig. 3. Fan hood of the lattice resistor

Fig. 4. Damages to resistor wires   **Fig. 5.** Cracks in the insulator

2.3   Suggested Lattice Resistor

As conventional lattice resistors experienced frequent damages to their wires with heat expansion, the recently suggested model reinforced the central part of the resistor, which is the most vulnerable part, with insulators to prevent damage. In addition, considering the temperature increase due to the narrow interval between the lattices, instead of the previous structure of 28 resistors (28S), as seen in Fig. 6 (a), the structure with 30 resistors (30S) was suggested, as seen in Fig. 6 (b).

The components of the conventional resistor wires were Ni/Cr/Fe with the proportions of 48/23/29%, whereas the suggested model excludes the Fe component, which has a low melting point and uses the Ni/Cr alloy at a ratio of 80/20%.

In addition, the suggested lattice resistor model was designed to operate in dead sections when Vacuum Circuit Breaker(VCB) and converter devices have a gate off status, and it also operates when the cable voltage exceeds 2,850 V and when a forced short-circuit or emergency resistor braking is applied.

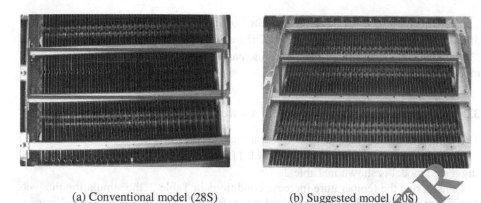

(a) Conventional model (28S)   (b) Suggested model (30S)

Fig. 6. Structure of lattice resistors

3   Simulation Results and Analysis

3.1   Calculation of the Increase in the Temperature of a Lattice Resistor

Temperature increases in the lattice resistors were calculated for both the conventional and suggested models during dynamic braking to consider the temperature increase due to the narrow intervals of the lattices.

The lattice resistor had six units of resistor wires that were serially connected with a resistance of 0.55 Ω per unit and a combined resistance of 3.3 Ω. The operating peak current (I_P) under the combined resistance (R_C) of 3.3 Ω and the operating voltage of 2,850 V was calculated as shown in equation (1). The amount of heat (Qcal) generated in the unit resistor with a resistance of 0.55 Ω for one second was calculated using equation (2), as follows:

$$Ip = V/R_C \tag{1}$$

$$Q_{cal} = 0.24I^2RT \tag{2}$$

Where in the specific heat (C) of the components of the resistor wire were 0.2079 cal/g℃ for Ni, 0.1178 cal/g℃ for Cr, and 0.1070 cal/g℃ for Fe.

The components of the conventional model (28S) were Ni/Cr/Fe with the proportions of 48/23/29%. The total mass (M) was 20.23 kg/m³, and the components of the suggested model (30S) were Ni/Cr at a ratio of 80/20% and a total mass (M) of 21.08 kg/m³.

The composite specific heat (Cs) of the conventional model (28S) was 0.1579 cal/g℃, and that of the suggested model (30S) was 0.1899 cal/g℃. The temperature increase (T) was calculated using equation (3).

$$Qcal = C_sMT \tag{3}$$

The calculation with equation (3) resulted in an increase in the final temperature of 30.82 °C/s for the conventional model (28S) and 24.59 °C/s for the suggested model (30S). It was found that the temperature increase was 6.28 °C/s slower in the suggested model than in the conventional model.

3.2   Thermal Energy Distribution in a Lattice Resistor

The temperature increase in the conventional model, under the conditions of no cooling fan and an initial temperature of 11 °C, is shown in Table 1. That of the suggested model is shown in Table 2.

Considering the temperature increase conditions in Table 2, the simulation that was performed with ANSYS, thermal analysis software, resulted in a thermal energy distribution based on the location of the lattice resistor for the conventional model, as seen in Fig. 7 (a), and suggested model, as shown in Fig. 7 (b). The given thermal energy distributions by location are listed in Table 3. The measured thermal energy distribution was lower in the suggested model, which implies that the thermal characteristics of the suggested model are superior to those of the conventional model.

Table 1. Temperature increase in the conventional model (28S)

Time [sec]	Temperature [°C]
0	11
2	72.64
4	134.28
6	195.92
8	257.56
10	319.20

Table 2. Temperature increase in the suggested model (30S)

Time [sec]	Temperature [°C]
0	11
2	60.18
4	109.36
6	158.54
8	207.72
10	256.90

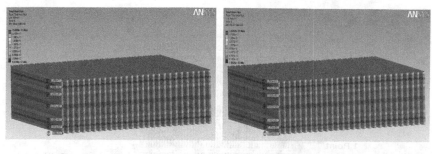

(a) Conventional model (28S)   (b) suggested Model (30S)

Fig.7. Thermal energy distribution by location in lattice resistors

Table 3. Thermal energy distribution by location

Location	Conventional Model	Suggested Model
①	1.9750e-11	1.5573e-11
②	2.8099e-12	2.7567e-12
③	1.4766e-11	1.1664e-11
④	4.2421e-12	3.4153e-12
⑤	1.4382e-11	1.1812e-11
⑥	2.8163e-12	2.3704e-12
⑦	1.8460e-11	1.5754e-11

4   Experiment Results and Analysis

4.1   Results of the Temperature Increase Experiment

Forced cooling of the Lattice resistor was performed with a cooling fan motor with a wind velocity of 2 m/s to keep the experiment conditions identical to those of the field, and the four spots at which the damages to the resistor wire were greatest in the field conditions with a surrounding temperature of approximately 11 ℃ were selected for the temperature measurement, as shown in Fig. 8.

The temperatures were measured with infrared thermometers because attached-type thermometers could not be used due to such harsh field conditions as high voltage, forced cooling, and limited spaces.

The results of the experiments on the conventional and suggested lattice resistors under the same conditions are listed in Tables 4 and 5.

The average temperatures appear to be almost similar, but the smaller temperature increase was measured in the suggested model.

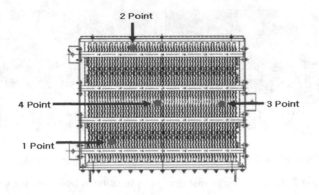

Fig. 8. Temperature measurement points

Table 4. Results of the conventional model experiment

Time (min.)	Measurement Point in the Resistor				
	1	2	3	4	Ave.
15	245	172	216	209	211
20	231	176	196	213	204
25	241	170	12	208	208
30	238	176	208	211	208

Table 5. Results of the suggested model experiment

Time (min.)	Measurement Point in the Resistor				
	1	2	3	4	Ave.
15	245	191	175	215	207
20	242	181	181	206	203
25	244	184	180	212	205
30	244	181	183	213	205

4.2   Field Test Results

The wave forms of the currents during the regeneration braking and dynamic braking that were performed in the field conditions of speed 60km for the conventional lattice resistor and the suggested lattice resistor were compared and analyzed.

A hicorder (HIOKI 8842, 16CH) and a clamp meter (HIOKI 3285, 2,000 A/1V) were used for the measurements, and the braking resistors of RF-1 and RF-2 in a motor block were selected as the measurement points.

Fig. 9 shows the graph of the current wave form of the motor block grid resistor during the regeneration braking of an express train, and Fig. 10 shows the results of the dynamic braking. The analysis of the current wave form, as seen in Fig. 9, shows that regeneration braking at low speeds in the field test yields a small amount of currents that are not very different with conventional Model (42 A) and suggested Model (40 A). Fig. 10 shows that the currents generated during dynamic braking in the field test were almost identical, and it is estimated that the two models have similar performance degrees with 120 A.

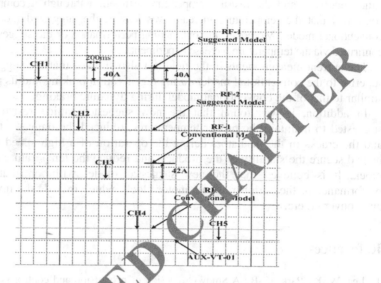

Fig. 9. Current wave graph in a lattice resistor during regeneration braking

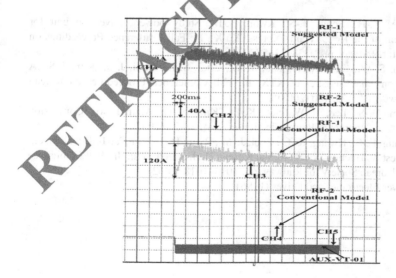

Fig. 10. Current wave graph in a lattice resistor during dynamic braking

5   Conclusion

In this study, a new suggested model for a motor block lattice resistor was suggested to prevent damages to the resistor wires due to the thermal expansion during regeneration braking in a high speed train. Resistors and insulators were added to the new lattice resistor after considering the temperature increase in the conventional models due to the narrow lattice intervals, and the resistor temperature estimation through a component analysis confirmed that the temperature increase was less in the suggested model than in the conventional model. Moreover, the outstanding performance of the suggested model was confirmed via the temperature increase experiment.

The current measurements in the field test also showed that the suggested model superior to the conventional model during regeneration braking and its performance is similar to that of the conventional model during dynamic braking.

In addition, it was found that the new suggested lattice resistor which was suggested to maintain the proper temperatures, reduced the damages to the resistors and the cracks in the insulators during the operation of a high speed train, and thus helped secure the stability of the products and reduce the temperature inside a motor block. It is believed that the new suggested model will contribute to the best performance of the peripherals in a motor block, which include the inverter, chopper and converter, etc.

References

1. Lee, W.-K., Park, K.-B.: A Study On Design of propulsion and control system for Korean High Speed Train. In: Spring Conference Proceedings on Korean Society for Railway, pp. 576–588 (2000)
2. Lee, E.-K., Lee, Y.-H., Song, Y.-S., Kwon, S.-B.: Study power conversion unit for propulsion system of the Korea Train eXpress (KTX). In: Fall Conference Proceedings on Korean Society for Railway, pp. 2338–2345 (2009)
3. Han, Y.-J., Kim, S.-W., Choi, K.-Y., Cho, M.-S., Choi, S.-K., Choi, J.-S., Kim, J.-S.: A Study on Traction Characteristics of KTX. In: Fall Conference Proceedings on Korean Society for Railway, pp. 175–180 (2003)
4. Kim, Y.-J., Kim, D.-S., Lee, H.-W., Seo, K.-D., Kim, N.-H.: Main Power Conversion Device Development. Journal of Power Electronics 2(4), 21–28 (1997)
5. Kno, J.-S., Chung, E.-S., Hwang, K.-C., Choi, J.-M., Ryoo, H.-J., Kim, Y.-J.: Development and Combined test of Traction system for the Korean High Speed Train. In: Fall Conference Proceedings on Korean Society for Railway, pp. 1013–1018 (2002)
6. Bose, B.K.: Power Electronics and Drives (1986)

Structure Vibration Analysis and Active Noise Control of a Power Transformer by Mobility Measurement

Young-Dal Kim[1], Jae-Myung Shim[1], Keun-Seok Park[1],
Yun-Mi Jeong[1], and Dae-Dong Lee[2]

[1] Department of Electrical Engineering, Hanbat National University,
Daejeon, Republic of Korea
{zeromoon,jmshim,jym0809}@hanbat.ac.kr,
smg-park@nate.com
[2] Department of Electrical Engineering, Hanyang University,
Seoul, Republic of Korea
ldd77@hanbat.ac.kr

Abstract. Most cases of power transformer failure are caused by physical factors linked to the transient vibrations of multiple 120 Hz combinations. In addition, the noise generated in the transformer from this vibration not only directly contributes to the worsening of the work environment but also causes psychological stress, resulting in the worsening of the workers' efficiency and of the living environment of the inhabitants around the power plant. Thus, to remedy these problems, the mechanical-excitation forces working on a power transformer were categorized in this study, and the mechanical-damage mechanism was identified through the vibration transfer paths acting on machines or structures. In addition, a study on active noise cancellation in a transformer using the FXLMS algorithm was conducted to develop a system that is capable of multiple-sound/channel control, which resulted in the active noise reduction effect when applied on the field.

Keywords: Active Noise Control, Filtered-XLMS, Power Transformer, Structure Vibration Analysis.

1 Introduction

In transformers, a multiple combination of 120 Hz electrical frequencies is generated by the magnetostriction in the internal iron core which is emitted externally through the transformer tank's outer wall. Here, the resonance greatly increases if the transformer tank's resonant frequency is the same as the frequency of the magnetostriction which is caused by the transformer's internal magnetic field. To prevent such a resonance phenomenon, forced dampening can be added to the tank system, or the resonance can be controlled by adjusting rigidity and mass.

Adding damping to a large structure, however, such as a transformer tank, is difficult from the viewpoint of cost and manufacturing, and therefore, mass and rigidity adjustment is performed on the tank's mass, and soundproof walls have been installed recently.

T.-h. Kim et al. (Eds.): CA/CES³ 2011, CCIS 256, pp. 75–85, 2011.
© Springer-Verlag Berlin Heidelberg 2011

Such methods are feasible for high-frequency noises but cause a huge economic burden on blocking low-frequency noise. Thus, much effort is being done internationally to put a newly proposed method called Active Noise Control (ANC) to practical use [1-3]. Here, Ross [4] researched on the control of the transformer noise in the transformer room while Morgan studied how to perform active noise control in a three-dimensional space [5].

Currently, while noise cannot be removed within the entire space, it is possible to establish local silence areas [6]. Here, much effort is being done to implement active noise control with a single system while avoiding a complicated acoustic system [7-9].

Therefore, through this study, we intend to contribute to the noise reduction in large transformers by analyzing the type of vibration in the transformer tank via mode analysis and developing the ANC system for application in field transformers.

2   Power Transformer Structure Vibration Analysis and ANC Algorithm

2.1   FEM on ANSYS

In the ANSYS/SOLID187 Used in this study, the prism/tetrahedral element was not used. The boundary condition of Young's modulus was 200 GPa (based on cast carbon steel), density was 7,800 kg/m3, and the Poisson's ratio was set at 0.32. The node size for using Block Lanczos as a mode method was 173,249, and the element size was set at 87,016. ANSYS was used as the analysis tool while using a tetrahedron forming a mesh.

A free mesh is advantageous in forming an irregular-type mesh on a complex form, such as a transformer tank. In addition, by adding a shape-dependent mesh (smart-sized mesh), the no. of meshes of the entire model was set. By using the finite-element model (FEM) in Fig. 1(a), the mesh shape in Fig. 1(b) was obtained. As shown in Fig. 1(a), the part contacting the ground surface through the entire transformer tank's weight showed almost no vibration-related displacement and thus assigned a fully fixed constraint while excluding the influence of insulator oil.

Fig. 2(a) was analyzed at the natural-mode shape of 118.1 Hz, where the resonance condition was local and did not affect the transformer. Fig. 2(b) was analyzed, however, at the natural-mode shape of 121.3 Hz, where the transformer was not greatly affected, and it was found that vibrations could be induced at the bushings.

Fig. 2(c) was analyzed at the natural-mode shape of 238.2 Hz, where the resonance condition was local and did not affect the transformer. Fig. 2(d) was analyzed at a natural-mode shape of 241.1 Hz, where resonance occurred at the transformer's upper side.

It was found that there is a possibility of large vibration in various bushing areas. The analysis of the transformer's structural and dynamic-response characteristics, which was done at the natural mode, resulted in the detection of resonant frequencies near 120 and 240 Hz. It is thus concluded that there is a possibility of induced vibrations.

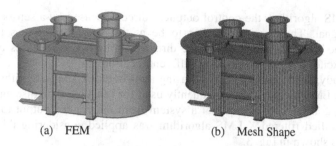

(a)   FEM   (b)   Mesh Shape

Fig. 1. Shape of power transformer

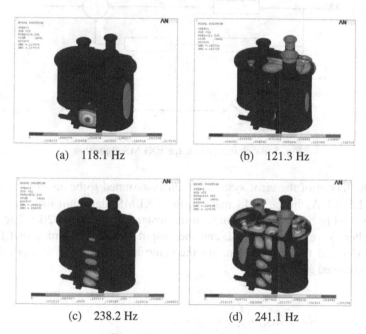

(a)   118.1 Hz   (b)   121.3 Hz

(c)   238.2 Hz   (d)   241.1 Hz

Fig. 2. Shape of natural mode

2.2   Filtered-X LMS Algorithm

For active control of the noise generated by large transformers, methods such as the feedback and feed forward control algorithm are used as well as hybrid control algorithms that improve the stability and control performance by combining the advantages of the two. In the noise produced by large transformers, the flux changes 120 times per second according to the 60 Hz frequency signal, and the noise is caused by the core and coil. In addition, as the noise transfer path is time-varying according to various factors, such as temperature, moisture, and obstacles, accurate modeling is difficult. The reference signal, however, can be easily measured from the transformer's vibrations or current, and control of complex structures is possible using such reference signal. In addition, it is recommended that control be performed using the effective feed forward method.

In the LMS algorithm, the control output is directly sensed by a sensor measuring the error signal. Thus, the sensor has to be at the same location as the exciter. However, the LMS algorithm cannot be directly applied in most cases because the additional exciter and the sensor are at different locations.

In this study, control was performed using the filtered-X LMS algorithm, which is based on the LMS method that is frequently used for reducing the noise and vibration of large transformers. Assuming that a system from the control output to the sensor exists, a modified filtered-X LMS algorithm was applied considering this. Its block diagram is as shown in Fig. 3.

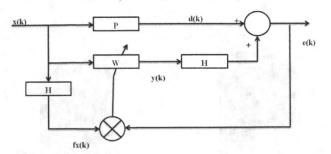

Fig. 3. Block diagram of the FXLMS algorithm

$\hat{H}$ is the model of the error system, which is assumed to be an FIR filter with a length of LK +1 As in the LMS method, the FXLMS algorithm uses the steepest-descent method to minimize the square of the instantaneous error e2(k). The input of the controller W is the x(k) signal, and the output is y(k). Assuming that the error system model and the error system are the same as in the LMS method, the error signal is expressed as in Eq. (1).

$$e(k) = d(k) + \sum_{j=0}^{L_k} h_j y(k-j)$$

$$= d(k) + \sum_{i=0}^{L} \sum_{j=0}^{L_k} h_i w_i (k-j) x(k-i-j)$$

$$(1)$$

Meanwhile, the coefficient of the applied filter can be derived using Eq. (2).

$$\omega_i(k+1) = \omega_i(k) - \mu \bar{N}_i(k) \qquad (2)$$

If it is assumed that $\omega_i(k) \approx \omega_i(k-1) \approx \cdots \approx \omega_i(k-L_h)$ is satisfied, that is, that the coefficient changes slowly, the instantaneous slope is calculated as in Eq. (3).

$$\nabla_i(k) = \frac{\partial e^2(k)}{\partial \omega_i(k)} = -2e(k) \sum_{j=0}^{L_k} h_i x(k-i-j) \tag{3}$$

Thus, the equation with the updated filter coefficient is given as in Eq. (4). Here, $fx(k)$ is the reference signal that passed the error system model.

$$\omega_i(k+1) = \omega_i(k) - 2\mu e(k) \sum_{j=0}^{L_k} h_i x(k-i-j) \tag{4}$$

$$= \omega_i(k) - 2\mu e(k) fx(k-1)$$

3   ANC System Configuration and Transformer Noise Analysis

3.1   ANC System Configuration

The overall hardware block diagram of the ANC system is shown in Fig. 4 and was implemented as shown in Fig. 5. First, a noise that resembles the transformer noise source was generated in the lab, and then ANC was applied to observe the noise cancellation effect according to the control output and location of the error microphone. In addition, for the field experiment, a system supporting up to 20 channels was built as shown in Fig. 6. A test was then performed by applying up to 15 channels on a currently operating 154(kV) 60(MVA) 3 phase transformer. In addition, to measure and analyze the noise of the large-scale transformer, measurement was performed at the error microphone located at the right side, as shown in Fig. 6.

The noise map for each frequency is shown in Fig. 7. The measurement results showed the following maximum values at each frequency: 20 Hz - 95.55 dB, 240 Hz - 82.59 dB, 360 Hz - 84.07 dB, 480 Hz - 80.62 dB, 600 Hz - 75.05 dB and 720 Hz - 72.56 dB.

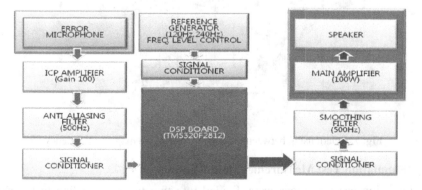

Fig. 4. ANC system diagram

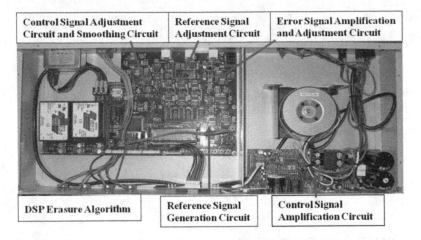

Fig. 5. ANC system prototype

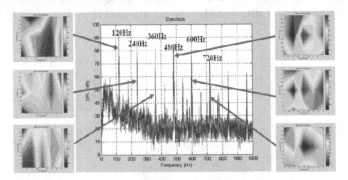

Fig. 6. Multichannel ANC system

Fig. 7. Relationship between the transformer noise map and frequency

3.2   Simulation Test Measurement and Analysis

The simulation test conditions were divided into two types, according to the noise, control output, and location of the error microphone, and the data were measured for the single-tone control frequencies of 120 and 240 Hz. First, for the simulation test conditions, the noise signal of speaker, the reference generation control output of speaker, and the error microphone's signal location were placed on a straight line, as shown in Fig. 8, and were then measured with an oscilloscope. As a result, at the single-tone frequencies of 120 and 240 Hz, the measurements were as shown in Fig. 9-10 and Table 1. The noise decreased by microphone output waveform the most at 240 Hz, up to 22.3 dB, as shown in Fig. 10.

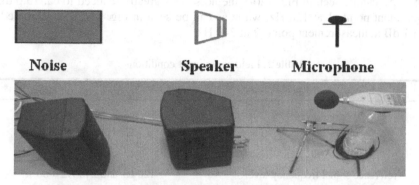

Noise   **Speaker**   **Microphone**

Fig. 8. Simulation test conditions

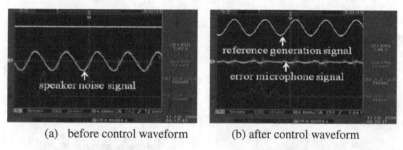

(a)   before control waveform   (b) after control waveform

Fig. 9. Simulation test measurement waveforms of 120Hz

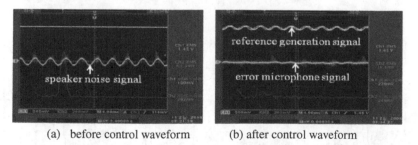

(a)   before control waveform   (b) after control waveform

Fig. 10. Simulation test measurement waveforms of 240Hz

Table 1. Measurement results at the simulation test conditions

control conditions	before control	after control	decrement
120 Hz	80.8 dB	69.7 dB	11.1 dB
240 Hz	80.8 dB	58.5 dB	22.3 dB

3.3   Field Experiment Measurement and Analysis

The field test conditions were as shown in Table 2. As can be seen at the right side of Fig. 6, control was performed at 15 locations, while the noise was measured at four points, as shown at the right and left sides of Fig. 6. The data measurement results for the single-tone control frequencies of 120 and 240 Hz are shown in Fig. 11-14 and Table 3. As can be seen in Fig. 12(a), the noise was greatly reduced to ca. 13.0 dB at measurement point -1 at 120 Hz, while as can be seen in Fig. 14(b), it decreased by ca. 25.1 dB at measurement point -2 at 240 Hz.

Table 2. Field experiment conditions

control items	control conditions
shutter door conditions	closed
control frequency	120 Hz and 240 Hz
main AMP gain	50 %
reference signal frequency level	120 Hz and 240 Hz = 80 %
reference signal total level	80 %

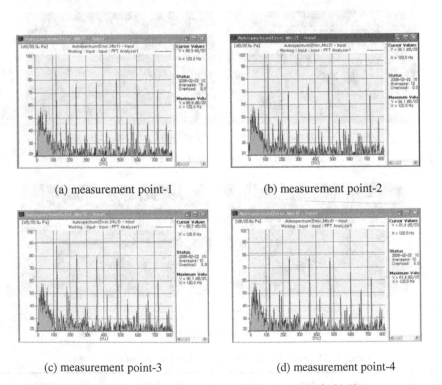

(a) measurement point-1

(b) measurement point-2

(c) measurement point-3

(d) measurement point-4

Fig. 11. Measurement waveforms before control of 120 Hz

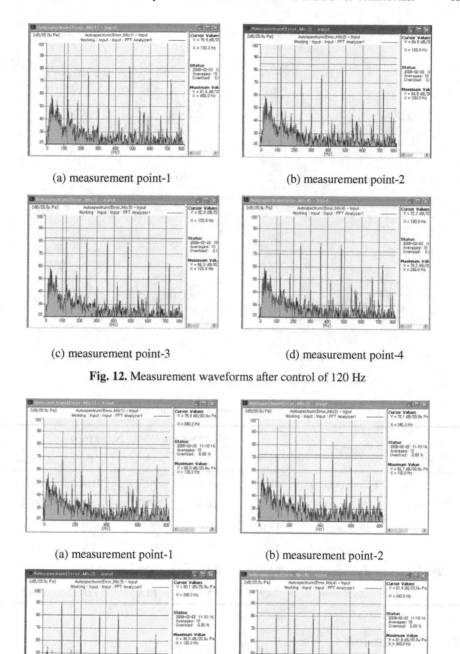

(a) measurement point-1

(b) measurement point-2

(c) measurement point-3

(d) measurement point-4

Fig. 12. Measurement waveforms after control of 120 Hz

(a) measurement point-1

(b) measurement point-2

(c) measurement point-3

(d) measurement point-4

Fig. 13. Measurement waveforms before control of 240 Hz

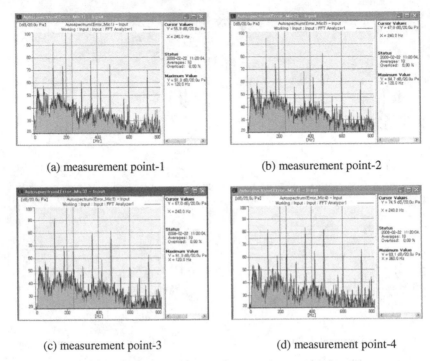

    (a) measurement point-1   (b) measurement point-2

    (c) measurement point-3   (d) measurement point-4

Fig. 14. Measurement waveforms after control of 240 Hz

Table 3. Measurement results under the field test

control conditions	controls	Measurement Point / Noise (dB)				
		1	2	3	4	average
120 Hz	before control	89.9	94.1	90.7	81.4	89.0
	after control	76.9	84.5	82.0	72.2	78.9
	decrement	13.0	9.6	8.7	9.2	10.1
240 Hz	before control	76.8	72.1	80.1	81.9	77.7
	after control	55.9	47.0	67.0	74.9	61.2
	decrement	20.9	25.1	13.1	7.0	16.5

4   Conclusion

In this thesis, the structural vibration of a single-phase transformer was analyzed through mobility measurement while performing simulated and field experiments on transformer noise reduction during operation, using an active noise control system on which the FXLMS algorithm was applied. As for the transformer's resonance test results, the natural mode analysis of the transformer's structural and dynamic-response characteristics revealed resonant frequencies near 120 and 240 Hz. It is thus concluded that vibrations may be caused. In addition, the measurement of the field transformer data on the single-tone control frequencies of 120 and 240 Hz when the developed ANC system was used showed that the transformer noise was reduced by at least 13.0 and 25.1 dB.

As shown here, if the new technology will be applied to currently operational transformers, it is expected that not only the complaints of inhabitants near the substations but also the occupational diseases of the workers in the substations or power plants can be reduced, thereby greatly contributing to the improvement of work efficiency

References

1. Chaplin, G.B.: Method and apparatus for canceling vibration. U. S. Patent, No. 4, pp. 441–489 (1984)
2. Eriksson, L.J., Allie, M.C., Bremigan, C.D.: Active noise control using adaptive digital signal processing. In: Proc. ICASSP, New York, pp. 2594–2597 (1988)
3. Warnaka, G.E., Poole, L., Tichy, J.: Active attenuator. US Patent 4 473. 906, September 25 (1984)
4. Ross, C.F.: An algorithm for designing a broadband active sound control system. J. Sound and Vibration 80(3), 373–380 (1982)
5. Morgan, D.R., Thi, J.C.: A delay less sub band adaptive filter architecture. IEEE Trans. on Signal Proc. 43(8), 1819–1830 (1995)
6. Tokhi, M.O., Leitch, R.R.: Active Noise Control. Clarendon Press, Oxford (1992)
7. Efron, A.J., Han, L.C.: Wide-area adaptive active noise cancellation. IEEE Trans. on Circuits and System-II: Analog and Digital Proc. 41(6), 405–409 (1994)
8. Graupe, D., Efron, A.J.: A Output-Whitening Approach to Adaptive Active Noise Cancellation. IEEE Trans. on Circuit and Systems 38(11), 1306–1313 (1991)
9. Oppenheim, A.V., Zangi, K.C., Gaupe, D.: Single-Sensor Active Noise Cancellation. IEEE Transactions on Speech and Processing 2(2), 285–290 (1994)

Estimation of Deterioration Degree in Overhead Transmission Lines by Tension Load Analysis

Dae-Dong Lee[1], Jae-Myung Shim[2], Young-Dal Kim[2], and Dong-Seok Hyun[1]

[1] Department of Electrical Engineering, Hanyang University,
Seoul 133-791, Republic of Korea
ldd77@hanbat.ac.kr, dshyun@hanyang.ac.kr
[2] Department of Electrical Engineering, Hanbat National University,
Daejeon 305-719, Republic of Korea
{jmshim,zeromoon}@hanbat.ac.kr

Abstract. When a forest fire hits a mountainous area, the life of an overhead transmission line is affected by the heat, extinguishing water, chemicals, and dust. The life of a wire depends on the combination of these elements. Generally, how a conductor wire is affected by forest fire can be analyzed only when the forest fire is accurately modeled and its effects identified. In Korea, however, there are few studies that were conducted based on a forest fire model for transmission lines. There have not been any results from analyzing actual test specimens that were exposed to forest fire. In this study, an artificial dust experiment device was designed and used in the tests because the deterioration characteristics from a forest fire and dust cannot be directly analyzed. The device is set to show field conditions. ACSR 410 mm^2 were used as test specimens. These wires are commonly used for overhead transmission lines in Korea and now are used to analyze tensile strength. In addition, the transmission line samples were collected from the field where a forest fire occurred. They were then compared with the experiment data to estimate their degree of deterioration.

Keywords: ACSR, overhead transmission lines, estimation of deterioration degree, tension load, artificial flame, forest fire.

1 Introduction

The deterioration of the aluminum stranded conductors steel reinforced (ACSR) wire progresses according to the interactions among various factors including the wire material, manufacturing method, wiring condition and the surroundings [1-2]. The ACSR is usually employed in extra-high voltage overhead distribution and transmission lines.

Overhead transmission lines in Korea are mostly located in the mountainous areas. When a forest hits a mountainous area, galvanized steel wires and aluminum stranded wires in the transmission lines directly or indirectly exposed to fire will deteriorate due to the flame and heat, which may cause line-to-line or grounding faults [3-6].

T.-h. Kim et al. (Eds.): CA/CES^3 2011, CCIS 256, pp. 86–95, 2011.

Accordingly, the forest fire significantly reduces the life of the wire because the overall tension load of a wire can decrease according to diverse corrosion types caused by flames. It is necessary to analyze how much overhead transmission lines deteriorated from the forest fire.

Because the characteristics of the ACSR change when it is affected by fire, the wire must be replaced or reinforced. There are, however, just a few studies worldwide on the degree of wire deterioration. No precise replacement standard exists. Therefore, further studies on this sector are urgently needed [7].

As it is difficult to analyze wire characteristics after the flame and dust from forest fire have affected the wires, an environment that was similar to the actual field situation was assumed in this study. Dusts were deposited on the new 410 mm^2 ACSR sample wire using an artificial dust experiment device at different distances and temperatures. This was done to analyze the tensile strength of the ACSR conductor based on temperature.

In addition, the transmission line samples were collected from the field in Korea where forest fires have actually occurred. They were then compared with the experiment data to estimate the degree of deterioration.

2   Structure and Experiment Method of an ACSR

2.1   Structure and Corrosion of ACSR

As shown in Fig. 1 the ACSR 410 mm^2 used in the experiment had an inner layer of 7 galvanized steel wire strands and two layers of 26 light aluminum element wires. The latter two layers carried the current and the seven former layers bore the mechanical tension [8]. The zinc layer that covers the galvanized steel wire is melted by heat, and this accelerates the atmospheric corrosion of the steel wire. The aluminum element wire is also corroded because of galvanic corrosion from the contact of the steel wire without the zinc layer with the aluminum wire. The galvanic corrosion occurs inside the ACSR, and its resultant defects cannot be detected visually.

Due to the galvanic corrosion inside the ACSR, however, the cross-section of the aluminum element wires decreases. Consequently, several types of corrosion by exposure to flames reduce the overall tension load of the ACSR and also greatly reduce its life and increase the power loss in the transmission lines [9-10].

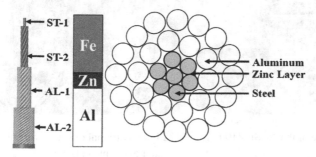

Fig. 1. Structure of the ACSR 410 mm^2

2.2   Experiment Method

Using conductors that had been installed and used for a certain time to verify the changes in the mechanical characteristics of ACSR 410 mm^2 power transmission cables due to forest fire would not yield accurate reference data, since complex corrosion would have already progressed to some extent on the collected cable.

There are no standards for forest fire models or simulations at present. In this study, an artificial dust experiment device was designed and manufactured, as shown in Fig. 2, Oak trees 5 kg, which are common in Korea and 50 cm ACSR used for the experiment. Wire-dust distances were set at 20 cm, 40 cm, 60 cm, and 80 cm. As an additional experiment, ambient temperature was kept constant at 500°C for 15 min, and the tension characteristic was analyzed using the experiment data.

As shown in Fig. 3 it was verified with the naked eye that the specimens were damaged by flame and dust. The specimens were then cooled at normal temperature.

The ambient temperature was measured with four clearance lengths that ranged from 20 cm to 80 cm, at 20cm intervals. The temperature measurements were conducted at ST-2, the area between ST-2 and AL-1, and at AL-2. The measured temperature data were monitored and collected using a notebook via a data collection device.

To check the mechanical characteristics of the specimen, tension test were conducted according to the Korean (Industrial) Standards. Average data were obtained from the tests with five specimens, and used for the results analysis. For ST-1, which was the innermost spot, average values were not obtained, as there was only one specimen, and the value was not used in this test.

The small wires were identified as follows: ST-1: galvanized steel wire, ST-2: galvanized steel stranded wire, AL-1: inner aluminum stranded wire layer and AL-2: outermost aluminum stranded wire layer.

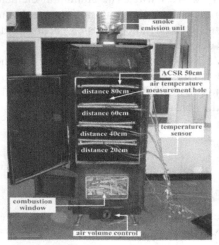

Fig. 2. Structure of the ACSR 410 mm^2

Fig. 3. Artificial dust experiment device (after experimental)

2.3   Experiment Method for the Specimens Affected by Forest Fire

To analyze the tension load characteristic of 410 mm² ACSR affected by forest fire, as the overhead line conductor, the wires that deteriorated from the flames were collected from three sections and cut into five pieces with a length of 50 cm. The tension test was conducted according to the Korean (Industrial) Standards in the same manner as with the new wire to analyze its mechanical characteristics. An average value was obtained from the tension tests for fifteen specimens.

To reduce errors in the test data, the average value of five measurements in the same condition were used as the mechanical characteristic of the wire was analyzed. The aluminum wires (AL-1 and AL-2), which were directly affected by the flames as they were positioned in the outer layers, were excluded from the test, and the tension characteristic of only the galvanized steel wire (ST-2), which supplied tension load, was analyzed. For the galvanized steel core (ST-1), which was the innermost spot, average values were not obtained as there was only one specimen. The value was not used in this test.

3   Experiment Results and Analysis

3.1   Temperature Test Results Analysis

Fig. 4-7 show the temperature data with reference to the wire-dust clearances of 20 cm, 40 cm, 60 cm, and 80 cm when the 5 kg Oak tree was burnt using the artificial experiment device. These figures show the temperature data scanned in real time with 10 seconds as one interval. In the figures, 20, 40, 60, and 80 represent the clearances of 20 cm, 40 cm, 60 cm, and 80 cm, respectively. The ambient and surface temperatures of the wire are also shown.

In the representation of the surface temperature, ST-2/AL-1 represents the area between the galvanized steel wire (ST-2) and the inner aluminum stranded wire (AL-1); AL-1/AL-2, the area between the inner aluminum stranded wire (AL-1) and the outer aluminum stranded wire (AL-2); and AL-2, the outer aluminum stranded wire (AL-2).

From the temperature data in Fig. 4−7 the analysis results of the temperature data showed that the ambient temperature started to increase from about 250 sec and continued until it reached 720 sec, and then gradually decreased. The wire surface temperature started to increase from 500 sec to 1,000 sec, and then gradually decreased.

The ambient temperature and wire surface temperature fell below 100°C after about 4,500 sec. This seems to have been because the ambient temperature increase preceded the wire surface temperature increase due to the convection heat in the artificial dust experiment device, whereas the flame and dust gradually transferred heat to the wire surface.

The highest ambient temperature according to the diverse wire-flame distances was about 699°C. At a wire-flame distance of 20 cm, as shown in Fig. 4 the highest wire surface temperature was 480°C for ST-2/AL-1, 510°C for AL-1/AL-2, and 505°C for

AL-2. At a wire-flame distance of 40 cm, as shown in Fig. 5 the highest wire surface temperature was 439°C for ST-2/AL-1, 378°C for AL-1/AL-2, and 453°C for AL-2.

At a wire-flame distance of 60 cm, as shown in Fig. 6 the highest wire surface temperature was 403°C for ST-2/AL-1, 418°C for AL-1/AL-2, and 428°C for AL-2.

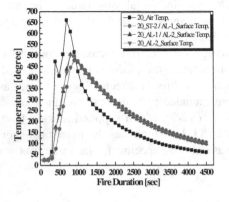

Fig. 4. Temperature data by 20 cm distance

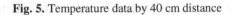

Fig. 5. Temperature data by 40 cm distance

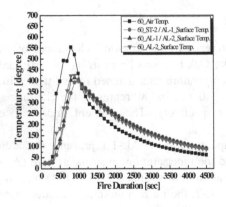

Fig. 6. Temperature data by 60 cm distance

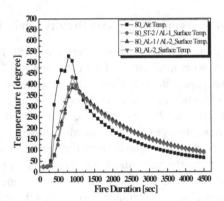

Fig. 7. Temperature data by 80 cm distance

At a wire-flame distance of 80 cm, as shown in Fig. 7 the highest wire surface temperature was 444°C for ST-2/AL-1, 387°C for AL-1/AL-2, and 401°C for AL-2.

These data indicate that a wire deteriorated more as the flames came closer to the wire, and deteriorated less as the flames went farther. In Fig. 7 however, the surface temperature on ST-2/AL-1 with a clearance of 80 cm was slightly higher than those on other wires even though its clearance was longest. This seems to have been caused by the error from the un-uniform shape of the flames.

Fig. 8-11 show the temperature data with reference to the clearances of 20 cm, 40 cm, 60 cm, and 80 cm when the oak tree was burned using the artificial experiment device. Ambient temperature was kept constant at 500°C for 15 min.

The ambient temperature with reference to the clearance was kept almost constant at 500°C for 900 sec, but the highest temperature on the wire surface significantly varied.

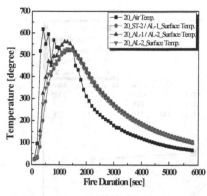

Fig. 8. Temperature data by 20 cm distance (500 degree kept)

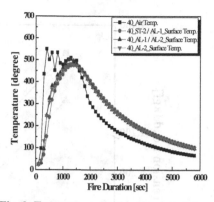

Fig. 9. Temperature data by 40 cm distance (500 degree kept)

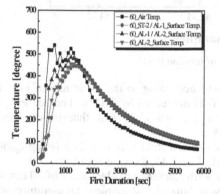

Fig. 10. Temperature data by 60 cm distance (500 degree kept)

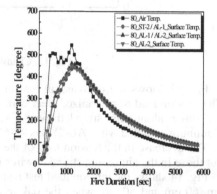

Fig. 11. Temperature data by 80 cm distance (500 degree kept)

As shown in Fig. 4-7 show the highest temperature on the wire surface was 532°C for 20 cm, 484°C for 40 cm, 456°C for 60 cm, and 452°C for 80 cm, which showed that the highest temperature on the wire surface was inversely proportional to the clearance.

In addition, the highest surface temperatures of AL-1 spots were slightly higher than those of AL-2, though all of them were positioned in the inner layer. This seems to have been caused by heat that was slowly emitted in the air due to the deterioration over a long time. The temperature data, however, were negligible because they were not significant.

3.2   Mechanical Characteristics and Analysis

Fig. 12 shows the tension load test results with reference to clearances of 20 cm, 40 cm, 60 cm and 80 cm, When the 5 kg oak tree was burned the changes in the clearances did not significantly influence the tension load of the galvanized steel wire (ST-2), but significantly influenced those of the aluminum stranded wires (AL-1 and AL-2).

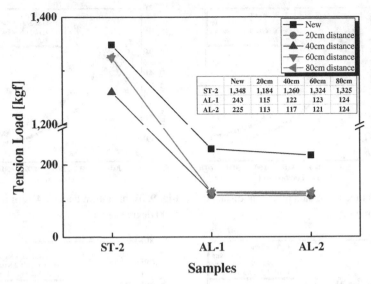

Fig. 12. Changes of tension load

Fig. 13 shows the decrease in tension load according to the clearance in Fig. 12 The tension load of galvanized steel wire (ST-2) decreased by 2-12%. The decrease in the inner aluminum stranded wire (AL-1) was 49-53%, and that in the outer aluminum stranded wire (AL-2) was 45-50 %.

The decrease in the tension load of the galvanized steel wire (ST-2) was negligible, but those in the aluminum stranded wires (AL-1 and AL-2) were about 45-53 %.

Fig. 14 shows the tension load test results with reference to clearances of 20 cm, 40 cm, 60 cm and 80 cm, when the oak tree was burned and ambient temperature was kept constant at 500°C for 15 min. The changes in the clearances did not significantly influence the tension load of the galvanized steel wire (ST-2) (Fig. 12), but significantly influenced those of the aluminum stranded wires (AL-1 and AL-2).

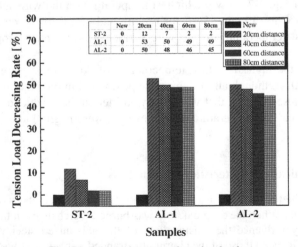

Fig. 13. Decreasing rate of tension load

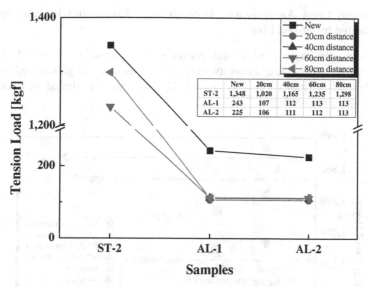

	New	20cm	40cm	60cm	80cm
ST-2	1,348	1,020	1,165	1,235	1,298
AL-1	243	107	112	113	113
AL-2	225	106	111	112	113

Fig. 14. Changes of tension load (500 degree kept)

Fig. 15 shows the decrease in tension load according to the clearances in Fig. 14 The tension load of galvanized steel wire (ST-2) decreased by 4-24%. The decrease in the inner aluminum stranded wire (AL-1) was 53-56%, and that in the outer aluminum stranded wire (AL-2) was 50-53%.

If tension load decreases by 20%, it represents the life limit. From Fig. 12-15 the test results indicate that the galvanized steel wire (ST-2) was not significantly damaged by the artificial dust because it was located in the innermost layer of the wire. The aluminum stranded wires (AL-1 and AL-2) were significantly damaged because they were located in the outer layers. Besides, the aluminum stranded wires (AL-1 and AL-2) must be replaced as their life limit had already exceeded.

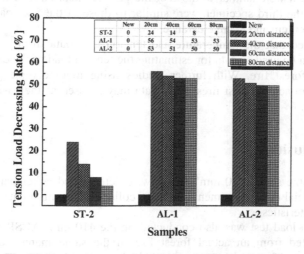

	New	20cm	40cm	60cm	80cm
ST-2	0	24	14	8	4
AL-1	0	56	54	53	53
AL-2	0	53	51	50	50

Fig. 15. Decreasing rate of tension load (500 degree kept)

3.3   Tension Load Analysis and Deterioration Estimation for the Specimen Affected by Forest Fire

Fig. 16 shows average tension load data for the galvanized steel wire (ST-2) during an actual forest fire. The figure shows average tension load of the galvanized steel wire (ST-2) when the 5 kg oak tree was burned. The data were analyzed by dividing the specimens into three sections.

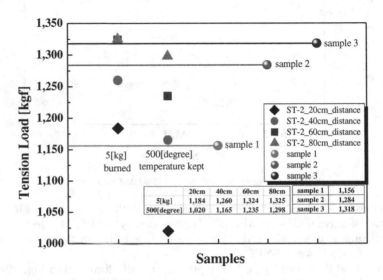

Fig. 16. Flame suppositions of forest fire samples

As shown in Fig. 16, the test result of the first specimen was similar to that of the oak tree that was kept at 500℃ with a 40 cm clearance, and the test results of the second specimen were similar to those of the oak tree kept an 80 cm clearance. The test results of the third specimen were similar to those of the 5 kg oak tree that was burned with a 60 cm and 80cm clearance.

It is expected that the temperature and tension load data from the artificial dust experiment can be used as data for estimating the tension load of the deteriorated wire in an actual forest fire. With further studies using more diverse parameters and specimens from actual forest fires, these data may be used as the basic data for wire life estimation.

4   Conclusion

In this study, the sound 410 mm² ACSR wire deteriorated as temperatures changed using an artificial dust experiment device to collect temperature data and analyze its tension characteristics.

The tension load test was also conducted on the 410 mm² ACSR wire specimens that deteriorated from an actual forest fire in the same manner as the artificial deterioration test. The results were comparatively analyzed.

The measurement of the data that examined the tension load characteristics of the ACSR wire exposed to artificial dust and flames showed that there was almost no change in the tension load of the galvanized steel wire (ST-2) because it existed inside and was not exposed to flame and dust. The tension load of the aluminum stranded wires (AL-1 and AL-2), however, significantly decreased according to the wire-flame clearances.

In addition, specimens from the actual forest fire field were compared with the laboratory data to estimate the degree of deterioration of specimens.

It is expected that the resulting analysis data may be used as data for estimating refurbishment life of deteriorated ACSR wires.

References

1. A selection of project Power distribution administration, Korea Electric Power Research Institute, KRC-92D-001 (1992)
2. Influence of Air pollution on Power System, Korea Electric Power Research Institute, KRC-92C-S05 (1993)
3. Electric Power Research Institute, Transmission Line Reference Book, 345 kV and Above/Second Edition (1989)
4. West, H.J., Mcmullan, D.W.: Fire Induced Flashovers of EHV Transmission Lines. In: IEEE-PES Winter Meeting, New York, Paper A73047-2 (February 1978)
5. Kim, S.-D.: An Experimental Study on a Solenoid Eddy Current Sensor to Inspect Deteriorations in Overhead Distribution Lines. Journal of the Korean Institute of Illuminating and Electrical Installation Engineers 13(1), 77–85 (1999)
6. Kim, Y.-K., Chang, S.-K., Cho, S.-I.: Effects of Corrosion Environment on Mechanical Properties of Catenary Wires. Korean Society for Railway 5(1), 32–39 (2002)
7. Kojima, Y., Fukuda, J., Kumeda, T., Iinuma, J., Endo, M.: Corrosion Detector Robot for Overhead Transmission Line. Fujikura Technical Review (21), 74–83 (1992)
8. Jeong, J.-K., Kang, J.-W., Kang, Y.-W., Shim, E.-B., Kim, J.-B.: Experimental Detections of the Aluminum Layer Corrosions for ACSR Transmission Ground Wires. Journal of the Korean Institute of Electrical Engineers 46(7), 1102–1108 (1997)
9. Influence of Air pollution on Power System, Korea Electric Power Research Institute, KRC-92C-S05 (1993)
10. The Development of System for ACSR Life-Time Estimation, KEPRI, TR.97EJ02. J2000.16 (2000)

Structural and Electrical Properties of High Temperature Polycrystalline Silicon Films on Molybdenum Substrate

Hyun-il Kang[1], Won-suk Choi[1], Yeon-ho Jung[1],
Hyun-suk Hwang[2], and Do-young Kim[3]

[1] Division of Electrics, Electronics and Control Engineering, Hanbat National University,
Daejeon 305-719, Republic of Korea
{hikang,wschoi,yhjoung}@hanbat.ac.kr
[2] Department of Electrical Engineering, Seoil University,
Seoul 131-702, Republic of Korea
konae@seoil.ac.kr
[3] Division of Electrics, and Electronics Engineering, Ulsan College,
Ulsan 680-749, Republic of Korea
dykim@uc.ac.kr

Abstract. For the photovoltaic application, a technique of high temperature crystallization was proposed to change from amorphous to polycrystalline silicon. We investigated the structural and electrical properties of the poly-Si thin films on Molybdenum (Mo) substrate using a direct resistive heating process. The hydrogenated amorphous silicon films were crystallized in the temperature range of 750°C to 1050°C. As the crystallization temperature increases, the intensity of the peaks for (111) orientation has strongly observed. Improvement of the crystallinity over 75% has been noticed. Photo conductivity and dark conductivity decreased with the increase in substrate temperature.

Keywords: Molybdenum, Direct resistive heating (DRH), Sputtering, Photosensitivity.

1   Introduction

In recent years, there has been considerable interest in development of the high performance polycrystalline silicon (poly-Si) owing to their applications such as the organic light emitting diodes, liquid crystal displays, thin film transistors (TFTs), and solar cells [1-3]. The poly-Si thin films are very useful for the fabrication of very large area and low cost solar cell. The commonly used techniques to obtain poly-Si film are solid phase crystallization (SPC) and metal induced crystallization (MIC). Among these methods, SPC method using a thermal treatment of the a-Si films in hot-wall furnace requires high temperature in range from 600 to 1000°C and long time above 10 hours [4]. However, it is very difficult to fabricate high performance poly-Si at a temperature over 600°C because of the high-temperature durability of glass substrate [5]. MIC has the disadvantages such as high initial cost, process complexity and the metal residues remain after crystallization process [6]. Therefore, new

T.-h. Kim et al. (Eds.): CA/CES³ 2011, CCIS 256, pp. 96–101, 2011.
© Springer-Verlag Berlin Heidelberg 2011

technique for Si crystallization is needed. As high temperature process also is not used for glass substrate because of the low softening points under 450°C. Furthermore, we need to change the substrate from glass to metal sheet which is possible to endure high temperature. However, high temperature process is required to get high crystallization volume fraction so called crystallinity.

In this paper, we report the growth of poly-Si on flexible metal substrate such as molybdenum for the photovoltaic application using a direct resistive heating (DRH) crystallization of amorphous silicon (a-Si) layer. The structural and electrical properties of the poly-Si film transistor above high temperature (>750°C) were investigated.

2   Experiments

Molybdenum (Mo) substrate of about 150 μm thickness was treated with the solutions of H_3PO_4 and HNO_3 for etching the natural oxide layer. This step is followed by the rinsing with DI water and drying with nitrogen gas. A layer of a-Si of thickness about 310 nm was deposited by sputtering. Sintered pure Si of 99.999% (Cerac Co.) of 2 inch diameter was used as sputtering target. Pre-sputtering was performed for 10 min for target surface cleaning.

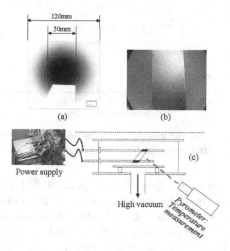

Fig. 1. Experiment schematics diagrams (a) uniform area, (b) as-deposited Si on Mo substrate, and (c) DRH crystallization heater

From the Fig. 1(a), we determined the uniform area size as 50 mm × 50 mm because of small target size. We also exhibited the real images of deposited Si on Mo substrate in the Fig. 1(b). In order to crystallize deposited a-Si layer on the Mo substrate, we connected the Mo substrate with the electrode to apply high electric currents. And then, the Mo substrate was heated from 750°C to 1050°C by DRH process, as shown in the Fig. 1(c). We defined DRH as the self-heating of thin Mo substrate by an electric thermal dissipation without a hot-wall or graphite heating. The substrate temperature was measured by infrared pyrometer to control accurate temperature. The crystal volume fraction of the poly-Si film was measured by Raman scattering spectroscopy. The crystal structure of the films was analyzed using X-ray diffraction (XRD, Mac Science M18XHFSRA, Cu target, 1.54 •, Ni filter). The electrical conductivity was obtained using a Keithley 617 programmable electrometer.

3   Results and Discussion

In order to observe the crystallinity of Si thin film as a function of the crystallization temperature, we carried out Raman spectroscopy. Raman spectroscopy and the calculated crystalline volume fraction (X_c) of crystallized poly-Si films as a function of the crystallization temperature are shown in Fig. 2.

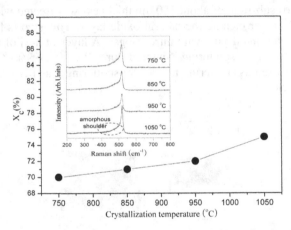

Fig. 2. Raman spectroscopy and the calculated crystalline volume fraction Xc of crystallized poly-Si films as a function of the crystallization temperature

All of the samples showed a clear Raman peak at 521 cm^{-1}. But the shoulder observed around 480 cm^{-1} indicates the mixed phase of crystalline and amorphous Si. We calculated X_c using the peak at 480 cm^{-1} which indicates amorphous silicon and the peak at 521 cm^{-1}, that indicates single crystal silicon. The origin of the intermediate peak at 500 cm^{-1} is considered to be caused by distribution of crystalline phase size because the small size of crystallites induces a breakdown of the wave-vector selection rule. The crystalline volume fraction X_c can be expressed by following formula [7].

$$X_c = \frac{I_{520} + I_{500}}{I_{520} + I_{500} + \sigma I_{480}}$$

where I_{480}, I_{500} and I_{520} are intensities of the peaks 480 cm^{-1}, 500 cm^{-1}, and 520 cm^{-1}, respectively, and σ is the ratio of the integrated Raman cross section for a-Si to crystalline Si. We assumed that grain size was small and it is possible to hold $\sigma = 1$ in the present analysis. It was observed that X_c of the films varied with crystallization temperature from 71.8% at the 850 °C to 75.2% at the 1050 °C.

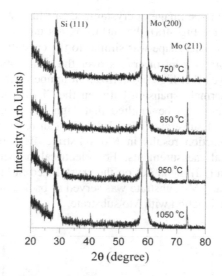

Fig. 3. The X-ray diffraction pattern as a function of crystallization temperature, (a) 750℃, (b) 850℃, (c) 950℃, and (d) 1050℃

Figure 3 shows the X-ray diffraction pattern as a function of crystallization temperature. The peaks at the angle of 28° represent the Si (111) orientation of samples. Other peaks are induced from the Mo substrate. As the crystallization temperature increases, the intensity of the peaks for (111) has all the same values. But the symmetry of peak is deficient about samples and high full width half maximum (FWHM) over 0.42°.

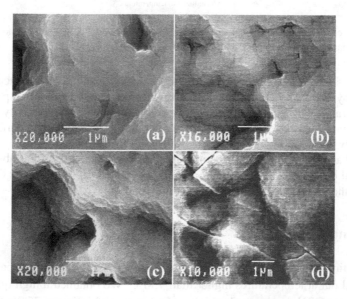

Fig. 4. The surface morphology of crystallized Si on the Mo substrate, (a) 750℃, (b) 850℃, (c) 950℃, and (d) 1050℃

Figure 4 shows the surface image of crystallized Si films. When the crystallization temperature is low like the Fig. 4(a), the surface is not uniform though remained the super-cooled large grain. This shape was similar to the crystallized sample at 950 °C. But, Si surface incorporates a lot of cracks over the temperature of 1050 °C. From these results, we observed that high crystallization temperature caused the formation of crack induced by thermal expansion between the Si film and Mo substrate. The reason of crack formation can be implied that high temperature has an effect on diffusion of Mo atoms of substrate. The Mo atoms can react with Si atoms at high temperature that the reaction results in Mo substrate. This result has been made clearer by the electrical measurements. For electrical property measurement, we deposited an Aluminum (Al) metal dot on the crystallized Si layer. Al electrode was served as front contact and Mo substrate was served as back contact. Al metal formed automatically the ohmic junction with Mo substrate.

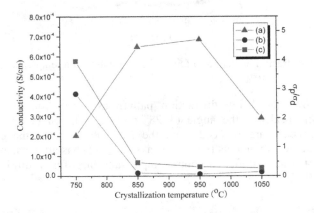

Fig. 5. The electrical properties of crystallized Si on the Mo substrate, (a) photosensitivity (σ_p/σ_d), (b) dark conductivity (σ_d), and (c) photo conductivity (σ_p)

Figure 5 shows the photosensitivity, dark conductivity and photoconductivity when irradiated by 100 mW halogen lamp, as a function of crystallization temperature. As the temperature increases, dark conductivity and photoconductivity decrease. However, photosensitivity increases with temperature. The decrease in dark and photo conductivity is caused by the decrease mobility of the crystallized Si films. This result indicates that high crystallization temperature leads to increase in the absorption of light. It will be expected that low dark and photoconductivity result in the dependence of crack rather than crystallization effect at the 1050°C.

4   Conclusion

Crystallization of hydrogenated a-Si film on the Mo substrate of thickness 150 μm was carried out at temperatures higher than 750°C. We obtained a high quality poly-Si films using DRH process and a high crystal volume fraction of 75.2% at 1050 °C. The experimental results show that higher crystallization temperature leads to greater absorption of light. The higher crystallization temperature also results in the incorporation of the cracks on Si surface. The proposed high temperature technique using Mo substrate is promising for poly-Si thin film transistors process.

References

1. Deng, W., Zheng, X.: Modeling of kink effect in polycrystalline silicon thin-film transistors. Solid-State Electronics 53(6), 669–673 (2009)
2. Lee, E.-K., Lee, Y.-H., Song, Y.-S., Kwon, S.-B.: Polymers for flexible displays: From material selection to device applications. Progress in Polymer Science 33(6), 581–630 (2008)
3. Chen, Z.W., Jiao, Z., Wu, M.H., Shek, C.H., Wu, C.M.L., Lai, J.K.L.: Microstructural evolution of oxides and semiconductor thin films. Progress in Materials Science 56(7.4), 901–1029 (2011)
4. Budini, N., Rinaldi, P.A., Schmidt, J.A., Arce, R.D., Buitrago, R.H.: Influence of microstructure and hydrogen concentration on amorphous silicon crystallization 518(18), 5349–5354 (2010)
5. Noda, S., Nagano, K., Inoue, E., Egi, T., Nakashima, T., Imawaka, N., Kanayama, M., Iwata, S., Toshima, K., Nakada, K., Yoshino, K.: Development of large size dye-sensitized solar cell modules with high temperature durability. Synthetic Metals 159(21), 2355–2357 (2009)
6. Park, J., Kwon, S., Jun, S.-I., Ivanov, I.N., Cao, J., Musfeldt, J.L., Rack, P.D.: Stress induced crystallization of hydrogenated amorphous silicon. Thin Solid Films 517(11), 3222–3226 (2009)
7. Wu, X.L., Siu, G.G., Tong, S., Liu, X.N., Yan, F., Jiang, S.S., Zhang, X.K., Feng, D.: Raman scattering of alternating nanocrystalline silicon/amorphous silicon multilayers. Synthetic Metals 69(4), 523–525 (1996)

An Improved Method for High-Precision Measurement Using Recursive WLS

Jihyun Ha, Wooram Lee, and Kwanho You

Department of Electrical Engineering,
Sungkyunkwan University, Suwon, 440-746, Korea
hjh3436@skku.edu, {wooram,khyou}@ece.skku.ac.kr

Abstract. The heterodyne laser interferometer has been widely used in ultra-precision measurement fields. However, the periodic nonlinearity error caused by frequency mixing restricts the precise measurements at nanometer level. We use a nonlinearity compensation method based on the recursive weighted least square (RWLS) algorithm. Using the compensation method, we can obtain the optimal compensation parameters of nonlinearity of heterodyne laser interferometer. To apply the RWLS, the measurement process of the laser interferometer is modeled as a state equation. The effectiveness of the RWLS approach is verified through the comparison with the reference values in some simulations.

Keywords: laser interferometer, recursive weighted least square method, nonlinearity, error compensation, precision measurement.

1 Introduction

Recently the nano-technology has become more and more important part to realize the cutting-edge technology. Especially, the laser interferometry has been widely used in measurement area due to the several good features such as long measurement range, nano-scale precision, and adjustable set-up. As typical examples of the use of laser interferometry, there are semiconductor manufacture, metrology and optical fiber industry. Such a nano-metrology system also has a crucial role on the overall industry as well as the specific area mentioned above.

There are several types of interferometer for the appropriate purposes. It can be categorized as Michelson interferometer and Tyman-green one according to the types of light-source. Michelson interferometer uses one or two stabilized laser and Tyman-green one uses the parallel rays. Between these two, the Michelson type interferometry is widely used in recent days. Michelson types of interferometer can be specified as two main classes which is homodyne laser interferometer and heterodyne one. The first one, the homodyne interferometer, uses single frequency stabilized laser as a light source, and the other is heterodyne one which uses two orthogonal frequencies. In this paper, we focus on a heterodyne laser interferometer because it is more accurate in measurement at high frequency ranges and has a better signal-to-noise-ratio (SNR) and stability from external noise than homodyne one. Regarding

T.-h. Kim et al. (Eds.): CA/CES³ 2011, CCIS 256, pp. 102–111, 2011.

the systematic structure, the optical set-up of heterodyne one is easier than the other one. In spite of the high accuracy of the heterodyne laser interferometry, there are still difficulties for the ultra-precision in the measurement of heterodyne laser interferometer. The measurement result is influenced by the two factors which are the environmental noise and the nonlinearity error in the laser interferometer system.

The environmental noise happens because of the changes of air refraction rate which is mainly caused by the irregular atmospheric temperature, pressure, humidity and air density. The wavelength of a light source is not affected in the vacuum, however, the wavelength in the atmosphere is changed due to the change of air refraction rate. The factors which decide the extent of environmental error are related to the accuracy of compensation method, the condition of measurement circumstance and the level of environmental change. Air refraction problem can be generally resolved by Edlen's formula [1]. However, there are still some problems. The formula is somewhat complicated and we need extra sensors to apply the rule for different set-up of the laser interferometry. Therefore, the error caused by the environmental factors can be restricted by the system isolation from the external circumstances which corrupt the accurate result. When the environmental noise is eliminated by the method mentioned above, we still have a problem to solve for the precise measurement. There are nonlinearity errors which interrupt the accuracy of the interferometry.

The nonlinearity errors are related to polarization-mixing and frequency-mixing. The polarization-mixing means the incomplete separation of the polarization with the same frequency in homodyne laser interferometer. The frequency-mixing is occurred due to the elliptical polarization, non-orthogonal property of the polarizing radiations and imperfect alignment of the polarizing beam-splitter (PBS) [2]. In recent days, a variety of researches have been studied to improve the degree of measurement precision of the laser interferometer as applying different methods which minimize the nonlinearity error in the laser interferometer.

As one solution to minimize or compensate the nonlinearity error, Olyaee [3] compensated for the nonlinearity of the heterodyne laser interferometer using the adaptive algorithms such as the least mean squares (LMS), normalized least mean squares (NLMS), and recursive least squares (RLS). It is also testified that the RLS algorithm can obtain the optimal modeling parameters of nonlinearity errors. Lee [4] demonstrated the efficiency of the extended kalman filter (EKF) which compensates for the nonlinearity errors by comparing the results of the algorithm with the experimental one for the heterodyne laser interferometer. Also, Heo [5] represented the new combined compensation algorithm which adopts recursive least square method and neural network back-propagation algorithm to improve the measurement accuracy and reduce the chattering effect.

In this paper, we propose the recursive weighted least square algorithm to minimize the nonlinearity error which is caused by frequency-mixing of the heterodyne laser interferometer. The WLS algorithm is a method which finds the optimal estimation value only once using the covariance value of given data. However, when the new measured sample data is added to the existing one, the RWLS which is the improved version of WLS is a method to calculate the new covariance matrix. After that, we find the optimal estimation repeatedly using the RWLS method.

We discuss briefly the nonlinearity error in the heterodyne interferometer in Section 2. Section 3 explains about the RWLS approach to compensate for the nonlinearity error. The simulation results for the performance of the RWLS algorithm are given in Section 4. Conclusions appear in Section 5.

2   Nonlinearity Error Modeling in Heterodyne Laser Interferometer

In the laser interferometer system demanding the high resolution property, even the nano-scale error can influence on the accurate measurement results. Under the assumption that the prime error which is caused by the inappropriate installation is resolved, there are two main factors which affect the ultra-precision results of measurement. Those are environmental noise and nonlinearity error.

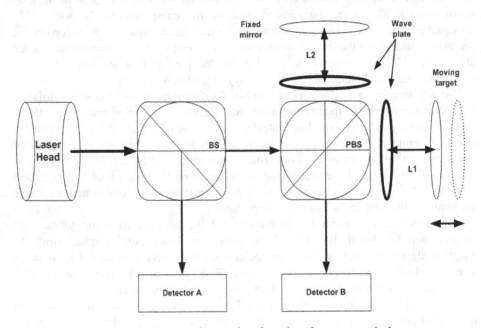

Fig. 1. Schematic diagram of heterodyne laser interferometer optical set-up

The environmental noise can be restricted through shielding the system and using the auxiliary sensors. After that, we consider that the nonlinearity error interrupts the ultra-precision measurement. Fig. 1 shows the fact that two orthogonally polarized beams with magnitude (A , B) and frequencies (f_1 , f_2) proceed to a non-polarizing beam splitter (BS). Using the received signal by the photo detector A, we can express the intensity of the input signal (I_r) as [4]:

$$I_r \propto \frac{1}{2}(A^2 + B^2) + AB \cos[2\pi\Delta ft + (\varphi_B - \varphi_A)] \tag{1}$$

where Δf is $f_2 - f_1$ and φ_A, φ_B are the initial phase values.

If it is an ideal case, there is no frequency-mixing where two splitted beams through the PBS are reflected in a fixed mirror and moving mirror independently to each other. However, the intensity signal measured by photo detector have an error portion caused by frequency-mixing in the real situation. The beam (Af_1), going through the reference path (L2), is mixed with the nonlinear component βf_2 and other beam passing through measurement path (L1) is mixed with the component αf_1. The intensity of an input signal (I_m) obtained from the photo detector B can be represented in terms of the electric field as follows. The DC components and initial phase factors are eliminated.

$$I_{m,AC} \propto AB\cos(2\pi\Delta ft + \varphi) + (A\beta + B\alpha)\cos(2\pi\Delta ft) + \alpha\beta\cos(2\pi\Delta ft - \varphi) \qquad (2)$$

Using a lock-in amplifier (LIA) which includes the functions of the phase shift, power divider, multiplier and low pass filter (LPF), the two intensity signals can be transformed to the different intensity signals in a quadrature form.

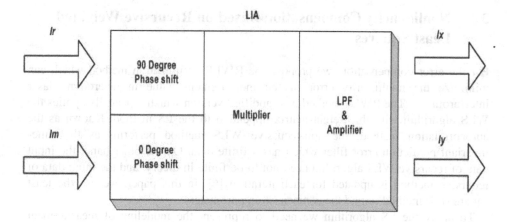

Fig. 2. The functions of a lock-in amplifier

I_r and $I_{m,AC}$ are applied as input signals to the power divider. After those signal's passing through the multiplier, the two output signals are as follows:

$$I_{m,AC}I_r = \cos(2\pi\Delta ft)[AB\cos(2\pi\Delta ft + \varphi)$$
$$+ (A\beta + B\alpha)\cos(2\pi\Delta ft) + \alpha\beta\cos(2\pi\Delta ft - \varphi)] \qquad (3)$$

$$I_{m,AC}I_r \exp(j\frac{\pi}{2}) = \sin(2\pi\Delta ft)[AB\cos(2\pi\Delta ft + \varphi)$$
$$+ (A\beta + B\alpha)\cos(2\pi\Delta ft) + \alpha\beta\cos(2\pi\Delta ft - \varphi)] \qquad (4)$$

Finally, after passing through the low pass filter as a final outcome, we can obtain the quadrature signals of I_x and I_y.

$$I_x \propto \frac{AB + \alpha\beta}{2} \cos\varphi + \frac{A\beta + B\alpha}{2} \tag{5}$$

$$I_y \propto \frac{AB - \alpha\beta}{2} \sin\varphi \tag{6}$$

As an ideal case, we can represent the two intensity signals in a quadrature form. The intensities of I_x and I_y without nonlinearity error are generally represented as follows:

$$I_x = \frac{AB}{2} \cos\varphi \tag{7}$$

$$I_y = \frac{AB}{2} \sin\varphi \tag{8}$$

3   Nonlinearity Compensation Based on Recursive Weighted Least Squares

For the error compensation, we propose the RWLS optimization method which can minimize the nonlinearity error of the measurement value in heterodyne laser interferometer. The RWLS method is a modified version which repeatedly applies the WLS algorithm with the weight-matrix appended to the LS method. Known as the autocorrelation method, the non-recursive WLS method performs as the time-invariant prediction error filter which has a finite data. On the other hand, the input data of recursive WLS algorithm need not to be finite in theory, and the input data of recursive method is updated for each iteration [6]. In this paper, we use the least square (LS) method to find the compensation parameters.

To apply the LS algorithm we need to represent the modeling of measurement process. We assume that the moving mirror proceeds with a constant velocity. Denote the distance by d and the regular velocity by v, respectively. We can express the relationship of the movemental displacement as $d = vt$. However, the moving mirror is influenced by the delicate vibration and other external factors in the real situation. Under this situation, the displacement measured in the laser interferometer is not uniform. Including the non-uniform factors, the displacement equations are represented as follows.

$$d(k+1) = d(k) + s_t v(k) \tag{9}$$

$$v(k+1) = v(k) + \delta(k) \tag{10}$$

where s_t is the sampling time and δ is the velocity error contaminated by the external factors. The unexpected factors restrict the measurement of the ultra-precision distance. In the laser interferometry system, the displacement is expressed by the phase (φ). Considering the vibration, we can express the phase as follows.

$$\varphi(k+1) = \varphi(k) + (s_t / \sigma) v(k)$$
$$= \varphi(k) + \Delta\varphi(k) \tag{11}$$

where σ is $\lambda / (4\pi n)$. Considering the relationship of the phase and the intensity, the intensity I_x and I_y can be represented in terms of the phase. Using the phase update in (11), we can rewrite the state model for a moving target as follows:

$$\hat{I}_x(k+1) = \left(1 + \frac{\alpha\beta}{AB}\right)\cos(\varphi(k) + \Delta\varphi(k)) + \frac{A\beta + \alpha B}{AB} \tag{12}$$

$$\hat{I}_y(k+1) = \left(1 - \frac{\alpha\beta}{AB}\right)\sin(\varphi(k) + \Delta\varphi(k)) \tag{13}$$

With the results of $I_x(k) = \cos(\varphi(k))$ and $I_y(k) = \sin(\varphi(k))$, the state equation can be represented as:

$$\begin{bmatrix} \hat{I}_x(k+1) \\ \hat{I}_y(k+1) \end{bmatrix} = \begin{bmatrix} \left(1 + \frac{\alpha\beta}{AB}\right)\cos\Delta\varphi & -\left(1 + \frac{\alpha\beta}{AB}\right)\sin\Delta\varphi \\ \left(1 - \frac{\alpha\beta}{AB}\right)\sin\Delta\varphi & \left(1 - \frac{\alpha\beta}{AB}\right)\cos\Delta\varphi \end{bmatrix} \begin{bmatrix} I_x(k) \\ I_y(k) \end{bmatrix} + \begin{bmatrix} 1 \\ 0 \end{bmatrix} \frac{A\beta + B\alpha}{AB} \tag{14}$$

$$\begin{bmatrix} \hat{I}_x(k+1) \\ \hat{I}_y(k+1) \end{bmatrix} = \begin{bmatrix} \cos\Delta\varphi I_x(k) - \sin\Delta\varphi I_y(k) & 1 \\ -\sin\Delta\varphi I_x(k) - \cos\Delta\varphi I_y(k) & 0 \end{bmatrix} \begin{bmatrix} \frac{\alpha\beta}{AB} \\ \frac{A\beta + B\alpha}{AB} \end{bmatrix}$$
$$+ \begin{bmatrix} \cos\Delta\varphi I_x(k) - \sin\Delta\varphi I_y(k) \\ \sin\Delta\varphi I_x(k) + \cos\Delta\varphi I_y(k) \end{bmatrix} \tag{15}$$

$$\begin{bmatrix} \hat{I}_x(k+1) - \cos\Delta\varphi I_x(k) + \sin\Delta\varphi I_y(k) \\ \hat{I}_y(k+1) - \sin\Delta\varphi I_x(k) - \cos\Delta\varphi I_y(k) \end{bmatrix} = \begin{bmatrix} \cos\Delta\varphi I_x(k) - \sin\Delta\varphi I_y(k) & 1 \\ -\sin\Delta\varphi I_x(k) - \cos\Delta\varphi I_y(k) & 0 \end{bmatrix} \begin{bmatrix} \Gamma \\ \Delta \end{bmatrix} \tag{16}$$

where $\Gamma = \alpha\beta / AB$, and $\Delta = (A\beta + B\alpha) / AB$.

After that, to apply the LS algorithm we change the equations (12) and (13) as the form of $Mx = l$. The matrix equation is

$$M = \begin{bmatrix} \cos(\varphi(k)+\Delta\varphi(k)) & 1 & 0 \\ 0 & 0 & \sin(\varphi(k)+\Delta\varphi(k)) \end{bmatrix}$$

$$x = \begin{bmatrix} a & h & q \end{bmatrix}', \quad l = \begin{bmatrix} I_x \\ I_y \end{bmatrix} \tag{17}$$

where a^*, h^* and q^* mean the nonlinearity parameters. We can represent the value of x by the following equation.

$$x^* = \left(M^T M \right)^{-1} M^T l \tag{18}$$

Using the equation (18), we can obtain the optimal parameters of a^*, h^* and q^* of I_x and I_y. Before implementing the RWLS algorithm we define the new estimation value $\tilde{I}_x$ and $\tilde{I}_y$ from the optimal parameters which is obtained by the results of LS algorithm. After that, using the appropriate weighted value we can apply the RWLS method. The weighted value is set to the value of remaining error of the LS algorithm. $\tilde{I}_x$ and $\tilde{I}_y$ are represented as follows:

$$\tilde{I}_x = a^* I_x + h^*$$
$$\tilde{I}_y = q^* I_y \tag{19}$$

To apply the RWLS algorithm, we define the error matrix. Using that matrix, we can rewrite the equation about the $\tilde{I}_x$ and $\tilde{I}_y$.

$$e = \begin{bmatrix} e_x & e_y \end{bmatrix}$$
$$= \begin{bmatrix} \hat{I}_x - \tilde{I}_x & \hat{I}_y - \tilde{I}_y \end{bmatrix} \tag{20}$$

$$Mx + e = I_{xy} \tag{21}$$

where I_{xy} is $[I_x, I_y]'$. The optimal compensation variable x^* is represented like this

$$x_n^* = x_{n-1}^* + (M_{n-1}^T E_{n-1} M_{n-1} + m_n^T e_n m_n)^{-1} m_n e_n^{-1}(I_{xy(n)} - m_n x_{n-1}^*) \tag{22}$$

where $x_{n-1}^* = (M_{n-1}^T E_{n-1} M_{n-1})^{-1} M_{n-1}^T E_{n-1} I_{xy}$, E_n is the covariance matrix of error one, m_n is the n-th measurement value and e_n is the covariance value of error of the n-th data from initial value. Finally, using the result of RWLS algorithm, we can rebuild the optimal I_x^* and I_y^* as follows:

$$I_x^* = \frac{\hat{I}_x - h^*}{2a^*} AB, \quad I_y^* = \frac{\hat{I}_y}{2q^*} AB \tag{23}$$

From the equation (23), we can obtain the compensated phase and displacement values as follows:

$$\varphi^* = \tan^{-1} \frac{I_y^*}{I_x^*} \tag{24}$$

$$\Delta L = \frac{\varphi^* \lambda}{4\pi n} \tag{25}$$

4   Simulation results

In this section we prove the efficiency of the RWLS algorithm. For the demonstration of the RWLS performance, we have simulated using a MATLAB program. We set the simulation conditions as follows; the mean of wavelength is 0.6329912 nm, amplitude A and B are 1 Volts, respectively and air refractive index is 1.00000002665.

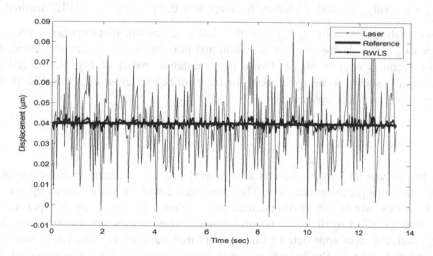

Fig. 3. Nonlinearity error compensation using RWLS algorithm

In Fig. 3, the dotted thin line denotes the uncompensated laser signal which contains the white Gaussian noises and the dashed thick line represents the compensated signal using the RWLS method and the line which is stationary at 40 nm is a reference signal during the sampling period of 13 seconds. We have shown that the RWLS method minimizes the nonlinearity error of a heterodyne laser interferometer.

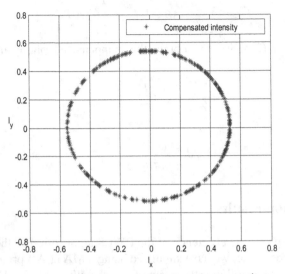

Fig. 4. Lissajous figure of final I_x^* and I_y^*

The intensity I_x^* and I_y^* which is compensated by using the RWLS method is drawn on the 2-dimension in Fig. 4. In the ideal case, the shape of drawing is a perfect shape of a circle. However, with the additional portion by the nonlinearity error, the result becomes oval in shape. Given the simulation result of Fig. 4, the RWLS algorithm is shown to be appropriate for the nonlinearity error compensation in the heterodyne laser interferometer.

5   Conclusion

The heterodyne laser interferometer as a powerful tool in the nano-metrology system needs the ultra-precision accuracy. The nano-scale accuracy is influenced by several error factors which are environmental and nonlinearity errors. In this paper, we excluded the effect by the environmental noise to treat only the nonlinearity error. We suggested the new approach to find the optimal parameters which minimize the nonlinearity error in the heterodyne laser interferometer. The performance of the RWLS algorithm is demonstrated with simulation results. The RWLS algorithm is recursively applied to the situation when the new sample data are added to the existing one. In the future study, we apply the algorithm to the real data which are generated by the experiment.

References

1. Birch, K.P., Downs, M.J.: An Updated Edlen Equation for the Refractive Index of Air. Metrologia, 155–162 (1993)
2. Wu, C., Su, C.: Nonlinearity in Measurement of Length by Optical interferometry. Meas. Sci. Technology 7, 62–68 (1996)
3. Olyaee, S., Abadi, M., Hamedi, S., Finizadeh, F.: Adaptive Algorithm for Nonlinearity Modeling in Laser Heterodyne Interferometer. In: 2010 IEEE Symp. Communication Sys., pp. 665–669 (2010)
4. Lee, W., Kim, D., You, K.: Improved Measurement Accuracy of a Laser Interferometer: Extended Kalman Filter Approach. IEICE Tr. Fundamentals E93-A(10), 1820–1823 (2010)
5. Heo, G., Lee, W., Choi, S., Lee, J., You, K.: Adaptive Neural Network Approach for Nonlinearity Compensation in Laser Interferometer. In: Apolloni, B., Howlett, R.J., Jain, L. (eds.) KES 2007, Part III. LNCS (LNAI), vol. 4694, pp. 251–258. Springer, Heidelberg (2007)
6. Lopez-Valcarce, R., Dasgupta, S.: On the Stability of the Inverse Time-varying Prediction Error Filter Obtained with the RWLS Algorithm. In: ICASSP, vol. 3, pp. 1673–1676 (1999)

Formal Verification of DEV&DESS Formalism Using Symbolic Model Checker HyTech

Han Choi[1], Sungdeok Cha[1], Jae Yeon Jo[2],
Junbeom Yoo[2], Hae Young Lee[3], and Won-Tae Kim[3]

[1] Korea University, Seoul, Republic of Korea
{issubi,scha}@korea.ac.kr
[2] Konkuk University, Seoul, Republic of Korea
{tm77,jbyoo}@konkuk.ac.kr
[3] Electronics and Telecommunications Research Institute,
Daejeon, Republic of Korea
{haelee,wtkim}@etri.re.kr

Abstract. A hybrid system is a dynamical system reacting to continuous and discrete changes simultaneously. Many researchers have proposed modeling and verification formalisms for hybrid systems, but algorithmic verification of important properties such as safety and reachability is still an on-going research area. This paper demonstrates that a basic modeling formalism for hybrid systems, DEV&DESS is an easy-to-use input front-end of a formal verification tool, HyTech. HyTech is a symbolic model checker for liner hybrid automata, and we transformed an atomic DEV&DESS model into linear hybrid automata. We are now developing translation rules from DEV&DESS models, including a coupled DEV&DESS, into linear hybrid automata, through various case studies.

1 Introduction

A hybrid system is a dynamical system whose behavior is a combination of continuous and discrete dynamics [5]. The discrete parts naturally model modes of operation of the system, while the continuous dynamics model physical interactions with themselves or environment, such as automotive controllers, avionic systems, defense modeling and simulation, medical equipments and controllers.

Researches on modeling, analysis and verification of hybrid systems can be classified into two classes, one starting from finite state machine (FSM) and the other originating from continuous system controls. Timed automata [3], (linear) hybrid automata [1,4], DEV&DESS [22] and CHARON [2] are modeling methods for hybrid systems, which belong to the first class. They have also been applied to various domains [11,7,20,13,14] relevantly. UPPAAL [21], HyTech [12] and KRONOS [10] are algorithmic verification tools developed for model checking. UPPAAL uses timed automata which is a finite automaton augmented with a finite number of clocks, which are real-valued variables changing continuously with a constant rate 1(one). HyTech can handle more general kinds of hybrid systems since it uses linear hybrid automata. The second class has developed

T.-h. Kim et al. (Eds.): CA/CES³ 2011, CCIS 256, pp. 112–121, 2011.

out of researches in continuous dynamics and system control. Many researches[1] have been proposed to specify and verify hybrid systems from the viewpoint of control automation. Efficient application of these techniques, however, is rather limited to specific scopes, because of their inherent complexity. In particular, Checkmate [8], d/dt [6] and level set method [16] allow verification on more general dynamics than HyTech, but still have the hard problem of scalability.

DEV&DESS have been typically used as a fundamental formalism of other extended ones (e.g. CHARON and ECML [15]), since it deals with only basic behavior of hybrid systems without visual syntax. Therefore, verification of the hybrid system modeled in the DEV&DESS formalism using HyTech is a good starting-point of developing modeling and verification tools for hybrid systems, which a research institute in Korea, ETRI (Electronics and Telecommunications Research Institute) does. We first transformed the model of DEV&DESS formalism into a form of linear hybrid automata. While transforming the DEV&DESS formalism into linear hybrid automata, we found and resolved many semantic gaps between the two formalisms. We, however, still have several obstacles to overcome, and we are currently focusing on resolving them.

The outline of the paper is as follows. We briefly review the basics of the DEV&DESS formalism and the HyTech symbolic model checker in Section 2. It includes a brief introduction to linear hybrid automata. Section 3 explains hybrid systems modeled with DEV&DESS, and transformation into linear hybrid automata and formal verification using HyTech are explained in Section 4. In Section 5, we summarize out considerations on the translation from DEV&DESS into linear hybrid automata and the problems to be solved. Section 6 concludes the paper.

2   Background

2.1   DEV&DESS Formalism

The *discrete event and differential equation specified system (DEV&DESS)* [18,17] formalism is a system theoretic formalism [22] for modular, hierarchical, combined discrete/continuous system modeling. The DEV&DESS formalism is defined as follows[22,18]:

$$DEV\&DESS = \langle\ X^{discr},\ X^{cont},\ Y^{discr},\ Y^{cont},\ S,\ \delta_{int},\ C_{int},\ \delta_{int},\ \lambda^{discr},\ ta,\ f,\ \lambda^{cont}\ \rangle$$

where,

- X^{discr} and Y^{discr} are the set of discrete input and output from DEVS
- X^{cont} and Y^{cont} are the structured set of continuous value inputs and outputs
- $S = S^{discr} \times S^{cont}$ is the cartesian product of continuous and discrete states
- $\delta_{ext} : Q \times X^{cont} \times X^{disc} \rightarrow S$ is the external state transition function, where $Q = \{(s^{discr}, s^{cont}, e) | s^{discr} \in S^{discr}, s^{cont} \in S^{cont}, e \in R_0^+\}$ is the set of total states with the elapsed time e

---

[1] See the website http://wiki.grasp.upenn.edu/hst/index.php?n=Main.HomePage managed by U. Penn.

- $\delta_{int} : Q \times X^{cont} \to S$ is the internal state transition function
- $C_{int} : Q \times X^{cont} \to Bool$ is the state event condition function
- $\lambda_{discr} : Q \times X^{cont} \to Y^{discr}$ is the discrete event output function
- $\lambda_{cont} : Q \times X^{cont} \to Y^{cont}$ is the continuous output function
- $f : Q \times X^{cont} \to S^{cout}$ is the rate of change function
- $ta : S^{discr} \to R_0^+ \cup \infty$ is the time advance function

The semantics of the DEV&DESS are informally described as follows:

1. **Intervals $\langle t_1, t_2 \rangle$ with no events:** Only S^{cont} and e change. λ^{cont} is operating throughout the interval.
2. **A state event occurs first at time t in interval $\langle t_1, t_2 \rangle$:** δ_{int} is executed to define a new state. e is set to 0, and λ^{discr} is called to generate an output event at time t. λ^{cont} is calculated from time t_1 to t.
3. **A discrete event at the external input port occurs first at time t in interval $\langle t_1, t_2 \rangle$:** δ_{ext} is executed to define a new state at time t. e is set to 0, and λ^{cont} is calculated from time t_1 to t.

Fundamental of DEV&DESS is to understand how the discrete part is affected by the continuous part (See [22] for detials). Events occur whenever a condition specified on the continuous elements becomes true. In the interval between events, the continuous input, state and output values change continuously.

2.2   HyTech and Linear Hybrid Automata

HyTech [12] is a symbolic model checker for linear hybrid automata [4]. As other model checkers [9], it checks a formal model of a system automatically for correctness with respect to requirements. It also provides parametric analysis. If a system model has parameters whose values are not decided yet, then HyTech can compute necessary and sufficient conditions on the parameter's value.

Hybrid automata[1] has been a background formalism of various modeling and verification tools for hybrid systems. However, since the hybrid automata model is too expressive to be proved automatically by model checkers with reasonable computational cost, HyTech uses a restricted class of hybrid automata, which called linear hybrid automata. A hybrid automaton is a linear hybrid automaton if it satisfies following two requirements:

1. **Linearity:** For every control mode $v \in V$, $flow(v)$, $inv(v)$ and $init(v)$ are finite conjunctions of linear inequalities.
2. **Flow independence:** For every control mode $v \in V$, $flow(v)$ is a predicate over the variables in $\dot{X}$ only and does not contain any variables from X.

With linear hybrid automata, the HyTech symbolic model checker verifies safety properties and analyzes correct conditions for parameters. Many embedded systems which belong to hybrid systems, on the other hand, may be not the linear hybrid automata. They are not apt to meet the constraints above. In such cases, we carefully have to approximate or abstract the system model into linear hybrid automata. However, from a practical point of view, we still face a number of important hybrid systems which are classified into linear hybrid automata.

3   Hybrid System Modeling

To demonstrate our approach, we modeled an atomic DEV&DESS model for a simple barrel filler system originated in [22]. Since there is no visual representation in the DEV&DESS formalism, we used graphical notations proposed by [19] for better understanding. In graphical notations, states mean the phases which are mutually exclusive state space[22], while solid and dotted transitions symbolize external and internal events, respectively. ⟨Fig.1⟩ denotes the DEV&DESS model for a barrel filler system. The formal definition of DEV&DESS model is skipped for the limit of space.

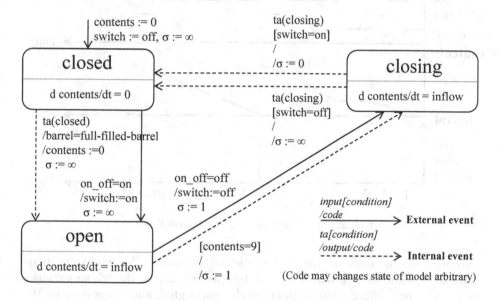

Fig. 1. An atomic DEV&DESS model for the Barrel Filler

The system fills a barrel with a certain rate of inflow while the valve of pipe is opened. When the barrel is filled up, it stops filling, then puts the full-filled barrel out. This process involves changing the barrel with a new empty one. The valve of the system can be changed by signal from the input port '*on_off*', the external event, or by the state event occurred when '*contents*' becomes a cutoff value while the valve is opened; the cutoff value is set as 9 for prevention of overflow because of the assumption that the capacity of a barrel is 10 liter. The continuous variable '*contents*' represents the level of water, increasing its value continuously with derivative. Its derivative is the same as the continuous input '*inflow*' while the valve is not closed. We also assumed the inflow of water is decreased as half, from 0.5 to 0.25, when the valve is closing since the valve is not fully opened. The variable '*switch*', which contains the last signal value of input '*on_off*', is used for differentiation the two events that change the state of the valve, since '*contents*' is the only available information. The '*σ*' which is renewed at every phase changes, represents result of time advanced function.

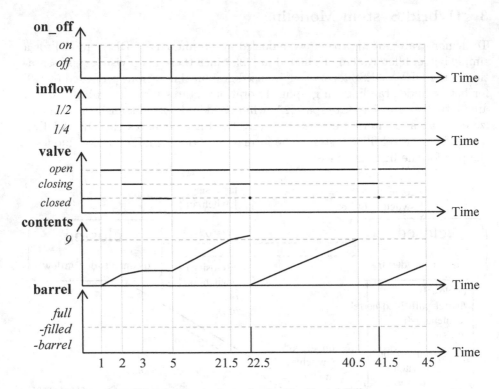

Fig. 2. The trajectories for the Barrel Filler

In order to guarantee the correct behavior of the barrel filler model, we made a simple scenario for the barrel filler system as ⟨Fig.2⟩. In the whole scenario, the model starts filling a barrel twice by the 'on' signal, and stops once by the 'off' signal. Even though the value of '*contents*' stops increasing occasionally by the '*on_off*' signal, as time goes on, the state event is occurred whenever the '*contents*' reaches at 9. The state event causes the model puts a 'full-filled-barrel' out when the valve is closed, and the series of processes above are repeated immediately after a barrel is produced.

For translation the barrel filler model into linear hybrid automata, it is needed to confirm whether the model satisfies the conditions of linear hybrid automata or not, since it is one of the necessary condition for translation. First, the rate of change function '*f*' is influenced only by the input '*inflow*'. Although '*inflow*' has different value according to the state of the valve, it has constant value while system stays in the same state. Therefore continuous state variable '*contents*' always increases linearly under same phase, meaning that the model has '*flow independence condition*' of linear hybrid automata. Second, it is able to find out all possible phases and its changes, since all events and states of the model are decidable. Thus every condition of concerned variables in phases can be expressed by conjunction of linear inequalities, and we can assure that the model above satisfies the '*linearity*' of linear hybrid automata.

4   Verification Using HyTech

This section demonstrates that properties of barrel filler model can be verified with HyTech through translation into linear hybrid automata model. We introduce the translated linear hybrid automata first.

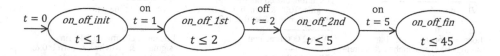

Fig. 3. Automata for discrete input '*on_off*'

The main issue faced during translation was that hybrid automata[1] doesn't have any notations to express I/O behavior, different from the DEV&DESS formalism. Thus we used an additional automaton, as described in ⟨Fig.3⟩, which shows the same behavior with the input '*on_off*'. The variable '*t*' is a clock for global time, and the automaton coordinates with the barrel filler automata through synchronization labels 'on', 'off'.

The barrel filler model with explained scenario can be translated into a linear hybrid automaton as depicted in ⟨Fig.4⟩. The variable '*e*' represents the elapsed time in DEV&DESS and it is compared at every control mode with the variable '*σ*' for checking occurrence of time event. ⟨Fig.5⟩ shows an excerption of the state trace from 0 to 22.5 time unit by the HyTech execution. The value '−1000'

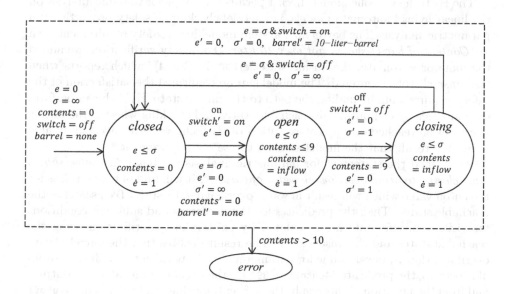

Fig. 4. A linear hybrid automata model for the barrel filler model

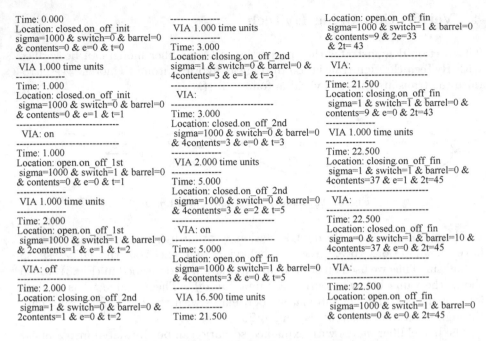

Fig. 5. Reachable states for the barrel filler model

is used for representing infinity since HyTech doesn't support such expression. Analysis on the result confirmed that the translated linear hybrid automaton shows the same behavior with the DEV&DESS model illustrated in ⟨Fig.2⟩.

The HyTech symbolic model checker performs a couple of valuable analysis on the linear hybrid automata models, i.e., model checking of safety properties and parametric analysis. The barrel filler system model has a safety requirement such as '*Content of barrel should not over 10 liter*'. For safety verification, we added the monitor automata, the unsafe state '*error*' in ⟨Fig.4⟩, which reports when the '*unsafe*' state is entered. The model can be confirmed the satisfaction of the safety requirements by finding the path to the unsafe state. HyTech can perform such analysis by computing all reachable states and checking whether the unsafe state can be reached or not. By execution of HyTech, we were successfully able to get the result that the model satisfies the safety requirement.

We defined the statement for parametric analysis as '*When the valve should start closing to avoid overflowing water of barrel?*'. It will find out constraints for the cutoff value which will result in water overflowing. First, HyTech searches the reachable states. Then the predicates for the necessary and sufficient conditions for visiting unsafe state are calculated by existential quantification using the reachable states and the unsafe state. The result denotes that the barrel always overflows, that is, unsafe value for parameter cutoff. As executed with such series of processes, the predicate '4cutoff > 39' for the unsafe cutoff value was output, and from the negation of this result, the safe cutoff value can be derived, '4cutoff <= 39'. It also implies if the cutoff value is 9.75, then the model puts a ten liter filled barrel exactly.

5   Further Considerations on the Translation from DEV&DESS into Linear Hybrid Automata

Components structuring DEV&DESS and linear hybrid automata are different from each other, and we need to map one to the other appropriately while keeping their behavioral equivalence. First of all, we used the concept of 'phase[22]' in the DEV&DESS formalism to compose control modes which are the fundamental elements of linear hybrid automata. The biggest challenge for the translation is how to express I/O behavior of the DEV&DESS formalism in linear hybrid automata. Our solution in the paper is to use parallel automata which shows the same behavior with the original input trajectories of the DEV&DESS model. The basic ideas for translation are as follows:

– The variable 'e' is added to symbolize the elpased time in DEV&DESS. Its value is refreshed at every every control mode changes.
– The variable 'σ' is used for time advanced function 'ta'.
– A labeling function '$init$' is derived from initial condition.
– A labeling function '$flow$' is derived from change of rate function 'f' with continuous input value.
– A labeling function '$jump$' is derived from state and external events. The conditions for time event is also included at every control mode.
– A labeling function 'inv' is derived from state events and time events.

Based on the guidelines above, we could translate the DEV&DESS model into an equivalent linear hybrid automata model successfully. We could also perform formal verification of HyTech on the translated models too. We, however, found some problems which should be resolved for more seamless translations.

– In the case that the external and internal events conflict in DEV&DESS model, assignment the order of priority between jump conditions is difficult, since hybrid automata does not provide any such semantics. Therefore, It may happen that exploring unintended trajectories of transformed automata.
– If the continuous input trajectories are the form of stairs, figuring out the whole input trajectories is required before translation even if it satisfies '$flow$ independece condition'. It is due to that the phase may map to the several control modes, not one by one, since HyTech doesn't allow using variables to express rate condition.

6   Conclusion

This paper translated an atomic DEV&DESS model for a barrel filler system into linear hybrid automata, and then performed model checking of safety requirement and parametric analysis using the HyTech symbolic model checker. Translation from the DEV&DESS formalism into linear hybrid automata has its won significance, since verification tools dealing with DEV&DESS have not been proposed while DEV&DESS has been used as a basic formalism for various modeling tools, such as CHARON and ECML. Therefore, if the translation is well defined and a mechanical translator is also supported, then verifying the model can be done by using existing tools such as HyTech. We are now developing translations for coupled DEV&DESS formalism to linear hybrid automata and transition rules for the broad applications.

Acknowledgement. This work was supported by the IT R&D Program of MKE/KEIT [10035708, "The Development of CPS(Cyber-Physical Systems) Core Technologies for High Confidential Autonomic Control Software"]. This research was partially supported by the National IT Industry Promotion Agency (NIPA) under the program of Software Engineering Technologies Development.

References

1. Alur, R., Courcoubetis, C., Halbwachs, N., Henzinger, T.A., Ho, P.H., Nicollin, X., Olivero, A., Sifakis, J., Yovine, S.: The algorithmic analysis of hybrid systems. Theoretical Computer Science 138(1), 3–34 (1995)
2. Alur, R., Dang, T., Esposito, J., Hur, Y., Ivančić, F., Vijay Kumar, I.L., Mishra, P., Pappas, G.J., Sokolsky, O.: Hierarchical modeling and analysis of embedded systems. Proceedings of the IEEE 91(1), 11–28 (2003)
3. Alur, R., Dill, D.L.: A theory of timed automata. Theoretical Computer Science 126 (1994)
4. Alur, R., Henzinger, T.A., Ho, P.H.: Automatic symbolic verification of embedded systems. IEEE Transactions on Software Engineering 22(3), 181–201 (1996)
5. Antsaklis, P.J., Stiver, J.A., Lemmon, M.D.: Interface and Controller Design for Hybrid Control Systems. In: Antsaklis, P.J., Kohn, W., Nerode, A., Sastry, S.S. (eds.) HS 1994. LNCS, vol. 999, pp. 462–492. Springer, Heidelberg (1995)
6. Asarin, E., Dang, T., Maler, O.: The d/dt Tool for Verification of Hybrid Systems. In: Brinksma, E., Larsen, K.G. (eds.) CAV 2002. LNCS, vol. 2404, pp. 365–770. Springer, Heidelberg (2002)
7. Balluchi, A., Benvenuti, L., Benedetto, M., Pinello, C., Sangiovanni-Vincentelli, A.: Automotive engine control and hybrid systems: challenges and opportunities. Proceedings of the IEEE 88(7), 888–912 (2000)
8. Chutinan, A., Krogh, B.H.: Verification of Polyhedral-Invariant Hybrid Automata Using Polygonal Flow Pipe Approximations. In: Vaandrager, F.W., van Schuppen, J.H. (eds.) HSCC 1999. LNCS, vol. 1569, pp. 76–90. Springer, Heidelberg (1999)
9. Clarke, E.M., Grumberg, O., Peled, D.A.: Model Checking. MIT Press (1999)
10. Daws, C., Olivero, A., Trypakis, S., Yovine, S.: The Tool Kronos. In: Alur, R., Sontag, E.D., Henzinger, T.A. (eds.) HS 1995. LNCS, vol. 1066, pp. 208–219. Springer, Heidelberg (1996)
11. Esposito, J.M., Kim, M.: Using formal modeling with an automated analysis tool to design and parametrically analyze a multirobot coordination protocol: A case study. IEEE Transactions on Systems, Man and Cybernetics, Part A: Systems and Humans 37(3), 285–297 (2007)
12. Henzinger, T.A., Ho, P.H., Wong-Toi, H.: Hytech: a model checker for hybrid systems. Software Tools for Technology Transfer 1(1-2), 110–122 (1997)
13. Henzinger, T.A., Wong-Toi, H.: Using Hytech to Synthesize Control Parameters for a Steam Boiler. In: Abrial, J.-R., Börger, E., Langmaack, H. (eds.) Dagstuhl Seminar 1995. LNCS, vol. 1165, pp. 265–282. Springer, Heidelberg (1996)

14. Kim, T.G., Sung, C.H., Hong, S.Y., Hong, J.H., Choi, C.B., Kim, J.H., Seo, K.M., Bae, J.W.: Devsim++ toolset for defense modeling and simulation and interoperation. The Journal of Defense Modeling and Simulation: Applications, Methodology, Technology 8(3), 129–142 (2011)
15. Lee, D.A., Lee, J.H., Yoo, J., Kim, D.H.: Systematic verification of operational flight program through reverse engineering. In: International Conference on Advanced Software Engineering & Its Applications (submitted, 2011)
16. Mitchell, I., Tomlin, C.J.: Level Set Methods for Computation in Hybrid Systems. In: Lynch, N.A., Krogh, B.H. (eds.) HSCC 2000. LNCS, vol. 1790, pp. 310–323. Springer, Heidelberg (2000)
17. Praehofer, H.: Systems Theoretic Foundations for Combined Discrete Continuous System Simulation. Ph.D. thesis, Department of Systems Theory, University of Linz, Autria (1991)
18. Praehofer, H., Auernig, F., Reisinger, G.: An environment for devs-based multiformalism simulation in common lisp/CLOS. Discrete Event Dynamic Systems: Theory and Application 3, 119–149 (1993)
19. Praehofer, H., Pree, D.: Visual modeling of devs-based multiformalism systems based on higraphs. In: Simulation Conference Proceedings, pp. 595–603 (December 1993)
20. Tomlin, C., Pappas, G., Sastry, S.: Conflict resolution for air traffic management: a study in multiagent hybrid systems. IEEE Transactions on Automatic Control 43(4), 509–521 (1998)
21. UPPAAL (2010), http://www.uppaal.com/
22. Zeigler, B.P., Praehofer, H., Kim, T.G.: Theory of Modeling and Simulation. Academic Press (2000)

DVML: DEVS-Based Visual Modeling Language for Hybrid Systems[*]

Hae Young Lee, Ingeol Chun, and Won-Tae Kim

CPS Research Team, ETRI
Daejeon 305-700 Republic of Korea
haelee@ieee.org

Abstract. This paper proposes a visual modeling language for a large-scale hybrid system based on discrete event system specification formalism. Within theproposed language, basic model diagrams define the hybrid behavior of systems, whilethe structure can be represented through coupled model diagrams. The language can visually define large-scale hybrid systems without a sacrifice of formal semantics, and does not require the users to have programming skills. A prototype of the modeling and simulation environment based on an extended version of the language has been implemented.

Keywords: Visual modeling language, discrete event system specification (DEVS), DEV&DESS,hybrid system modeling, cyber-physical systems.

1 Introduction

Discrete event system specification (DEVS) formalism [1], which is a theoretically well-grounded means of expressing modular discrete event simulation models, has gained increasing popularity in recent years [2]. Various DEVS-based modeling and simulation (M&S) environments [3,4] have been developed to tackle complex problems through a broad array of domains. However, in most of these environments, the users must write models in certain programming languages, such as Java and C++, with predefined libraries. This therefore results in their relatively limited adoption within the industry [5].

Recently, several DEVS-based graphical modeling approaches [5-7] have been proposed to make DEVS more accessible to a wider community. A DEVS graph [6], which permits the users to write DEVS models using state machines, was proposed by Christen et al., and was later adopted in graphical modeling editors of CD++Builder [5]. Traoré proposed a DEVS-driven modeling language [7] that considers functional, dynamical, and static aspects of systems in a graphical way. However, they have addressed only the graphical modeling of discrete systems, while most large-scale systems, such as cyber-physical systems (CPS) [8,9], involve hybrid processes combining both continuous and discrete phenomena.

---

[*] This work was supported by the IT R&D Program of MKE/KEIT [10035708, "The Development of CPS (Cyber-Physical Systems) Core Technologies for High Confidential Autonomic Control Software"].

T.-h. Kim et al. (Eds.): CA/CES³ 2011, CCIS 256, pp. 122–127, 2011.

This paper proposes a visual modeling language (DVML) that enables graphical modeling of hybrid systems, based on discrete event and differential equation systems (DEV&DESS) formalism developed by Praehofer [10]. In DVML, a hybrid system can be defined using two different kinds of diagrams: a basic model diagram and coupled model diagram. The hybrid behavior of systems can be graphically defined using basic model diagrams, while coupled model diagrams can describe the structure of the systems. For hybrid systems modeling, by using DVML, the users are no longer required to have programming experience. A prototype of a DVML-based modeling and simulation environment is introduced at the end of this paper.

2   DEVS-Based Visual Modeling Language (DVML)

This section presents the proposed modeling language, DVML, in detail.

2.1   Basic Model Diagram (BMD)

DVML specifies a basic DEV&DESS model using a basic model diagram (BMD). A BMD is depicted as an empty rectangle with the name of the model at the top left. All elements that belong to a BMD are shown within the rectangle.

Each basic model interacts with its external environment by passing continuous values or discrete events through its I/O ports. Each port is represented by a small rectangle drawn on the border of the BMD, with the textual notation for the ports. The notation is defined by the following Backus-Naur Form (BNF) expression:

$<port>::=`[`<port-type>`]`<port-name>`:`<data-type>$

$<port-type>::=`[C]`|`[E]`$

'[C]' is specified for continuous value ports. For a discrete event port, '[E]' is specified and its value can be either a predefined event (an element of $<data-type>$) or $\emptyset$ (nonevent). An input port and an output port are drawn as a small empty rectangle and a small filled rectangle, respectively. A discrete event port can be accessed only within transitions, while continuous value ports can be accessed at any time.

In DVML, the specification of the behavior of a basic model is organized around the phase variable in an enumerated type of programming language. The phase variable denotes some type of representative state that the model remains in. In each phase, an enumerator in the variable is rendered as a rounded rectangle along with its name. The initial phase is depicted as a small filled circle.

Other state variables are denoted by text strings in the notation defined by the following BNF expression:

$<state-variable>::=`[`<variable-type>`]`<variable-name>`:`<data-type>$

$<variable-type>::=`[C]`|`[D]`$

'[C]' is specified for continuous state variables, while '[D]' is specified for discrete state variables, which are updated by discrete events.

A transition from a source phaseto a target phase is renderedas an arc that connects them, with a textual notation for transitions. The notation is defined by the following expression:

<transition>::=[<transition-name>]['['<transition-condition>']']['/'<state-definition>]]

<transition-condition> is a Boolean expression that specifies the firing condition of the transition. A transition is performed if and only if the model is in the source phase and if the firing condition is true. If the firing condition for a transition is not specified, the transition is immediately performed whenever the model is in the source phase. A <state-definition> is an expression that defines a new state and/or generates outputs. The expression is executed when the transition fires. The firing condition for the initial transition must not be specified so that the transition can be immediately fired. The initial values for state variables and continuous output ports must be specified within <state-definition> of the initial transition. Consequently, the model actually starts in the target phase of the transition with the initial values.

A constraint is an algebraic or ordinary differential equation (ODE) that defines continuous behavior or computes continuous states. If a constraint is within a phase (i.e., a phase constraint), the constraint is enabled only when the model is in that phase.

2.2   BMD Example

Figure 1 illustrates a sample BMD for a barrel filler described in [1]. The sample model has two input ports: *Inflow*, a continuous value input port ('[C]') in *double* (real) data type, and *On*, a discrete event input port ('[E]') in *bool* (Boolean) data type. The value of the port *On* is read only within the conditions of two transitions, *StartFilling* and *StopFilling*. Three output ports, *Level*, *Room*, and *Barrel*, belong to the model. Port *Barrel* is written using *Barrel = BarrelID* in order to generate an output event when transition *GenerateBarrel* fires. The model has three phases: *Ready*, *Filling*, and the initial phase. A continuous state variable ('[C]'), *Capacity*, and a discrete ('[D]') state variable, *BarrelID*belong to the model. The former and latter variables store the capacity of a barrel and the identifier of the current barrel, respectively.

Continuous value output port *Room* is updated using the following algebraic equation:

$$Room = Capacity - Level \qquad (1)$$

While the model in *Ready* phase is updated by the following ODE:

$$\partial Level / \partial t = 0 \qquad (2)$$

That is, the current barrel is not filled. If the model is in *Ready* phase and receives an event true through *On*, transition *StartFilling* is fired. While the model is in *Filling*, *Level* is updated as follows:

$$\partial Level / \partial t = Inflow \qquad (3)$$

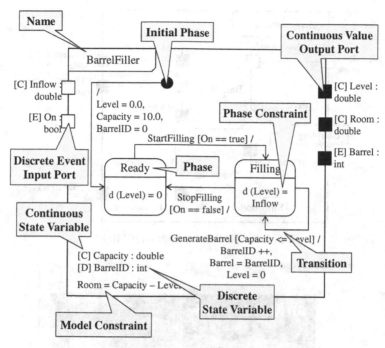

Fig. 1. Basic model diagram (BMD)

Thus, the current barrel is filled by *Inflow*. *GenerateBarrel* is fired if the model is in *Filling* phase and the value of *Level* is equal to or greater than the value of *Capacity* (i.e., if the current barrel is fully filled with content). Through the transition, the value of *BarrelID* increases in order to give the next barrel a new identifier, and the value of *Level* is set to 0 (an empty barrel). If the model is in *Filling* phase and receives a false through *On*, then *StopFilling* is fired.

2.3   Coupled Model Diagram (CMD)

A DEV&DESS coupled model is specified as a coupled model diagram (CMD) in DVML. Ports are drawn by small rectangles on the border with the textual notations. Each sub-model is depicted as a rectangle with its name. A coupling from a source port to a target port is rendered as an arc connecting them. When two ports are coupled, their types and data types must match.

2.4   CMD Example

Figure 2 shows a sample CMD for a barrel generator. The model consists of two sub-models, *BarrelFiller* (illustrated in Fig. 1) and Controller. A single external input coupling, three external output couplings, and two internal couplings are rendered as arcs.

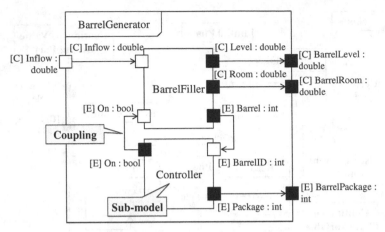

Fig. 2. Coupled model diagram (CMD)

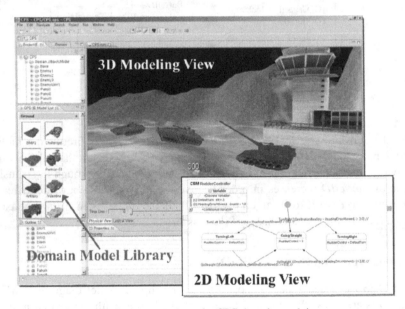

Fig. 3. A screenshot of a CPS domain modeler

3   DVML-Based Modeling Environment

We have implemented a prototype of a DVML-based CPS M&S environment. Figure 3 shows a screenshot of the modeling environment prototype, called *CPS domain modeler*, which is an Eclipse plug-in. Hybrid systems can be modeled with ease, by drag-and-dropping DVML elements (e.g., transitions, phases, and so on). That is, by using a CPS domain modeler, the users are not required to have programming experience in the modeling of hybrid systems. Models described in DVML are stored in a model base, called a *CPS domain model library*, together with 3-D objects. The modeler also provides a 3-D modeling environment. Within the modeler, a large-scale CPS can be easily composed by drag-and-dropping of 3-D objects embedding a hybrid behavior. CPS models can be executed on our DEV&DESS-based hybrid simulation environment, and their execution results can be reviewed by using a 3-D visualizer.

4   Conclusions and Future Work

In this paper, we proposed the formalism-based language for large-scale hybrid systems that can provide full graphical modeling capabilities without a sacrifice in formal semantics. A prototype based on DVML has been implemented for CPS. DVML is still being developed for a complex CPS. In the next version, some extensions for autonomic computing support will be included. We will also study the formal verification of DVML models.

References

1. Zeigler, B.P., Paraehofer, H., Kim, T.G.: Theory of Modeling and Simulation, 2nd edn. Academic Press (2000)
2. Feng, B., Wainer, G.: A NET Remoting-Based Distributed Simulation Approach for DEVS and Cell-DEVS Models. In: Proc. DS-RT 2008, pp. 292–299 (2008)
3. Adevs, http://www.ornl.gov/~1qn/adevs/
4. DEVSim++, http://smslab.kaist.ac.kr/
5. Bonaventura, M., Wainer, G., Castro, R.: Advanced IDE for Modeling and Simulation of Discrete Event Systems. In: Proc. SpringSim 2010 (2010)
6. Christen, G., Dobniewski, A., Wainer, G.: Modeling State-Based DEVS Models in CD++. In: Proc. ASTC 2004 (2004)
7. Traoré, M.K.: A Graphical Notation for DEVS. In: Proc. SpringSim 2009 (2009)
8. Lee, E.A.: Cyber Physical Systems: Design Challenges. In: Proc. ISORC 2008, pp. 363–369 (2008)
9. Park, J., Yoo, J.: Hardware-Aware Rate Monotonic Scheduling Algorithm for Embedded Multimedia Systems. ETRI Journal 32(5), 657–664 (2010)
10. Praehofer, H.: System Theoretic Formalism for Combined Discrete-Continuous System Simulation. International Journal of General System 19(3), 226–240 (1991)

Fast Discovery Scheme Using DHT-Like Overlay Network for a Large-Scale DDS

Sung-Yoon Chae[1], Sinae Ahn[1], Kyungran Kang[1],
Jaehyuk Kim[2], Soo-Hyung Lee[2], and Won-Tae Kim[2]

[1] Department of Computer Engineering, Ajou University, Suwon, Korea
{unichae,kacey,korykang}@ajou.ac.kr
[2] ETRI, Daejeon, Korea
{jhk0330,soohyung,wtkim}@etri.or.kr

Abstract. Data distribution service (DDS) is a middleware for data distribution and supports large-scale applications such as Internet service and military systems. However, the reliability and quality of service feature of DDS standard requires an entity to have the complete picture of the participants and endpoints in the network. Thus, the discovery process of the DDS is not scalable and causes noticeable long delay as the number of entities in the network increases. In this paper, we present a scalable fast discovery scheme by exploiting the DHT-like overlay network. Our scheme integrates the participant and endpoint discovery processes and significantly reduces the number of messages for the discovery process. Simulation results indicate that our scheme is faster and requires quite less overhead compared with the simple discovery protocol (SDP) of the DDS standard.

Keywords: DDS, DHT-like overlay network, fast discovery.

1 Introduction

DDS[1] is the open standard for data distribution for real-time systems. Many real-time applications DDS has been deployed a small networks. Recently, DDS has been deployed large-scale distributed systems[2]. For example, P2P applications like KaZaa and Skype are connecting millions of users.

An essential point for building a global data-centric space for data distribution is the discovery process between participants and endpoints in DDS entities. As grown the network complexity, discovery process becomes a new challenge for real-time operations. The current discovery protocol in the standard, SDP, properly works in only small networks in terms of participants and endpoints. SDP uses multicast message delivery. It causes multicast storm and messages are probably dropped by full of buffer. retransmissions of dropped messages make delivery with a long delay when crowded joins of nodes are happened in the network.

Fast and scalable discovery is one of the most important features in a large-scale DDS. In this paper, we propose fast discovery scheme which is designed for scalable in terms of the number of nodes. First, we present DHT-like overlay network

T.-h. Kim et al. (Eds.): CA/CES³ 2011, CCIS 256, pp. 128–137, 2011.

construction[3]. It makes our scheme more scalable and efficient. Then, specific algorithms for events are described. The goal of our scheme is to reduce the number of exchanged messages by network construction and integrated discovery for participants and endpoints.

This paper organized as follows. In section 2, DDS discovery protocols are briefly studied as related works. Our scheme is described and evaulated through section 3 and 4. Finally, section 5 concludes the paper.

2   Related Works

Simple discovery protocol (SDP) specifies in DDS standard[4]. SDP is defined simple participant discovery protocol (SPDP) and simple endpoint discovery protocol (SEDP). The discovery process is started with PDP to discover other participants. In SPDP, participant discovery message is periodically sent to already discovered peers. SPDP discovery message contains information, such as protocol version, address and port number, for communications between participants.

After participant discovery, endpoint information is exchanged. SEDP protocol sends the endpoint information to all participants and they receive every discovered participant's endpoints information.

In the SDP, each participant communicates directly to every other participant and maintains the connections for checking liveness periodically. A critical limitation is that total number of exchanged messages has order of $O(P*E)$, where P is the number of participants and E is the number of endpoints in the network.

[5] propose improve DDS discovery process using a compact informaiton by bloom filter. By using bloom filters, total number of sent messages is P*P instead of P*E. However, there can be false positives in endpoints mapping.

3   Fast Discovery Scheme

There are two entities to discover in DDS, participants and endpoints. Participant represents the application. It acts as an entry point of application and a container for the other entity objects, such as endpoints. Endpoint is an object responsible for data distribution and receiving published data.

The DDS discovery protocol must discover every participants and endpoints in real-time. In other words, discovery protocol enables participants to obtain iunformation about the existence and attributes of all the other participants and endpoints in the network. That is, every participant obtains a complete picture of all participants and endpoints.

Therefore, we construct DHT-like overlay network so that reduces overheads for exchanging discovery messages between every other nodes in the network. Our scheme constraints the number of directly connected nodes and message packing Using DHT-like overlay network, limited connections: Each node connects only successors instead of all nodes. network traffic: burst network traffic caused by multicast storm can be preserved. We need to spread these discovery messages not to use a multicast protocol. Total number of sent messages for discovery process is reduced by message packing.

The basic idea of our scheme is as follows: First, construction of DHT-like overlay network. Second, each node in the network set their successor table using *ID* of the node and *maxID*. Third, exchanging QoS information of participants and endpoints when periodical and trigered events occurred.

3.1   Network Model and Message Delivery

In order to access the overlay network, a node(participant) makes a query to the bootstrap server. We construct DHT-like overlay network with largest ID (*maxID*), which is informed a bootstrap server. *maxID* of the network will be maintained by the bootstrap server. Then, the node has given a unique ID in the network. Fig. 1 shows an example of overlay network with 16 nodes from node-1 to node-16.

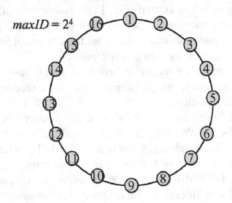

Fig. 1. A fully populated overlay network with 16 nodes is constructed with *maxID*=16. Each node has a unique *ID* from the bootstrap server.

When a node accesses the network, the node constructs successor table for discovery process with a given *ID* and *maxID* of the network. Successor table for node i is constructed like Tabel 1. A node has $\lceil \log_2(maxID) \rceil$ successors, and each node of successors is forwarding a message generated by the node to its own successor nodes in limit range. In other words, A message is broadcasted through successor nodes in multi-hop.

Table 1. Successor Table for node i

Index	Successor *ID*	Limit range
0	$i + 2^0$	$(i + 2^0, i + 2^1 - 1)$
1	$i + 2^1$	$(i + 2^1, i + 2^2 - 1)$
...	...	...
j	$i + 2^j$	$(i + 2^j, i + 2^{j+1} - 1)$
...	...	...
$\log_2(maxID) - 1$	$i + 2^{\log_2(maxID) - 1}$	$(i + 2^{\log_2(maxID) - 1}, i + 2^{\log_2(maxID)} - 1)$

Successor table is updated when *maxID* of the network is changed. The bootstrap server monitors population of the overlay network and makes it enlarge or reduce according to the number of nodes in the network. Then, *maxID* will be changed and informed to all nodes in the network.

To avoid duplicated message delivery we use DHT broadcast[6] message delivery which is proposed by El-Ansary *et al.*. Unlike broadcast in network layer, DHT broadcast messages are delivered through intermediate nodes, which are successors. Broadcast messages through intermediate nodes are only forwarded in limit of the node. Thus, Each message contains limit by the forwarding node. It is guaranteed there is no duplicated or missed transmission with respect to all active nodes in the overlay network, because successors of the source response packed ACK to confirm successful transmissions.

In Fig. 2, DHT broadcast messages are delivered from node 3 to all nodes. Each transmission of DHT broadcast is able to run on unicast. We guarantee reliable transmissions that uses reliable transport layer protocols, such as TCP/IP. Node 4, 5, 7, 11 that are received DHT broadcast message forward the message to their successors under limit which is contained in the broadcast message. Node 4 receives broadcast message from node 3 with limit (4, 4). Then, node 4 . On the other hand, node 11 also receives broadcast message from node 3 with limit (11, 2). Then, node 11 forwards the broadcast message to its successors in limit, node 12, 13 and 15. At last, broadcast message is forwarded through three intermediate nodes (node 11, 15, 1) to node 2.

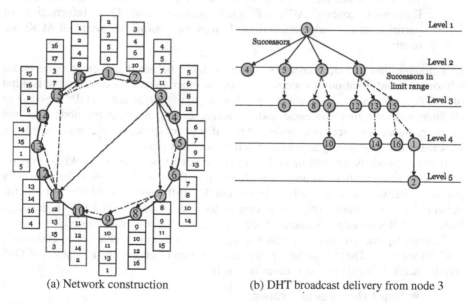

(a) Network construction   (b) DHT broadcast delivery from node 3

Fig. 2. There are 16 nodes in the network (a). For each node, corresponding successor table is shown (b). In this example, DHT broadcast messages are forwarded from node 3 to all nodes through multi-hop. There are totally 15 transmissions.

3.2   Discovery Process

Discovery processes both sides, a new joining node and exist nodes, at the same time. As outlined above, the node that is about access the network makes a query for the bootstrap server. Then, join process is operated by the node. Join process is described as follows:

- **Step 1 (Initialization):**
  The node makes and sends a query to get information of *ID* and *maxID* to the bootstrap server. Also mapping function from *ID* to address is given for discovery message delivery.
- **Step 2 (Successor table construction):**
  The node constructs successor table with *ID* and *maxID*, and assign limit range for each successor. Successor table has $\lceil \log_2(maxID) \rceil$ rows. Successor nodes are selected without QoS information of other nodes, so that blind search at the first time.
- **Step 3 (Message generation):**
  The node generates JOIN messages for each successor in limit range like Message (JOIN, originator, source, destination, limit range).
- **Step 4 (Exchanging messages):**
  The node sends JOIN messages to successors with DHT broadcast delivery. JOIN message contains originator, source, destination and limit range.

  The node waits for receiving responses of JOIN message from successors. Responses contain ACK of JOIN message and QoS information of participants and endpoints in limit. Join process is finished when all ACKs are received.

It is notable that a node constructs successor table before discovering other nodes without QoS information of successor nodes. In other words, successor table is a list of *ID*s that constraints communications. A new joining node sends JOIN message to all successors whether successor node is active or not, because the node does not know presence of successor nodes. After discovery process, the node sends or forwards messages to only active node in the successor table.

If the network is not full of nodes, DHT broadcast delivery is working properly because of using participant presence information. Detailed description for a partially populated network will be available in section 3.3. If the node would like to leave the network, leave process, which is a similar to join process with LEAVE message instead of JOIN message, is operated without waiting for responses in step 4.

Second, Update process is operated when a node recognises changes of endpoint's QoS information. They could be creation and deletion of endpoints or changes of QoS requirements. Update process is described as follows:

- **Step 1 (Message generation):**
  When the node recognises changes of endpoint's QoS information, it makes UPDATE message to inform other nodes. UPDATE message contains originator, source, destination, limit range and QoS information.

  Message (UPDATE, originator, source, destination, limit range, QoS information).

- **Step 2 (Exchanging messages):**
The node sends UPDATE messages to successors with DHT broadcast delivery, and waits for receiving responses of UPDATE message from successors.
- **Step 3 (Setting the timer):**
The node resets timer with T, which is predefined timer value.
Update process is finished when all ACKs are received.

Update process only occurs when a new endpoint is created, an endpoint is deleted and QoS requirement of endpoint is changed in the node. In other words, no event occurred until timer is expired, the node sends HEARBEAT messages to successors instead of UPDATE message. HEARTBEAT message only contains originator, source, destination and limit range. It helps other nodes to keep up-to-date information about active nodes in the network. Therefore, the node resets the timer with T in step 3, because UPDATE message delivery solves liveness of the node to all active nodes in the network.

At last, response process will be described here. When a node receives a message, following steps are taken.

- **Step 1 (Updating information):**
When a node receives a message, it parses the message and stores QoS information of senders if the message type is JOIN or LEAVE or HEARTBEAT.
The node updates QoS information of the endpoints if the message type is UPDATE.
- **Step 2 (Message generation):**
The node makes ACK message with packing QoS information of active nodes in limit range.
The node also makes forwarding messages for each case (JOIN or UPDATE or HEARTBEAT).
- **Step 3 (Exchanging messages):**
The node replies ACK message to the sender, and broadcasts forwarding messages made in step 2 to its successor nodes in limit range.

In SDP, a new joining node sends join message to all nodes in the network and receives corresponding responses from them. That is, total number of exchanged messages is $2(P-1)$, where P is the number of nodes in the network. On the other hands, our scheme consumes only $(P-1) + \log_2 P + \alpha$, where α is the number of fragmentations caused by ACK message packed with QoS information.

In terms of scalability, our scheme consumes an order of $O(P \log_2 P)$ exchanged messages, while SDP has order of $O(P*P)$ exchanged messages being required to finish discovery process in the network with P nodes. This is a major reduction of the number of messages. Messages are packed when response message generated for JOIN message in step 2.

3.3   Message Formats

We define four types of message, JOIN, LEAVE, UPDATE and HEARTBEAT, and two types of events, triggered and periodic. The message has extra fields such as message type, originator, sender, receiver, limit range and QoS. Originator represents the *ID* that generates the message. Sender/receiver represents *ID* to send/receive the message, respectively. QoS field is filled in JOIN, UPDATE and ACK for JOIN message.

Table 2. Types of events and messages

Type of events	Event	Message	Response
	Participant creation	JOIN	ACK with QoS information
Triggered	Participant deletion	LEAVE	No ACK
	Endpoint creation/deletion/change	UPDATE	ACK
Periodic	Participant timer expired	HEARBEAT	ACK

Table 2 shows relations of events and types of message. When events occurred, corresponding message generated and sent. Only response of JOIN message is Piggybacked ACK with data, while responses of UPDATE and HEARBEAT messages are just ACK with no information. As we mentioned section 3.2, HEARTBEAT message is sent by the node that has no changed QoS information of endpoints within T.

3.4   Failure Recovery

If the network is not fully populated, broadcast messages are probably failure to deliver to the forwarder. There are two recovery mechanisms, receiver and sender-initiated. Receiver-initiated recovery occurred when sender does not know whether nodes are active or not. In other words, when a new joining node sends a JOIN message to its successor nodes, its successor nodes recover if there are failure nodes in the successor nodes. Simple way to recover failure in case of receiver-initiated is that every receiver checks liveness of next successor node. If next successor node is not active, the receiver expands forwarding limit range. If there is only one active successor node in extreme case, the node forwards it to all active nodes in the network.

In case of sender-initiated recovery, forwarding nodes already have complete picture of the network. Then, forwarding nodes select active nodes as successor nodes. Fig. 3 shows an sender-initiated recovery example of join process when node3 joins the network. An example, node 3 as an originator of JOIN message broadcasts the message to all nodes in the network. Node 3 makes JOIN messages for each successor, and unicast delivery to each successor. In this example, node 15 is leaved the network before node 3 is accessed. In this case, sender-initiated recovery processes when node11 receives broadcast message from node 3 with limit range (11, 2).

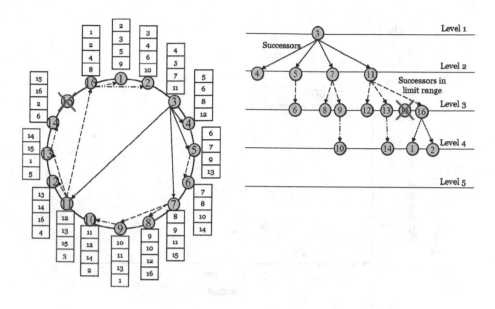

(a) Network construction   (b) DHT broadcast delivery from node 3

Fig. 3. DHT broadcast in a partially populated network (a). We assume that node 15 is a failure node, and sender-initiated recovery processed in node 11.

4   Performance Evaluations

We use overlay simulator, OverSim, for experimentally evaluations. It is scalable and efficient simulator in large-scale overlay network. The simulations have been performed in randomly generated overlay network with N from 16 to around 5000 where N is the total number of nodes in the network. We evaluate the number of messages to be exchanged varying the number of nodes.

4.1   Simulation Result

A set of tests has been run on random events occurred. We set a maximum message size as 1500 bytes and QoS information for each node 300 bytes. We construct a global data structure as the bootstrap server to maintain network information, such as *maxID*, in the simulator.

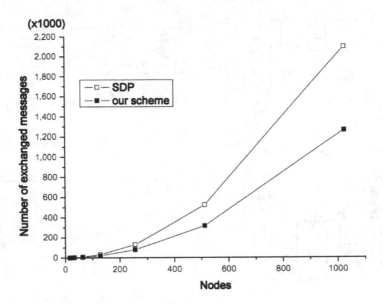

Fig. 4. The result shows total number of exchanged messages to finish discovery process with respect to the number of nodes in the network

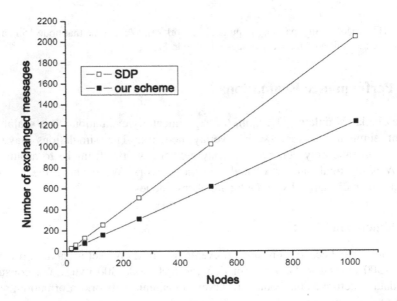

Fig. 5. The result shows the number of exchanged messages at a node to finish discovery process with respect to the number of nodes in the network

Fig. 4 and 5 show the comparison results SDP and our scheme in terms of the number of exchanged messages. We can see significantly reduction of the number of messages compared to SDP. We evaluate the total number of exchanged messages to finish discovery process from 16 nodes to 1024 nodes joining in Fig. 4, and the average number of exchanged messages to finish discovery process at an individual node by increasing nodes from 16 to 1024.

The overall results show that our scheme reduces the number of messages than SDP. This is because integrated participant and endpoint discovery and packed message on responses. The reduction of messages is related delay of discovery process. We will also evaluate the delay of discovery process, and make a scale of simulation environment up to 10^4 nodes in future work.

5   Conclusion

In this paper, we present important features about discovery process in a large-scale DDS. To support scalability, our proposed scheme use DHT-like overlay network constructions and message packing. Based on the overlay network, we describe our specific algorithms for each case of event.

The evaluation has been performed through OveSim overlay simulator by varying the number of nodes in the network. The results show that our scheme generates and exchanges much less number of messages compared to SDP.

Acknowledgement. This work was supported by the IT R&D Program of MKE/KEIT [10035708, "The Development of CPS (Cyber-Physical Systems) Core Technologies for High Confidential Autonomic Control Software"].

References

1. Object Management Group. Data Distribution Service for real-time systems specification, version 1.2 (2007)
2. RTI DDS, http://www.rti.com
3. Stoica, I., Morris, R., Karger, D.R., Kaashoek, M.F., Balakrishnan, H.: Chord: a scalable peer-to-peer lookup service for internet applications. ACM SIGCOMM (2001)
4. Object Management Group. The real-time publish-subscribe wire protocol DDS interoperability wire protocol specification, version 2.1 (2009)
5. Javier, S., Lopez-Soler, J.M., Povedano-Molina, J.: Scalable DDS discovery protocols based on bloom filters. In: Realtime and Embedded Systems Workshop (2007)
6. El-Ansary, S., Alima, L., Brand, P., Haridi, S.: Efficient broadcast in structured P2P networks

Approach to Generating Monitoring Code toward Advanced Self-healing[*]

Jungmin Park[1], Sung-Hwa Hong[2], and Ingeol Chun[3]

[1] Dept. of Software Engineering, Dongyang Mirae University
62-160 Gocheok-dong, Guro-gu, Seoul, 152-174, Korea
jmpark@ece.skku.ac.kr
[2] Dept. of Information and Communication Engineering,
Mokpo National Maritime University
91 Haeyangdaehang-Ro Gocheok-dong,
Mokpo-si, Jeollanam-do, 530-729, Korea
amipro90@gmail.com
[3] Dept. of Embedded SW Research,
Electronics and Telecommunications Research Institute (ETRI)
138 Gajeongno, Yuseong-gu, Deajon, 305-700, Korea
igchun@etri.re.kr

Abstract. System administrator deals with many problems, as computing environment becomes increasingly complex. Systems with ability to recognize system states and heal to resolve these problems offer a solution. Much experience and knowledge are required to build a self-healing system. Self-healings have inherent difficulties. Much attention has recently been focused on self-healing ability that recognizes problems arising in a target system. However, if a system wants to provide self-healing functionalities, there are many loads such as target system analysis and system environment analysis for external problem. Thus, this paper proposes using deployment diagram for self-healing approach to determine problem arising in external environment. The UML deployment diagram is widely used for resource specification of a system and generally designed in the system design phase. The approach proposes of 1) analysis for associations between software and hardware; 2) generating a monitor using constraints in deployment diagrams; and 3) adding the monitor to the component after adapting it to the specific software architecture. As proof of the approach, we automatically generate a resource monitor automatically, and used a video conference system. We illustrate how the method detects anomalies using the example.

Keywords: Monitor, self-adaptive, UML.

---

[*] This work was supported by the IT R&D Program of MKE/KEIT(10035708), "The Development of CPS(Cyber-Physical Systems) Core Technologies for High Confidential Autonomic Control Software".

T.-h. Kim et al. (Eds.): CA/CES[3] 2011, CCIS 256, pp. 138–148, 2011.
© Springer-Verlag Berlin Heidelberg 2011

1   Introduction

Distributed computing systems are continuously increasing in complexity, and it is difficult to analyze and resolve system problems. The first solution to these problems is for humans to manage the system [1]. The second is for the system to recognize the problem and resolve it. 40% of computer system errors are the mistakes of the manager [2]. Current system management processes should be improved. The self-healing systems are an improvement on the human based system management process [3]. Self-healing systems can recognize and diagnose system problems and autonomously recover the system. Critical systems consider the design and the cost of the additional self-adaptive modules in order to achieve reliability, error tolerance and availability [4]. Self-adaptive modules applied to critical systems improve system performance.

In this paper, we describe an approach to generate the resource monitor automatically by using a UML diagram. The approach consists of the following steps:
- **step1:** Analyzing associations between software and hardware
      in the UML deployment diagram of a component.
- **step2:** Generating the resource monitor using constraints specified
      by the de signer in the diagram.
- **step3:** Adding the monitor to the component after adapting the component's
      structure.

Through these steps, resource monitor can be generated automatically using the deployment diagram for a target system. It is useful in implementing the resource monitor for the component because it reduces additional work for monitoring the resources.

Component developers just simply modify parts of the monitor generated automatically for adaptation and can easily add healing strategies to it. For illustrating the approach, we tested our method by adapting a video conference system for evaluation. We can see that the monitor generated by our method works correctly when a resource problem occurred. The next section of the paper describes related work. Section 3 presents the approach in more detail. Section 4 illustrates evaluations for the approach. The paper ends with a summary in Section 5.

2   Related Work

This section describes a self-healing component architecture [5,6] and an Autonomic Failure-Detection algorithm [7], which is one of the failure detection methods.

2.1   Layered Software Architecture for Self-healing Component

In Layered Software Architecture, Each self-healing component consists of a healing layer and a service layer.[5,6] The service layer performs tasks requested by another task or component in the system. It also contains active objects, connectors, and passive objects, which are accessed by active objects. The active object can execute another active object or a passive object. In contrast, a passive object is called only by an active object. It cannot perform independently unless another object calls it. The connectors transfer messages to or from tasks and synchronize them. The healing layer makes a decision that an object in the service layer of the component becomes sick, the healing process is launched via connectors. This architecture has the following features.

- The architecture can identify an object with faults.
- Healing strategies for each object are pre-made.
- The architecture does not allow detailed mistakes.
- Only faults that occurred in the component can be detected.

2.2   Autonomic Failure Detection Algorithm

Mills et al. [7] proposed an algorithm that detects failures automatically. In the approach, objects and devices that need to be observed send a signal to the monitor periodically, similarly to a human's heartbeat. The monitor can manage many components. It determines whether the object or device has a problem by checking the signal over time. Let H_p represent the period of a signal. The maximum time for detecting faults will then also be H_p. However, faults can occur at any time during the signal period. The average time for detecting faults is $H_p / 2$. This algorithm can identify whether an object has problems or not in a very short time. However, it has an overhead cost because it requires frequent communication to exchange the signal between the monitor and the objects.

3   Approach Architecture for Generating Resource Monitor

In this paper, we present an improved self-healing component architecture that can recover resource problems. We do not focus on inner problems in this paper because this is covered by Shin et al.[5,6] The resource in this case could be independent of the software. The monitor measures the state of resources periodically and decides whether self-healing policies should be adopted or not. For this, we used a modified "heartbeat" algorithm. The algorithm sends the signal to resources. Through this mechanism, the resource monitor can measure values and detect anomalies. The architecture can be divided into an analyzing phase and a generation phase. Figure 1 illustrates the flow of structure. The architecture can be divided into an analyzing phase and a generation phase. Figure 1 illustrates the flow of structure.

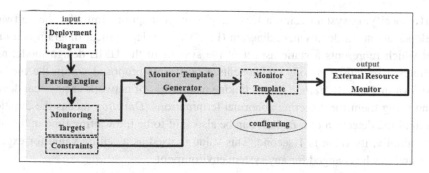

Fig. 1. Architecture for generating resource monitor

- **UML Deployment Diagram:** This is the input of the architecture. The diagram is transformed into an XMI (XML Meta-Interchange)[8,9].
- **XMI Parser:** The XMI parser analyzes resource constraints of and associations with the resource. In the analyzing phase, the outputs are monitoring targets and constraints. These outputs are parsed in XML format.
- **Monitor Template Generator:** The monitor template generator uses the output of the XMI parser. It generates a monitor template, which detects device problems or resources selected for monitoring. This template is implemented in the specific language.
- **Configuring:** The monitoring template code need to be modified for adaptation. The software developer configures it for the structure of software.
- **Resource Monitor:** The resource monitor generated by the approach can be adapted to the software directly.

Mills et al. [7] proposed an algorithm that detects failures automatically. In the approach, objects and devices that need to be observed send a signal to the monitor periodically, similarly to a human's heartbeat.   Fig2 shows our process composed of 4 steps in this section.

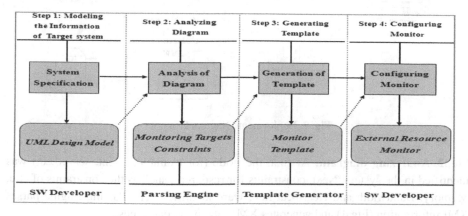

Fig. 2. Process of approach (4-steps)

Step1. Specifying system using a UML deployment diagram: Initially, the software developer creates a deployment diagram (Fig. 3). The deployment diagram is a diagram which represents a static aspect of the system in the UML design model and illustrates associations among components. Constraints proposed within the method are shown in Table 1. *Method* means linking techniques of network or physical devices and using them for detecting abnormal terminations. *Duration* means the duration time until the detection of a fault. It can be also said to be the waiting time in the method; initially, its value is 1 second. This value is used as a setting value for experiments and can be changed for any system environment.

Table 1. List of constraints

Contents	Input	Unit
CPU usage	0.0 ~ 1.0	Percent
Memory usage	0.0 ~ 1.0	Percent
Heartbeat	0.1 ~ 1.0	Second
Bandwidth	User defined minimum bandwidth	KB/s
Method	User defined connection type	
Duration	Duration time for detecting fault	Second

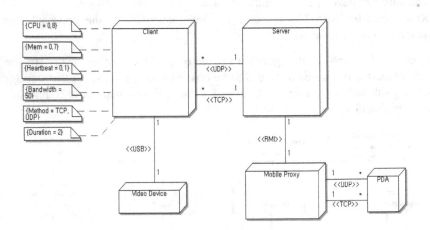

Fig. 3. Deployment Diagram Example

Step2. Analyzing diagram: At first, the node (for example, client, server etc) was identified in the system. Next, constraints for resources, such as the constraints of cpu, Memory, Bandwidth and Heartbeat rate, were identified. The Parsing Engine parses XMI information (Fig 4) and generates XML about the two types.

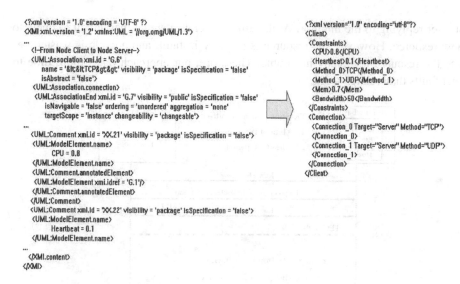

Fig. 4. XMI Information and constraints model derived from a deployment diagram

Step3. Generating monitor template: In this step, the template for an executable resource monitor was generated by using the information analyzed in the previous step. The Template Generator *(TG)* performs the generation of a monitor by analyzing the XML generated by the Parsing Engine. It also generates fault processing and anomaly detection routines for each constraint. (Fig. 2)

Step4. Composing monitor: In this step, a developer modifies the resource monitor according to the software environment. The fault processing handler or guidelines are actually implemented in the monitor template generation level by the approach. It also performs customization regarding parts needed and parts modified. Afterwards, a resource monitor is added to the self-healing layer or component. The architecture can be divided into an analyzing phase and a generation phase. Figure 1 illustrates the flow of structure. The architecture can be divided into an analyzing phase and a generation phase.

3.1   Problem Detection Algorithm

This section describes the parts that were adapted to the autonomic fault-detection algorithm relate to our approach (Fig. 5). The resource monitor in the self-healing layer judges the state of the system as abnormal if a reply is sent to the devices or resources and does not return in the period. It was also regarded as abnormal if the values of the resource violated a constraint. In this context, a self-healing layer should construct a reconfiguration plan and perform it. Unlike related works, L_{max} and L_{avg} are 1.5 times longer than before because the monitor sends the signal first. The monitor determines that a resource is still in the normal state if a fault has occurred just after replying to the monitor. At this time, it sends a signal that tells it to cycle to a new resource. However, the resource is actually in fault, and a cycle is wasted because the resource is already in trouble. Therefore, our approach takes more time to detect faults than related work.

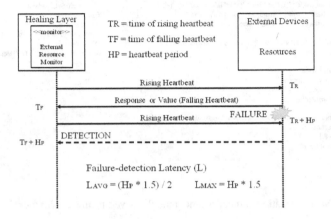

Fig. 5. Error Detection Algorithm

3.2   Self-healing Components Including Resource Monitor

Resource monitoring is illustrated in Fig. 6. The device and self-healing component architecture featured resource monitoring. Devices and the modified architecture available to resources monitoring the self-healing component architecture were designed by E. Shin [2, 3]. Resource monitoring is illustrated in Fig. 6. The device and self-healing component architecture featured resource monitoring. Devices and the modified architecture available to resources monitoring the self-healing component architecture were designed by E. Shin [2, 3].

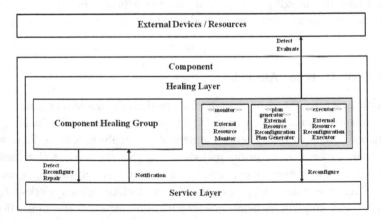

Fig. 6. Proposed Self-healing Component Architecture

Six objects used for healing referred components and three objects used for detecting resources and reorganizing is added in this architecture. The added objects are divided into three parts. : *External Resource Monitor, External Resource Reconfiguration Plan Generator, and External Resource Reconfiguration Executor. External Resource Monitor* checks the status of external devices and resources. *External Resource Reconfiguration Plan Generator* makes organizational plans for service levels in accordance with external situations. *External Resource Reconfiguration Executor* executes the plans. The purpose of the External Resource Reconfiguration Plan Generator is to make plans that prevent other well-operating objects from being affected by other resources by isolating objects that are easily influenced by resources, similar to the organization of the component plans. The Self-healing Controller that controls objects in the self-healing layer governs the resource reconfiguration executor to perform a reconfiguration of the service layer. When it comes to external errors, it performs in the same way and allows anomalies of the service layer by minimizing resources.

4   Implementation and Evaluation

We present an improved self-healing component architecture that can recover resource problems. We do not focus on inner problems in this paper because this is covered by Shin et al.[3,4,5] The resource in this case could be independent of the software. The monitor measures the state of resources periodically and decides whether self-healing policies should be adopted or not. For this, we used a modified "heartbeat" algorithm. The algorithm sends the signal to resources. Through this mechanism, the resource monitor can measure values and detect anomalies. Also, to evaluate the algorithm, we implemented the basic design of a video-based conference system. The purpose of this system was to successfully conduct a video-based conference. During the meeting, the client should not be interrupted by external problems of the software. In this paper, the purpose was to check whether the client detected errors that arose from the software's external problems after automating the resource monitor and applying it to the client in the video-based conference system.

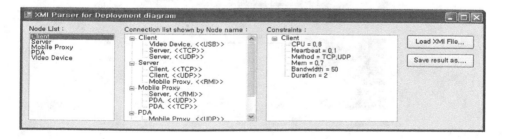

Fig. 7. Parsing Engine Prototype

To evaluate this approach, we implemented clients of a video conferencing system based on .NET Framework 2.0. We used C# with the implements in MS Windows XP. We used Borland Together for UML modeling. The server was implemented by Java2 SDK 1.4. The client additionally used DirectShow.NET for the video device. A deployment analyzer and resource monitor template were also implemented in C#. Fig. 3 illustrated the deployment diagram that we used. Fig. 7 and Fig. 8 illustrate the Parsing Engine prototype and Template Generator.

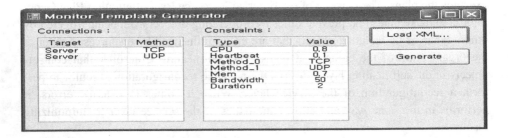

Fig. 8. Template Generator Prototype

4.1   Normal Case and Abnormal Case

-Normal case - Resource monitor continues to monitor the resource unless resource performs its work without any anomalies.
-Abnormal case - Monitor detects an abnormal state when the measured value was over the normal range or the connection with the other resources was accidentally terminated. Figure 9 illustrates any case when the CPU usage was in excess of 80%. we did not focus on self-healing strategies. Therefore, strategies for healing the faulty state were generated by the administrator.

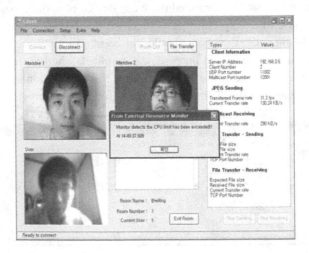

Fig. 9. Detection of anomalies of CPU by monitor

4.2   Objective of Evaluation and Results

The purpose of the evaluation is to determine whether the approach recognizes error situations or not within a designated time in applied purpose systems and to compare applied target systems with not applied to the system, if errors occur in the resources. We used programs such as the benchmarking program and forced server determination in the case of extreme situations in the system. Additionally, we added a routine that immediately reports the time when errors occur in the client, and a routine that prints the error time in a resource monitor in pursuit of the accuracy of the Failure-Detection Latency evaluation. The detection results for various constraints are listed in Table 2. The error detection time, which was estimated for the CPU for 10 times, is shown in Fig. 10.

Table 2. Experimental results of Monitoring

Check list	Constraints	Success of detecting
CPU usage	Max 80%	Success
Memory usage	Max 70%	Success
Bandwidth usage	Min 50KB/s	Success
Network connection	Abnormal network determination	Success

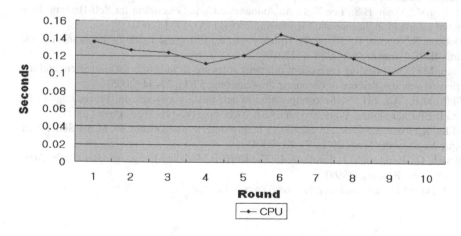

Fig. 10. Error detection time of resource monitor

As a result of the evaluation, the resource monitor detected the four items that constraints are set up. Even though there were differences in the average fault detection time, we were able to verify that the resource monitor could detect it within the maximum fault detection time.

5   Conclusion

Critical systems require the design and implementation of self-healing modules to boost reliability, fault-tolerance, and availability. This paper proposed an approach to reduce the efforts of a self-healing developer and offered a software architecture that detects the resources available. Until now, developers had to do more effort to implement the monitor which checks resources for the software. In this study, we confirmed that we could make resource monitors automatically that can include a self-healing component by a deployment diagram. To evaluate these, we arranged a prototype component and confirmed whether the detection monitor operated correctly when an abnormal situation occurred. However, we could not overcome a high overhead since signals must be exchanged frequently if errors are to be detected. To solve this problem, a study that investigates self-regulating cycles of exchanging signals between monitors is needed. The study of automation in self-healing strategies for recovering from faulty states remains future work.

References

1. Garlan, D., Cheng, S.W., et al.: Rainbow: Architecture-Based Self-Adaptation with Reusable Infrastructure. IEEE Computer 37(10), 46–54 (2004)
2. Autonomic Computing. IBM, http://www.research.ibm.com/autonomic
3. Park, J.M., Youn, H.S., Lee, E.S.: An Autonomic Code Generation for Self-Healing. Journal of Information Science and Engineering 25(6), 1753–1781 (2009)
4. Dobson, S., Sterritt, R., Nixon, P., Hinchey, M.: Fulfilling the vision of autonomic computing. IEEE Computer 43(1), 35–41 (2010)
5. Shin, M.E.: Self-healing component in robust software architecture for concurrent and distributed systems. Science of Computer Programming 57(1), 27–44 (2005)
6. Shin, M.E., An, J.H.: Self-reconfiguration in self-healing systems. In: Proceedings of the 3rd IEEE International Workshop on EASE 2006, pp. 106–116. IEEE Press (2001)
7. Mills, K., Rose, S., et al.: An autonomic failure-detection algorithm. ACM SIGSOFT Software Engineering Notes 29(1), 79–83 (2004)
8. Booch, G., Rumbaugh, J., Jacobson, I.: The Unified Modeling Language User Guide. Addison Wesley, Reading (1999)
9. XMI Online Document, http://www.omg.org/xml

Layer-3 Emulator Design for Efficient Protocol Debugging and Validation

Jinkyeong Kim[1], Sunggeun Jin[1,*], and Jae-Min Ahn[2]

[1] ETRI
[2] Chungnam National University

Abstract. It is necessary to implement new protocols on time in order to follow the fast evolving wireless communication technologies. For the purpose, we design layer-3 emulator providing a fast way to establish experimental environments to validate the correctness of protocol implementation. The emulator emulates layer-3 protocols with the interpretation of properly described scripts, and hence, it reacts to a wireless communication system as a peer side. We practically utilize the emulator in order to validate the correctness of our implementations for 3GPP layer-3. In near future, we plan to apply our emulator to the state-of-the-art Medium Access Control (MAC) technology for very high throughput wireless communication system in 60 GHz band.

1 Introduction

We face an era that new wireless technologies evolve fast than ever before. Accordingly, it is highly encouraged that on-time-implementation for the fast evolving technologies such as IEEE 802.11 Wireless Local Area Networks (WLANs) [1], 3GPP Long Term Evolution (LTE) [4], and IEEE 802.16 Wireless Metropolitan Area Networks (WMANs) [3, 2].

However, typical wireless communication systems comprise of many complicated subsystems, each of which owns its protocol stack for its purpose, and the subsystems are interconnected for functional cooperation. When a new protocol is implemented for a subsystem, the other subsystems related to the new protocol should be employed to validate the newly implemented protocol works well in a peer-to-peer communication environment.

It implies that debugging and validation for wireless communication system is different from that for general purpose software development since it is possible to debug general purpose software without a counterpart required for a peer-to-peer environment. Therefore, the debugging and the validation may consume a large portion of time since a set of subsystems should be prepared for proper operation.

In order to alleviate the overhead for the debugging and the validation, we design an emulator, which can mimic layer-3 for wireless communication systems.

* This research was supported by the KCC (Korea Communications Commission), Korea, Under the R&D program supervised by the KCA(Korea Communications Agency)(KCA-2011-09913-04006).

T.-h. Kim et al. (Eds.): CA/CES[3] 2011, CCIS 256, pp. 149–153, 2011.

For the emulator, we design a script language, with which, any types of layer-3 protocols can be described irrespective of wireless communication standards. In fact, script languages are already used for simulators as *ns-2* shows an exemplary model.

However, when the proposed script language is utilized, our emulator has obvious difference from the existing simulators in that proposed script language is capable of describing procedural sequences of wireless protocols while script languages of the existing simulators are used to build simulation environments and scenarios. In our experiments, we utilize the emulator to validate layer-3 protocol for 3GPP mobile stations, and hence, we make scripts which enable our emulator to operate as a 3GPP base station.

This paper is organized as follows: in Section 2, we explain how we design our emulator. In Section 3, we show our experiments and validation utilizing our emulator after we develop 3GPP layer-3 protocols. In Section 4, we conclude this paper.

2   Emulator Design

Fig. 1 shows the architecture of our emulator. As shown in this figure, the emulator consists of User Interface (UI) block, *Script Interpreter* block, *Generic Input/Output (IO) Interface* block, *Layer-2* module, *Communication* block, Adaptive Multi-Rate (AMR) codec, and *Message Editor*. Prior to the discussion of *Script Interpreter*, we explain the other blocks briefly.

The emulator is developed for Windows Operating System (OS), and hence, *UI* module is designed to support graphical interactive user interface environment. Our emulator is used to verify the operation of 3GPP mobile station as it emulates a 3GPP base station. For the purpose, we adopt the 3GPP layer-2 protocol, shown as *Layer-2* module to support wireless link connection. The layer can be replaced with other corresponding link protocols if this emulator is employed for other wireless standards. *Generic IO Interface* block is designed to provide consistent functional interface for *Script Interpreter* block no matter what link protocol is employed. *Communication* block takes the role of transmitting data physically. It could be wireless modem or ethernet depending on

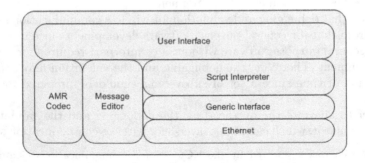

Fig. 1. The architecture of the designed emulator

experimental environment. The *AMR* codec is used for voice communication when 3GPP calling procedure is completed successfully.

The *Message Editor* provides a graphical user interface to edit layer-3 message. It is capable of parsing the structure and the union data types of 'C' language, so that users have only to prepare 'C' language header files containing the data types for the layer-3 message.

The *Scrip Interpreter* interprets scripts, which describe procedural sequences for layer-3 protocols. The proposed script language supports the features summarized as follows: (1) syntax for iteration is supported in the same manner to the 'C' language; (2) the language provides event handling operations to manage internal events generated by timers and functions; (3) layer-2 operations are encapsulated and configured by generic input/output functions, namely, 'receive,' 'transmit,' 'open,' and 'close.' Each link connection in layer-2 is handled with identity number similar to the file descriptor; (4) the language supports conditional statement and variables capable of containing layer-3 messages are compared with each other by using equity operator, namely, '=;' (5) timers are provided to support the operations having deadline; (6) the language enables emulator to serve multiple peers, of which instance is created by variable declaration; (7) the procedure flow can be changed by using 'goto' statement.

Fig. 2 shows an exemplary script that the emulator as an base station transmits Radio Resource Control (RRC) message to two mobile stations. For mobileSTA1, the emulator transmits request message and wait for response message until messageWaitingTime timer is expired. Next, the emulator does the same operation for the mobileSTA2 twice. However, in this case, the emulator recognizes whether mobileSTA2 replies with response message timely, and if so, it checks the response message is correct by comparing the message with the prepared one.

"RequestData.RRC" and "ResponseData.RRC" are not character strings but file names designating the files containing practical data. Therefore, the variable TxRRC contains the data stored in "RequestData.RRC." file. The *open* function creates an Radio Link Control (RLC) connection with default configuration. There are three parameters for the function such as "UnAcknowledgeMode," "AcknowledgeMode," and "TransparentMode", each of which corresponds to the RLC link type. The RLC connections are identified by unique ids returned by *open* function.

The *waitevent* () function suspends the emulator from proceeding to the next script until an internal event occurs. The predefined variable 'event' indicates the types of the internal events. In this example, the next procedures are determined depending on the type of event, which occurs earlier than the other.

In spite of the efforts, we made for the emulator, it has two shortages as follows: (1) the emulator does not support array type for variable declaration; (2) it is not possible for users to define new function procedure by using the script language. However, the shortages are minor to be improved soon.

```
 1:  timer messageWaitingTime = 10 ms;
 2:  terminal mobileSTA1, mobileSTA2;
 3:  data TxRRC = "RequestData.RRC";
 4:  connection cid1, cid2;
 5:  count i;
 6:
 7:  cid1 = mobileSTA1.open "UnAcknowledgeMode";
 8:  cid2 = mobileSTA2.open "AcknowledgeMode";
 9:
10:  set messageWaitingTime {
11:    mobileSTA1.transmit cid1, TxRRC;
12:    mobileSTA1.receive cid1, RxRRC;
13:  }
14:
15:  for ( i = 0; i < 2; i ++ ) {
16:    set messageWaitingTime {
17:        mobileSTA2.transmit cid2, TxRRC;
18:    }
19:
20:    waitevent ();
21:
22:    if (event == 'DATA_RECEPTION') {
23:        mobileSTA2.receive cid2, RxRRC;
24:      if (RxRRC == "ResponseData.RRC") {
25:        print "Response message arrives successfully";
26:      }
27:      goto Next;
28:    }
29:    if (event == 'TIMER_EXPIRATION') {
30:      print "Response message is not received";
31:    }
32:    Next:
33:  }
```

Fig. 2. Exemplary usage of the proposed script language

3 Experiments

We conduct experiments to validate whether 3GPP mobile stations, which we developed, work correctly by using the emulator providing the role of a 3GPP base station. However, the mobile stations were not equipped with wireless modem since the development of the mobile stations was not completed. Inevitably, the emulator and the mobile stations communicate with each other via ethernet interface. Nevertheless, the experimental environment does not influence the working of the emulator since it deals with only layer-3 protocol independent to link quality or reliability.

We first prepare the scripts for our experiments in order to verify 3GPP mobile stations' basic operations, namely, power-on, power-down, call initiation, and call termination. We observe that each operation is successfully verified by the emulator. When the call initiation is completed successfully, we talk to each other with the emulator and mobile station thanks to the AMR codec in the emulator. Next, we combine the scripts into a single one to observe the overall behavior of the mobile stations from power-on to power-down. Here as elsewhere, the emulator successfully manages the operation without any problem.

4 Conclusion and Future Work

We build a flexible and powerful emulator emulating layer-3 protocol. By using the emulator, it is possible to conduct various experiments to validate mobile stations' operations since rich experimental scenarios are easily established due to the proposed script language.

References

1. IEEE 802.11-2007, Part 11: Wireless LAN Medium Access Control (MAC) and Physical Layer (PHY) Specifications (Revision of IEEE Std 802.11-1999) (June 2007)
2. IEEE 802.16m, Part 16: Air Interface for Broadband Wireless Access Systems: Advanced Air Interface (May 2011)
3. IEEE 802.16-2009, Part 16: Air Interface for Broadband Wireless Access Systems (May 2009)
4. 3GPP, Technical Specification 3G TS 36.300 version 10.0.0 (June 2010)
5. http://isi.edu/nsnam/ns/index.html

A Schema Digest Based Metadata Encapsulation Architecture with Shared String Tables

Bong-Jin Oh[1], Sunggeun Jin[2], EuiHyun Baek[2], and KwanJong Yoo[1]

[1] Department of Computer Science, Chugnam National University, Korea
kjy@cnu.ac.kr
[2] Electronics and Telecommunications Research Institute, 138 Gajeongno, Yuseong-gu, Daejeon, 305-700, Korea
{bjoh,sgjin,ehbaek}@etri.re.kr

Abstract. We propose a simple but efficient encapsulation architecture that is used to encode Extended Markup Language (XML) based service information for a TV Anytime (TVA) metadata delivery model. In the proposed architecture, a schema digest and common string tables are applied to multiple fragments while the existing scheme utilizes an independent individual string table for each fragment. The experimental results show that we can achieve significant improvements compared with the existing architecture through the schema digest and common string tables.

Keywords: Metadata encoding, metadata encapsulation, TVA metadata delivery model.

1   Introduction

Extended Markup Language (XML) [1] based service descriptions are used widely by many international digital broadcast standards due to their extensibility and readability [2]. TV-Anytime (TVA) [3] defines the schema and delivery model for the XML based contents guide (CG) between server and clients. We call documents described using XML as TVA descriptions.

The TVA descriptions are fragmented into independent sub-descriptions (fragments), and encapsulated into containers to be delivered to clients. Encoding methods such as Efficient XML Interchange (EXI) [4] and Gnu-ZIP (GZIP) are also used to encode TVA descriptions into a binary XML format during encapsulation [5].

The EXI encoding method is extended to evaluate our proposed methods due to its good performance among schema-based algorithms with string tables. The schema-based methods including EXI and Binary Format of Metadata (BiM) are affected by both the size and pattern of elements in the XML schema. Moreover, the string table-based methods like EXI and fast-info set are sensitive to string patterns in XML documents. In this letter, we propose an efficient encapsulation architecture using a schema digest that optimizes the schema by including only those elements needed to create TVA descriptions stored at the server. Common string tables are also used to increase the string hit ratio among fragments encoded into the same containers. These

T.-h. Kim et al. (Eds.): CA/CES³ 2011, CCIS 256, pp. 154–159, 2011.

two proposed methods improve the encoding performance when fragments are encapsulated, as compared with original EXI used to evaluate the proposed scheme.

2   EXI Encoding Method

The EXI method relies on the grammar generated from the schema when encoding TVA fragments. Fig. 1 shows an exemplary EXI automata graph for XML schema.

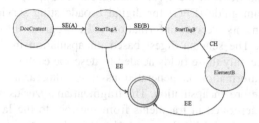

Fig. 1. EXI automata graph

An EXI-encoded stream consists of event codes, encoded values, and an EXI header. Event codes are assigned to each direct link between two nodes of the schema automata. The event codes are used to move the current node to the target node according to input tokens, and the size of the event code depends on the number of links from the source node to the target nodes as follows:

$$\text{Event code size} = \lceil \log_2 (N) \rceil, \tag{1}$$

where N is number of directly connected target nodes.

Event codes are inserted into an encoded stream whenever the current node is moved to other nodes. Some nodes may have several types of values, such as the date, numerical identifier, string, etc. If moved nodes have their values, and the values to be embedded into EXI stream are encoded according to their type (in this letter, it is assumed that every node value is a string), then the complete encoded stream is described as follows:

We assume that T is a set of tokens described in TVA descriptions, and is represented by

$$T = \{t_n \mid 0 \leq n \leq N\}, \tag{2}$$

where n is an index designating a token.

We assume that P (T) is a path consisting of all nodes traversed according to the input tokens in T, L is a link traversed by T, and L (t) is the number of nodes directly connected to a node moved by t_n:

$$\text{P (T)'s size} = \text{EXI header} + \sum_{t \in T} \lceil \log_2 (L(t)) \rceil + \sum_{t \in T} encode \ (Value_t), \tag{3}$$

where L (t) is the number of target nodes directly connected from $node_t$, and encode (value$_t$) is the size of encoded value of $node_t$.

The encoded size is affected by L (t) and encoded size of values. This paper also is focused on providing efficient methods related with L (t) and encoding string values.

3   The Proposed Metadata Encapsulation Scheme

Typically, the TVA descriptions for CG depend on the service provider's own policies. Together with mandatory fields, most descriptions use only a few fields among many optional fields of the TVA schema. For example, TVA descriptions for an electronic program guide (EPG) for digital broadcasting services may use only three types of fragments: service information (SI), program information (PI), and schedule fragments. The schema digest based encapsulation method optimizes the TVA schema to have only those fields needed to describe each service provider's CG descriptions. The information is generated as a bit flag array generated from a fragment analyzer before encapsulation. The fragment analyzer uses shallow traversal to search elements described in fragments from the root to the last leaf node. If an element is found, then set the bit flag mapped to the element to 1; otherwise, the bit flag is set to 0. The child nodes of parents set at 0 are not contained in the bit flag array, as it is clear that they are not described in the fragments.

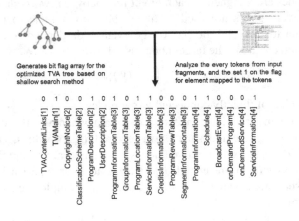

Fig. 2. Schema digest of TVA schema

Figure 2 shows the bit flag array as a schema digest of a TVA schema with the three kinds of fragments for EPG described above (SI, PI, and schedule fragments) with a depth of 4. 19 bits are needed to represent the optimal digest, which may not be critical overhead for EXI streams.

The schema digest method improves the size of the EXI encoder as follows. If M is a set optimized by removing nodes not traversed by any tokens in T, then $M \subseteq L$ and $M(t) \in M$ for all $t \in T$, and therefore we can calculate the effect factor ef as follows:

$$e_f = \left(\sum_{t \in T} \lceil \log_2 (M(t)) \rceil \middle/ \sum_{t \in T} \lceil \log_2 (L(t)) \rceil \right) \tag{4}$$

The average $M(t) \leq L(t)$ as M is a subset of L, and therefore $e_f \leq 1$. Thus, we can decide whether the schema digest method is sufficiently effective.

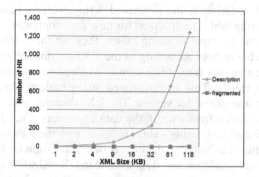

Fig. 3. String hit number according to XML size

The TVA delivery model has performance degradation problems caused by fragmentation. Most encoding methods including EXI are affected by the size of the TVA descriptions. Figure 3 shows more string hits occur on large descriptions rather than small ones. Large descriptions also lose their string hit ratio when they are fragmented, as the fragments are encoded independently during encapsulation.

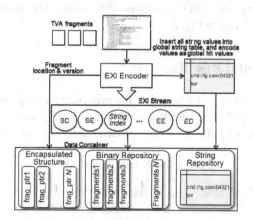

Fig. 4. Common string table based EXI encoder

This paper proposes a scheme to avoid performance degradation using shared string tables stored at the containers. The tables have a role in helping the encoder keep the string hit ratio across fragments of the same containers, as shown in Fig. 4. When encoding string values, the common string table method integrates fragments of the same containers as a large TVA description logically; nevertheless, the fragments are physically independent.

The TVA data container is composed of encapsulation structure and binary repository. The proposed architecture adds the string repository to the data containers to store the shared string tables. Whenever encoding and encapsulation of fragments for a data container is finished, the generated string table is inserted into the data container and new string table is initialized for new data container.

If string-type tokens are input in string tables, they are then embedded into an EXI stream with string table indices according to the EXI's global hit rule. Otherwise, the EXI encoder puts the strings into string tables, and embeds the indices into an EXI stream as global hit values. That is, the shared string table method makes all string values of fragments into global hit values. The EXI decoder loads the string table in order to decode all encoded fragments in the data containers. Encoded string values in EXI streams are replaced with string values indexed with the locations of the tables.

The proposed method can improve the effects of compression by keeping same string patterns among physically independent fragments using shared string tables as follows:

$$\text{Optimized P (T)'s size} = \text{EXI header} + e_f \sum_{t \in T} \lceil \log_2(L(t)) \rceil +$$

$$\sum_{i=1}^{N_s} L_i + \lceil \log_2(N_s) \rceil \times \left(\sum_{i=1}^{N_s} f_i \right),$$ (5)

where N_s is the size of a string table shared by multiple fragments, L_i is the length of the ith string, and fi is the hit ratio.

Based on (3) and (6), we can know that (3) has almost $\lceil L_i - \log_2(N_s) \rceil \times \left(\sum_{i=1}^{N_s} f_i \right)$ more string value encoding size than (5), because the average hit number in each fragment is almost 0 or 1, as shown in Fig. 3.

4   Experimental Results

To evaluate the encoding performance of the proposed method, we compared it to the original EXI and GZIP methods. We used TVA descriptions provided by BBC in 2010, and the Siemens EXIficient 0.6 was extended for the use of global string tables.

Table 1. Experimental environments

Environments	Contents	
Host	1.5Ghz CPU, 1G RAM, UMPC	
Analyzing Software	EXIficient 0.6 based simulator over JDK1.6	
Test XML data	PIs published by BBC from 2010.08.31 to 09.08	XML's size is from 1KB - 61KB, 118KB (generated by two 59KB PIs)
	Containers with fragmented BBC's PIs with size 1KB-118KB	
Compared Algorithms	EXI 1.0 (EXIficient's original algorithm is used)	
	GZIP (JDK GZIPOutputStream is used)	

The proposed method shows a 30-40% better performance than the original EXI, which is likely because shared string tables increase the encoding performance and the schema digest optimizes the schema, thus reducing node's average event code size.

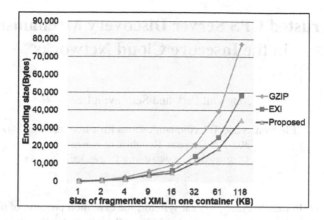

Fig. 5. Encoding size according to XML size

5   Conclusion

This paper proposed an efficient metadata encapsulation method for a TVA-based CG delivery system. We optimized the schema using a schema digest learned from TVA descriptions intended for delivery to clients. Common string tables were used to share string values among fragments encapsulated into the same containers. The methods showed improvement in both the compression rate and encoding time compared to the original EXI methods. This is caused by keeping the sociality of the string patterns among multiple fragments, and using the schema digest to optimize the schema for TVA descriptions.

Acknowledgments. This work was supported by the IT R&D program of MKE/KEIT, [KI001877, Locational /Societal Relation-Aware Social Media Service Technology].

References

1. W3C: Extensible Markup Language (XML) 1.0, 5th edn. W3C Metadata Schemas Ver. 1.3 (2002)
2. Kim, S.K., Jeong, J.G., Kim, H.G., et al.: A Personal Videocasting System with intelligent TV Browsing for a Practical Video Application Environment. ETRI Journal 31(1), 10–20 (2009)
3. TV-Anytime Forum: TVA Specification S-3 on Metadata, Part B: System Aspects in a Unidirectional Environment Ver. 1.3 (2002)
4. W3C: Efficient XML Interchange (EXI) Format 1.0: W3C Candidate Recommendation (2009)
5. Kim, M.J., Park, M.S., Yang, S.J., et al.: System Aspects of TV-Anytime Metadata Codec in a Uni-directional Broadcasting Environment. In: Proceedings International Symposium on Consumer Electronics (2007)

Trusted CPS Server Discovery Mechanism in the Insecure Cloud Networks

Jongyoul Park and Seungyun Lee

Electronics and Telecommunications Research Institute,
305-700 Daejeon, Republic of Korea
{jongyoul,syl}@etri.re.kr

Abstract. In mobile cyber-physical systems, the execution program of physical system including remote robotics should be a flexible and self-manageable to control behaviors from remote system. However, the physical system is not safe in the view point of security because we assume that the physical system can be infected by a malicious people. Since the core program should be protected and we have to guarantee the secure connection between CPS client and CPS server. This paper addresses the security issues regarding remote code such as CPS client. In addition, we propose the CPS server discovery mechanism based on the secure group management for cloud based CPS system.

Keywords: mobile CPS, cyber-physical systems, remote code, secure group, access management, key pairing, key coupling.

1   Introduction

Since the development of smart device, the numbers of mobile cyber-physical applications have grown steadily due to the generalization of device sensors such as GPS, microphones, and cameras. The cyber-physical system has a process to react upon the remote signal and it also impacts the physical world [1].

Recent application area of cyber-physical system becomes various such as health care, environment scanning, situation detection, traffic control and patients monitor [2-9]. Traditionally, specialized embedded system is cheap and simple but these systems do not meet the user requirement such as flexibility and UI accessibility. In addition, customized functions are required for low battery consumption or high functionality [10]. To satisfy these requirement, mobile code and cloud computing is good standing technologies because they can provide a flexible and self-control ability in the remote machine. Basically it is inherent characteristics of mobile code, but mobile cyber-physical system requires direct and immediate control by the near computing resources such as Fig. 1.

The increasing popularity of wireless Internet and device has set new trends and techniques for the upcoming environment. The most significant change of new computing paradigm is mobility and clouding. In the cyber-physical system, the remote code updated in the embedded or smart devices with the self-control, and the control logics of system are distributed into the cloud computers instead of proprietary servers.

T.-h. Kim et al. (Eds.): CA/CES³ 2011, CCIS 256, pp. 160–168, 2011.

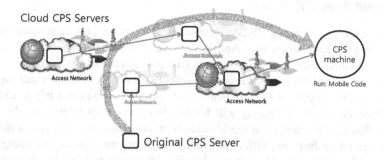

Fig. 1. Cloud based mobile cyber-physical system, the original CPS server is located outside of cloud computing and CPS machine looks well maintained and secure computer in the cloud network, and the selected server controls the CPS machine and the control logic is transported from original CPS server.

To achieve this goal, we propose group based secure server discovery and code encryption mechanisms to provide a mobility and security.

2   Group Based Trusted Server Management

Cloud computing should be connected with each other and can provide us new computing environments that make it possible to use a computer and network in anywhere and anytime without special recognition of those existence.

Secure utilization of cloud computing is not easy. The resource of cloud computing is shared by everybody, who is not known others. A client wants to use it in personal or private work such as web browsing, teleconferencing, e-learning, remote assistance and arrange a schedule with a mobile device. However, normal cloud computing is not safe since it is not private and isolated, and it is public in aspect of security. To make it secure or private, there needs a group management.

Client, or mobile devices, should find a secure and trusted computer to entrust their server work in cloud based CPS. Hence the entrusted computer as safe as a client entrusts his server work, is separately managed by protocols, and thus it should be found easily among clouded and anonymous computers, which is different with general and cloud server. In this regarding, the members are composed of two different groups. One is a trusted server group, which consists of trusted servers, and the other is general server group. Especially every member of the trusted group shares the same public key and private key at any time, when a client requests an entrustment, anyone of the server group can decrypt the entrustment message and invoke CPS server logic. In a distributed environment, large group management should be scalable and efficient [11-12]. Basically we use a 4-node tree based approach for the server group management, and some nodes are split again into 4 sub-group's capacity. Otherwise some nodes are merged into one node. The key distribution and leave/join protocol is given in the chapter 3 regarding more detailed description.

2.1   Cloud Based CPS Scenario

Cloud computing has many diverse scenarios and could play a role of specific scenario from the application area. And so we assume that the computational situation as follows and also essential composition of scenario is same or similar one.

Alice, he is an end-user of this scenario, want to spend his summer vacation in exploring the upper reaches of the Amazon. Therefore he just makes a trip to there. He believes that the cloud computing will be an alternative way to prepare the urgent situation. When he has arrived at the Manaus International Airport he gets a message. The message came from his office and requests an urgent scanning of energy consumption of Brazil branch. He found a scanning machine and can be operated with CPS modules.

Alice wants to control the machine himself, but he doesn't know the way to operate it. Current it is only operated by the branch officer. Therefore the machine is running under the control of branch office. However, if Alice can install CPS code into the machine, then it has a connection with the server computers and the head office can control it.

Previously, in this case, only technician control the physical machine but mobile cyber-physical system can be applied and server machine remotely control it. Some case, raw monitoring data are sent to the main server and real-time analysis is possible. There are still two problems. One is network delay. Long distance network cause a network loss and delay due to the multi-hop connection. If the server can move to the client side, then the real-time and stable control is possible. In addition, the discovery time of trusted computers also reduced. Another problem is end-to-end encryption, to guarantee the confidentiality they have to share a common key for encryption.

Thus, we propose cloud based mobile CPS, it is moving the server from the head office to the branch office in conceptually.

2.2   Group Management and Trusted CPS Server Discovery

Fig. 2 denotes the system components for cloud based CPS. In this case, there are four different objects and it is defined as follows;

Mobile device: totally CPS machine, but the essential and tiny processing unit is identified with mobile device within CPS machine.
Cloud network: it is a network for the cloud computing and interconnects distributed computers. This controls and assigns some work to each server.
Secure/Insecure server: certified or well managed server systems. Which server is trust or not is another problem. In this paper, we assume cloud network manages the group.

In the Fig. 2, first the mobile device 1 connects to cloud network in the cloud services, and connection with the assigned server. The mobile device 1 send an encrypted code to the server, if the server can decrypt it, then it is secure one, otherwise the server is insecure and cloud network 1 finds another server to decrypt it. In case of mobile

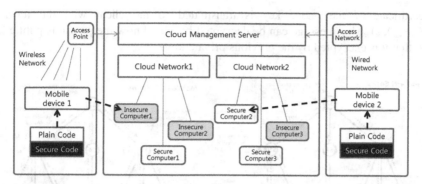

Fig. 2. Overall system configuration for the cloud based CPS, shows the relation of mobile device, cloud network and trusted server group. In geographically, mobile CPS machine 1 is strongly closed.

device 1 is request another one, and mobile device 2 find a secure one. We discover the trusted servers by checking the key because the trusted and secure server has a common key (private key of the group). And also they has one more common key to secure communication between trusted computers, it is a symmetric key. The mobile device 1 broadcasting the request message to the whole cloud servers and also the selection of which server can do it, is decided by the cloud management server.

The trusted server management is based on the group protocol, which is consisted of join and leave protocol.

3   Key Distribution and Group Join/Leave Protocols

Fig. 3 show how to distribute private and public key to server and client group members as stated before. Conceptually the key distribution procedure of the server group is broadcast of a new key from a leader to all child nodes. First of all, one server makes a specific group and adds other members using the join protocol. Otherwise leave protocols are used for the banishment of a member. And then all group members can share a symmetric key and public/private key pair in the Fig. 3.

In detail, Key distribution is occurred when a new member added or old members are removed. When a new member ($S11$) is added, old members receive the new key K_{1-11} which is encrypted using the previous symmetric key K_{1-8} and when the old server S_{12} is leaved, updates sub-group key K_{10-12}, it is a key of the sub-group including the S_{12}, to new one K_{10-11}. New sub-group key is encrypted with individual keys K_{10}, K_{11} in the sub-group and distributed to members S_{10}, S_{11} of the new sub-group. And then new group key K_{1-10} is also distributed to all members with encrypted form using each sub-group key K_{1-3}, K_4 and K_{10-11}. In this time, first a pair of private and public key is generated and then the group key K_{1-10} is also generated from the private key. Especially the certificate of public key is issued by the Certificate Authority. We assume that there has a certificate authority in order to supervise all groups.

Therefore all member of the server group receive a group key pair, a private key and a certificate of public key. Conspicuously the group key pairs are saved on the server and the certificate of the public key is transmitted to the client with the form of $S_{pri}^{n-1}(C(S_{pub}^{n}),...)$. This message can be decrypted by who know the previous public key due to that it is encrypted by the previous private key.

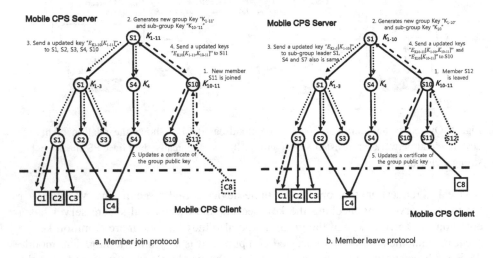

a. Member join protocol   b. Member leave protocol

Fig. 3. There are two protocols for group key distribution. One is join protocol when a new member is added. The other is leave protocol when some members leave or change.

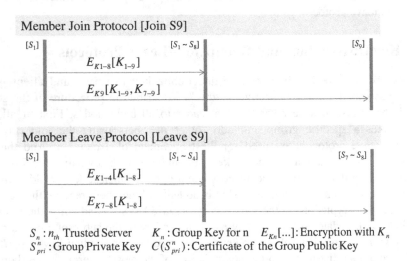

$S_n : n_{th}$ Trusted Server K_n : Group Key for n $E_{Kn}[...]$: Encryption with K_n
S_{pri}^{n} : Group Private Key $C(S_{pri}^{n})$: Certificate of the Group Public Key

Fig. 4. Detailed protocol of member join and member leave. The trusted group members can share the three key, a symmetric key, certificate of the group public key and group private key.

Finally, server group and client group has respectively a pair of private and key. A member of the client group encrypts something with the public key and any one of the server group can decrypts it using the corresponding private key. In a word the client sends a request message, which is encrypted by the public key. A member of the server group can decrypt it because trusted servers know the corresponding private key.

4   Code Encryption with Group Key

The cloud based CPS provides a way to formulate a group of trusted members; they can share same key and privileges. A mobile code needs a secure computation such as "update of secure modules" and "make a secure communication channel between CPS client and CPS server". In the CPS client, a secure part of mobile code should be protected because it includes how to decide in any given state and the code itself is important.

Mobile codes, which are CPS client code, are divided into three parts: a normal code, secure code and restricted code. The normal code is a plain text code. It is serialized, transported and executed in any servers even if the system is attacker. The Secure code, on the other hand, is encrypted by a group key of the trusted group. The secure code is opened to every trusted server when it arrived in the server. Last restricted codes are delivered to the head office server, which is real CPS server with encrypted form. These codes used for the testing and reporting the CPS client status.

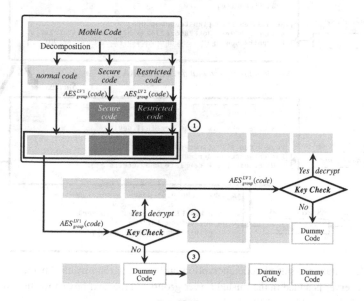

Fig. 5. There are three divided code and its encryption. The output case is also three 'normal only', 'normal and secure code' and 'whole code'.

In Fig. 5, mobile codes are decomposed according to the type of the code. If a server has a legal key, which is a group key of the trusted members, the encrypted codes can be decrypted. Otherwise, the server can execute only normal codes without secure or restricted codes.

5   Implementation

Fig. 6 shows the screen shot of the implementation. We also used 128-bit AES algorithm as a group key, the top of the figure shows the CPS client. Here, some codes of the mobile code are encrypted using $AES_{group}(code)$ and represented as "Encrypted Code [D00A600E8A00BC10A ...]". The mobile code moved to the AKIRA server. It decrypts the mobile code using the corresponding key [TrustedGroup.der], which is $AES_{group}(code)$.

Finally, the full and original code is reconstructed by the following sequence of operations: decryption, de-serialization and program loading. To represent a full code, we insert a message printing code in the encrypted code. In Fig. 6, the message is printed as follows;

RTN: result [Work complete and success!!] or
RTN: result [Work fail – invalid key!!]

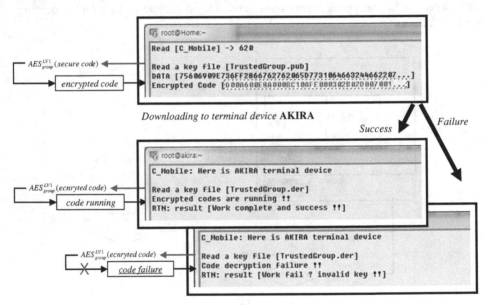

Fig. 6. Implementation result of code encryption and trusted group management. First success box is AKIA server is added in the trusted server group and the next box show the fail case, the AKIA server is removed from the trusted server group.

6   Conclusion

The CPS technology is a very useful, but also it is an easy to break the confidentiality of CPS client. Especially in case that a CPS client uses cloud computers, he cannot guarantee his job is secure or not. To resolve the problem, we propose a secure group management and code encryption scheme. And also we introduce an asymmetric key structure for the group key management. The member of group divided into server group and client group.

Server group takes a pair of key, public key and private key of the group. Client group takes only a certificate of the public key and it is not public. Therefore, anyone who knows the certificate of public key makes a code encryption. In addition, we provide a way to find a trusted server in cloud environment in order to resolve the restriction of mobile application in a hash chain based approach. And finally, mobile applications are divided into normal and secure parts. Therefore secure parts of mobile code can be encrypted.

Acknowledgements. This work has been supported by the ICT standardization program of KCC, [2011-PK10-01] Development of IPTV Standard for Next Generation.

References

1. Sztipanovits, J.: Composition of Cyber-Physical Systems. In: 14th Annual IEEE International Conference and Workshops on the Engineering of Computer-Based Systems, ECBS 2007, pp. 3–6. IEEE Press, New York (2007)
2. Saponas, T., Lester, J., Froehlich, J., Fogarty, J., Landay, J.: iLearn on the iPhone: Real-Time Human Activity Classification on Commodity Mobile Phones. University of Washington CSE Tech Report UW-CSE-08-04-02 (2008)
3. Froehlich, J., Dillahunt, T., Klasnja, P., Mankoff, J., Consolvo, S., Harrison, B., Landay, J.: UbiGreen: Investigating a Mobile Tool for Tracking and Supporting Green Transportation Habits. In: Proceedings of the 27th International Conference on Human Factors in Computing Systems, pp. 1043–1052. ACM (2009)
4. Thompson, C., White, J., Dougherty, B., Schmidt, D.: Optimizing Mobile Application Performance with Model-Driven Engineering. In: Proceedings of the 7th IFIP Workshop on Software Technologies for Future Embedded and Ubiquitous Systems (2009)
5. Jones, W.D.: Forecasting Traffic Flow. IEEE Spectrum 38(1), 90–91 (2001)
6. Rose, G.: Mobile Phones as Traffic Probes: Practices, Prospects, and Issues. Transport Reviews 26(3), 275–291 (2006)
7. Mohan, P., Padmanabhan, V., Ranjee, R.: Nericell: Rich Monitoring of Road and Traffic Conditions Using Mobile Smartphones. In: Proceedings of the 6th ACM Conference on Embedded Network Sensor Systems, pp. 323–336. ACM, New York (2008)
8. Leijdekkers, P., Gay, V.: Personal Heart Monitoring and Rehabilitation System Using Smart Phones. In: Proceedings of the International Conference on Mobile Business, p. 29 (2006)
9. White, J., Turner, H.: Smartphone Computing in the Classroom. IEEE Pervasive Computing 10(2), 82–86 (2011)
10. Whtie, J., Clarke, S., Groba, C., Dougherty, B., Thompson, C., Schmidt, D.C.: R&D Challenges and Solutions for Mobile Cyber-physical Applications and Supporting Internet Services. Journal of Internet Services and Applications 26(2), 4–6 (2009)
11. Wong, C., Gouda, M., Lam, S.: Secure group communications using key graphs. IEEE/ACM Transactions on Networking 8(1), 16–30 (2000)
12. Baugher, M., Canetti, R., Dondeti, L., Lindholm, F.: MSEC Group Key Management Architecture. IETF Internet Draft (September 2003)

13. Hohl, F.: Time Limited Blackbox Security: Protecting Mobile Agents From Malicious Hosts. In: Vigna, G. (ed.) Mobile Agents and Security. LNCS, vol. 1419, pp. 92–113. Springer, Heidelberg (1998)
14. Sander, T., Tschudin, C.: Towards Mobile Cryptography. In: IEEE Symposium on Security and Privacy, pp. 215–224 (1998)
15. Yee, B.: A Sanctuary for Mobile Agents. In: Ryan, M. (ed.) Secure Internet Programming. LNCS, vol. 1603, pp. 261–273. Springer, Heidelberg (1999)
16. Stinso, D.R.: Collision-free Hash Function. Cryptography Theory and Practice, pp. 234–236. CRC Press (1995)
17. NIST: Recommendation for Key Management –Part 1: General (revised), NIST Special Publication 800-57, p. 63 (2007)
18. Sahner, R., Trivedi, K., Puliafito, A.: Performance and Reliability Analysis of Computer Systems. Kluwer Academic Publishers (1996)
19. Dikaiakos, M., Samaras, G.: A Performance Analysis Framework for Mobile Agent Systems. In: Toussaint, M.-J. (ed.) Ada-Europe 1994. LNCS, vol. 887, pp. 180–187. Springer, Heidelberg (1994)

Hybrid Middleware Architecture Supporting an Active Service Provisioning

Yu-Seok Bae, Bong-Jin Oh, Tai-Yeon Ku, and Eui-Hyun Paik

Electronics and Telecommunications Research Institute,
218 Gajeong-ro, Yuseong-gu, Daejeon, 305-700, Korea
{baeys,bjoh,kutai,ehpaik}@etri.re.kr

Abstract. This paper presents the hybrid middleware architecture that accommodates both Web-based and Java-based interactive N-screen services in the broadband IP network. In addition, it supports an active service provisioning that automatically configures service environments through terminal provisioning with TR-069 protocol and service provisioning with SD&S/BCG. The proposed architecture provides middleware stacks, based on the common service platform, such as Web middleware and ACAP-J based Java middleware.

Keywords: Hybrid Middleware, Terminal Provisioning, Service Provisioning, TR-069, SD&S/BCG.

1 Introduction

In the broadband IP network, one of the most promising areas is the interactive services. Recently, IPTV service providers in Korea are trying to extend their business domains to the Web services in addition to the traditional Java-based broadcast services to support interactive N-screen services. Besides, many researches and developments on the effective service delivery to provide broadcast and broadband services are being established. Moreover, it is essential to provide IP-based terminals for interactive N-screen services with efficient auto configuration about service environments to support easy-of-use and easy-of-management. Furthermore, the effective delivery mechanisms of service-related information applicable to bidirectional IP network are being introduced in various domains.

Google launched Google TV [1], connecting Web with TV which allows viewers to access Internet applications such as Web searches and other Internet content to video entertainment on their televisions in addition to traditional broadcast, and is built on top of the Android platform and the Chrome Web browser .

The Hybrid Broadcast Broadband TV (HbbTV) [2] aims at harmonizing the broadcast and broadband delivery of entertainment to the end consumer through connected TVs and set-top boxes.

The Open IPTV Forum (OIPF) [3] aims to specify a common and open end-to-end solution for supplying a variety of IPTV and Internet multimedia services to retail-based consumer equipment at home.

T.-h. Kim et al. (Eds.): CA/CES³ 2011, CCIS 256, pp. 169–175, 2011.

The TR-069 (Technical Report 069) [4] is a terminal management protocol through communication between Customer Premises Equipment (CPE) and Auto Configuration Servers (ACS) based on the bidirectional SOAP/HTTP protocol.

The Service Discovery and Selection (SD&S) [5] is an XML-based protocol for service discovery defined by DVB-IPI. HTTP and DVBSTP (DVB SD&S Transport Protocol) are used to deliver SD&S documents over an IP network. Moreover, DVB-IPI defines the Broadband Content Guide (BCG) [6] that uses the TVAnytime to describe service information and program detail information.

In this paper, we propose the hybrid middleware architecture that integrates Web middleware and ACAP-J [7] broadcasting middleware. In addition, we describe active service provisioning coupled with the hybrid middleware that supports terminal provisioning using the TR-069 protocol and service provisioning based on SD&S/BCG.

2   Hybrid Middleware Architecture

Fig. 1 shows system architecture for hybrid middleware supporting active service provisioning for interactive N-screen services.

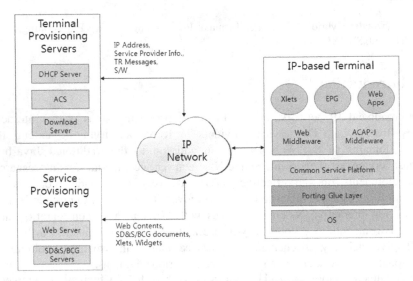

Fig. 1. System Architecture for Hybrid Middleware

The Terminal Provisioning (TP) Servers perform a series of operations such as automatic IP allocation based on DHCP (Dynamic Host Configuration Protocol), information delivery related to service provider, TR message transmissions for auto configuration, and S/W downloads.

The Service Provisioning (SP) Servers provide Web contents and widgets for Web middleware, Xlets for ACAP-J middleware, and service-related information and application information based on the SD&S/BCG.

Fig. 2 shows the proposed hybrid middleware architecture that supports Web-based and Java-based interactive services with active service provisioning.

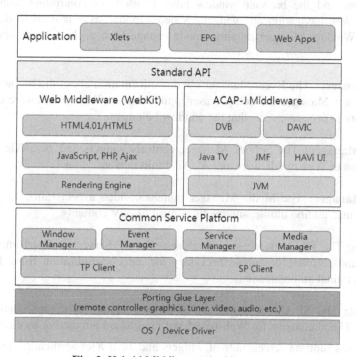

Fig. 2. Hybrid Middleware Architecture

Porting Glue Layer (PGL): The PGL is a platform-independent abstraction layer which allows it to be highly portable and provides neutral APIs about remote controller, graphics, tuner, video and audio, and etc.

Common Service Platform (CSP): The CSP is a common infrastructure layer for the hybrid middleware in order to accommodate Web middleware and ACAP-J based Java middleware. In addition, it includes two components for terminal provisioning and service provisioning to support active service provisioning.

Web Middleware: The Web Middleware uses WebKit [8], open source Web browser engine, which supports rendering about Web contents with XML, HTML, JavaScript, CSS, Ajax, PHP (PHP: Hypertext Preprocessor), and etc.

ACAP-J Middleware: The ACAP-J Middleware is basically based on the GEM (Globally Executable MHP) [9] and provides an execution engine for performing Java-based applications known as Xlets using Java APIs such as DVB, DAVIC, Java TV, HAVi UI, and so on.

Meanwhile, the CSP consists of six components to support hybrid middleware and their purposes are described as follows.

Window Manager: The Window Manager controls three kinds of window layers to handle Java, browser, and video. Java window layer is used for handling Java Xlet applications, and the browser window layer is used for controlling Web contents including Web navigation and widgets. Video window layer is used to display A/V contents. Window Manager monitors mode change such as Java mode and Browser mode.

Event Manager: The Event Manager obtains information about the topmost window from Window Manager and delivers user input events to Web middleware or ACAP-J middleware to process events that the window belongs to.

Service Manager: The Service Manager controls widgets and Java Xlets with the cooperation of Web middleware and ACAP-J middleware.

Media Manager: The Media Manager manages video aspect ratio, scaling, video output format, audio volume, and media control of A/V contents.

TP Client: The TP Client receives IP addresses of SP Servers and performs firmware upgrade and software download necessary for auto configuration from TP Servers through terminal authentication.

SP Client: The SP Client also receives service-related information based on the SD&S/BCG and contents for Web-based and Java-based interactive services.

Fig. 3 shows runtime screenshots of widgets and Java Xlet application based on the hybrid middleware.

Fig. 3. Screenshots of Widgets and Java Xlet application

3   Active Service Provisioning

In this section, we describe active service provisioning that automatically configures service environments through terminal provisioning and service provisioning. Terminal provisioning deals with a series of procedures that are necessary for N-screen terminals to select service providers and to provide auto configuration after connecting to broadband IP network. Service provisioning plays a role in delivering SD&S/BCG documents, Web contents, widgets, and Xlet applications as shown in Fig. 1.

3.1 Terminal Provisioning

Fig. 4 shows a sequence diagram of terminal provisioning between IP-based terminal and TP Servers.

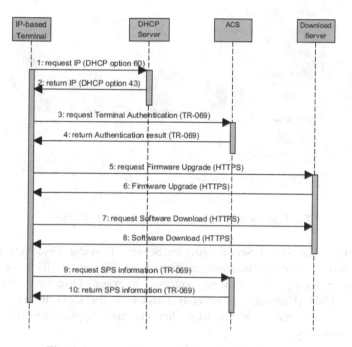

Fig. 4. Sequence Diagram of Terminal Provisioning

IP-based terminal requests IP address allocation using DHCP option 60 (Class-identifier) with device type information. DHCP Server sends reply message using DHCP option 43 (Vendor specific information) about service provider identifier, ACS IP address, and NTP (Network Time Protocol) server address. Next, IP-based terminal requests terminal authentication to ACS using TR-069 message with terminal identifier, model, serial number, certificate information, and provisioning status. ACS investigates the certificate and provisioning status using managed objects defined for terminal authentication and returns authentication result message with configuration information including IP address of Download Server (DS). After that, IP-based terminal performs firmware upgrade and software download necessary for terminal setup from DS. Finally, IP-based terminal receives the IP addresses of SP Servers for service provisioning.

3.2   Service Provisioning

Fig. 5 shows software architecture for delivering SD&S/BCG documents between SD&S/BCG Servers and SP Client.

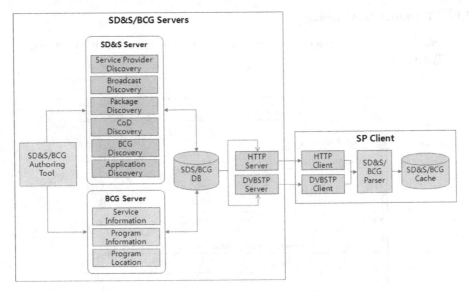

Fig. 5. Software Architecture for SD&S/BCG Delivery

SD&S Server: The SD&S Server provides Service Provider Discovery (SPD) for delivering service provider information, Broadcast Discovery (BD) for broadcast information including IP multicast address, Package Discovery for package information, CoD (Contents-on-Demand) Discovery for CoD information, BCG Discovery for information about BCG Server, and Application Discovery for application signaling.

BCG Server: The BCG Server provides service information and program detail information using three kinds of tables. Service Information contains information such as title, genre, owner, logical channel number, and region control code. Program Information includes information such as program name, genre, synopsis, and descriptions. Program Location contains schedule information of programs.

SD&S/BCG Servers uses HTTP and DVBSTP protocols to transfer SD&S/BCG documents to SP Client. First of all, SP Client receives SD&S documents including SPD and BD from SD&S Server and SD&S/BCG Parser stores service provider information and broadcast information to SD&S/BCG Cache by interpreting SD&S documents. Besides, SP Client identifies BCG Server's IP address using BCG Discovery. Likewise, SP Client receives BCG documents from BCG Server and obtains service information and program detail information using SD&S/BCG Parser, and also stores their information to SD&S/BCG Cache. SP Client delivers their information to Web middleware and ACAP-J middleware so that they compose their own EPG (Electronic Program Guide). In this architecture, we use W3C EXI (Efficient XML Interchange) encoding in the compression of generated SD&S/BCG documents to reduce network traffic.

Meanwhile, we implemented ACAP-J middleware and CSP components in the set-top box with BCM7405 chipset and used the Apache Web Server (AWS), PHP, Ajax, and JavaScript are used to transfer Web contents, widgets, and Xlet applications. In addition, we provide Eclipse-based authoring tool and emulation tool for Java Xlet applications, and generated applications are uploaded to the AWS. Their information is also reflected to the Application Discovery for application signaling.

4   Conclusions

In this paper, we proposed the hybrid middleware architecture supporting active service provisioning. The hybrid middleware architecture integrates WebKit-based Web middleware and ACAP-J based Java middleware with the cooperation of CPS and PGL. Moreover, terminal provisioning using TR-069 protocol is efficient to support auto configuration, monitor and synchronize end-user terminals, and highly applicable to N-screen service domains. Furthermore, service provisioning uses SD&S/BCG based on the extensible XML schema. Therefore, it is also effective to define and transfer metadata using SD&S/BCG through broadband IP network. Future work includes design and development of more sophisticated architecture that accommodates heterogeneous middleware in order to provide more efficient collaboration with N-screen terminals.

Acknowledgments. This work was supported by the IT R&D program of MKE/KEIT, [10039202, Development of SmartTV Device Collaborated Open Middleware and Remote User Interface Technology for N-Screen Service].

References

1. Google TV, http://www.google.com/tv/
2. ETSI TS 102 796: (V1.1.1) Hybrid Broadcast Broadband TV (2010)
3. Open IPTV Forum, http://www.oipf.tv/
4. Broadband Forum: TR-069 Amendment 3 - CPE WAN Management Protocol v1.2 (2010)
5. ETSI TS 102 034: (V1.4.1) Digital Video Broadcasting (DVB); Transport of MPEG-2 TS Based DVB Services over IP Based Networks (2009)
6. ETSI TS 102 539: (V1.2.1) Digital Video Broadcasting (DVB); Carriage of Broadband Content Guide (BCG) information over Internet Protocol (IP) (2008)
7. ATSC A/101A: Advanced Common Application Platform (2009)
8. The WebKit Open Source Project, http://www.webkit.org/
9. ETSI TS 102 819: (V1.4.1) Digital Video Broadcasting (DVB); Globally Executable MHP version 1.0.3 (GEM 1.0.3) (2008)

Performance Evaluation of Reliable Real-Time Data Distribution for UAV-aided Tactical Networks

Jongryool Kim[1], KeyongTae Kim[2], Soo-Hyung Lee[2], and JongWon Kim[1]

[1] Networked Computing Systems Lab.,
Gwangju Institute of Science and Technology (GIST)
Gwangju, Korea
[2] Dept. of Embedded Software Research,
ETRI Daejeon, Korea

Abstract. In this paper, by taking the example of reliable real-time data distribution for UAV(unmanned aviation vehicle)-aided tactical networks, we discuss how to evaluate the relationship of CPS networking performance and resource consumption by building a trace-driven simulation environment.

Keywords: Cyber-physical systems, reliable real-time multicasting, resource awareness, and UAV-aided tactical networks.

1 Introduction

CPS (cyber-physical system) is a kind of real-time system that has a tight combination between the system computation and physical elements [1]. CPS networking, designed as networking of interacting elements with physical input and output, requires reliable real-time data distribution (i.e., one to many transport) among CPS nodes [2]. This CPS networking needs to accommodate the specific QoS (quality of service) requirements of selected CPS domains, which demand diversified tradeoffs between targeted performance and incurring resource consumption. That is, for the success of real-world CPS applications, we should select and deploy a reliable data distribution scheme while paying extra attention to the incurring resource consumption.

Thus, in this paper, based on a trace-driven simulation method, we discuss how to evaluate the tradeoff of resource-aware CPS networking. Actually, this on-going investigation extends our previous work in [3] by improving the simulation environment. By taking UAV-aided tactical networks [4] as an example CPS domain, we simulate with ns-2 [5] a reliable real-time data distribution scenario that employs LDPC (low dencity parity check) FEC (forward error correction). The resulting simulation results based on the trace-driven simulation allow us to analyze the tradeoffs between the resulting performance and its resource consumption.

T.-h. Kim et al. (Eds.): CA/CES³ 2011, CCIS 256, pp. 176–182, 2011.

2   Resource-Aware CPS Networking

In a real-world there is limited resource capacity, and this resource limitation affects the performance of data distribution. To enhance the reliability of real-time data distribution, most of theoretical proposals concentrate on challenges like network-adaptive reliable multicasting without seriously considering their computational overhead [6,7]. The basic conflicting tradeoff between reliability performance vs resource consumption (including time, i.e., deadline) is quite often set as out of scope. However, in order to realize more practical solutions for real-world CPS domains, we should accomplish reliable data distribution while considering incurring resource consumption to satisfy diverse requirements. We believe that if we can understand the required resources better, we can improve the control of these resource consumptions and thus can achieve the targeted performance level.

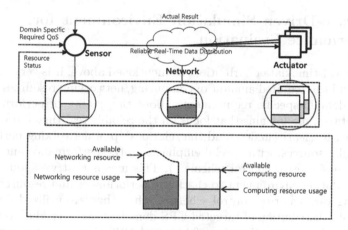

Fig. 1. Conceptual diagram for resource-aware reliable data distribution

Fig. 1 depicts the high-level concept for resource-aware reliable real-time CPS networking. To realize reliable real-time data distribution, we need to understand the required (computing and networking) resources that can satisfy the domain-specific performance requirements. Also, domain-specific performance should reflect the quality characteristics of deployed applications or services for given CPS domain. Domain-specific performance can be described and measured as achieved application qualities including deadlines, achieved networking QoS values (i.e., bandwidth/loss/delay), and so on. Finally, by utilizing following key methods, we are trying to achieve the resource-aware CPS networking.

– *Modeling*: To quantitatively relate the amount of resources and estimated quality of performance, we need to establish a systematic understanding about this relationship via *modeling*. Various aspects of modeling should be achieved depending on the target domain.

- *Monitoring*: To measure and recognize current resource status (e.g., originally available and consumed), appropriate *monitoring* methods are required for all the monitored resources, which can allow us to decide the level of *monitoring* based on resource properties. Also, we should measure the achieved domain-specific performance in terms of various quality measures.
- *Adaptation*: About the domain-specific quality of performance as well as the resource consumption, we need to minimize the differences between requested requirements and achieved (sometimes estimated via modeling only) estimations. Usually we perform various adaptations on the available quality-affecting parameters (e.g., the amount of resources to be used for each targeted adaptation task) for resource-aware CPS networking. We also review the output results of performed adaptations so that we can adjust the adaptation loop according to the differences between the expected and achieved results.

3   A Trace-Driven Simulation Environment for Performance Evaluation

For reliable real-time data distribution, as mentioned above, it is very important to understand the required amount of computing/networking resources that can satisfy the domain-specific requirements about the quality of performance. In the CPS networking domains that focus on the reliable real-time data distribution, we need to clearly understand the relationship of networking performance and required resources, with special emphasis on the performance and resource tradeoff of chosen error control scheme(s). This means that we should setup a realistic simulation environment to check the performance and resource tradeoff of employing various error control schemes, when they are utilized for reliable real-time data distribution of targeted CPS domains. However, due to real-time constraints and resource diversity of targeted CPS domains, it is quite challenging to setup a realistic simulation environment for reliable real-time data distribution [8]. In general, it is known that network simulations with tools like ns-2 can cover localized approximated (but effective) simulations by building customized effective networks at low cost. We however, only with ns-2 network simulations, cannot check the practical performance (e.g., encoding/decoding time and throughput) of error control schemes, since it lacks practical consideration on the consumed resources (in terms of computing and networking). That is, the performance and resource consumption results from ns-2 only networking simulations cannot directly reflect the real-world computing aspects. In other words, the required *modeling* cannot be effectively accomplished by the ns-2 only simulations. Therefore, in order to understand the CPS networking performance tightly tied with current resource status, we use the following trace-based simulation environment with emulation effects as shown in Fig. 2.

In Fig. 2, at the server-side, we encode original data by using a selected FEC encoder. Before conducting network simulations, real FEC encoding is performed to the provided original data based on assigned parameters. As a result, we

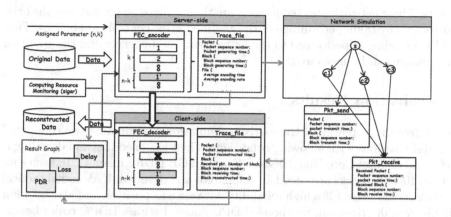

Fig. 2. Overview of trace-driven simulation for reliable data distribution

have trace file(s) containing the various aspects of FEC encoding (e.g., encoded time of each packet, average encoding time, average encoding rate, and so on). For given parameters, the results of FEC encoding are separately stored and thus can provide the limited *modeling* effect to quantitatively relate the amount of resources and estimated quality of performance. Then, these trace results together enable the decision on the required *adaptation* (i.e., network-adaptive selection of FEC encoding parameters). At the same time, we monitor the status of computing resources such as CPU, memory, and disk I/O by using a sigar (system information gatherer and report) tool [9] during FEC encoding and FEC decoding.

In this paper, continuing our previous work in [3], we simulate the UAV-aided WiMax networks based on the WiBro version of WiMax IEEE 802.16. Each FEC-encoded packet is matched with a generated packet of network simulations and this matching information is recorded in the trace file. Through network simulations, we make trace files based on the setting of network topology, which contain packet sequence numbers and sending/receiving time of each packet for given network simulations. By referring this information, we check the specific amount of network delay and loss for each simulated packet. Also, sinc current ns-2 does not support the simulation of individual bit-errors on a time scale shorter than the packet duration[1], to check the performance of byte-level FEC, we implement a new module that calculates the numbers of bit and burst errors per packet according to the BER (bit error rate) variation (with respect to time) and records the bit error information of each packet in the trace file.

Also at the client-side, we decode FEC-encoded data by using a selected (and matching) FEC decoder. During the network simulations, some packets are lost or delayed or corrupted (i.e., get error bits). This information is recorded in the trace file that is generated from the network simulations. Based on it, we make the nework affected (i.e., lost, delayed, corrupted) version of FEC-encoded

---

[1] The number of bit errors per packet is not calculated or recorded.

packets. These network-affected packets are then utilized to reconstruct the original packets by taking advantage of the assumed error control capabilities. That is, FEC decoding is performed to the network-affected packets and the resulting performance can be measured.

4   Evaluation Results

To evaluate the potential of trace-driven simulation environment, we conducted several simulations with following conditions. The FEC-encoding and decoding is performed on Intel Core Duo 2.0Ghz PCs with 2GB DDR2 memory. In each simulation, 100,000 blocks are encoded, simulated, and decoded. UAV-aided tactical network should transmit a high reliability data such as position and attitude. For reliable data distribution, we choose LDPC codes, because LDPC codes belong to a class of powerful error correcting codes that can achieve near-capacity error correcting performance. For LDPC decoding, iteration threshold of 3 is used and the number of checks per row and column is fixed to 3. Note that, as discussed earlier, to quantify the amount of resources for each error control module, we match it with the real usage of resources.

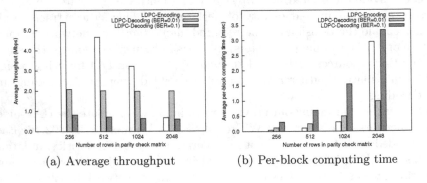

(a) Average throughput   (b) Per-block computing time

Fig. 3. Throughput and time performance of LDPC FEC computing

From the PCs at both server and client sides, the throughput and time of LDPC FEC computing are measured, respectively. Fig. 3(a) shows the FEC-encoding throughput of LDPC computing that is checked during the trace-driven simulation. As we increase the size of PCM (parity check matrix), it shows the lower encoding throughput. The FEC-decoding throughput of LDPC computing is affected from the BER of underlying network. The trace-driven simulation can show the average per-block encoding and decoding time of LDPC computing. Fig. 3(b) shows the corresponding encoding and decoding time per block. The per-block encoding time also increases as the size of parity check matrix increases. As expected, the number of decoding iterations needs to increase to correct more bit errors when BER is increased at the cost of increased decoding time.

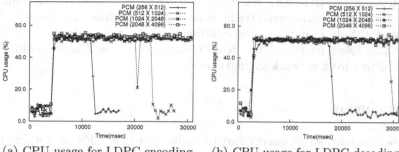

(a) CPU usage for LDPC encoding.   (b) CPU usage for LDPC decoding.

Fig. 4. CPU usages for LDPC computing

During LDPC encoding and decoding, the trace-driven simulation can show the status of computing resource such as CPU, memory, and disk. From Fig. 4(a) and Fig. 4(b), we can check the corresponding CPU usages for LDPC encoding and decoding, respectively. Based this, we can link the impact of consumed resources to the networking performance.

Fig. 5 and Fig. 6 show the respective packet delivery ratio and the end-to-end delay when we use LDPC on the simulated network topology mentioned

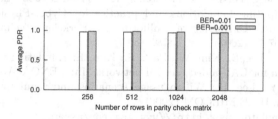

Fig. 5. Networking performance: Packet delivery ratio

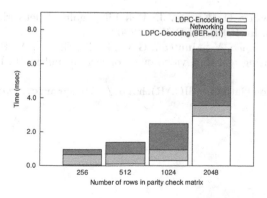

Fig. 6. Networking performance: End-to-end delay

in [3]. Reliable real-time data distribution from a UAV node to three mobile nodes is simulated. Background traffic is also generated from non-participating mobile nodes. Note that the end-to-end delay in Fig. 6 contains the encoding and decoding delays measured from real PC computing as well as the networking delay measured from network simulations.

5   Conclusion

This paper explains an on-going effort to realize practical CPS networking that can support reliable real-time data distribution while considering resource awareness. Currently we focus on how to understand the tradeoff of CPS networking performance and resource consumption and how to evaluate it by adopting a trace-driven simulation environment.

Acknowledgments. This work was supported by the IT R&D Program of MKE/KEIT [10035708, The development of CPS core technologies for high confidential autonomic control software].

References

1. NSF Workshop on Cyber-Physical Systems, http://varma.ece.cmu.edu/cps/
2. Lee, E.A.: Computing foundations and practice for Cyber-Physical Systems: A preliminary report. University of California at Berkeley, Technical report no. UCB/EECS-2007-72 (2007)
3. Kim, J., Kim, K., Lee, S., Kim, W., Park, S., Kim, J.: Simulating reliable real-time data distribution for UAV-aided tactical networks. In: VENOA Workshop (2011)
4. Lee, J., Shim, Y., Lee, H.: WiBro usage scenarios and requirements in tactical environment. In: IEEE MILCOM (2006)
5. The network simulator- ns-2, http://www.isi.edu/nsnam/ns
6. Floyd, S., Jacobson, V., Liu, C.G., McCanne, S., Zhang, L.: A reliable multicast framework for light-weight sessions and application level framing. IEEE Trans. Networking (1997)
7. Ghaderi, M., Towsley, D., Kurose, J.: Reliability gain of network coding in lossy wireless networks. In: IEEE INFOCOM (2008)
8. Xu, C., Fallon, E., Qiao, Y., Muntean, G.M., Li, X., Hanley, A.: Performance evaluation of distributing real-time video over concurrent multipath. In: IEEE WCNC (2009)
9. System Information Gatherer (SIGAR), http://www.hyperic.com/products/sigar

Multi-level Access Control for GeoContents

Sun Rae Park[1], Jong Suk Ruth Lee[1], Kum Won Cho[1], and Kyu-Chul Lee[2,*]

[1] Korea Institute of Science and Technology Information,
245 Daehak-ro, Yuseong-gu, Daejeon, Korea
[2] Chungnam National University, 99 Daekah-ro, Yuseong-gu, Daejeon, Korea
`{srpark,jsruthlee,ckw}@kisti.re.kr, kclee@cnu.ac.kr`

Abstract. The environment changes in the Internet and network technology have enabled real-time services of higher-quality and larger-size content. The convenience of digital content has increased the demands on content, but because of the nature of digital content that can be duplicated unlimitedly, the issues on security and copyright have come to the fore. In the meanwhile, new technologies to control access to the digital content based on usages and permissions for identical digital content are emerged. This paper proposes multi-level access control using Delta compress algorithm and by granting access control based on usages and permissions of content, it prevents the illegal use of GIS data and protects and maintains digital content consistently.

Keywords: Multi-level access control, GeoContents, DRM, Vector data, Raster data, Delta compress.

1 Introduction

The environment changes in Internet and network has enabled real-time services that provide a huge amount of high quality digital content[1]. As digital technology and communication technology are becoming more common, end users can create, modify and distribute digital content with few efforts. The convenience of digital content has increased the demands on content, but because of the nature of digital content that can be duplicated unlimitedly, the issues on security and copyright[2] have come to the fore. Especially, GIS data has been extended to GeoContents concept which includes digital contents related to geographic information and it is expanded into many different forms of data.

Copyright protection is needed because of high production cost and importance of information. Due to the nature of security in GIS data (classified into closed, open, and restricted), access to GIS data is different based on its usage and access level.

This paper proposes a Multi-level access control technique to protect the copyright of GeoContent which provides in various forms and to control the access of GeoContent based on access level. When Multi-level access control has access to GeoContent to use GeoContent, it provides access to GeoContent that corresponds to its access level. Multi-level access control technique using Delta compress algorithm

---

* Corresponding author.

T.-h. Kim et al. (Eds.): CA/CES³ 2011, CCIS 256, pp. 183–190, 2011.

is also easily applied to GIS data that is provided in various forms. In particularly, it can be applicable to Vector data and Raster data as well as file formats which don't have Layer and Object.

2   Multi-level Access Control

The proposed Multi-level access control is a technique that controls access to GeoContent based on its usage and access level. It enables to control access to the resources in not only a server area but also local personal computers.

Multi-level access control for GeoContents in GIS must satisfy following conditions.

- Support various file formats.
- Support layer-level access control.
- Support object-level access control.
- Support access control for Vector data as well as Raster data.

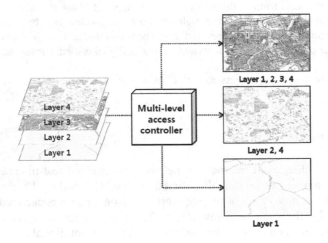

Fig. 1. Layer access control

Figure 1 illustrates the concept of the layer-level access control. It grants access to specific layers in GIS data consisting of a number of layers based on its usage. As shown in figure, different scenarios for the GIS data consisting of layer 0, layer 1, layer 2 and layer 4 may exist as follows.

1) All the layers are used.
2) Two layers, layer 2 and 4 are used.
3) Only layer 1 is used.

In the three scenarios of layer access control, layers which had access to use were all the same layers but it granted three different access to the layers based on the usage.

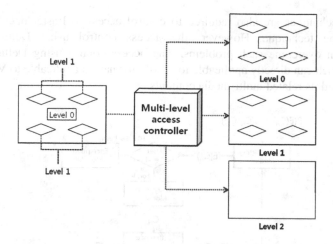

Fig. 2. Object access control

Figure 2 explains the concept of object-level access control and possible scenarios. The access to the objects in the GIS data is granted according to user classes. For the GIS data consisting of a rectangle of class 0 object and diamond of class 1 object, the following scenarios can exist.

1) In case of access control for class 0 objects, a user of class 0 is authorized to access all the objects.
2) In case of access control for class 1 objects, a user of class 1 is authorized to access all the diamonds of class 1 object except the rectangle of class 0 object.
3) A user of class 2 is not authorized to access any objects in diamond of class 0 and rectangle of class 1 objects.

In the three scenarios of object access control, objects which had access to use were all the same objects but it granted or denied access in three different ways based on access level.

3   Multi-level Access Control Implementation

To provide the access control to individual objects and layers in GIS data, the highest-level data and the Delta, which is compressed by extracting from the differences between the highest-class and lower-class GIS data, are packaged in a GeoContent together. The users receiving such packaged GeoContent are licensed according to their usage and access level.

When Geo-processing techniques are used to control access to GeoContent, an engine that can interpret the file format used in the GeoContent is needed. For example, to control access to Shapefile, we need an engine interpreting the Shapefile format. Similarly, to control access to Drawing file, we need an engine which can interpret the Drawing file format. It means that engines that are able to interpret the files should be added as the file formats to control access increase. In addition, image processing techniques are also required to control access to Raster data, instead of geo-processing technique. However, the access control using Delta compress algorithm can overcome such problems. The access control using Delta compress algorithm which can directly applicable to all file formats is applicable to Vector data, Raster data and its related multi-media contents.

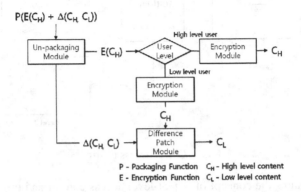

$P(E(C_H) + \Delta(C_H, C_L))$

P - Packaging Function C_H - High level content
E - Encryption Function C_L - Low level content

Fig. 3. Flow of Multi-level access control

Figure 3 illustrates the fundamental flow in a Multi-level access controller that controls access based on access levels. When a user attempts to access packaging P(E(CH) + Δ(CH, CL)), the Multi-level access controller separately interprets the encrypted E(CH) and difference extracted Δ(CH, CL) through un-packaging module. A high-level user is allowed access to CH content restored by decrypting E(CH) depending on user level. In the case of low-level users, they can access to CL content through the decryption of encrypted E(CH) and difference patch with difference extracted Δ(CH, CL).

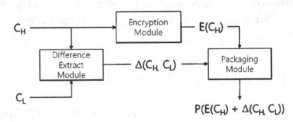

$P(E(C_H) + \Delta(C_H, C_L))$

Fig. 4. Flow of Multi-level access control packaging

Figure 4 illustrates a fundamental flow in Multi-level access control packaging. The Multi-level access control packager produces Delta Δ(CH, CL) by difference extracting between two input data of High level content (CH) and Low level content (CL). Because CH is confidential information to be protected, it is encrypted using encryption module and then the encrypted E(CH) and difference extracted Delta Δ(CH, CL) are packaged in the Multi-level DRM content format. Delta Δ(CH, CL) data can be protected with encryption according to importance.

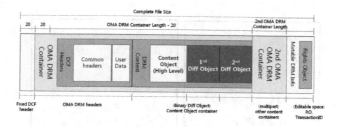

Fig. 5. Multi-level access control packaging format

Figure 5 shows DRM file packaging format to support Multi-level access control. The DCF format [7] of OMA was extended to support all file formats. OMA DRM Container box contains a DCF headers box and protected content box and Delta Compress box was added to support Multi-level access control. In order to support Multi-level Delta Compress box is composed of structure that can be added as many as the number of multi-levels.

4   Experimental Results

This section describes the result of multi-level access controller which controls access of layers, or objects in specific area based on usage and access level of the GIS data. Results of access control are also presented for image file of raster data.

Table 1. Layer information by access level

Layer Name	Type	Access Level					Note
		0	1	2	3	4	
APA	Polygon	O	O	O	O	O	
BDA	Polygon	O	O	O	O	O	
EAA	Polygon	O	X	O	X	X	Only class 0
RPG	Polygon	O	X	X	O	X	can access to
RPM	Polygon	O	X	X	O	X	protected
TLL	Line	O	O	X	X	X	object
WAA	Polygon	O	X	X	X	X	

Table 1 shows the layer information about access levels used in this paper to control access to individual layers. Class 0 has access to APA, BDA, EAA, RPG, RPM, TLL and WAA layers. Level 1 has access to APA, BDA, and TLL layers. Level 2 has access to APA, BDA, and EAA layers. Level 3 has access to APA, BDA, RPG and RPM layers. Lastly, Level 4 has access only to APA, BDA layers.

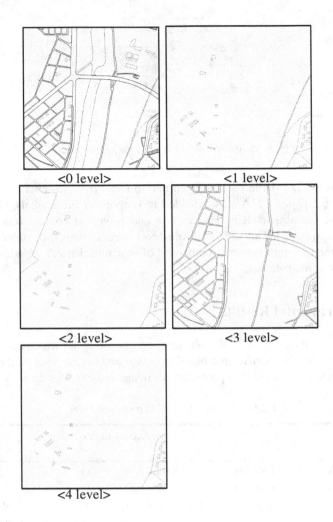

Fig. 6. Access control result of Layer units

Figure 6 is a visualized image of layers using GIS application in order to check the access control results of layers from class 0 to class 4 based on usage and access levels.

<0 level>   <3 level>

Fig. 7. Access control result of Object units

Figure 7 is an image captured the access control result of protected object based on class 0 and class 3 for usage and access levels. In the left figure, objects in the red oval are only granted to a user with access level 0. If a user with access level 3 attempts to access to protected objects as shown in the right figure, since a user has no access control to them, it appeared to be no objects. BDA layer is accessible to all levels, but protected object where BDA layer is presented is only accessible to a user with access level 0. However, the users with other levels except level 0 can't be accessible to protected objects.

5   Conclusions

GIS data is digital content that requires high production costs for initial construction and it is transformed into different digital content according to its usage or access level. For such GIS data a technique is needed for copyright protection and access control based on usage. GIS data is able to control access with Geo-processing technique, but an engine which can interpret GIS data file format which supports the access control. This means that an engine should be supported for file formats on Shapefile and Drawing file and the additional work is needed for newly added file format. Image-processing technique is needed for raster image instead of Geo-processing technique. To solve these issues, this paper proposed Multi-level access control technique and Delta compress algorithm, and DRM content packaging format were proposed as a method to construct Multi-level access controller. Because Multi-level access controller using Delta compress proposed in this paper is applied to all digital content in the same way, the same application is possible to raster image without additional work for file format. The Multi-level access control is also applicable to the file formats that do not support layer or object concept.

In the future, we will look into methods to improve the performance of Multi-level access control and efficient management systems. Our future work will also include Multi-level access control technique applicable to not only file-based but also streaming-based digital content.

References

1. Park, J.-H., Yoon, K.-S., Jeon, K.-P.: A Study on Steaming Service for Content Protection. In: Proc. KCAC, vol. 1(1), pp. 198–201 (2003)
2. Jeong, Y., Yoon, K., Ryou, J.: A Trusted Key Management Scheme for Digital Rights Management. ETRI Journal 27(1) (February 2004)
3. Burns, R.C., Long, D.D.E.: Efficient Distributed Backup with Delta Compression. In: Proc. IOPADS 1997, pp. 26–36 (1997)
4. Mount10 Data Continuity Architects, White Paper FastBIT™ Binary Patching vs. Block Technology Release: 1.0 (October 2004)
5. Trendafilov, D., Memon, N., Suel, T.: zdelta: An Efficient Delta Compression Tool. Technical Report TR-CIS-2002-02, Polytechnic University, CIS Department (June 2002)
6. Heirbaut, J.: JojoDiff - diff utility for binary files, http://jojodiff.sourceforge.net/
7. DRM Content Format, Open Mobile Alliance, Approved ver 2.1 (2008)

Self-Managed System Development Method for Cyber-Physical Systems

Ingeol Chun[1], Jinmyung Kim[1], Won-Tae Kim[1], and Eunseok Lee[2]

[1] Embedded Software Research Department
Electronics and Telecommunications Research Institute (ETRI)
138 Gajeongno, Yuseong-gu, Deajon, 305-700, Korea
[2] Department of Electrical and Computer Engineering, SungKyunKwan University (SKKU)
300 Cheoncheon-dong, Jangan-gu, Suwon, 440-760, Korea
{igchun,jm.kim,wtkim}@etri.re.kr, leees@skku.edu

Abstract. Cyber-Physical Systems is a major currently challenging domain that handles extremely tight integration of and coordination between information world and physical resources. In CPS, people want to acquire useful information and control actual systems anytime and anywhere. However it is not possible all the time because the physical world where systems are deployed has much uncertainty and uncontrollable conditions. To solve those problems, systems in CPS could be more intelligent in the adaptation. In this paper, we propose self-managed system development method for Cyber-Physical Systems to deal with uncertainty and uncontrollable condition. The self-managed system based on the proposed approach can reason about its state and environment, and adapt itself at runtime automatically and dynamically in response to changes.

Keywords: Autonomic Computing, Self-Managed System, Cyber-Physical System, High Reliable System.

1 Introduction

People want to retrieve useful information and control systems anytime and anywhere automatically in the physical world where they lived. That makes numerous sensing and actuating systems embody in the physical world with every daily life and systems more complex than before. However, it is very difficult to make complete and reliable systems because of complexity and the unpredictable nature of the physical world where the systems operates.

The starting point of this research is to understand the characteristics of the physical world. The physical world has much uncertainty and uncontrollable conditions. However, in general development method, uncertainty and uncontrollable conditions are not allowed. Moreover, all of the user requirements and the system states are well-defined and described in requirement specification documents. The differences of the system design philosophy make it impossible to make systems suitable to the physical world. Hence, new and innovative approaches to build self-managed systems are strongly needed[2]. Cyber-Physical System(CPS) is a good

T.-h. Kim et al. (Eds.): CA/CES³ 2011, CCIS 256, pp. 191–194, 2011.

example to apply our research because it is a major currently challenging domain that deals with extremely tight integration of and coordination between computational systems and physical resources. The systems in CPS have always been held to a higher reliability and predictability standard than general-purpose computing systems that operates in strict and fixed environment, and must be smart and reliable to unexpected conditions and adaptable to system failure[1], because the application fields of CPS are the mission-critical or the safety-critical system as shown in fig. 1.

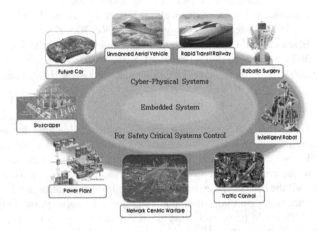

Fig. 1. Application Fields of Cyber-Physical Systems

In this paper, we introduce new system development method to make self-managed systems based on self-adaptation technologies. The primary reason why self-adaptive systems are needed is the increasing cost of handling the complexity of software systems to achieve their goals. Traditionally, most researches have been focused on software verification and validation (V&V) based on its internal quality attributes. However, in recent years, there has been an increasing demand to handle these issues at runtime[3]. Researchers in this area have proposed several solutions to incorporate adaptation mechanisms into software systems. IBM started the autonomic computing initiative in 2001 to build self-adaptive computing systems to overcome the rapidly growing complexity problem. The main reason for large blue-chip companies, like IBM, being interested in autonomic computing is the need to reduce the cost and complexity of owning and operating an IT infrastructure[4, 5]. Thereafter Rainbow framework[6], MADAM[7], ML-IDS[8], etc. are introduced.

2   Self-Managed System Development Method

We propose 4 steps to make self-managed systems for CPS as shown in fig. 2. The system modeling step is the starting point to make complete system. To design the system, the understanding of its characteristics is strongly needed. Differing from conventional information systems, the systems in CPS consists of a combination of discrete and continuous features and is called hybrid system. The hybrid system is divided into a discrete part, a continuous part and an interface governing the interaction of the two[9]. In order to design a hybrid system, a hybrid modeling language is needed. We selected ECML(ETRI CPS Modeling Language) developed by ETRI (Electronics and Telecommunications Research Institute) as a system modeling language[2].

Fig. 2. Self-managed System Development Method

The second step is to extract knowledge from the system model. To implement self-managed systems, we make 4 types of knowledge - Normal Status Table(NST), Potential Fault Table(PFT), Adaptation Policy Table(APT), Adaptation Strategy Table(AST). NST*(NST=<Cartegory, NSC name, BMD name, PMD name, State name, Condition>)*, PFT*(PFT=<PF name, CMD name, Substructure name, Description>)* and APT*(APT=<Policy name, NSC name, Priority, Strategy command, Parameters>)* are derived from the system model while AST*(AST=<Strategy name, Description, Type>)* is predefined according to the adaptation capability of a target system.

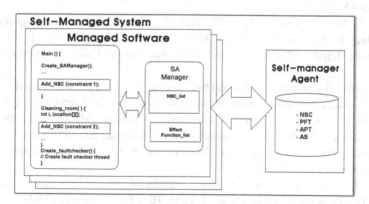

Fig. 3. Architecture of Self-Managed System

Next step is to generate adaptation code. We propose a self-managed system that consists of the managed software and the self-manager agent. Managed software consists of the main function and SAManager thread that achieves the internal adaptation cooperated with the self-manager agent. The self-manager agent gathers massive distributed data from widespread sensors and SAManager in managed software. If a system encounters an anomaly, the self-manager constructs and executes adaptation plans to achieve the management goals in accordance with the policies and rules in effect. Final step is to implement system with a conventional programming language. Fig. 3 shows the architecture of a self-managed system.

3   Conclusion

The adaptation is to handle uncertainty and unpredictable situation of the physical world. The self-adaptation technology to make self-managed systems is a new paradigm to increase the robustness of systems. The objective of the self-managed system is to provide seamless service and to avoid unexpected operation reliably. In this paper, we propose the method for making an agent based self-managed system to satisfy user requirements and overcome the system failure. Especially, we proposed 4 steps that cover from acquiring user requirements to implementing a self-managed system easily.

In future work, to prove the efficiency and the reliability of proposed approach, we will measure the effectiveness of our research quantitatively according to metrics defined in ISO/IEC 9126 (Software Engineering - Product Quality).

Acknowledgments. This work was supported by the IT R&D Program of MKE/KEIT [10035708, " The Development of CPS(Cyber-Physical Systems) Core Technologies for High Confidential Autonomic Control Software"].

References

1. Chun, I., Lee, H., Kim, W., Park, S., Lee, E.: Smart Home Service Robot applying self-adaptation technologies. In: IEEE International Conference on Consumer Electronics, pp. 853–854 (2011)
2. Chun, I., Kim, J., Lee, H., Kim, W., Park, S., Lee, E.: Faults and Adaptation Policy Modeling Method for Self-adaptive Robots. In: Kim, T.-h., Adeli, H., Robles, R.J., Balitanas, M. (eds.) UCMA 2011, Part I. CCIS, vol. 150, pp. 156–164. Springer, Heidelberg (2011)
3. Salehie, M., Tahvildari, L.: Self-adaptive software: Landscape and research challenges. ACM Transaction on Autonomous and Adaptive Systems 4(2), Article 14 (May 2009)
4. Appleby, K., Fakhouri, S., Fong, L., Goldszmidt, G., Kalantar, M., Krishnakumar, S., Pazel, D., Pershing, J., Rochwerger, B.: Oceano—SLA-based management of a computing utility. In: Proceedings of the IFIP/IEEE International Symposium on Integrated Network Management, pp. 855–868 (2001)
5. Tuttle, S., Batchellor, V., Hansen, M.B., Sethuraman, M.: Centralized risk management using Tivoli risk manager 4.2., Technical report, IBM Tivoli Software (2003)
6. Garlan, D., Cheng, S.-W., Huang, A.-C., Schmerl, B., Steenkiste, P.: Rainbow: Architecture-based self-adaptation with reusable infrastructure. IEEE Computing 37(10), 46–54 (2004)
7. Floch, J., Hallsteinsen, S., Stav, E., Eliassen, F., Lund, K., Gjorven, E.: Using architecture models for runtime adaptability. IEEE Software, 62–70 (2006)
8. Al-Nashif, Y., Kumar, A.A., Hariri, S., Qu, G., Luo, Y., Szidarovsky, F.: Multi-Level Intrusion Detection System (ML-IDS). In: International Conference on Autonomic Computing, pp. 131–140 (2008)
9. Park, J., Yoo, J.: Hardware-Aware Rate Monotonic Scheduling Algorithm for Embedded Multimedia Systems. ETRI Journal 32, 657–664 (2010)

DSUENHANCER: A Dynamic Update System for Resource-Constrained Software

Dong Kwan Kim, Won-Tae Kim, and Seung-Min Park

CPS Research Team, Embedded SW Research Department
Electronics and Telecommunications Research Institute
Daejeon, Korea
{dgkim,wtkim,minpark}@etri.re.kr

Abstract. Dynamic Software Update (DSU) is an advanced software practice to change a running program with imposing negligible service interruption while updating. In this paper, we present DSUEnhancer, a DSU implementation for resource-constrained C programs like embedded software. DSUEnhancer generates a patch file off-line and loads it into the dynamic memory of an updated program on-line. In particular, DSUEnhancer is relatively lightweight in terms of memory and CPU usage and runs on the ARM architecture with the *gcc* cross compiler.

Keywords: Dynamic Software Update, Patch File, Patch Generation, Patch Injection.

1 Introduction

Dynamic software update (DSU) refers to the process of changing the software code of a running program to support software evolution while the program runs. A DSU system changes the code of a computer program while it runs, thus saving the programmer's time and using computing resources more productively [1]. Most DSU systems are based on in-place updating, in which patches are loaded into memory area of a running process [2]. In other words, their approach to dynamic updating is to add patches to an updated process itself at runtime. Since software developers often create their programs without considering dynamic updating during software development phase, it is necessary to inject some updating facilities to the programs before they are deployed on the operating environment. In in-place updating systems, a custom compiler enables an updated application to be updateable by inserting special code (e.g., update management code) or annotations. Another necessary part of the in-place updating system is a patch generator that produces patches containing program modifications. The patch generator compares the old and new versions of a program to identify differences between them. In addition, most in-place updating systems provide safe update points where a program could be updated safely without causing unexpected behavior.

Unlike the in-place updating, state transfer-based updating [2] performs updates without applying patches into a running process. In state transfer-based updating, a

T.-h. Kim et al. (Eds.): CA/CES³ 2011, CCIS 256, pp. 195–201, 2011.

new version of an updated program is executed separately while an old version is running. The state of the old process is transferred to the new process. Therefore, there is no need to patch the running old process for updating. Once the new process is running after state transfer, the old process will be killed. The key element of this updating technique is to transfer runtime state between the old and new processes. State transfer-based updating can be safer than in-place updating in that the old process remains untouched during updating.

This paper introduces DSUEnhancer, a new DSU implementation for resource-constrained programs. DSUEnhancer supports the in-place updating and changes a running program loaded in memory to perform updates without program restart. DSUEnhancer dynamically updates programs which run on the ARM architecture [3]. It also supports the need for rollback. The original version of an application can be executed using the update rollback. In DSUEnhancer, it is not necessary to manipulate source code or binary code to inject some update management code such as directives, annotation, and special functions.

The rest of this paper is structured as follows. Section 2 introduces DSUEnhancer. In Section 3, we present existing dynamic updating mechanisms and systems. In Section 4, we present the concluding remarks and outline the future work directions.

2 DSUEnhancer

We present the system architecture of DSUEnhancer and the flow of updating on the fly.

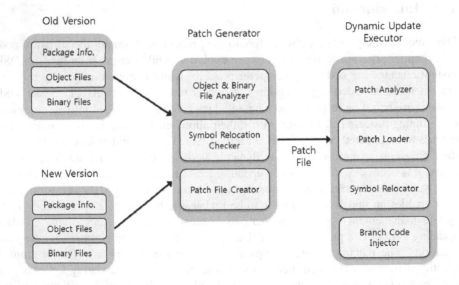

Fig. 1. DSUEnhancer architecture

Figure 1 shows the architecture of DSUEnhancer that consists of a patch generator and a dynamic update executor. For dynamic updates, DSUEnhancer generates patch files before update requests are triggered. The patch generator is responsible for making patch files. It identifies differences between the old and new versions of an updated program. Since the size of the patch file affects system performance during updating, it is efficient to construct the patch file as small as possible. The patch generator consists of an object/binary file analyzer, a symbol relocation checker, and a patch file creator as seen in Figure 1. The update request makes DSUEnhancer to change a running program by loading the generated patch file at runtime. The dynamic update executor allocates unused heap area and loads patch content to that area on the fly. When function updates have been completed, all the calls to an old function are switched to the new version of that function. The dynamic update executor consists of a patch analyzer, a patch loader, a symbol relocator, and a branch code injector.

2.1   Patch Generation

Figure 2 depicts the procedure of generating patch files through the patch generator. The input of the patch generator is old and new application programs. The object and binary files of the input programs are created through the compilation and link phases.

There are two types of differencing: object and binary differencing. The object/binary file analyzer collects not only the differences at the code level but also the structural ones at the architecture level. Prior to comparing the old with new version, the object/binary file analyzer obtains the necessary update information such as binary file names, execution symbols, and object file names. The object/binary file analyzer is intended to catch modification update and addition update of new variables and functions.

Recall that DSUEnhancer loads the updated code to the dynamically reserved memory space of the target program. Therefore, it is necessary to relocate the updated symbols due to the difference between memory address allocated in the binary file and physical memory address. The symbol relocation checker stores all the relocation symbols from the object files according to their names and types. For read-only data, DSUEnhancer extracts them in a function and then attaches them at the end of the function code.

Finally, the patch file creator generates a patch file containing update information and symbol relocation information.

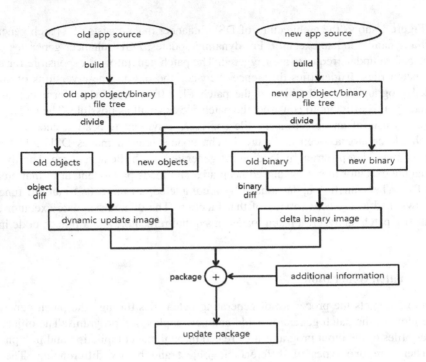

Fig. 2. Generating patch files

2.2   Patch Injection

To make changes to running programs without service interruption, the dynamic update executor applies the patch file to the program on the fly. The dynamic update executor consists of a patch analyzer, a patch loader, a symbol relocator, and a branch code injector. The dynamic update executor applies updates to the running program according to the steps shown in Figure 3.

The patch analyzer extracts necessary update information by analyzing the header of a patch file and assorting the patch of each section by function ((1) in figure 3). The patch loader will allocate dynamic memory ((2) in figure 3) and load the classified patch to reserved memory area ((3) in figure 3). If the symbol relocation is needed with a function, the patch analyzer stores the information about the symbol relocation ((4) in figure 3). The symbol relocator will use such information to relocate symbols. Finally, the branch code injector will write a *branch* instruction at the head of the changed function ((5) in figure 3). The branch instruction depends on the computer architecture where DSUEnhancer is working.

The patch loader allocates unused heap memory where the patch content will be loaded. Some modified Linux system calls are used to enable a DSUEnhancer process to reserve memory space for another at runtime. The system calls take the process identifier of an updated process and allocates memory area for that process on the fly.

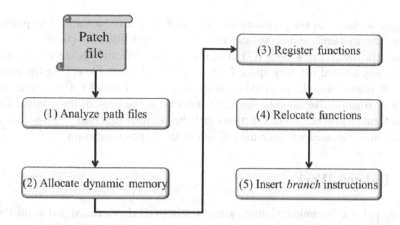

Fig. 3. Applying updates to running programs

The *ptrace* system call is used to load the patch content into the pre-allocated memory. The information of the allocated memory space is logged for possible update rollback.

Some symbols of an updated program are required to be relocated so that the loaded patch can be executed correctly. For the relocatable symbol using a relative address, the symbol relocator computes the relative address by considering the address of an updated function as well as the address and offset of a corresponding new function. In the case of an absolute address, the symbol relocator searches an absolute address from the symbol table of the updated program. To execute the patch, the function call to an old function should be delegated to a new function. The branch code injector inserts a branch instruction into the entry point of the old function so that all function calls to that old function jump to the new function. The insertion of the branch instruction is also performed by the *ptrace* system call. Once the new function has been completed, the right next instruction of the call to the old function will be executed.

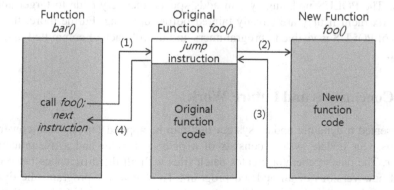

Fig. 4. Dynamic updates by injecting *jump* instruction

Figure 4 illustrates the proposed mechanism for dynamic updates. The patch generator of the dynamic update system generates a patch file that contains differences between the old and new code ((1) in figure 4). The dynamic update system allocates dynamically unused memory space for the generated patch file ((2) in figure 4). The patch file is loaded in the reserved memory area ((3) in figure 4). The system inserts a branch instruction like jump to the patch function at the head of the original function ((4) in figure 4). When other functions call the original function, the inserted branch instruction is executed and then the call jumps to the patch function.

3   Related Work

Ginseng [4] is a dynamic updating system for both single-threaded and multi-threaded C applications. Ginseng consists of a compiler, a patch generator, and a runtime system; the Ginseng compiler generates an updateable executable and checks if changes to a running program violate type-safety, the Ginseng patch generator automatically creates patch code representing differences of two versions of C software, and the Ginseng runtime system applies the changes to the program when a safe update point has been reached. To make target applications updateable, Ginseng inserts type wrappers and function indirections into them. For safe and timely changes to multi-threaded programs, the enhanced Ginseng compiler [5] induced more update points from the safe update points specified by programmers.

Similar to Ginseng, UpStare [6] is composed of a compiler, a patch generator, and a runtime. To update active functions immediately, UpStare uses *call stack reconstruction*, which unrolls the call stack of an original version and reconstructs it for a new one. UpStare also supports updates to multi-threaded C programs and allows for arbitrary updates of functions.

POLUS [7] allows the coexistence of both the old and new versions of data and calls synchronization functions on the state whenever there is a write access to either version of the data. To achieve such state synchronization, POLUS uses the debugging API provided by operation systems to control and modify the state of a running process. The POLUS updating system adds special recovery code to target applications to fix them if they are already tainted before updating. Furthermore, the patch process of POLUS is visible to programmers and the rollback of committed updates is allowed.

4   Conclusions and Future Work

We presented a dynamic update system that can be applied for resource-constrained programs. Our update system consists of a patch generator and a dynamic update executor. The patch generator creates patch files with all the differences between the old and new versions of an updated program. To change the program, the dynamic update executor allocates unused heap area and loads the patch file into that area. The proposed update system is relatively lightweight in terms of memory and CPU usage and runs on the ARM architecture with the *gcc* cross compiler. To verify

DSUEnhancer, we plan to apply it to cyber-physical systems [8]. Cyber-physical systems, next-generation embedded systems, often run in resource-constrained environments and are needed to ensure high reliability at runtime. As the support of seamless service and reliability has become an indispensable part of cyber-physical systems, we believe dynamic software updating can benefit software developers in maintaining these systems.

Acknowledgments. This work was supported by the IT R&D Program of MKE/KEIT [10035708, "The Development of CPS(Cyber-Physical Systems) Core Technologies for High Confidential Autonomic Control Software"].

References

1. Kim, D., Tilevich, E., Ribbens, C.J.: Dynamic software updates for parallel high-performance applications. Concurrency and Computation: Practice and Experience 23(4) (March 2011)
2. Hayden, C., Smith, E., Hicks, M., Foster, J.: State Transfer for Clear and Efficient Runtime Updates. In: Workshop on Hot Topics in Software Upgrades (HotSWUp) (April 2011)
3. Seal, D.: ARM Architecture Reference Manual, 2nd edn. Addison-Wesley Professional (2001)
4. Neamtiu, I., Hicks, M., Stoyle, G., Oriol, M.: Practical dynamic software updating for C. In: ACM Conference on Programming Language Design and Implementation (June 2006)
5. Neamtiu, I., Hicks, M.: Safe and timely dynamic updates for multi-threaded programs. In: ACM Conference on Programming Language Design and Implementation (June 2009)
6. Makris, K., Bazzi, R.A.: Immediate multi-threaded dynamic software updates using stack reconstruction. In: USENIX Annual Technical Conference (June 2009)
7. Chen, H., Yu, J., Chen, R., Zang, B., Yew, P.: POLUS: A Powerful Live Updating System. In: International Conference on Software Engineering (May 2007)
8. Lee, E.A.: Cyber physical systems: Design challenges. In: International Symposium on Object/Component/Service-Oriented Real-Time Distributed Computing (ISORC) (May 2008)

Evaluation of Real-Time Characteristics for Mission Critical Systems Using Hierarchically Profiled Petri Net

Hyunsang Youn[1], Ingeol Chun[2], and Eunseok Lee[1]

[1] Department of Electrical and Computer Engineering,
Sungkyunkwan University
wizehack@gmail.com, leees@skku.edu
[2] Department of Software Research,
Electronics and Telecommunications Research Institute (ETRI),
South Korea
igchun@etri.re.kr

Abstract. Development of mission-critical systems requires the verification and the validation (V&V) considering limited time, available resource and costs to analyze the possibility of mission accomplishment in system development life cycle. In this paper we propose a Petri Net based modeling formalism, called Hierarchically Profiled Petri Net (HPPN), which provides a unified solution for above problems through the profiled firing rule in which the state evolves according to the state transition rule. Additionally we propose an analysis technique, which represents the multi-aspect based state enumeration that considers the state of token and the state of marking. Expressive and analysis capabilities of the model are demonstrated with reference to an intercontinental ballistic missiles (ICBM) scenario.

Keywords: Critical Systems, Verification and Validation, Real-time Schedulability, Hierarchically Profiled Petri Net.

1 Introduction

Due to the criticality of applications involved, it is important issues to analyze the expected dependability characteristics of systems during all phases of their development cycle [7]. Several researchers have evolved their techniques to the verification and validation (V&V) at the early stage of the life cycle, such as Petri-Net [1] and Process Algebra [2]. In particular, discrete time process algebra is used to model a set of recurring real-time tasks scheduled and to support schedulability analysis [3]. However, stochastic characterization of this formalism does not cover the variability of temporal parameters such as task release times and computation times. Real-time system characteristics require more elaborate verification and validation technique due to stochastic evaluation both correctness and the dependability in real-time systems. However, in the classical literature, above modeling formalisms do not cover the required characteristics. Generally the development of time-critical systems

T.-h. Kim et al. (Eds.): CA/CES³ 2011, CCIS 256, pp. 202–212, 2011.
© Springer-Verlag Berlin Heidelberg 2011

requires the verification of real-time characteristics such as Effective Time, Effective Deadline, Real time scheduling, Preemption, Dynamic Scheduling, etc.

Petri Net based methods are generally applied as a unified formal specification framework, to support the analysis of both functional and nonfunctional properties of systems. Many modeling formalisms based on Petri Net have been created to support system analysis and design, such as Stochastic Petri Net (SPN)[4], Colored Petri Net (CPN)[5], Time Petri Net (TPN)[6].

Generalized Stochastic PN (GSPN) allows two types of transitions to be used: immediate and timed [8]. Once enabled, immediate transitions fire in zero time. Timed transitions fire after a random exponentially distributed firing delay as in the case of SPN. However, it is inconvenient for expressing timing constraints of the systems. CPN allows a color that specifies the type of tokens. These characteristic are convenient for specifying complex concurrent systems and usefully applied to describe the transaction of target system. Samuel Kounev proposed a methodology for analyzing the performance of distributed component system using HQPN [11]. This offers very well to modeling distributed component-based system, such as modern e-business application. However it is difficult to represent a state transition and consistency of processed transaction. E-HQPN extends the concept of HQPN to allow the identification of the state of transactions processed in concurrent system [10]. Another formalism for V&V that considers the temporal properties is spTPN[9]. The approach provides the verification of soft deadlines, which lead to probabilistic analysis, for real-time systems. This approach has the limitation, which is the reduced expressive power for the distributed and diverse tasks.

In this paper, we propose a Petri Net modeling formalism with the analysis techniques. The modeling formalism, that we call Hierarchically Profiled Petri Net (HPPN), is characterized by the use of a profiled firing rule and colored token added attributes. This formalism provides powerful expression for the real-time characteristics and enables discrete time based modeling.

2 Hierarchically Profiled Petri Net

Hierarchically Profiled Petri Net (HPPN) consists of the combination of the characteristics of TPN and CPN. Additionally, HPPN assigns attributes to the color of token and profiled firing rule.

2.1 Syntax

Definitiaon1. A HPPN is an 12-tuple. HPPN = (S, Q , P, T, C, I+, I-, I*, M_0, W, attr, e), where:

- S, Q, P, T, I+, I-, I*, M_0, C is equal to the syntax of HQPN
- attr = ($attr_1$, $attr_2$,..., $attr_n$) is a set of attribute which is respectively assigned to color function optionally.
- e is a set of trigger event for transition.
- W = (W_1, W_2, (w_1, w_2, ..., $w_{|n|}$)), where:

- W_1 is a mapping called static interval, W_1: $C(t_i) \rightarrow N \times N$, where N is the set of nonnegative rational numbers
- W_2 is a mapping called firing profile.
- $w_{lil} \in [C(t_i) \rightarrow R]$ such that $\forall c \in C(ti)$: $wi \in R+$ is interpreted as a rate of a negative exponential distribution specifying the firing weight specifying the relative firing frequency due to color c,

2.2   Semantics

The state of a HPPN is a pair s=<M, t(e)>, where M is a marking and t(e) is a vector associating each transition t with a discrete time to fire. The state evolves according to a state transition rule defined through token selection probability, priority. A transition is enabled if each of its input places contains at least one token none of its inhibiting places contains any token. Once a transition T fires, the marking M is replaced by M' obtained by remove a firing set F_i from each input place connected by each transition, and by adding a firing set F_o to each output place of each transition.

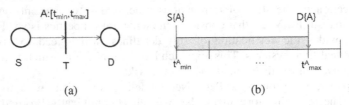

(a)   (b)

Fig. 1. Single token selection, (a) HPPN model for single token selection, (b) Transition time

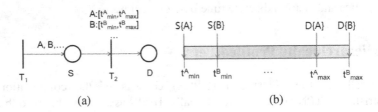

(a)   (b)

Fig. 2. Token selection from the plural numbers of token, (a) HPPN model for selecting token A or B, (b) Transition time for each token

The duration for firing time is decided between maximum time and minimum time allocated to firing mode. For example, in fig.1(a), transition T removes token A of place S and deposits the token A to place D. Transition T is fired between time clock t_{min} and t_{max}. Assuming that token A must remove by 3 seconds, we allocate the value A:[0, 3] for the firing time of the token. Figure 1(b) shows dense time model that place D has a token A before time t^A_{max}. In fig2(b), token A or B is randomly selected, if they are in the place S and progress time is between t^B_{min} and t^A_{max}. Definition 2 explains the priority assignment for the configuration of firing set under ordinary place.

Definition 2. Token c at Time t1 has higher priority than token A at Time t_0 under a transition T

$$\text{if } \forall c \in C(t), t_0 \subseteq t \text{ and } t_1 \subseteq t, \forall t_1 > t_0, \text{ then } Prio(c, t_1) > Prio(c, t_0)$$

Queueing Place has scheduling mode to sort added tokens according to their priority. Fig.3(a) shows the graphical notation of queueing place. Transition t_1 of fig.3(b) selects a token and then dispatch it to priority queue. T_1 has the scheduling mode such as EDF and LST [9]. Priority Queue removes a token from the queue and then adds the token to P_2 if P_2 is empty. T_2 fires when P3 is empty. The dotted arrow line is drawn when T_2 has firing profile, which explains in section 2.3.1.

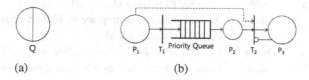

(a)   (b)

Fig. 3. Queueing Place, (a) a shape of queueing place, (b) the international implementation of a queueing place

2.3   Remarks

A transition fires a so-called firing profile in which defines a firing set of token and firing condition. A token can include attributes involved in the state representation of it. This marks a difference with respect to most colored extensions of petri net.

Definition 3. Token c_j described in firing profile has absolutely higher priority than other tokens

$$\text{if } \forall c_j \in C(t_j) \text{ and } \forall c_i \subseteq C(t_i) \text{ then } Prio(c_i, t_i) < Prio(c_j, t_j)$$

In HPPN, the processing of some events that have highest priority is represented by using firing profile. Definition 3 explains the priority of tasks described by firing profile.

```
Annotated_Element_Name {
        PreCondition{
                condition expression;
        }
        Action{
                action expression;
        }
        PostCondition{
                condition expression;

        }
}
```

Fig. 4. firing profile

Firing profile is the set of conditions and actions. If the state of system satisfies firable condition (pre-condition), the transition performs the set of described actions. If the marking of the system satisfies the post—condition that is represented in the profile, the transition is compeleted. But if the marking does not satisfy the condition, the transition is in progressing state. Figure 4 shows a temple of firing profile.

Table 1. Transition function

Function	Mean	Example
deposit(Place)	Add token	- deposit(P1{c1(a1, a2, a3), c2(a1, a3, a5)}); Add token c_1 and c_2 to place p_1 with set of attributes c1(a1, a2, a3) and c2(a1, a3, a5)
remove(Place)	Delete token	- remove (P1{c1(a1, a2, a3), c2(a1, a3, a5)}); Remove token c_1 and c_2 which have each attribute $c_1(a_1, a_2, a_3)$ and $c_2(a_1, a_3, a_5)$ of place p_1.
tick(number)	No operation	- tick(3); Wait for 3 time units, it gurrentees that another transition does not fire during waiting time.
sleep(number)	No operation	- sleep(3); Wait for 3 time units, it does not gurrentee that another transition does not fire during waiting time.

Action exprestion describes essential fuction of transition. We can express add or delete token in designed places. Additionally, we can represent 'No operation' using tick() function and sleep() function. Table 1 shows transition funciton to describe action expression. Condition expression of firing profile represents the marking of place. Table 2 shows basic notation to describe condition expression. We use operator such as AND, OR, NOT to describe condition expression more powerfully. Table 3 shows the set of operators.

Table 2. Condition function

Function	Meaning	Description & Example
pos()	Positive	- pos(P1{c1,c2}); There are token c1 and c2 in place P1.
neg()	Negative	- neg(P1{c1,c2}); There are not token c1 and c2 in place P1
prec()	Precise	- prec(P1{c1,c2}); There are only token c1 and c2 in place P1

Table 3. Operators

Operator	Mean	Description & Example
&	AND	- $pos(P_1\{c_1,c_2\})$ & $neg(P_1\{c_3,c_4\})$ There are both tokens c_1 and c_2 in plae P_1, but not c_3 and c_4 in the place.
|	OR	- $pos(P_1\{c_1,c_2\})$ | $pos(P_1\{c_3,c_4\})$ There are ether tokens c_1 and c_2 or tokens c_3 and c_4 in place P_1.
~	NOT	- $\sim pos(P_1\{c_1,c_2\})$ There are not tokens C_1 and C_2 in place P_1.

In HPPH, Token has attributes that explain the state of it. The state of token can be represented as follows: Color (attr$_1$, attr$_2$,..., attr$_n$).

The description of each state of tokens helps to understand the behavior of system. Espicially, the description bridges the gap to interpret the analysis results of mathemitical model.

3   Analysis

In this section, we introduce the enumeration method of stochastic state space and provides the schedulability analysis technique. The evolution of an HPPN generates the states of a descrete time stochastic process, which are pairs s=<M, t(e)>, where M is a marking and t(e) is a vector of probability mass function for times to fire of transitions enabled by M. Given sates s=<M, t(e)> and s'=<M', t'(e')>, the transition across the two states is represented through the relation $s \xrightarrow{e,u} s'$, where e is an event and u is a measure of probability. In HPPN, the generation of the new marking requires firing set, clock event and friring event.

Clock Event (CE) is an event which leads time to fire. Transition connected to output place allocates maximum clock time (C_{max}) and minimum clock time (C_{min}) to firing time per colored token. Transition generates CE per static time between C_{min} and C_{max}. CE is a pair of CE=<ATE, RTE>, where RTE is the number of relative time event allocated to tokens described in Fig.1 [C_{min}, C_{max}]. ATE is the number of absolute time event, which means the number of clock event from the initial marking of system to the current marking. CE allocates a token to firing set F_I and F_O. The allocation algorithm is as follows:

Step1. Finding ATE$_{MIN}$ and ATE$_{MAX}$
Step2. If ATE is equal to ATE$_{MIN}$, Then allocating C$_O$ that has C$_{MIN}$ and C$_{MAX}$ to F$_O$
Step3. Allocating C$_I$ which is related to C$_O$ to F$_I$

Firing set F at descrete time t are pairs F_t=<F_I, F_O>, where F_I is a input firing set that is a set of tokens that will be newly added to related placeses at time t. F_O is a output firing set that will be removed from related placesses at time t. Considering firing profile, Ft is set of input parameters of deposit() and remove() functions. Firing event is enabled when ATE allocated for the token is between ATE_{MIN} and ATE_{MAX}. Firing event remove F_O from output places and then add F_I to input places. The probability of firing event is enabled.

In HPPN, an enabled transition t is said to be *schedulable* under it remove all of the tokens in the output place for limited time allocated for each tokens. However an enabled transition t is *not schedulable* under it does not remove the tokens in the output place. We provides folloing theroem to find the defect with regard to schedulability in system.

Theorem 1. Let's assume that firing profile does not allow multiple token selection. If there is a transition T which output place P has more than two separate tokens, and their firing probability is 1, the transition T is not schedulable under a given time.

Proof 1. If P_T(t, A)=P_T(t, B)=1, current time t=t_{max} and only one token is moved by one transition.

4   Case Study

In this section, we evaluate the modeling and the analysis capability of HPPN from the launching scenario of intercontinental ballistic missile (ICBM).

4.1   Scenario

ICBM follows a ballistic trajectory that includes three phases that are the boost phase, the mid-course phase, and the terminal phase. In this examination we do not allow the interception of the missile in terminal phase. Therefore the missile is incepted in the boost and mid-course phase. In this simulation we find minimal numbers of simultaneously fired ICBM to hit the command center of enemy. We set the following input to ICBM simulator.

- Attacker fires the missile in the launching ramp after a countdown from ten.
- The time to get out of the boost phase in trajectory is between 160~180 seconds after the missile is fired.
- The time that ICBM is in the mid-course phase is between 20~25 minutes.
- The time that ICBM is in the terminal phase is between 20~30 seconds.
- The target of ICBM is either a commend center or an intercept missile base.
- An intercept missile base attacked by ICBM does not fire any more.
- Enemy intercepts four ICBMs in the boost phase using four combat planes after 8~12 seconds.
- The aegis destroyer of enemy fires five anti-ballistic missiles concurrently when ICBM is in the mid-course phase.

- ICBM does not attack the combat planes and the destroyer.
- The anti-ballistic missiles that the destroyer fires intercepts ICBM after 10~20 seconds.
- The intercept missile base in the ground fires simultaneously three anti-ballistic missiles at 20 second intervals after the aegis destroyer fires the anti-ballistic missiles.
- The anti-ballistic missiles that fires in the ground intercept ICBM after 80~90 seconds.

4.2   Model Validation

We built the HPPN model of ICBM scenario depicted in Fig.5. Places "BoostP", "MidP" and "TermP" mean the boost phase, the mid-course phase and terminal phase. Places "CCP" and "MIBP" are the command center and the missile intercept base which are the targets of ICBM. Places "AirP", "ShipP" and "G_launcherP" represent the combat airplanes, the aegis destroyer and anti-ballistic missile base. Place "G_InterceptedP" is a space to represents the intercepted ICBM by the anti-ballistic missiles. Place "WaitP" is the waiting space for ICBM that can be fired simultaneously. Place "ReadyP" is the space to deposit ICBM that is being countdown. Token "m" denotes the anti-ballistic missile. Token "I" denotes ICBM, which has following attributes.

I (Target, Phase, Operation)

Attribute "Target" is either "mib" that means the missiles interceptor base or "cc" that means command center. Attribute "Phase" is the current location. It has one of the

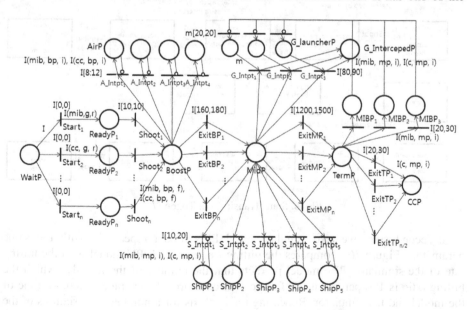

Fig. 5. HPPN model for ICBM Shooting Scenario

following five values: "bp" that means the boost phase, "mp" that means the mid-course phase, "tp" that means terminal phase, "g" that means the ground and "t" that means the target. Attribute "Operation" represents the current behavior, which has one of the following two values: "r", "f" and "b". Symbol "r" describes the missile is in the ready state. Symbol "f" represents the missile is flying. Symbol "b" means the missile is boomed at target.

In HPPN, transition can change the attributes of token. For example, transition "Start" changes the state of token "I" (ICBM) from waiting to ready; setting the target and starting the countdown. Transition "Shoot" fire the ICBM. Transition "ExitBP" has the trajectory of ICBM change from the boost phase to the mid-course phase. Transition "ExitMP" has the trajectory of ICBM change from the mid-course phase to the terminal phase. Transition "ExitTP" has the ICBM move to the target. The fire of transition "A_Interpt" means that intercepts ICBM by the combat planes. The fire of transition "G_Interpt" means that intercepts ICBM by the missile anti-ballistic missile base. The fire of transition "S_Interpt" means that intercepts ICBM by the aegis destroyer. The state transition flow is depicted in Fig.6.

The model developed in this section is new validated by comparing its predictions against measurements on the simulator. In first step to get the experimental results, we repeatedly execute the simulator with various number of ICBM concurrently fired. The metrics considered are the number of the missiles simultaneously fired the target of the fired missiles, the number of intercepted missiles, the number of experiments, success ratio for hitting the command center and the execution time of the simulator.

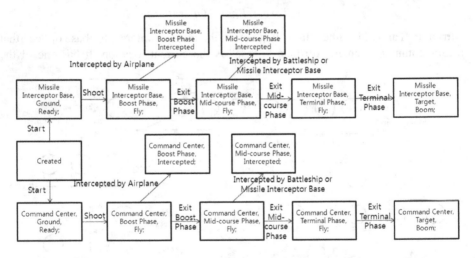

Fig. 6. State Transition of Token *"I"*

In second step, we also simulate our HPPN model repeatedly with the same parameters. Figure 7(a) compares the hitting rate of our HPPN model with the hitting rate of the simulator. The model predicts that the number of the missiles which the hitting ratio is 100 percent is 55. Figure 7(b) compares the average execution time of the model and the simulator. Repeating the analysis for a number of variations of the input parameters shows the results of similar accuracy.

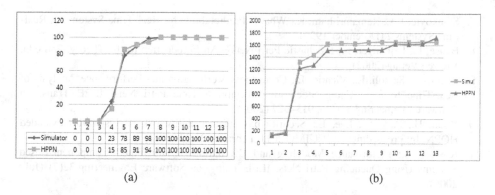

(a)   (b)

Fig. 7. Comparing Correctness of HPPN based model with the experimental results of simulator, (a) Comparing Hitting Rate, (b) Comparing Execution Time

5   Conclusion

In this paper, we proposed Hierarchically Profiled Petri Net (HPPN) that provides the verification of correctness for real time systems. HPPN showed following three characteristics. Firstly HPPN provided powerful natation to represent real time properties such as time limitation, static/dynamic preemption. Secondly HPPN extended the color function of token. Each token had attributes to represent the state transition of each token. It could be used to bridge the gap between real system and the model. Lastly the evolution of HPPN based system model generates discrete time state space. The state space provides a useful tool which supports verification of correctness for time-critical systems.

Acknowledgments. This work was supported by the IT R&D Program of MKE/KEIT [10035708, "The Development of CPS (Cyber-Physical Systems) Core Technologies for High Confidential Autonomic Control Software"].

References

1. Küngas, P.: Petri Net Reachability Checking Is Polynomial with Optimal Abstraction ·Hierarchies. In: Zucker, J.-D., Saitta, L. (eds.) SARA 2005. LNCS (LNAI), vol. 3607, pp. 149–164. Springer, Heidelberg (2005)
2. Hennessy, M.: Algebraic Theory of Processes. The MIT Press, ISBN 0-262-08171-7
3. Vereijken, J.J.: Discrete-time process algebra. Eindhoven University of Technology (1997) ISBN 90-386-0541-2
4. Ajmone-Marsan, M.: Stochastic Petri Nets: an Elementary Introduction. In: Rozenberg, G. (ed.) APN 1989. LNCS, vol. 424, pp. 1–29. Springer, Heidelberg (1990)
5. Jensen, K.: Coloured Petri Nets. In: Brauer, W., Reisig, W., Rozenberg, G. (eds.) APN 1986. LNCS, vol. 255, Springer, Heidelberg (1987)
6. Berthomieu, B., Dim, M.: Modeling and verification of time dependent systems using time Petri nets. IEEE Trans. on Software Engineering 17(3) (March 2000)

7. Stankovic, J.A., Ramamritham, K.: What Is Predictability for Real-Time Systems. J. Real-time Systems 2 (December 1990)
8. Bause, F., Kritzinger, F.: Stochastic Petri Nets—An Introduction to the Theory, 2nd edn. Vieweg Verlag (2002)
9. Bucci, G., Sassoli, L., Vicario, E.: Correctness Verification and Performance Analysis of Real-Time Systems Using Stochastic Preemptive Time Petri Nets. IEEE Trans. on Software Engineering 31(11), 913–927 (2005)
10. Youn, H., Park, C., Lee, E.: Security based survivability risk analysis with extended HQPN. In: Proceedings of ICUIMC 2011, February 21-23 (2011)
11. Kounev, S.: Performance Modeling and Evaluation of Distributed Component-Based Systems Using Queueing Petri Nets. IEEE Trans. on Software Engineering 32(7) (July 2006)

Communication Entities Discovery
in Complex CPS System

Soo-Hyung Lee[1], JaeHyuk Kim[1], Won-Tae Kim[1], and JaeCheol Ryou[2]

[1] Embedded Software Research Department,
Electronics and Telecommunications Research Institute, Daejeon 305-700, Korea
{soohyung,jhk0330,wtkim}@etri.re.kr
[2] Department of Computer Science & Engineering, Chungnam National University,
Daejoen 305-764, Korea
jcryou@cnu.ac.kr

Abstract. This paper presents the detailed design of node discovery method based on Data Distribution Service (DDS) for Cyber–Physical System (CPS) applications. Even though DDS has been standardized by Open Management Group (OMG), OMG DDS is not sufficient for developer to implement DDS as a communication and control middleware of CPS. It does not provide not only precise specification of its procedure and message coding rule but interoperability between the different implementations. We designed EDDS (ETRI DDS) based on OMG DDS for implementation and interoperability. In this paper, we present the discovery procedure, state of EDDS discovery and the discovery message scheduling issue of huge complex CPS system in bootstrapping phase.

Keywords: CPS, DDS, Discovery, Middleware, Publish/Subscribe.

1   Introduction

The revolutionary technology advances in pervasive computing, networking and chip processing are leading new paradigm of embedded system called cyber-physical systems (CPS). CPS is comprised of many sensors, actuators and some processing units. All these components are tightly connected with each other to form single complex system. The information about the physical system or the physical world is gathered from sensors. The information is forwarded to the processing units to analyze the current state and to decide the response method. The processed results are fed back to the actuators for controlling physical system or to the sensors for adjusting the level of information to be gathered. Nowadays computing, communication, and intelligence capabilities converge into many physical systems in the most of industry fields[1], CPS   include high confidence medical systems, power grid, intelligent building, military system, environmental control system, transportation, and other critical infrastructure control. CPS will provide us the better means to understand and control the physical system. As result it will transform the way of interacting with physical world [2].

T.-h. Kim et al. (Eds.): CA/CES[3] 2011, CCIS 256, pp. 213–219, 2011.

As all components in CPS are tightly coupled with each other, the reliable and continuous communication capability is the one of most important things to make CPS successful. CPS consists of huge number of communication elements, the discovery of each node to make communication association can be a critical problem. There are a number of traditional pub/sub middleware technologies such as Common Object Request Broker Architecture Event Service and Notification Service [3], Java Message Service [4], and other proprietary middleware products. However, all these event-based services have some problems in real-time and Quality of Service (QoS) capabilities and require high computing capabilities, thus none of these cannot be adopted in resource constrained environment such as CPS. We adopted OMG DDS as a CPS communication and control middleware. The OMG DDS [5-6] specification does not define discovery procedures and message coding rule precisely and does not provide interoperability between different implementations. It can have performance problem when each node are discovering other nodes in bootstrapping phase of complex huge CPS system. So the DDS discovery protocol needs to be re-designed for implementation.

The paper is organized as follow. Section 2 gives the required background and section 3 presents the design of discovery procedure. Node discovery message scheduling issue in domain level will be presented in section 4 and finally we conclude this paper and suggest future work in section 5.

2   Background

DDS is an open specification defined by OMG and provides data-based message distribution service in real time. In DDS the data to be shared among the nodes is defined as Topic. The DDS can also control the data exchange characteristics using 22 QoS parameters defined in specification.

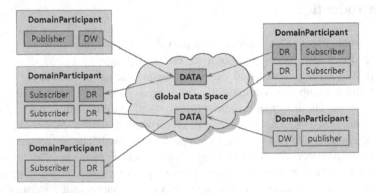

Fig. 1. The DDS – Conceptual Architecture

Fig. 1 illustrates the overall DDS architecture. A *DomainParticipant* is the entry point for the communication in a specific domain and is the root entity of all other entities in the specific node. A *Publisher* is responsible for the publication of data message and *Subscriber* is responsible for the reception of data streaming from its subscribed publisher. Publisher and Subscriber is some kind of container class containing several *DataWriters* (DW) and *DataReaders* (DR) respectively. The DataWriters and DataReaders, uniquely associated with a specific topic, are the communication endpoint. A key benefit of DDS is that nodes are completely decoupled in time, space.

CPS sub-system has many networked sensors, actuators and some processing units. The information about physical environment is gathered from sensors and forwarded to some processing units. The processed results are fed back to the actuators to control physical systems and to the sensors for controlling the understanding level. A CPS system which is perfectly operated as a complete system can be a sub-system of another lager CPS system.

For example, an up-to-date vehicle is a networked, computerized system rather than a just mechanic system. It has many electronic control units (ECUs) that control up to hundreds of sensors and actuators [7]. Each ECU controls some function of vehicle autonomously, such as power trains, breaking systems, temperature control systems, and etc. These ECUs are connected with each other via some shared/private bus or car area network, making vehicle operate reliably and harmoniously as a single system. Such vehicle will be connected with the other vehicle or to some infrastructure leading to smart highways. In smart highways, most of the vehicles in the road will be connected via wireless networks and then some information about the road situation such as accident or traffic state will be gathered into a central control system from the vehicles. Processed information will be given to the some vehicles to take another path avoiding traffic jams or accidents. Such smart high way could be another more complex CPS system. Each vehicle is a small scale CPS system itself, and can be also sensor/actuator of smart highway CPS system at the same time.

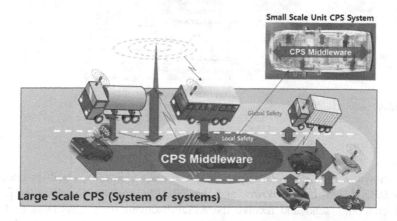

Fig. 2. The Example of CPS System – Smart Car: Small-Scale CPS and Smart-Highway: Large-scale complex CPS

3   Design of Discovery Procedure

In DDS, discovery procedure is composed of 2 phases: Participant Discovery Protocol (PDP) and Endpoint Discovery Protocol (EDP). In the PDP phase, every node in the same domain are discovering the Participant of each node's by sending and receiving Participant DATA sub-messages using multicast protocols. PDP phase uses best-effort communication. In the EDP, the publication DATA message or the subscription DATA message is exchanged between nodes to find out the communication endpoint – DataWrtiter or DataReader using reliable unicast method. EDP message includes both the required QoS and the Topic information. Topic is the data type that DataWriter/DataReader wants to produce/consume. However PDP and EDP is simple protocol, it is too abstracted to implement and it does not support the various environments. For example, if all Participants in the same CPS domain start the discovery procedure at same time, it can raise problems like the data congestion. Therefore it needs some scheduling method for discovery message transmission in the bootstrapping phase in domain level.

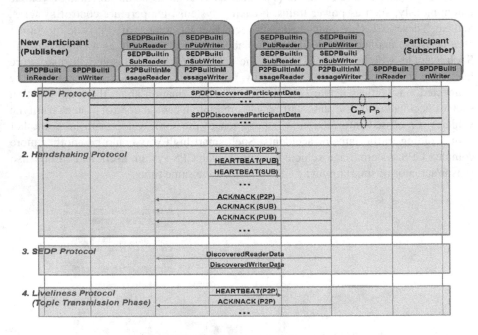

Fig. 3. The EDDS Discovery Procedure

As shown in Fig. 3, the Participant in every node creates two built-in Endpoints - the *SPDPbuiltinParticipantWriter* and the *SPDPbuiltinParticipantReader* for PDP. These endpoints send and receive the SPDPdiscoveredParticipantData to find out Participant of other node in the same DDS domain. The communication method in the PDP is the best-effort, the PDP message can be lost. In our design, PDP messages are transmitted several times (C_{IP}) with the random back-off period (P_P) for the faster discovery. If remote participants are discovered, Handshaking procedure is started to check whether remote node's endpoint is ready for EDP or not by sending HEARBEAT message and receiving ACK/NACK message each other. If remote node is ready, the EDP is carried out using DiscoveredReaderWriterData messages. These messages are exchanged using reliable DDS transmission mechanism, so messages are exchanged just one time. After EDP, Topic transmission phase is initiated where the messages for application data are exchanged. During Topic transmission phase, discovery module checks the liveliness of remote endpoint by exchanging HEARTBEAT and ACK/NACK message periodically.

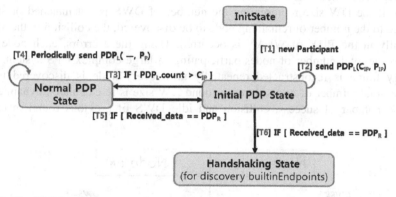

Fig. 4. The EDDS PDP State, where PDP_L means the local PDP message to send and PDP_R means the received remote PDP message

Fig. 4 illustrates the EDDS PDP state transition. If a Participant is created (T1), it starts the initial PDP state. It uses discovery configuration parameters such as the number of initial PDP messages (C_{IP}) and minimum period between PDP messages (P_{IP}) to send PDP messages to the Participant of other remote nodes (T2). If the Participant receives the remote PDP message during T2 state, it changes its state to the handshaking state (T6) to check the liveliness of built-in endpoints. If it does not receive the remote PDP message (T3), it moves to the normal PDP state that sends PDP message periodically. In Normal SPDP state, if the participant receives remote PDP message then it processes same procedure as in initial PDP state, and then it moves to the next state.

4   PDP Message Scheduling in Bootstrapping Phase

DDS initially setup full communication association between participating nodes. The nodes comprising a CPS are tightly coupled with each other to provide CPS system's target function as a single complex system. There might be no time difference between each node's bootstrapping i.e., it is possible that all nodes start node discovery procedure at the same time This aspect can make node discovery that is carried out in CPS bootstrapping phase worse and more difficult. The key is to distribute the node discovery message as even as possible using each node's own information without central control system or broker.

To cope with this problem, the logical discovery message frame can be constructed and frame is composed of discovery window (DW), frame header and tail. DW is comprised of several discovery window slots (DWS) in turn. The DWS are assigned to each node respectively for transmitting node discovery message (NDM) using MAC frame in turn. Practically every node selects its own DWS within the DW using same algorithm such as hash function or random number generator. If each node knows the total number of node and it has an ideal uniform distribution function such as Hash function or Random Number Generator, each node can take DW size as much as the number of nodes and it selects its own DWS using the uniform distribution function. If the DW size representing the number of DWS is not matched or small compared to the number of remaining node to be discovered, the collision in the MAC and finally in the PHY of WLAN is occurred. Using these errors, each node can estimates the total number of nodes participating in large complex CPS system. The discovery frame is reconstructed repeatedly until every node is discovered using estimated total number of nodes. In each round DW size is re-calculated dynamically using the number of success, collision and idle DWS of previous round in every round.

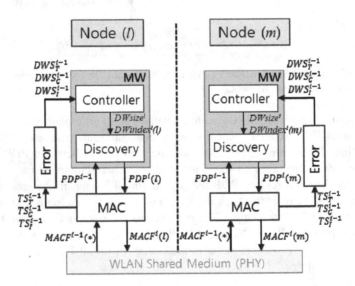

Fig. 5. The conceptual scheme of PDP message scheduling in domain level. The $DWS_{T,C,I}{}^{i}$ is the number of DWS which succeeds to send, fails due to collision and idle in round I respectively. TS is the number of LAN MAC frame in round i.

5   Conclusion

We have proposed a redesigned communication entity discovery scheme based on OMG DDS that we consider as communication middleware of large CPS system. Even though the DDS is OMG standard, it is not sufficient and complete to give precise information to implement and to provide interoperability. So we defined the message that can be used in discovering Participant in the node and discovering the Endpoints in the Participant. We also defined the procedure of message exchange and the state transition in PDP phase. We designed the conceptual scheme of PDP message scheduling between nodes that are participating in same CPS application domain at bootstrapping phase. We believe that the proposed scheme can be used in each node independently without any information sharing or central control method and can provide better performance, compared to the case of applying DDS discovery procedure directly into WLAN without any scheduling mechanism in the middleware. Future works include 1) the defining the coding rule of discovery message, 2) the more precise design of PDP message scheduling scheme and its performance analysis and 3) the implementation and the integration into DDS we are developing.

Acknowledgments. This work was supported by the IT R&D Program of MKE/KEIT [10035708, " The Development of CPS(Cyber-Physical Systems) Core Technologies for High Confidential Autonomic Control Software"].

References

1. Park, J., Yoo, J.: Hardware-Aware Rate Monotonic Scheduling Algorithm for Embedded Multimedia Systems. ETRI Journal 32, 657–664 (2010)
2. Lee, E.A.: Cyber Physical Systems: Design Challenges, Technical Report, University of California at Berkeley, Technical Report No. UCB/EECS-2008-8
3. Object Management Group: CORBA services specifications, http://www.omg.org/technology/documents/corba-services_spec_catalog.html
4. JMS, http://java.sun.com/products/jms/
5. Object Management Group: Data Distribution Service for Real-time Systems Ver. 1.2 (2007), http://www.omg.org/spec/DDS/1.2
6. Object Management Group: The Real-time Publish-Subscribe Wire Protocol, DDS Interoperability Wire Protocol Specification Ver. 2.1 (2009), http://www.omg.org/spec/DDSI/2.1/
7. Glas, M., Lukasewycz, M., Reimann, F., Haubelt, C., Teich, J.: Symbolic Reliability Analysis and Optimization of ECU Networks. In: Proceedings of Design, Automation and Test in Europe, pp. 158–163 (2008)

Key Distribution Method for Enhancing Secure Performances in Dynamic Filtering-Based Wireless Sensor Network

Byung Hee Kim and Tae Ho Cho

School of Information and Communication Engineering Sungkyunkwan University,
300 Cheoncheon-dong, Jangan-gu Suwon, Korea
{bhkim,taecho}@ece.skku.ac.kr

Abstract. Sensor nodes in many sensor network applications are typically deployed in open, wide, and unattended environments. In this environment, sensor nodes are easily compromised by adversaries. The adversary can use compromised nodes to inject a fabricated data into the sensor network. The injected fabricated data drains energy of sensor nodes and causes false alarms. A dynamic en-route filtering scheme is proposed to detect and drop the injected fabricated data. In this scheme, authentication keys used to verify event reports are redistributed to enhance the detection power. It is important to decide when to disseminate authentication keys since this phase consumes much energy. We propose a key distribution method to enhance detection power and reduce energy consumption. Simulation demonstrates that the proposed method is resilience and energy efficient.

Keywords: Sensor network, fabricated report, filtering scheme, detection power, fuzzy.

1 Introduction

Recent advances in sensor networks have enabled to be used sensor nodes in the real world applications such as military, target field imaging, weather monitoring, and distributed computing [1]. Sensor networks are usually comprised of many small sensor nodes and a few base stations. Sensor nodes detect interesting events and forward sensing information to the base station. They have physically limited processing power, small storage space, narrow bandwidth, and limited energy because of small size hardware.

These sensor networks are expected to be used in many applications. Many methods have proposed for sensor networks [3-5], but sensor networks still have some secure problems to use them in the real world [2].

In many sensor network applications, sensor nodes are deployed in open, wide and unattended environments. An adversary can easily compromise the deployed sensor nodes, because of these environments. They can inject fabricated reports containing

T.-h. Kim et al. (Eds.): CA/CES[3] 2011, CCIS 256, pp. 220–226, 2011.

bogus sensor readings or nonexistent events in the sensor networks with a malicious goal. The injected fabricated report will not only cause false alarms that waste real world response efforts, but also drain the finite amount of energy in a battery powered network [6-7]. The injected fabricated reports should be dropped en-route as early as possible to minimize the grave damage. The few elusive ones should be rejected at the base station [8]. The early dropping of the fabricated report leads to significant energy saving. Fig. 1 shows false data injection attacks.

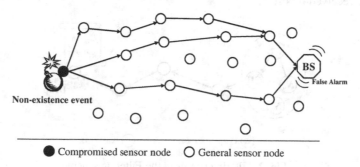

Fig. 1. False data injection attacks

Several security solutions and adaptation methods have been proposed to detect and drop injected fabricated reports. Yu and Guan's proposed method [9] is a dynamic en-route filtering scheme(DEF). In DEF, the determination when redistributing authentication keys is important, since the key exchange phase enhances the detection power that is the probability to filter out the fabricated reports and adaptation of the changed sensor networks. However, this phase consumes considerable energy of sensor nodes. Sensor nodes should conserve their energy and determine the time for redistributing keys considering the condition of the sensor network.

In this paper, we propose a key distribution method for enhancing the detection power while conserving energy. We use a fuzzy system to determine when keys should exchange. The proposed method can enhance detection power while conserving sensor node energy and provide sufficient resilience. The effectiveness of the proposed method is shown in the simulation results.

The remainder of the paper is organized as follows: Section 2 briefly describes the filtering scheme, DEF, and our motivation. Section 3 details the proposed method. Section 4 reviews the simulation result. Finally, the conclusions and future work are discussed in Section 5.

2 Background

A filtering-based secure method is proposed to overcome false data injection attacks. In this section, we briefly describe a filtering scheme, DEF, and our motivation.

2.1   Filtering Scheme

The filtering scheme is a secure method to detect and drop fabricated reports for sensor networks. In the filtering scheme, the sensor node cooperates with other sensor nodes to create an event report when sensing an interesting event. The event report, produced from event-sensing nodes, is verified using a message authentication code (MAC) by the forwarding nodes. When a forwarding node detects a false MAC, it drops the received report.

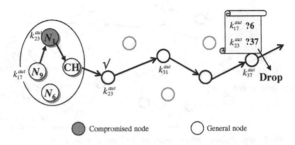

Fig. 2. Filtering phases in the Filtering scheme

2.2   Dynamic En-route Filtering Scheme (DEF)

Yu and Guan proposed DEF to detect and drop the fabricated reports in sensor networks. Sensor network topology can easily be changed, since sensor nodes are small and deployed in open environments. Therefore secure methods for sensor networks have to adapt to topology changes. DEF can deal with a dynamic topology and outperform other proposed methods. It also can reduce duplicated forwarding dates and energy consumption.

DEF comprises of three phase: pre-deployment, filtering phases, and post-deployment. The pre-deployment phase is executed before initial deployment. In this phase, each sensor node preloads a seed authentication key with security y-keys and one z-key randomly picked from the global key pool (Fig. 3).

The sensor node uses the authentication key to make and verify an event report. Besides, y-key and z-key are used to disseminate the authentication keys to other sensor nodes. When an interesting event occurs, event-sensing nodes send event

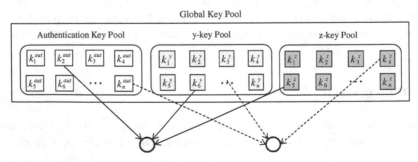

Fig. 3. The pre-deployment phase for disseminating keys

information with an MAC made from its authentication key and event information to its cluster head. In the filtering phase, sensor nodes in forwarding paths cooperate to detect and drop fabricated reports.

2.3   Motivation

In DEF, it is important to determine when to execute the post-deployment phase, since this phase enhances the detection power of sensor networks. However, this phase consumes a lot of sensor node energy. Sensor nodes have to conserve their energy, because the energy is limited resource and not easy recharged. There is a trade-off between detection power and energy consumptions. We propose a key a dissemination determination method using a fuzzy logic to determine the efficient time to execute this phase.

3   Key Distribution Method for Enhancing Secure Performances

3.1   Assumptions

We assume that a sensor network is comprised of a large number of sensor nodes and one base station. Each sensor node has a mechanism to organize the cluster automatically after deployment. We further assume that every sensor node has a unique identifier and verifies the broadcast message. The base station cannot be compromised and has a mechanism to authenticate a broadcast message.

3.2   Overview

Our proposed method uses two fuzzy systems to determine the point of the post-deployment phase. The first fuzzy system determines a fuzzy security value for disseminating authentication keys(FSVDK) considering the number of execute times to disseminate authentication keys(NET), distance from a cluster head to the base station(DCB), and the number of fabricated report(NFR). FSVDK is used to determine whether or not the post-deployment phase executes. Another fuzzy system determines a fuzzy security threshold(FST) considering the number of the fabricated reports(NFR), average energy of sensor nodes in a cluster(AEC), and the number of sensor nodes in a cluster(NSC). FSVDK is used to determine when to calculate the value of FSVDK. The proposed fuzzy system considers conditions of the sensor network and decides the optimal time to disseminate authentication keys.

3.3   Input Factors of the Fuzzy System

The fuzzy system determines FSVDK and FST by considering the state of the sensor networks. The labels in the fuzzy variables are presented as follows.

• NET = {FW(Few), MY(Many), VMY(Very Many)}.

• DCB = {NR(Near), AD(Around), AY(Away)}.

• NFR = {FW(Few), ME(Middle), MY(Many)}.

• FSVDK = {NCE(Nochange), CON(Consider), CE(Change)}.

• NFR = {FW(Few), ME(Middle), MY(Many)}.

• AEC = {VLW(Very Low), LW(Low), EN(Enough)}.

• NSC = {FW(Few), ME(Middle), MY(Many)}

• FST = {FW(Few), ME(Middle), MY(Many), VMY(Very Many)}.

We define fuzzy rules to use the fuzzy membership functions of defined parameters. Table 1 shows the some rules of the fuzzy rule-based system for determining FSVDK and FST.

Table 1. Fuzzy if-then rules for determining FSVDK and FST

RULE No.	FSVDK				FST			
	IF			THEN	IF			THEN
	NET	DCB	NFR	FSVDK	NER	AEC	NSC	FST
1	FW	NR	FW	CE	FW	LW	FW	VMY
3	FW	AD	MY	CE	FW	LW	ME	VMY
5	MY	AD	ME	CON	ME	LW	ME	ME
7	VMY	NR	ME	NCE	MY	LW	ME	ME
9	VMY	NR	MY	CON	VMY	EN	ME	FW

4   Simulation Evaluation

We use a virtual sensor network where 1000 cluster head are randomly distributed and 9000 sensor nodes are uniformly distributed. Each sensor node randomly picks five y-key from the y-key pool whose size is 100. It also randomly picks one authentication key and z-key. Cluster heads in the cluster regions forward the diffusion message of the authentication keys to forwarding nodes via ten hops. Each cluster head uses Hill Climbing to select the forwarding node to conserve forwarding energy. Five different MACs from event-sensing nodes in the same cluster are needed to make an event report. Each node consumes 16.25μJ to transmit and 12.5μJ to receive a byte. The size of an original report is 24bytes and each MAC size is 1byte. The size of each key is 4byte. To simulate our prosed method compared with other methods, a compromised node is randomly chosen and it makes a fabricated report. Furthermore, sensor nodes not operate when they exhaust their energy.

4.1   Simulation Results

We compare the result of the fuzzy-based period determination method(FPDM) with the number-based event report period determination method(NEPDM) and the number-based of fabrication report period determination method(NFPDM). The simulation results show the filtering ratio of fabricated reports and energy consumption of the sensor network.

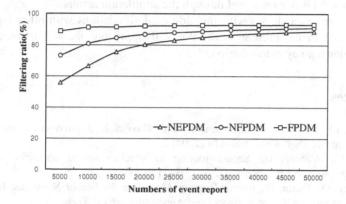

Fig. 4. The filtering ratio of fabricated report (fabricated MAC=3)

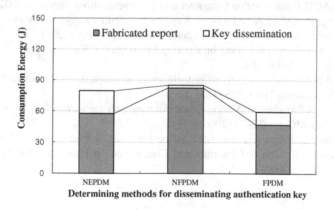

Fig. 5. Average energy consumption (fabricated MAC=3)

Our proposed method, FPDM, has effective detection power and consumes less energy compared with other methods. Simulation results show that FPDM is more efficient method than other methods.

5   The Conclusion and Future Work

In this paper, we have proposed the key distribution method for enhancing secure performances in dynamic filtering-based wireless sensor network. The proposed method uses fuzzy logic to determine when authentication keys should be disseminated. The fuzzy system is exploited to determine FSVDK by considering NET, DCB, and NRF that is used to determine whether or not the post-deployment phase executes. The fuzzy system determines FST considering NFR, AEC, and NSC used to determine when to calculate FSVDK to disseminate authentication keys. The proposed method can conserve consumption energy to diffuse authentication keys and enhance the detection power to filter fabricated reports. The effectiveness of the proposed method is demonstrated through the simulation results.

In our future research, we will run additional simulations with other input factors not considered in the present work. We will apply our method to other filtering schemes requiring key redistribution.

References

1. Akyildiz, I.F., Su, W., Sankarasubramaniam, Y., Cayirci, E.: A Survey on Sensor Networks. IEEE Commun. Mag. 40(8), 102–114 (2002)
2. Karlof, C., Wagner, D.: Secure routing in wireless sensor networks: attacks and countermeasures. Ad Hoc Netw. 1(2-3), 293–315 (2003)
3. Braginsky, D., Estrin, D.: Rumor Routing Algorithm for Sensor Networks. In: The First ACM Workshop on Sensor Networks and Applications, New York (2002)
4. Eschenauer, L., Gligor, V.D.: A key-management scheme for distributed sensor networks. In: The 9th ACM Conference on Computer and Communications Security (2002)
5. Liu, D., Ning, P.: Establishing Pairwise Keys in Distributed Sensor Networks. In: The 2nd ACM on Conference on Computer and Communication Security (2003)
6. Akkaya, K., Younis, M.: A Survey on Routing Protocols for Wireless Sensor Networks. Ad Hoc Netw. 3(3), 325–349 (2005)
7. Al-Karaki, J.N., Kamal, A.E.: Routing techniques in wireless sensor networks: a survey. IEEE Wireless Comm. 11(6), 325–349 (2005)
8. Li, F., Wu, J.: A Probabilistic Voting-based Filtering Scheme in Wireless Sensor Networks. In: Proc. of IWCMC, pp. 27–32 (2006)
9. Yu, Z., Guan, Y.: A dynamic en-route scheme for filtering false data injection in wireless sensor networks. In: The 3rd International Conference on Embedded Networked Sensor System, New York (2005)

The Application of the 0-1 Knapsack Problem to the Load-Shedding Problem in Microgrid Operation

Soojeong Choi[1], Sunju Park[2], and Hak-Man Kim[3]

[1] School of Business, University of Yonsei, Korea
crystal0208@yonsei.ac.kr
[2] School of Business, University of Yonsei, Korea
boxenju@yonsei.ac.kr
[3] Department of Electrical Engineering, University of Incheon, Korea
hmkim@incheon.ac.kr

Abstract. When a decentralized grid system such as microgrid is isolated, the system is vulnerable to power supply shortage. It is essential to address the load-shedding problem in islanded microgrid operation to maintain the system reliability. In this paper, we present an optimal load shedding model for microgrid. The model takes into account the customer values and the discrete characteristics of loads to meet the electrical energy requirement. The branch and bound algorithm to solve the 0-1 knapsack problem, one of the most widely-used combinatorial optimization algorithms, is used to capture the customer values and the discrete characteristics of loads. The objective of the model is to maximize customer values within given supply capacity. The case studies using the optimal load shedding model show how to estimate the customer values.

Keywords: microgrid, microgrid operation, demand side management, load management, load control, load-shedding, 0-1 knapsack problem.

1   Introduction

The deregulation in electricity market, which separates the power generation, transmission, and distribution, makes the market competitive. Although the competition may reduce operation cost, the power price and supply quality are subject to sharp fluctuation in new market. To buffer the effect of the price fluctuation and maintain power supply quality and flexibility, the decentralized grid system with distributed generation that is small scale power generation has been introduced. A microgrid is the decentralized grid system with distributed generation, storages, and loads as shown in Fig 1.

The decentralized grid system with distributed generation is physically disconnected or connected to the power grid. Although the system is physically connected to the power grid, it may enter the state of emergency. The major causes are the disturbance in power system, in distributed generation itself, and in interconnection when the system is isolated from the power grid [2]. The disturbance

T.-h. Kim et al. (Eds.): CA/CES³ 2011, CCIS 256, pp. 227–234, 2011.
© Springer-Verlag Berlin Heidelberg 2011

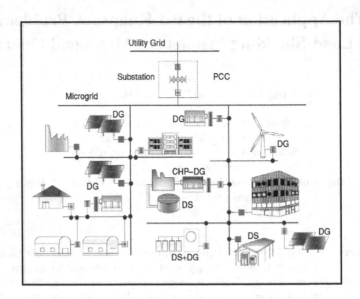

Fig. 1. Typical structure of a microgrid (adapted from [1])

causes the load-shedding problem. Therefore, it is essential to consider load-shedding problem in the decentralized system such as microgrid.

The load-shedding problem is to control the load as maintaining the system reliability. The studies on the load shedding or the load control, or the load management can be categorized into two groups, which are the direct load control by utilities and the indirect load control by subgroups that can be a load such as distribution and end-users [3]. In the direct load control, optimal load-shedding techniques in the bulk power system have been studied on the load-shedding cost [4, 5], on the profit of the utilities [3], and on the minimization of the variation in frequency [6]. In the indirect load control, an optimum load-shedding technique to reduce the total customer interruption cost is proposed [7]. The customer interruption cost was collected by postal survey. In [8], the Talmudic approach for the bankruptcy problem is used to solve the load-shedding problem based on the amount of the load needed by agents in islanded microgrid operation.

In the decentralize grid system as microgrid, the indirect load control is used. Since the system is smaller than the bulk power system, it is easy to capture customer values such as customer interruption cost in [7]. As moving into subgroups that can be a load, the load has discrete characteristic, not continuous one.

This paper proposes an optimal load-shedding model in islanded microgrid operation. The branch and bound algorithm to solve the 0-1 knapsack problem, one of the most widely-used combinatorial optimization algorithms, is used to reflect the customer values and the discrete characteristic. After the model is described, case studies using the model show how to estimate the value.

2   The Load-Shedding Problem and the 0-1 Knapsack Problem

2.1   The Branch-and-Bound Algorithm for the 0-1 Knapsack Problem

The 0-1 knapsack problem (KP) is to select a subset of n given items for maximizing total profit from the subset in a capacity c. Each item has a profit p_j and a weigh w_j, and the total weigh of the chosen items doesn't exceed the capacity c. The KP may be formulated as an integer programming problem and as a network flow problem. The integer linear programming problem for the KP is defined below [9].

$$Maximize\ z = \sum_{j \in N} p_j x_j \tag{1}$$

$$s.t \quad \sum_{j \in N} w_j x_j \le c \tag{2}$$

$$x_j \in \{0,1\} \quad (j \in N = \{1, 2, ..., n\}) \tag{3}$$

Since the KP is widely applicable problem from cargo loading situation to financial domain, the various algorithms to solve the KP have been studied in many years. One of the best-known algorithms is the branch and bound when the KP is formulated as the integer linear programming problem. In [10], Kolesar, Peter J. proposed a process to approach the optimal value in branch and bound algorithm where three stages are involved; preliminary, selection of a node for next branching, and computation of upper bounds. The algorithm employs the ordering method that is to list the items as the descending order of the ratio p_j / w_j and that is widely used in branch and bound algorithms, but it is slightly different on how to restrict the upper bounds.

2.2   The Optimal Load-Shedding Model Represented by the 0-1 Knapsack Problem

The load-shedding problem in islanded microgrid operation can be a good application of the 0-1 knapsack problem. This is because each customer value and discrete characteristic of the load is needed to be captured in microgrid operation. An optimal load-shedding model represented by the KP is proposed below as the integer linear programming model. The objective is to maximize total values of the subset from each load type of each customer in the available power supply S. The decision variable x_{ij} is the binary value on whether to choose the jth load type of the ith customer (if the jth load type of the ith customer is chosen, $x_{ij} = 1$; if not, $x_{ij} = 0$).

$$Maximize\ z = \sum_{j \in N} v_{ij} x_{ij} \tag{1'}$$

$$s.t \quad \sum_{j \in N} w_{ij} x_{ij} \le S \tag{2'}$$

$$x_{ij} \in \{0,1\} \quad (i \in I = \{1, 2, ..., n\},\ j \in J = \{1, 2, ..., m\}) \tag{3'}$$

I : the set of the customers, $i \in I = \{1, 2, ..., n\}$

J : the set of the load type of each customer I, $j \in J = \{1, 2, ..., m\}$

v_{ij} : the matrix of the values of the jth load type of the ith customer

w_{ij} : the matrix of the amount of the power of the jth load type of the ith customer

S : the total amount of the available power supplied in microgrid.

2.3   How to Estimate the Value

The value v_{ij} of the jth load type of the ith customer is important to model load-shedding problem because the value affects the optimal result. The chosen optimal subset differs depending on diverse assumptions of the value.

For practical approaches to getting the value, the value v_{ij} is assumed based on the environment. In the competitive environment, some customers want to maintain high quality of the power supply even though they have to pay high price and the others focus more on the power price than the quality of the power supply. In contrast, in the cooperative environment, they allocate the power to relatively important loads. The former assumption is reasonable to use bidding prices that are willingness to pay by each customer when the customer buys the power in the power market. The latter assumption is adequate to use identical or standard index when each customer presents his/her value on each load type. The reason to use standard index in the cooperative environment is that the index prevents the important load from exclusion when the bidding price is less competitive although the corresponding load types is important. The smaller the difference in standard index is, the more the importance of the amount of loads is emphasized.

3   The Case Study

To check the results of the proposed load-shedding model in the assumed environment, we have considered two case studies in the competitive environment and in the cooperative environment.

3.1   The Competitive Environment

The each value v_{ij} of the jth load type of the ith customer is assumed to be the bidding price by the customer. We also assume two customers ($n = 2$) and three load types ($m = 3$), thus there are total six load types. The total amount of the available power supply S is set to 30. Table 1 shows specific figures to be used in the optimal load-shedding model in accordance with the descending order of the ratio v_j / w_j.

Table 1. Figures on the value (v_{ij}) using bidding prices and the amount of the load (w_{ij}) according to the descending order of the ratio v_j / w_j.

No.	L_{ij}	v_{ij} ($)	w_{ij} (kWh)	v_{ij} / w_{ij}
1	L_{11}	10	10	1.00
2	L_{21}	8	9	0.89
3	L_{23}	2	3	0.67
4	L_{12}	5	8	0.63
5	L_{13}	3	5	0.60
6	L_{22}	4	10	0.40

The Fig 2 shows the process of searching the optimal solution or the possible feasible solution based on the branch and bound algorithm. As proceeding in sequence according to the listed number, the algorithm decides whether to choose the number corresponding to the load type. After checking the upper bounds associate with all nodes, the optimal subset of the load types is decided. As shown in Fig 2, the optimal subset which is comprised of the L_{11} , L_{21} , L_{23} , L_{12} is in node 12 ($x_{11}, x_{21}, x_{23}, x_{12} = 1$, $x_{13}, x_{22} = 0$). The objective value of the optimal subset is 25 dollars and the sum of the amount of the loads is 30 kWh that is equal to the total amount of the available power supply S.

3.2   The Cooperative Environment

Most of the data used in the competitive environment are also applied to the cooperative environment. The main difference is the value v_{ij} of the jth load type of the ith customer from the standard index, which makes the corresponding ratio v_j / w_j changed. We assume that there are three values; the biggest value is 3 and moderate vale is 2, and the smallest value is 1. The customer selects one of the three values in order to express a value of a load type. Table 2 shows the figures on the value (v_{ij}) using three standard indexes and the amount of the load (w_{ij}) according to the descending order of the ratio v_j / w_j.

As applying the same branch and bound algorithm in [10], we can get the optimal subset which is comprised of the L_{13} , L_{23} , L_{11} , L_{12} ($x_{13}, x_{23}, x_{11}, x_{12} = 1$, $x_{21}, x_{22} = 0$). The objective value of the optimal subset is 8 and the sum of the amount of the loads is 26 kWh that is smaller than the total amount of the available power supply S.

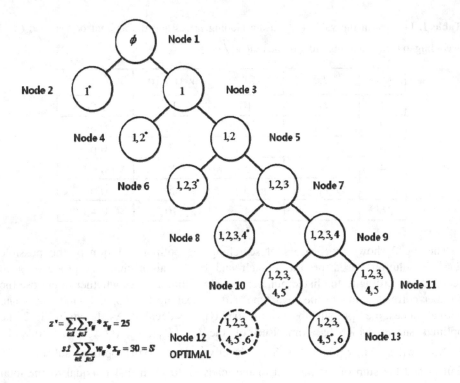

Fig. 2. The process to approach the optimal solution based on the branch and bound algorithm (k* means excluding the number in each node)

Table 2. Figures on the value (v_{ij}) using three standard indexes and the amount of the load (w_{ij}) according to the descending order of the ratio v_j / w_j

No.	L_{ij}	v_{ij}	w_{ij} (kWh)	v_{ij} / w_{ij}
1	L_{13}	2	5	0.40
2	L_{23}	1	3	0.33
3	L_{11}	3	10	0.30
4	L_{12}	2	8	0.25
5	L_{21}	2	9	0.22
6	L_{22}	2	10	0.20

3.3   Discussion

As shown in Table 3, the optimal subset differs depending on the used value v_{ij}. The variation on the value is wider in the competitive than in the cooperative environment, which makes the order of the ratio v_{ij} / w_{ij} differ. If the amount of the load is same, the wider the variation on the value is, the bigger the impact on ordering is. In Table 3, the difference in the optimal subset is L_{13} and L_{21}. The L_{13} that isn't included in the competitive environment is chosen in the cooperative environment. This is because the effect of the value is diminished and the L_{13} has relatively small amount of the load, thus the ratio is comparatively high in the cooperative environment. The L_{21} that is in the optimal subset in the competitive environment is excluded in the cooperative environment. The relatively large value L_{21} in the competitive environment is not useful in the cooperative environment. It is, therefore, essential to apply proper values in branch and bound algorithm.

Table 3. The comparison on the value (v_{ij}) and the amount of the load (w_{ij}), and the ratio v_j / w_j according to the assumed environment

L_{ij}	Competitive environment					Cooperative environment				
	No.	v_{ij}	w_{ij} (kWh)	v_{ij} / w_{ij}	x_{ij}	No.	v_{ij}	w_{ij} (kWh)	v_{ij} / w_{ij}	x_{ij}
L_{11}	1	10	10	1.00	1	3	3	10	0.30	1
L_{12}	4	5	8	0.63	1	4	2	8	0.25	1
L_{13}	5	3	5	0.60	0	1	2	5	0.40	1
L_{21}	2	8	9	0.89	1	5	2	9	0.22	0
L_{22}	6	2	10	0.60	0	6	2	10	0.20	0
L_{23}	3	2	3	0.67	1	2	1	3	0.40	1

4   Conclusion

In this paper, we apply the 0-1 knapsack problem into the load-shedding problem in islanded microgrid operation. The branch and bound algorithm is used to solve the KP. When we formulate the load-shedding problem as the KP, estimating the value of the load type is more subjective than the other parameters. To reasonably estimate the value, there are two possible assumptions; by the bidding price and the standard index. The two assumptions are proper to different environment, which is in competitive and cooperative environment. The case studies are conducted to compare the results in each environment.

Since the KP is widely used problem having discrete variables, there are lots of algorithms in order to solve the KP. Also, the branch and bound algorithm, one of the best-known algorithms for the KP, has diverse approaches to searching the upper bounds and the core subsets. In the future, we will deal with the various branch and bound algorithms to effectively and practically solve the load-shedding problem.

Acknowledgments. This work was supported by the Power Generation & Electricity Delivery of the Korea Institute of Energy Technology Evaluation and Planning(KETEP) grant funded by the Korea government Ministry of Knowledge Economy. (No. 20111020400220).

References

1. Katiraei, F., Iravani, R., Hatziargyriou, N., Dimeas, A.: Microgrids management. IEEE Power and Energy Magazine 6, 54–65 (2008)
2. Xu, D., Girgis, A.A.: Optimal load shedding strategy in power systems with distributed generation. IEEE Power Engineering Society Winter Meeting 2, 788–793 (2001)
3. Ng, K.-H., Sheble, G.B.: Direct load control-A profit-based load management using linear programming. IEEE Transactions on Power Systems 13, 688–694 (1998)
4. Hajdu, L.P., Peschon, J., Tinney, W.F., Piercy, D.S.: Optimum Load-Shedding Policy for Power Systems. IEEE Transactions on Power Apparatus and Systems PAS-87, 784–795 (1968)
5. Halevi, Y., Kottick, D.: Optimization of load shedding system. IEEE Transactions on Energy Conversion 8, 207–213 (1993)
6. Palaniswamy, K.A., Sharma, J., Misra, K.B.: Optimum Load Shedding Taking into Account of Voltage and Frequency Characteristics of Loads. IEEE Power Engineering Review PER-5, 39–39 (1985)
7. Wang, P., Billinton, R.: Optimum load-shedding technique to reduce the total customer interruption cost in a distribution system. IEE Proceedings-Generation, Transmission and Distribution 147, 51–56 (2000)
8. Kim, H.-M., Kinoshita, T., Lim, Y.: Talmudic Approach to Load Shedding of Islanded Microgrid Operation Based on Multiagent System. Journal of Electrical Engineering & Technology 6, 284–292 (2011)
9. Martello, S., Toth, P.: A New Algorithm for the 0-1 Knapsack Problem. Management Science 34, 633–644 (1988)
10. Kolesar, P.J.: A Branch and Bound Algorithm for the Knapsack Problem. Management Science 13, 723–735 (1967)

A Load-Shedding Scheme Using Optimization for Proportional Fairness in the Islanded Microgrid

Yujin Lim[1], Hak-Man Kim[2], Jaesung Park[3], and Tetsuo Kinoshita[4]

[1] Department of Information Media, University of Suwon,
2-2 San, Wau-ri, Bongdam-eup, Hwaseong-si, Gyeonggi-do 445-743, Korea
yujin@suwon.ac.kr
[2] Department of Electrical Engineering, University of Incheon,
12-1 Songdo-dong, Yeonsu-gu, Incheon 406-772, Korea
hmkim@incheon.ac.kr
[3] Department of Internet Information Engineering, University of Suwon,
2-2 San, Wau-ri, Bongdam-eup, Hwaseong-si, Gyeonggi-do 445-743, Korea
jaesungpark@suwon.ac.kr
[4] Department of Computer and Mathematical Sciences,
Graduated School of Information Science, Tohoku University,
Sensai 980-8577, Japan
kino@riec.tohoku.ac.jp

Abstract. In Islanded operation mode of the microgrid, one of solutions to meet the balance between supply and demand of power is load-shedding. The some of conventional schemes employ the game theoretic approach to solve the load-shedding problem. However, the schemes consider the load uses a continuous range of values to present its load demand, and ignore the discrete characteristic of the load demand. Thus, the waste of the power in loads may be happened and the balance of the power may be threaten. In this paper, we define the problem of the conventional schemes and propose the optimization solution for system efficieicy and proportional fairness.

Keywords: Microgrid, islanded microgrid, load-shedding, game theory, proportional fairness.

1 Introduction

Microgrid is a modern, small-scale version of the centralized electricity system [1-4]. It achieves specific local goals, such as reliability, carbon emission reduction, diversification of energy sources, and cost reduction, established by the community being served. Like the bulk power grid, the microgrid generates, distributes, and regulates the flow of electricity to consumers, but do so locally. It can create services at customer sites such as office buildings, industrial parks, and homes. The microgrid operates in grid-connected or in islanded operation mode [5-7]. The balance between supply and demand of the power is one of the most important requirements of the microgrid management. In grid-connected mode, the microgrid exchanges the power

T.-h. Kim et al. (Eds.): CA/CES³ 2011, CCIS 256, pp. 235–241, 2011.
© Springer-Verlag Berlin Heidelberg 2011

to an interconnected grid to meet the balance. On the other hand, in islanded mode, the microgrid should meet the balance by reducing power generation or shedding loads.

Load shedding is defined as the amount of load that must almost be instantly removed from a power system to keep the remaining portion of the system operational. This load reduction is in response to a system disturbance that results in a generation-deficiency condition. The disturbances include faults, loss of generation, system islanding, switching errors, and lightning strikes [8]. When dealing with the load-shedding, several items are taken into account. The most important of them are the definition of a minimum allowable frequency for secure system operation, the amount of load to be shed, the different frequency thresholds, and the number and the size of steps. When the amount of load to be shed for each load is decided, competing and conflicting claims of loads often limit the system performance. In some literatures [9-11], they construct the power system as a game between players. It is useful to re-examine the structure and objectives of the microgrid and to apply game theoretic techniques that capture the interactions and dependent relationships of the system players. It is also advantageous to think about each active component in the power system as an individual with objectives that may be in opposition with other components.

The conventional load-shedding schemes consider the load uses a continuous range of values to present its load demand. However, the load uses discrete values. Thus, if the amount of load to be shed is decided with no consideration of the discrete characteristic, the waste of the power in loads may be happened and the balance of the power may be threaten. In this paper, we define the problem and propose the optimization solution for system efficiency and proportional fairness. This paper is organized as follows. Section 2 defines the problem in the conventional load-shedding schemes. In Section 3 and Section 4, we consider two optimization problems, namely system efficiency optimization and proportional fairness optimization. In addition, we propose the solutions. Finally, conclusion and future work are drawn in Section 5.

2   Problem Definition

We consider a generic system model for load-shedding in islanded operating mode of the microgrid. The system is defined as a pair (L, P), where P is the vector of the amount of power supplied by N power generators and L is the vector of load demands claimed by M loads, i.e., $P=(P_1, P_2, ..., P_N)$ and $L=(L_1, L_2, ..., L_M)$. We assume that a central controller of the microgrid can accurately gather information about the power supplied and the load demands claimed. When $\sum_{m=1}^{M} L_m > \sum_{n=1}^{N} P_n$, the controller initiates load-shedding. As a result of load-shedding, the amount of load to be shed for each load is decided to maximize the fairness and performance in the system. Let S denote the vector of the amount of load to be shed for each load, i.e., $S = (S_1, S_2, ..., S_M)$. Let L^* denote the vector of the amount of available power for each load, i.e., $L^* = (L_1^*, L_2^*, ..., L_M^*)$ that is $L^* = L - S$.

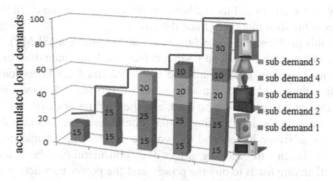

Fig. 1. The discrete characteristic of load demand

Conventional schemes to solve the load-shedding problem focus on the fairness of the rationing, but they overlook the characteristics of load demands. The limitation of the conventional load-shedding schemes is because they consider the load uses a continuous range of values to present its load demand. However, the characteristic is that the load demand increases in discrete, as shown in Fig. 1. In the figure, the load demand of a load (e.g., a residential load) is composed of five sub load demands to turn on home electronics, such as microwave, washing machine, TV, lamp, and fridge. The numbers in the bar chart indicate the amount of power claimed to run each machine, e.g., the washing machine needs the power 25 to run. In the case of the washing machine, the power less than 25 is useless because the machine does not run. The power greater than 25 is wasteful because the extra power to run the machine is also useless. Let L_1 denote the load demand of load 1, i.e., $L_1 = \{15, 25, 20, 10, 30\} = 100$. If the available power of load 1 through the load-shedding, i.e., L_1^* is 50, the load 1 can turn on microwave and washing machine, but the load cannot turn on TV. Besides, a part of the ration, i.e., the power 10 is useless, as shown in Fig. 2.

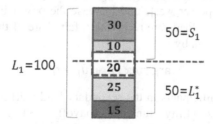

Fig. 2. The relationship between load claimed and load shed

To solve the limitation, we separate the performance optimization from load shedding scheme. That is, once L^* is decided by using conventional load-shedding schemes, regional load market for small-scale power trading is made among loads intending to buy the power or to sell the power. In our example, load 1 wants to buy the power from the other loads as many as a shortage to turn on TV, or it gives up to turn on TV and wants to sell its available power left to other loads. In this case, load 1 participates in the load market to trade the power.

We call this problem *the secondary load market problem* (SLMP). We design the system that is composed of a load trading center and loads intending to participate the secondary load market. First of all, the load concerned sends its load information, such as the amount of load demand, a list of sub load demands with their load priorities, the amount of load to be shed, and the bidding price (it can be selling price or buying price), to the load trading center. Then, the center decides the role of each load, such as seller or buyer, and the volume of business to maximize the system performance. Taking the bidding prices into consideration, the center assigns the power to sell among loads to buy the power, and the power transaction is completed.

3   System Efficiency Optimization Problem

Consider the load demand of a load as a set of K sub load demands, i.e., $L_i = \{l_i^1, l_i^2, \ldots, l_i^K\}$, and $L_i = \sum_{k=1}^{K} l_i^k$. Let l_i^k denote the k-th sub load demand of load i and the set is sorted by load priorities of sub load demands. We assume that the load priority of the sub load demand is given. If L_i^* is between $\sum_{k=1}^{p-1} l_i^k$ and $\sum_{k=1}^{p} l_i^k$ and $p \leq K$, load i can sell parts of its available power, i.e., L_i^s, to other loads and L_i^s is defined by

$$L_i^s \geq L_i^* - \sum_{k=1}^{p-1} l_i^k. \tag{1}$$

Otherwise, load i can buy the power, i.e., L_i^b, from other loads and L_i^b is defined by

$$L_i^b \geq \sum_{k=1}^{p} l_i^k - L_i^*. \tag{2}$$

To achieve system efficiency and fairness, we solve the optimization problem by using the game theory i.e., Nash bargaining solution [12-14]. The system efficiency indicates to reduce the power waste and increase the power utilization at loads. The fairness indicates whether loads are receiving a fair share of the power supplied. The bargaining solution is given by

$$\arg\max \prod_{i \in R}(u_i - t_i), \tag{3}$$

where R is the set of participants in the secondary load market and $R \leq M$. u_i is the individual participant's utility function (payoff) and t_i is the participant's disagreement payoff. We identify the relationship between load demand and benefit is that the load demand with higher priority is satisfied, the larger benefit the participant can get. With the relationship, the utility function u_i is defined by

$$1 - \alpha_i \cdot \log \left(\frac{L_i}{\sum_{k=1}^{K'} l_i^k}\right), \tag{4}$$

Where K' is number of sub load demands composing L_i^*, $K' \leq K$ and α_i is the sensitivity to the load priority of load i. The system efficiency optimization problem can be rewritten as

$$\arg max \prod_{i \in R}(u_i(\Gamma_i^{K'}) - \hat{L}_i^*), \tag{5}$$

where

$$u_i\left(\Gamma_i^{K'} = \sum_{k=1}^{K'} l_i^k\right) = 1 - \alpha_i \cdot \log\left(\frac{L_i}{\Gamma_i^{K'}}\right) \tag{6}$$

subject to

$$\sum_{k=1}^{K'} l_i^k \leq L_i \text{ and } \sum_{k=1}^{K'} l_i^k \geq \hat{L}_i^*. \tag{7}$$

$\hat{L}_i^*$ is the minimum requirement of the power allocated to load i and $\hat{L}_i^* \leq L_i$. For example, $\hat{L}_i^*$ is the sum of sub load demands with the highest priority. Given $\Gamma_i^{K'}$ from (5), if $\Gamma_i^{K'} > L_i^*$, then load i buys the power from other loads as many as $L_i^b = \Gamma_i^{K'} - L_i^*$. Otherwise, load i sells its available power to other loads as many as $L_i^s = L_i^* - \Gamma_i^{K'}$. Once the role of each participant and the volume of business are decided, the optimization problem to fairly divide the trading power is formulated in the following subsection.

4   Proportional Fairness Optimization

The power allocation is determined according to a proportional fairness criterion applied to the allocation per unit charge. It is shown that the system optimum is achieved when loads' choices of bidding prices and system's choice of allocations are in equilibrium. Suppose that if x_i is the power to be allocated to load i ($i \in R$) in the secondary load market, then this has utility $U_i(x_i)$ to the load. Assume that the utility is an increasing and strictly concave over the range $x_i \geq 0$. Under this model, the optimization problem is given by

$$max \sum_{i \in R} U_i(x_i). \tag{9}$$

Suppose that load i choose a bidding price to buy the power, w_i, and receives in return the amount of the power x_i proportional to w_i, say $x_i = \frac{w_i}{\lambda_i}$ where λ_i is regarded as a bidding price in unit to sell the power. Then the maximization problem for load i is as follows.

$$max \sum_{i \in R} U_i\left(\frac{w_i}{\lambda_i}\right) - w_i, w_i \geq 0 \tag{10}$$

Using the function $\frac{1}{w_i} \log x_i$, (9) is rewritten as

$$max \sum_{i \in R} \frac{1}{w_i} \log x_i \tag{11}$$

subject to

$$x_i = \sum_{k=1}^{K'} l_i^k \geq 0, C = \sum_{i \in R} L_i^b \geq \sum_{i \in R} x_i. \tag{12}$$

A vector of allocations $x = (x_i, i \in R)$ is proportionally fair if it is feasible, that is $x_i \geq 0$ and $C \geq \sum_{i \in R} x_i$, and if for any other feasible vector x^*, the aggregate of proportional changes is zero or negative:

$$\sum_{i \in R} \frac{x_i^* - x_i}{x_i} \leq 0. \tag{13}$$

Under the decomposition of (9) into the problems (10) and (11), the utility function $U_i(x_i)$ is not required by the system, and only appears in the optimization problem faced by load i. The Lagrangian for the problem is

$$L(x, z; \mu) = \sum_{i \in R} \frac{1}{w_i} \log x_i + \mu(C - \sum_{i \in R} x_i - z) \tag{14}$$

where $z \geq 0$ is a slack variable and μ is a Lagrange multiplier [15-17]. Then

$$\frac{\partial L}{\partial x_i} = \frac{1}{w_i \cdot x_i} - \mu, \tag{15}$$

and the unique optimum to the primal problem is given by

$$x_i = \frac{1}{w_i \cdot \mu}. \tag{16}$$

We solve $\mu(C - \sum_{i \in R} x_i) = 0$ and (16) and get the following as the optimal for the problem.

$$x_i = \frac{1}{w_i \cdot \sum_{i \in R} \frac{1}{w_i}} \tag{17}$$

5   Conclusions

The conventional load-shedding schemes overlook the discrete characteristic of load demands. Thus the waste of the power in loads may be happened and the balance of the power may be threatened. In this paper, we define the problem of the conventional schemes and propose the optimization solution for system efficiency and proportional fairness. Through the system efficiency optimization, the load intending to join the secondary load market decides to its role and the volume of business. Then, through the fairness optimization, the amount of power allocated of the load is fairly decided proportional to its bidding price.

References

1. Hatziargyriou, N., Asano, H., Iravani, R., Marnay, C.: Microgrids. IEEE Power Energy 5(4), 78–94 (2007)
2. Pogaku, N., Prodanovic, M., Green, T.C.: Modeling, Analysis and Testing of Autonomous Operation of an Inverter-based Microgrid. IEEE Trans. Power Electronics 22(2), 613–625 (2007)

3. Carrasco, J.M., Franquelo, L.G., Bialasiewiez, J.T., Galvan, E., Guisado, R.C.P., Prats, M.A.M., Leon, J.I., Moreno-Alfonso, N.: Power-electronic Systems for the Grid Integration of Renewable Energy Sources: A Survey. IEEE Trans. Power Electronics 53(4), 1002–1016 (2006)
4. Hatziargyriou, N.D.: Microgrids. IEEE Power Energy 6(3), 26–29 (2008)
5. Tsikalakis, A., Hatzargyriou, N.: Centralized Control for Optimizing Microgrids Operation. IEEE Trans. Energy Conversion 23(1), 241–248 (2008)
6. Kim, J.-Y., Jeon, J.-H., Kim, S.-K., Cho, C., Park, J.H., Kim, H.-M., Nam, K.-Y.: Cooperative Control Strategy of Energy Storage System and Microsources for Stabilizing the Microgrid during Islanded Operation. IEEE Trans. Power Electronics 25(12), 3037–3048 (2010)
7. Kim, H.-M., Kinoshita, T., Shin, M.C.: A Multiagent System for Autonomous Operation of Islanded Microgrids Based on a Power Market Environment. MDPI Energies 3(12), 1972–1990 (2010)
8. Shokooh, F., Dai, J.J., Shokooh, S., Tastet, J., Castro, H., Khandelwal, T., Donner, G.: Intelligent Load Shedding. IEEE Industry Applications Magazine 17(2), 44–53 (2011)
9. Weaver, W.W., Krein, P.T.: Game-Theoretic Control of Small-Scale Power Systems. IEEE Trans. Power Delivery 24(3), 1560–1567 (2009)
10. Kim, H.-M., Kinoshita, T., Lim, Y.: Talmudic Approach to Load-shedding of Islanded Microgrid Operation based on Multiagent System. KIEE Journal of Electrical Engineering & Technology (JEET) 6(2), 284–292 (2011)
11. Kim, H.-M., Kinoshita, T., Lim, Y., Kim, T.-H.: A Bankruptcy Problem Approach to Load-shedding in Multiagent-based Microgrid Operation. MDPI Sensors 10(10), 8888–8898 (2010)
12. Basar, T., Olsder, G.J.: Dynamic Noncooperative Game Theory, 2nd edn. Society for Industrial and Applied Mathematics, Philadelphia (1999)
13. Isaacs, R.: Differential Games: A Mathematical Theory with Applicationsto Warfare and Pursuit, Control and Optimization, 1st edn. Wiley, New York (1965)
14. Owen, G.: Game Theory, 3rd edn. Academic, New York (2001)
15. Kelly, F.P., Maulloo, A.K., Tan, D.K.H.: Rate Control for Communication Networks: Shadow Prices, Proportional Fairness and Stability. Journal of the Operational Research Society 49(3), 237–252 (1998)
16. Besada, M., Miras, M.: A Note on Lagrange Multipliers in the Multiple Constraint Case. Elsevier Economics Letters 75(1), 141–145 (2002)
17. Radunovic, B., Le Boudec, J.Y.: Rate Performance Objectives of Multihop Wireless Networks. IEEE Trans. Mobile Computing 3(4), 334–349 (2004)

Modeling and Analysis of Jeju Power System
with HVDC Using PSCAD/EMTDC

Hyun-Jae Yoo[1], Myong-Chul Shin[1], and Hak-Man Kim[2,*]

[1] Dept. of Electrical and Computer Engineering,
Univ. of Sungkyunkwan, Korea
{Yoohyunjae,mcshin}@skku.edu
[2] Dept. of Electrical Engineering,
Univ. of Incheon, Incheon, Korea
hmkim@incheon.ac.kr

Abstract. Recently, emerging power systems such as as wind farm, superconducting devices, smart grid, and microgrid have been challanged in Jeju Island, Korea. Modelling using Power System Computer Aided Design (PSCAD)/Electro-Magnetic Transient Design and Control (EMTDC) is suitable for detailed analysis of Jeju power system with the emerging technologies in detail. Especially, Jeju power system is interconnected with Korean main power system by High-voltage direct current (HVDC) transmission system to receive short power. In this paper, modelling of Jeju power system using PSCAD/EMTDC is described and generation system models and HVDC model are included. In addition, basic analysis studies are performed to evaluate the feasiblility of the model.

Keywords: Jeju power system, PSCAD/EMTDC modeling, HVDC model.

1 Introduction

Recently, emerging power technologies such as wind farm, superconducting devices, smart grid, and microgrid has been developing and testing in Jeju Island, Korea. Figure 1 shows the configuration of Jeju power system, which is interconnected with Korean main power system using a High-voltage direct current (HVDC) transmission system to receive short power from Korean main power system as shown in Fig. 1. Table 1 shows the detailed data of Jeju power system. Modelling using Power System Computer Aided Design (PSCAD)/Electro-Magnetic Transient Design and Control (EMTDC) is suitable for detailed analysis of Jeju power system with the emerging technologies in detail.

PSCAD/EMTDC models of Jeju power system, which have been developed in order to analyze emerging power system in Jeju Island in the near future, are presented in this paper. In order to evaluate feasibility of the models, dynamic behaviors of Jeju power system against disturbances are tested.

---

[*] Corresponding author.

T.-h. Kim et al. (Eds.): CA/CES³ 2011, CCIS 256, pp. 242–251, 2011.
© Springer-Verlag Berlin Heidelberg 2011

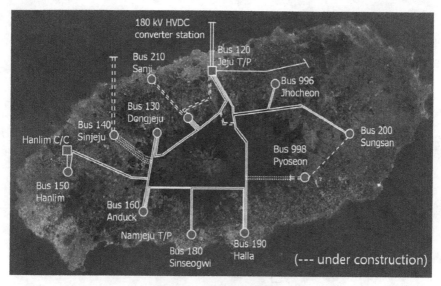

Fig. 1. Jeju power system

Table 1. Generator Control System of Jeju Power System

Power Plant	Generator	Type	Exciter	Governor
Jeju thermal power plants	Jeju GT #1	GENROU	IEEEX2	
	Jeju GT #2	GENROU	IEEEX2	
	Jeju T/P #2	GENROU	EXAC2	IEEEG1
	Jeju T/P #3	GENROU	EXAC2	IEEEG1
	Jeju DP #1	GENSAL	EXPIC1	DEGOV
	Jeju DP #2	GENSAL	EXPIC1	DEGOV
Hanlim combined cycle power plants	Hanlim GT #1	GENROU	EXPIC1	GAST2A
	Hanlim GT #2	GENROU	EXPIC1	GAST2A
	Hanlim ST #1	GENROU	EXPIC1	TGOV1
Namjeju thermal power plants	Namjeju TP #3	GENROU	EXST1	IEEEG1
	Namjeju TP #4	GENROU	EXST1	IEEEG1

2   Modeling Jeju Power System Using PSCAD/EMTDC

Figures 2 and 3 show developed exciter and governor models of Jeju power system using PSCAD/EMTDC, respectively.

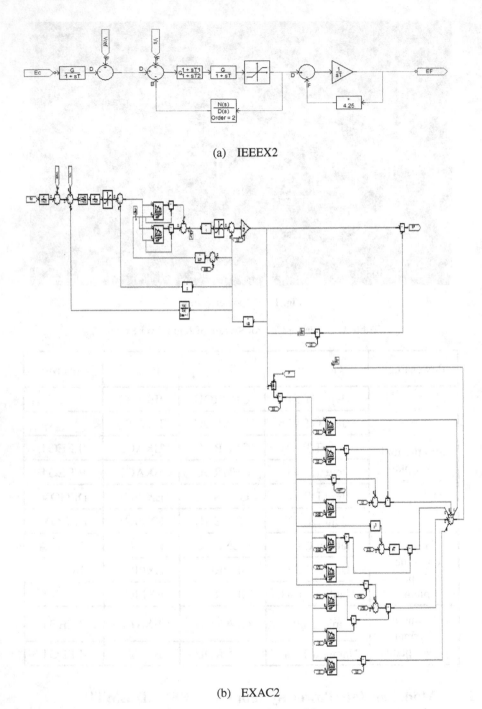

(a) IEEEX2

(b) EXAC2

Fig. 2. Developed exciter models

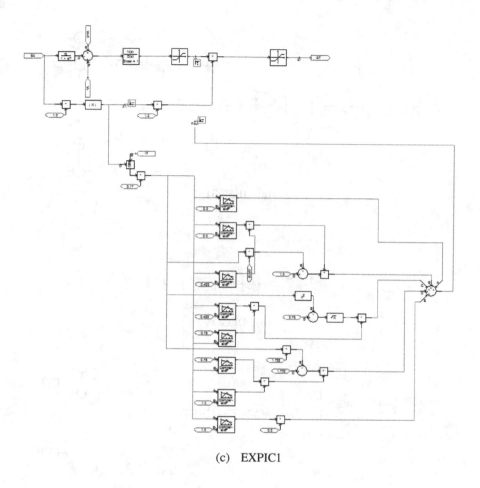

(c) EXPIC1

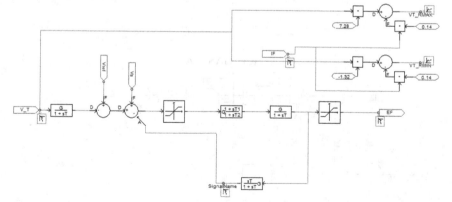

(d) EXST1

Fig. 2. (*Continued*).

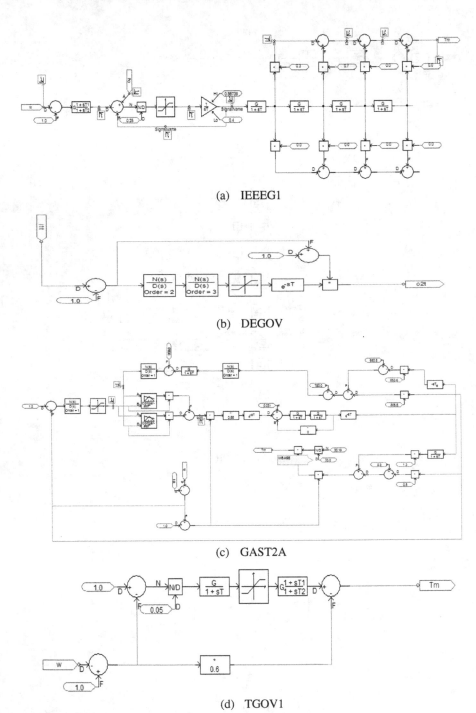

(a) IEEEG1

(b) DEGOV

(c) GAST2A

(d) TGOV1

Fig. 3. Developed governor models

Figures 4 and 5 show developed PSCAD/EMTDC models of the HVDC transmission system and the entail PSCAD/EMTDC model of Jeju power system, respectively.

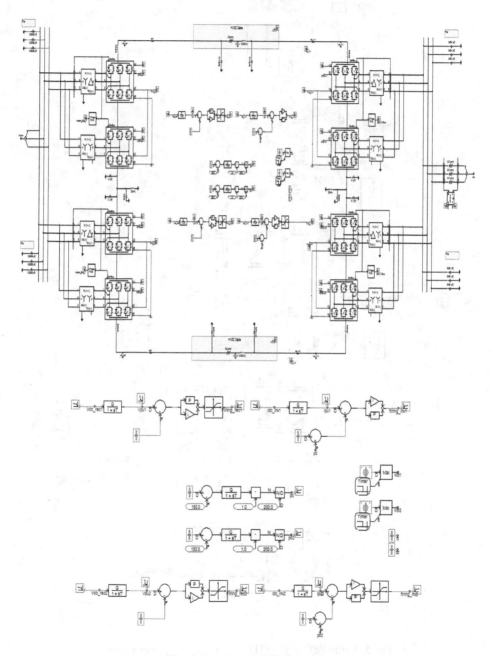

Fig. 4. Developed HVDC model

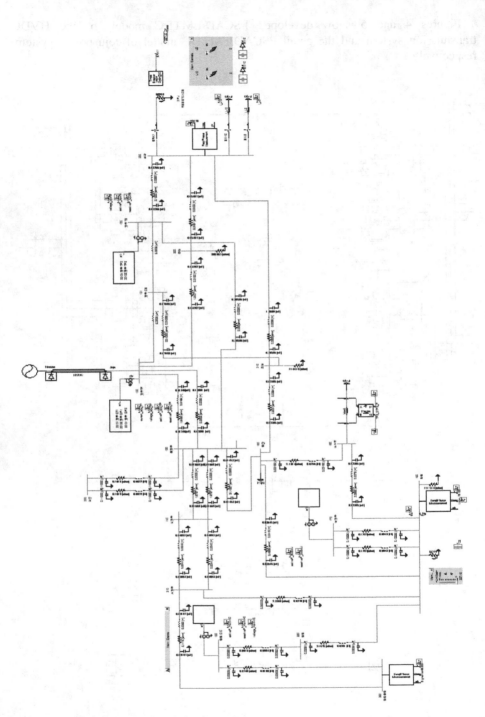

Fig. 5. Entire PSCAD/EMTDC model of Jeju power system

3   Simulation

In simulation, two cases are tested as follows:

a) Case 1: increasing load (10 MW) at bus 200 (Sungsan) at 5 sec.
b) Case 2: decreasing HVDC power from 150 MW to 145 MW at 5 sec.

3.1   Case 1

Figure 6 shows system frequency of Jeju power system by scenario of case 1. By sudden load decrease, frequency showed oscillation after 5 sec and then frequency recovered by load following of generators. Figure 7 shows real and reactive power flow in power line according to load following of generators.

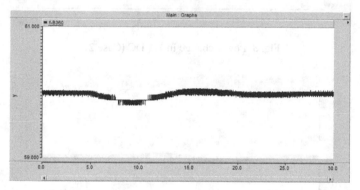

Fig. 6. System frequency of Jeju power system (Case 1)

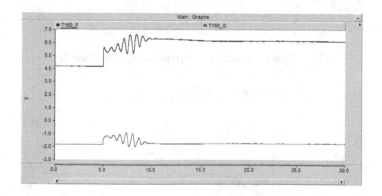

Fig. 7. Line power flow (Case 1)

3.2   Case 2

Figure 8 shows HVDC power by scenario of case 2. It is shown that HVDC power decreases from 150 MW to 145 MW at 5 sec according to the scenario. Fig. 9 shows the frequency of Jeju Island according to the change. It is shown that the frequency is recovered by load following of generators of Jeju Island. Fig. 10 shows increased output of generator TP#3.

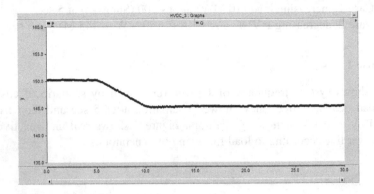

Fig. 8. Power change in HVDC (Case 2)

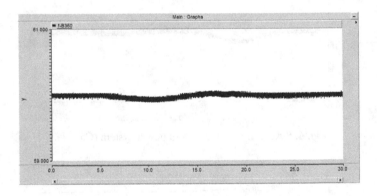

Fig. 9. System frequency of Jeju power system (Case 2)

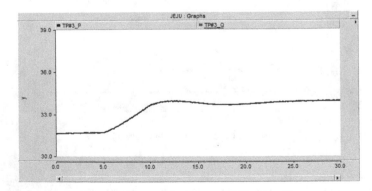

Fig. 10. Output of generator TP#3 (Case 2)

4   Conclusion

In this paper, the PSCAD/EMTDC models of Jeju power system have been introduced. PSCAD/EMTDC models of HVDC and its controller as well as exciters and governors have been developed to perform detailed transient and dynamic studies of Jeju power system with emerging systems in the near future. In order to evaluate the feasibility of the models, simulation tests have been performed. As a result, the dynamic behavior has been shown reasonably.

As future works, PSCAD/EMTDC models of wind farms will be developed. In addition, the effective control scheme for frequency control using HVDC against unstable output of wind farms will be studied.

References

1. Kunder, P.: Power System Stability and Control. McGraw-Hill (1994)
2. Kim, C.-K., Sood, V.K., Jang, G.-S., Lim, S.-J., Lee, S.-J.: HVDC Transmission. Wiley (2009)
3. User's Guide of PSCAD/EMTDC, Manitoba HVDC Research Center (2002)
4. Watson, N., Arrillaga, J.: Power Systems Electromagnetic Transients Simulation, The Institute of Electrical Engineers (2003)
5. Moon, S.-I., Park, J.-W., Pyo, G.-C.: Experience and Prospect of Wind Power Generation in Korea: Jeju Island Case. In: Proceedings of PES 2009 IEEE, Calgary, pp. 1–6 (July 2009)

Controller-Hardware-In-The Loop Simulation Based Analysis of Photovoltaic Power Generation System under Variable Conditions of Utility

Chulsang Hwang[1], Jin-Hong Jeon[2], Heung-Kwan Choi[2],
Jong-bo Ahn[2], Minwon Park[1], and In-Keun Yu[1]

[1] Dept. of Electrical Engineering, Univ. of Changwon, Korea
yuik@changwon.ac.kr
[2] Korea Electrotechnology Research Institute, Chang-won, Korea
jhjeon@keri.re.kr

Abstract. This paper presents a controller-hardware-in-the loop simulation (CHILS) based test system as a controller for testing phtovotaic (PV) power generation system. The analysis of grid-connected PV power generation system to observe the phenomenon and confirm the stability on the PV power generation system under the variable conditions occured in utility was performed. The utility is stable in the steady state but the utility condition can be changed by unexpected phenomenon. The effect of grid condition should be analyzed to make sure the stability of the grid-connected PV power generation system. The PV power generation system is connected to a utility grid through a inverter and several conditions of grid are modeled by using RTDS. A RTDS is employed to calculate the variable conditions of grid. The voltage source inverter (VSI) is controlled by a digital signal processor connected between gigabit transceiver analogue output card and a gigabit transceiver digital input card in the RTDS interface boards. Experiment results are presented and analyzed to show the effect of a variable conditions to the PV system.

Keywords: controller-hardware-in-the loop simulation, digital signal processor, photovoltaic power generation system, real time digital simulator.

1 Introduction

Environmental concerns about global warming, fossil fuel exhaustion and the need to reduce carbon dioxide emissions provide the stimulus to seek renewable energy sources. Specifically, solar energy has the advantages of no pollution, low maintenance cost, no installation area limitation and no noise due to the absence of the moving parts. However, high initial capital cost and low energy conversion efficiency have deterred its popularity. Therefore, it is important to reduce the installation cost and to increase the energy conversion efficiency of photovoltaic (PV) arrays and the power conversion efficiency of PV systems [1]. To improve the reliability and efficiency of operation of PV power generation system, it is necessary to analyze the effect of the PV power generation system when various grid conditions occur. In order to analyze the behavior of PV power generation system, the software-based simulation has been a

T.-h. Kim et al. (Eds.): CA/CES[3] 2011, CCIS 256, pp. 252–260, 2011.

general way because of the high expense of installation of system and the risk of real various grid conditions. However, the simulation result can not predict the actual controller performance. With CHILS, actual controller used in the real hardware system can be tested its operation with a simulation based PV power system [3]. The CHILS has been proposed to validate the controller performance under various conditions of utility grid before field test. In order to control the PV power generation system, a voltage source inverter (VSC) is used. For CHILS, a PV array, construction of VSI, connected utility grid and various grid conditions are modeled in a real time digital simulator (RTDS), a controller of VSI is designed in a digital signal processor (DSP). The DSP is connected to the RTDS through interface boards. The controller in DSP communicates with RTDS to operate the PV power generation. The simulation results show the impacts of a various conditions of utility grid such as over and under voltages, frequency fluctuations and so on.

2   PV Power Generation System

The PV power generation system typical diagram is shown in Fig. 1 Each component of the system is described in the following. The PV power generation system consists of a PV array, a diode, a DC-link capacitor, a VSI, a step up the VSI voltage to the nominal value of the utility grid and providing electrical isolation between the PV system and electric network. DC power generated from the solar array charges the DC-link capacitor. The grid connection inverter turns the dc into ac power, which has a sinusoidal voltage with the same frequency as the utility grid. The diode blocks the

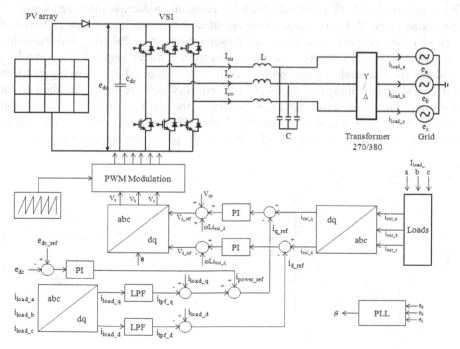

Fig. 1. Diagram of the PV power generation system

reverse current flow through the PV array. The transformer steps up the VSI voltage to the nominal value of the utility grid and providing electrical isolation between the PV system and electric network. Fig. 2 depicts all of system such as RTDS, DSP, display board and MC.

(a) RTDS   (b) DSP from HEX power   (c) Display board & MC

Fig. 2. Configurations of the hardware system

2.1   Voltage Source Inverter (VSI)

Fig. 3 presents the electrical configuration of the VSI for grid connection in RTDS/RSCAD. The circuit model includes a reverse current blocking diode, a DC-link capacitor, six IGBT switched VSI, a LC harmonic reduction filter, and a step-up transformer. The VSI supervises measurement and computation of data collected at sensors, power conversion of dc into ac, power regulation of PV array and protection from electric network faults. The power controller, as an upper level controller, regulates the real and reactive power of the grid-connected PV power generation system and returns its q and d-axis current orders, which are input s to the current controller. The lower level controller generates the desired values of Vq_ref and Vd_ref, the q and d-axis components of the VSI terminal voltage. The PWM generator creates the gating signals of IGBT1-6, the protection controller monitors the

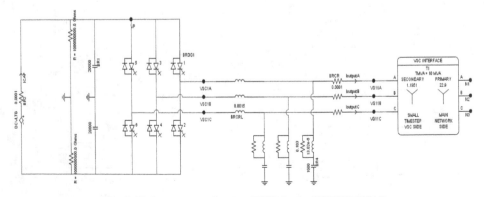

Fig. 3. Voltage source inverter (VSI) in the RTDS/RSCAD

terminal current of the VSI, the grid voltage and grid frequency determine the grid various conditions and grid tripping or closing signals to the MC switches.

2.2   Controller-Hardware-In-The Loop Simulation Test System

Fig. 4 shows a configuration of CHILS. The RTDS is a fully digital electromagnetic transient power system simulator capable of continuous, sustained real time operation [4]. That is, it can solve the power system equations fast enough to continuously produce output conditions that realistically represent conditions in the real network. The RTDS has been widely accepted as an ideal tool for the design, development and testing of power system protection and control schemes. Fig. 4 is a configuration of a controller-hardware-in-the loop simulation (CHILS) system for a real-time simulation. The CHILS system consists of the PV power generation system model realized by RTDS, real hardware based controller and communication emulator. The PV power generation system model, including PV array, the VSI, a transformer and utility grid is represented by RSCD software and plays a real time simulation. For the simulation, needed interface cards of the RTDS system are a GTIO card for a communication. The DSP receives a synchronization signal from a GTAO card in RTDS. After the control of VSI, DSP will send the PWM signals to a GTDI card in RTDS. The GTAO card and the GTDI card interfaced between the RTDS, magnetic contact switch and the DSP board.

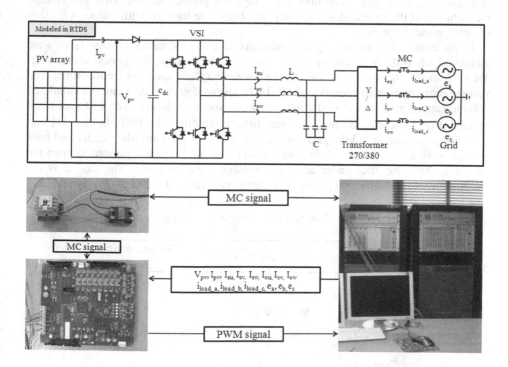

Fig. 4. Configuration of the CHILS

Table 1. Control parameters of the VSI

Signal	Propose	Signal	Propose
V_{pv}	MPPT	I_{su}	Control
I_{pv}	MPPT	I_{sv}	Control
e_a	PLL	V_{dc}	Control
e_b	PLL	MC	Switch ON/OFF

2.3   Digital Signal Processor

The voltage and current signals of the PV power generation system from RTDS are sent to an analog to digital converter of the DSP through GTAO card. The DSP generates proper PWM signals to control 6 switching devices of the VSI of the PV power generation system in the RTDS. The generated PWM signals are sent to the RTDS through GTDI card.

3   Simulation and the Results

In this simulation, the operation of protective control of grid connected three phase inverter for PV power generation system was tested with the transient grid condition when the grid voltage, frequency, and phase angle were suddenly changed. The simulated transient grid conditions were the fault protection time with the voltage magnitude and the over/under frequency, the fault ride through with sudden variation of voltage and frequency.

In the case 1, the transient grid conditions of over and under voltage level were simulated when the VSI was operated with its rated voltage, frequency, and power. Table 2 shows the each case of voltage level and their fault protection time. The voltage range of normal operation is 88~110% of rated grid voltage and the simulated voltage ranges of transient grid condition were under 88% and over 110% of rated voltage. Fig. 5 presents the results of real time simulation with DSP. In case 1-1 and 1-4, the MC disconnected the grid connection of VSI in 0.16 sec when under and over voltage were detected by DSP. In case 1-2 and 1-3, the MC was operated to open the circuit in 2.00 sec after under and over voltage were occurred. The case 2 is the simulation of operation range of VSI with variation of voltage magnitude and

Table 2. Case 1: Simulated fault protection time with the range of under/over voltage

Voltage (%)	Voltage (%)	Protection time (sec)
Case 1-1	$V < 50$	0.16
Case 1-2	$50 \leq V \leq 80$	2.00
Case 1-3	$110 \leq V \leq 120$	2.00
Case 1-4	$V \geq 120$	0.16

Table 3. Case 2: Simulated transient grid conditions with the variation of voltage magnitude and frequency

Case	Voltage (%) Frequency (Hz)	Voltage (V) Frequency (Hz)
Case 3-1	+8%	237.6
Case 3-2	-10%	198
Case 3-3	> 60.45	> 60.45
Case 3-4	< 59.35	< 59.35

Table 4. Case 3: Simulated fault protection time with the range of under/over frequency

Case	Frequency (Hz)	Protection time (sec)
Case 2-1	f > 60.5	0.16
Case 2-2	f<59.3	0.16

Table 5. Case 4: Changed grid voltage level conditions

Case	Change time (sec)	Voltage (V)
Case 4-1	10	238 → 220 → 238
Case 4-2	10	220 → 198 → 220

Table 6. Case 5: Changed phase angle of grid voltage

Case	Phase (°)	Voltage (V)
Case 5-1	0° → +10°	0° After 10s
Case 5-2	0° → -10°	0° After 10s
Case 5-3	0° → +120°	0° After 10s

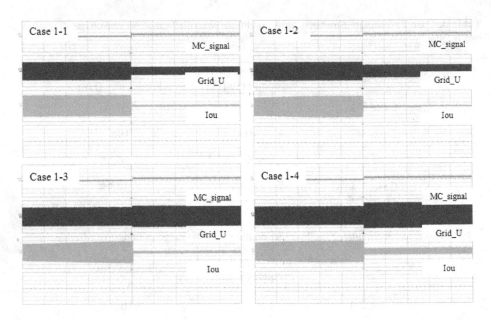

Fig. 5. Case 1: Simulation results of the MC operation with the range of under/over voltage

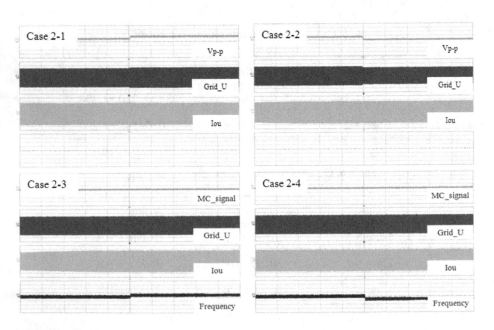

Fig. 6. Case 2: Simulation results of the MC operation with the range of under/over frequency and voltage

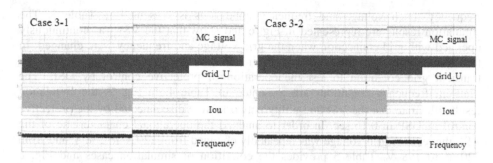

Fig. 7. Case 3: Simulation results of the MC operation with the range of under/over frequency

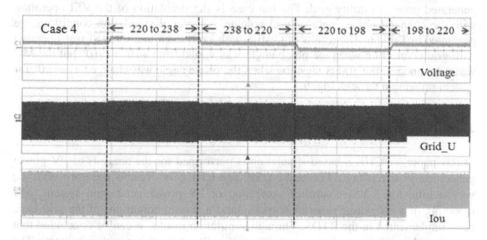

Fig. 8. Case 4 : Simulation results of the VSI operation with the changed grid voltage level

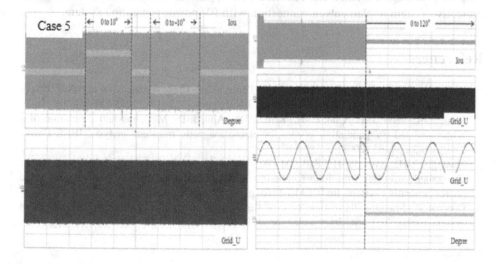

Fig. 9. Case 5: Simulation results of the VSI operation with the changed phase angle of grid voltage

frequency. Each voltage and frequency conditions is presented in Table 3. The simulation results are represented in Fig. 6 and show that the VSI was continuously operated with grid connection when the grid voltage and frequency were changed. In the simulation case 3, the ranges of under and over frequency were applied as the transient grid condition to test the operation of protective control by DSP. The transient frequency conditions are presented in Table 4. In Fig. 7, the simulation results illustrate that the VSI and utility network were disconnected by the protective control of DSP in 0.16 sec. In order to analyze the operational characteristic of the VSI, the level of grid voltage was repeatedly changed from 220 V to 238 V and from 220 V to 198 V. Table 5 provides the condition of simulation cases and Fig. 8 displays the simulation result of case 4. Even the voltage level was fluctuated from 198 V to 238 V, the MC was not disconnected and the VSI was transmitting the generated power to utility grid. The last case is the simulation of the VSI operation with the changed phase angle of grid voltage. The detail simulation conditions are presented in Table 6. The results of CHILS with DSP show that the VSI was operated with grid connection when the phase angle was varied from +10° to -10° but the MC was disconnected the grid connection when the phase angle was changed to +120° for system protection through Fig. 9.

4   Conclusions

In this paper, an CHILS based simulation is performed for the analysis of PV power generation system using RTDS and a DSP. The CHILS test results were proved to be very helpful for a VSI controlled protection of PV power generation system. The modeling of a PV power generation system and a several conditions of the grid have been implemented in the RTDS. Through simulation results, it can be concluded that the several conditions of the grid affect the PV power generation system. The proposed simulation method can effectively be applied to evaluate output control and protective system implements in connection with PV power generation system.

References

1. Kwon, J.-M., Kwon, B.-H., Nam, K.-H.: Three-phase Photovoltaic System With Three-Level Boosting MPPT Control. IEEE Power Electronics 23, 2319–2327 (2008)
2. Kim, S.-K., Jeon, J.-H., Cho, C.-H., Kim, E.-S., Ahn, J.-B.: Modeling and simulation of a grid-connected PV generation system for electromagnetic transient analysis. IEEE Power Energy 6(3), 54–65 (2008)
3. Hwang, C.-H., Kim, G.-H., Park, M.-W., Yu, I.-K., Park, J.-D., Yi, D.-Y., Lee, S.-J.: Controller-hardware-in-the loop simulation based transient analysis of PMSG type wind power generation system. In: ICEMS 2010, p. 69 (December 2010)
4. Forsyth, P., Maguire, T., Kuffel, R.: Real-time digital simulation for control and protection system testing. In: PESC 2004, vol. 1, pp. 329–335 (June 2004)

Dynamic Battery Modeling for Microgrid Operation

Gyeong-Hun Kim[1], Jin-Hong Jeon[2], Jong-Yul Kim[2],
Jong-Bo Ahn[2], Minwon Park[1], and In-Keun Yu[1]

[1] Dept. of Electrical Engineering,
Univ. of Changwon, Korea
[2] Dept. of Renewable Energy System,
Korea Electrotechnology Research Institute, Korea
jhjeon@keri.re.kr

Abstract. Operating shceme of a battery enenrgy storage system (BESS) is important for reliability and stability of a microgrid. The state of a battery has to be considred for operating scheme decision of the BESS because dynamic performance of the battery depends on state of charge (SOC), electrolyte temeperature, ambient temperature. In this paper, a lead-acid battery is modeled in PSCAD/EMTDC, and operating scheme of BESS is disscuessed. The parameter of battery is identified by using experimental data. The battery model can effectively be employed to model the microgrid for the operation shceme decision.

Keywords: dynamic battery model, microgrid, microgrid operation.

1 Introduction

A microgrid is a small-scale power system composed of renewable energy like as photovoltaic and wind power, diesel generator, energy storage system, and so on. A battery such as lithium-ion battery and lead-acid battery, electric double layer capacitor (EDLC), superconducting magnetic energy storage (SMES), flywheel, and fuel cell is used for energy storage system. Batteries are one of the most cost-effective energy storage devices available with energy stored electrochemically. The lead-acid battery energy storage system (BESS) is widely used because the lead-acid battery has low expense, long life span, durability, and the commercial availability of the technology.

There are many types of battery models such as simple battery model, modified model, Thevenin battery model, resistive Thevenin battery model, dynamic battery model, and so on [1]. The dynamic battery model is useful to considering for operating scheme decision of the BESS for microgrid. Because the battery voltage under SOC, depth of charge (DOC) is important for operating scheme decision of the BESS.

In this paper, the 250Ah dynamic battery which is composed of 12 V batteries (36 series) is modeled in PSCAD/EMTDC. The parameters of modeled battery are estimated real experimental result. The battery model can effectively be employed to model the microgrid for the operation shceme decision.

T.-h. Kim et al. (Eds.): CA/CES³ 2011, CCIS 256, pp. 261–266, 2011.
© Springer-Verlag Berlin Heidelberg 2011

2   Dynamic Model of Battery

A dynamic model of lead-acid battery is represented by an equivalent electric network as shown in Fig. 1 [2]. The dynamic battery model is considered a real interaction with ambient temperature, electrolyte temperature, battery voltage and current. The dynamic battery model consists of several resistance-capacitance (R-C) blocks, series resistance, and parasitic reaction branch.

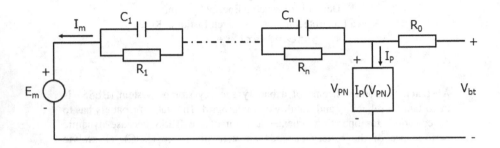

Fig. 1. Dynamic model of lead-acid battery

The internal voltage of battery cell (E_m) is function of SOC and electrolyte temperature. The resistance of R-C blocks ($R_1 \sim R_n$) is related with recovery voltage after charge and discharge. The capacitance ($C_1 \sim C_n$) is involved in the recovery time of voltage. The current of parasitic reaction branch is very small under most condition, except during charge at high SOC [3].

The SOC and DOC are given by

$$SOC = 1 - \frac{Q_e}{C(0,\theta)} \tag{1}$$

$$DOC = 1 - \frac{Q_e}{C(I_{avg},\theta)} \tag{2}$$

where Q_e is the extracted charge, $C(I, \theta)$ is the battery capacity. Q_e and $C(I, \theta)$ can be calculated as follows

$$Q_e(t) = \int_0^t -I_m(\tau)d\tau \tag{3}$$

$$C(I,\theta) = \frac{K_c C_0^* \left(1 + \dfrac{\theta}{-\theta_f}\right)^{\varepsilon}}{1 + (K_c - 1)\left(\dfrac{I}{I^*}\right)^{\delta}} \tag{4}$$

where $C_0{}^*$ is the no-load capacity at 0°C in Amp-seconds, θ_f is the electrolyte freezing temperature (-40°C), I^* is the nominal battery current, and K_c, ε, δ is a constant of a battery.

The internal voltage of battery cell (E_m) can be obtained through

$$E_m = E_{m0} - K_E(273 + \theta)(1 - SOC) \tag{5}$$

where E_{m0} is open circuit voltage under full-charge state, K_E is constant.

The terminal resistance (R_0) is function of SOC, and it is calculated by following equation.

$$R_0 = R_{00}(1 + A_0(1 - SOC)) \tag{6}$$

where R_{00} is the terminal resistance when the battery is fully charged, and A_0 is constant.

The resistance of R-C block is related with DOC, and R_1 is can be calculated as follow.

$$R_1 = -R_{10} \ln(DOC) \tag{7}$$

where R_{10} is constant.

The recovery time constant (τ_n) is decided by the capacitance in R-C block, C_n is obtained through

$$C_n = \frac{\tau_n}{R_n} \tag{8}$$

The current of parasitic reaction branch can be defined by function, related with electrolyte temperature and the branch voltage (V_{PN}), and it is given by

$$I_P = V_{PN} G_{P0} \exp\left[\frac{\left(V_{PN} / (\tau_p s + 1)\right)}{V_{p0}} + A_p\left(1 - \frac{\theta}{\theta_f}\right) \right] \tag{9}$$

where G_{p0}, τ_p, A_p is constant.

3   Parameters of Battery Identification

The battery stack which is composed of 12 V, 250 Ah batteries (36 series) is tested for identifying its parameters. The parameter is estimated by using the test results and datasheet of the battery.

The battery stack under fully charged condition is discharged during an hour, and the average discharge current is about 22.5 A. The voltage before discharge (start voltage), and the voltage after the recovery time (end voltage), the total discharge time, the average discharge current are represented Table 1.

Table 1. Battery discharge test result

Start voltage	End voltage	Difference	Average discharge current	Discharge time	Discharge capacity
472.76 V	462.58 V	10.18 V	22.87 A	3562 sec	22.63 Ah
462.58 V	457.05 V	5.53 V	22.80 A	3613 sec	22.88 Ah
457.05 V	451.58 V	5.47 V	22.92 A	3629 sec	23.10 Ah
451.58 V	447.03 V	4.55 V	23.46 A	3784 sec	24.66 Ah

$C(0,\theta)$ in (4) has to be calculated for obtaining SOC in (1). The electrolyte temperature is 0°C, and $C(0,\theta)$ is when the average discharge current is 0A. Hence, (4) is rewritten by

$$C(0,0) = K_c C_0{}^* 1^\varepsilon \tag{10}$$

The battery is available during 20 hours when the discharge rate is 0.05C and the temperature is 25°C in the datasheet. In case of the test, the battery can be discharged during 5 hours when the discharge rate is also 0.05C but the temperature is 0°C. Therefore, $C_0{}^* = 112.5$ Ah * 3600 sec = 405000 Asec, $\varepsilon = 1.645$. SOC can be calculated by using Table 1 and these parameters. Table 2 shows the calculated SOC in the test.

Table 2. SOC after the discharge test

No.	Start voltage	End voltage	Discharge capacity	SOC
1	472.76 V	462.58 V	45.24 Ah	100 to 79.89 %
2	462.58 V	457.05 V	45.75 Ah	79.89 to 59.56 %
3	457.05 V	451.58 V	46.20 Ah	59.56 to 39.03 %
4	451.58 V	447.03 V	49.32 Ah	39.03 to 17.11 %

K_E can be calculated by using (5) and Table 2. The calculated parameter K_E is shown in Table 3. K_E is not constant because the real battery is not linear to SOC. Hence, K_E is estimated to 0.098589 at 40 ~ 80% SOC.

Table 3. SOC after the discharge test

SOC	K_E
79.89	0.185436
59.56	0.099607
39.03	0.09757
17.11	0.07603

The parameters about terminal resistance (R_0) is calculated in (6) using the test results. Table 4 shows the terminal resistance in the test.

Table 4. Terminal resistance in the test

	Voltage	Current	SOC	Terminal resistance
Start of discharge	456.99	0	59.56	0.3672
	448.86	44.28		
End of discharge	428.61	46.08	39.03	0.3849
	437.48	0		

When the SOC is 59.56, 39.03, each terminal resistance is respectively 0.3672, 0.3849. Therefore, R_{00} is 0.3323, and A_0 is 0.2601 from (6).

The number of battery model's R-C block is one in this paper. R_1 is related with recovery voltage after discharge. The end voltage is 451.58 V in case of no. 3 test as shown in Table 2. In this test, the battery voltage is 428.61 V just before stopping the discharge and R_0 is 0.38454 Ω. R_1 can be calculated by (11).

$$R_1 = \frac{V_{end} - 428.61 - R_0 I}{I} \tag{11}$$

Hence, R_1 is 0.67 Ω and DOC is 38.07% in this time. R_{10}, the parameter of the battery, is 0.69 Ω in (7). Table 5 shows the parameters [4] of battery in this paper.

Table 5. Terminal resistance in the test

Parameter	Value	Parameter	Value
C_0^*	405000 Asec	R_{10}	0.69 Ω
ε	1.645	G_{p0}	2 pS
K_E	0.098589	K_c	1.18
R_{00}	0.3323 Ω	δ	1.40
A_0	0.2601	θ_f	- 40°C

4   Simulation Result

Dynamic battery model in Fig. 1 is modeled in PSCAD/EMTDC. The parameters of the modeled battery are used in Table 4. Fig 2 shows the simulation result comparison with experimental result. The shape of the simulation result's battery voltage is same with experimental result, but the error comes from the number of R-C block. The more accuracy of battery model, the more R-C blocks are needed. And the error is small enough to consider operating scheme of BESS for microgrid.

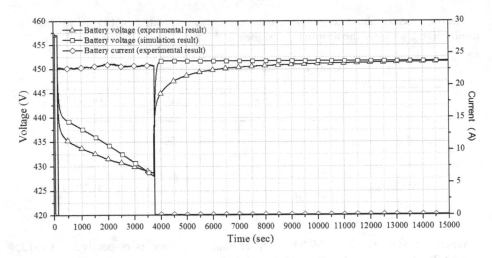

Fig. 2. Simulation result of battery voltage compared with experimental result

5   Conclusion

The 250Ah lead-acid battery is modeled in PSCAD/EMTDC. Some parameters of the real battery stack are estimated from experimental results. The simulation result is compared with experimental results. The error is small enough to decide operating scheme of BESS which is installed in a microgrid. In the future, the modeled battery with energy storage system will be applied to microgrid.

Acknowledgment. This work was supported by the Power Generation & Electricity Delivery of the Korea Institute of Energy Technology Evaluation and Planning (KETEP) grant funded by the Korea government Ministry of Knowledge Economy. (*No. 20111020400220*).

References

1. González-Longatt, F.M.: Circuitt Based Battery Models: A Review. In: Conference on CIBELEC (2006)
2. Barsali, S., Ceraolo, M.: Dynamic Models of Lead-Acid Batteries: Implementation Issues. IEEE Transactions on Energy Conversion 17(1), 16–34 (2002)
3. Moubayed, N., Kouta, J., El-Ali, A., Demayka, H., Outbib, R.: Parameter Identification of the Lead-Acid Battery Model. In: IEEE Photovoltaic Specialists Conference 2008, San Diego, USA, pp. 1–6 (May 2008)
4. Ceraolo, M.: New Dynamic Models of Lead-Acid Batteries. IEEE Trans. Power Systems 4(4), 1184–1190 (2010)

Simulation Analysis of Microgrid
Using Real Time Digital Simulator

Serim Heo , Gyeong-Hun Kim, Minwon Park, and In-Keun Yu

Dept. of Electrical Engineering, Univ. of Changwon, Korea
paku@changwon.ac.kr

Abstract. Microgrid is a new type of electric power grid which consists of distributed generation systems, energy storage devices and loads. It can operate either in grid-connected or islanded operation mode. Due to environmental pressure and enhanced demands on quality, security and reliability of electric power energy system, a microgrid has become a subject of special interest. In this paper, microgrid which has permanent magnet synchronous generator type wind power generation system, photovoltaic power genetation system, diesel generator, battery energy storage system (BESS), energy storage system (ESS) with an electric double layer capacitor (EDLC) and load was modeled using real time digital simulator. The modeled microgrid was simulated in both grid-connected and islanded operation mode. Simulation results represent that microgrid can supply high quality electric power to customers through the operation BESS and ESS with an EDLC. The modeled microgrid can be utilized to develop management system for a microgrid.

Keywords: microgrid, microgrid operation mode, ESS, BESS, microgrid system control.

1   Introduction

Nowadays, as the demand of the quality, security and reliability of the electrical energy and power supply has become increasingly higher, the traditional bulk grid can no longer meet the demand because of its own flaws. A microgrid is viewed as an alternative plan for this problem [1]. A microgrid can be defined as an integrated energy system consisting of distributed generators such as photovoltaic (PV) and wind power generators with power electronic converters, energy storage devices (i.e batteries, super-capacitor and flywheels) and customer loads, which can operate either in grid-connected or islanded operation mode [2-4]. A microgrid can improve security and flexibility, and therefore it will be the direction of future development. As an essential part of a microgrid, energy storage system plays an important role [5] for smoothing output power oscillation of renewable energy and so on. Simulation analysis of a renewable energy based microgrid using real time digital simulator (RTDS) is investigated in this paper. The modeled microgrid consists of PV power generation system, permanent magnet synchronous generator (PMSG) type wind

T.-h. Kim et al. (Eds.): CA/CES³ 2011, CCIS 256, pp. 267–275, 2011.

power generation system, battery energy storage system (BESS), energy storage system (ESS) with an electric double layer capacitor (EDLC), diesel generator and loads. The simulation results show the characteristics of BESS and ESS with an EDLC during either grid connected or islanded operation mode. The study results can effectively be utilized to develop management system for a microgrid.

2   Microgrid Modeling

In this paper, microgrid which consists of PMSG type wind turbine power generation system PV power generation system, diesel power generation system, Li-ion BESS, ESS with an EDLC and loads was modeled in RTDS.

2.1   Wind Turbine Power Generation System Modeling

The energy of wind can be expressed (1). Wind turbine can not use 100% of wind energy. If wind turbine absorbs total of wind energy then wind speed passing the wind turbine becomes 0. It is impossible because of continuous air flow. So C_p (Power coefficient) must be considered as (2). C_p is function of λ (tip ratio) and β (pitch angle) and is defined as (4).

$$P_{wind} = \frac{1}{2}v^2 \rho A \frac{ds}{dt} = \frac{1}{2} \rho A v^3 \tag{1}$$

$$P_{turbine} = C_p \cdot P_{wind} = C_p \cdot \frac{1}{2} \rho A v^3 \tag{2}$$

$$\lambda = \frac{R_{blade} \cdot \omega_{blade}}{v_{wind}} \tag{3}$$

$$C_p = \frac{1}{2}(\lambda - 0.022\beta^2 - 5.6) * e^{-0.17\lambda} \tag{4}$$

Where v is wind speed, ρ is air density, A is area of wind flow at wind turbine, R_{blade} is the length of blade and ω_{blade} means the rotation speed of blade.

The modeled PMSG type wind power generation system in this paper is controlled to operate at point of maximum power through Maximum Power Point Tracking (MPPT) control when wind speed is less than rated speed. In contrast, the more the wind turbine generates power, the bigger the capacity of power electronic converter is. However, it is rare to blow over the rated wind speed in Korea. Increasing capacity of power electronic converters is poor economic. Hence, when the wind speed is faster than rated wind speed, the rotation speed of wind turbine generators is restricted by controlling the pitch angle.

2.2   Photovoltaic Power Generation System Modeling

Voltage and current of solar cell change between open circuit voltage (Current = 0 A) and short current (Voltage = 0 V) according to load connected output terminal. Characteristics of solar cell voltage-current can be represented as (5) and (6).

$$I = I_{sc} - I_{os} \exp[\frac{q(V + IR)}{nKT}] - 1 - \frac{V + IR_s}{R_{sh}} \qquad (5)$$

$$I_{os} = AT^{\gamma} \exp\left(\frac{-E_g}{nkT}\right) \qquad (6)$$

Where I_{sc} is short current, R_s is series resistance, R_{sh} is shunt resistance, T is temperature of solar cell surface and A is area of solar cell. Because solar cell output changes according to insolation and temperature of solar cell, MPPT control is used to generate maximum power.

2.3   ESS with an EDLC Modeling

Output power of wind turbine and PV array changes according to the weather and the time. It causes frequency fluctuation. So ESS is needed in order to smooth output power fluctuation of renewable energy sources. In this paper, ESS with an EDLC is used to do that. EDLC is equivalent to EDLC bank. EDLC bank parameters are given in Table 1.

Table 1. EDLC bank parameters

Maximum voltage	Maximum storage energy	Capacitance
369 V	0.45 MJ	6.6 F

EDLC is charged and discharged by bi-directional DC/DC converter and DC-link capacitor is connected to the grid through inverter. If PV and wind power generation systems produce electric power more than the demanded then EDLC charges power from renewable energy sources (charge mode). In contrast, if PV and wind power generation systems produce electric power less than the demanded then EDLC supplies power for grid (discharge mode). Output power oscillation of renewable energy is smoothed by repeating charge or discharge mode of ESS with an EDLC. Fig. 1 and Fig. 2 show the basic structure and control block diagram for ESS with an EDLC. There is DC capacitor between bidirectional DC/DC converter and 3 phase inverter and voltage of DC capacitor is controlled by 3 phase inverter. Also, inverter converts DC into AC to connect 3 phase ac grid.

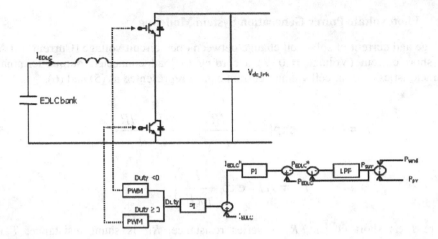

Fig. 1. Basic structure and control block diagram of bidirectional DC/DC converter for ESS with an EDLC

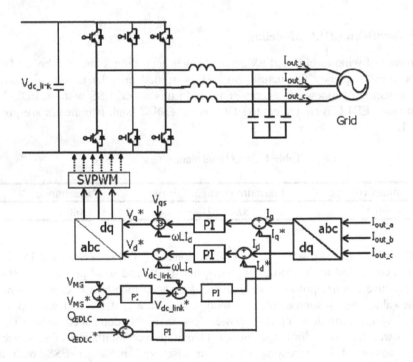

Fig. 2. Basic structure and control block diagram of grid-connected inverter for ESS with an EDLC

2.4   Li-ion BESS Modeling

In this paper, Li-ion BESS operates to maintain frequency of microgrid under islanded operation mode and outputs power as much the ordered value from energy management system (EMS) under grid-connected operation mode but EMS was not considered. Basic structure of BESS is the same as the power converter for ESS with an EDLC. In this paper, a simplified BESS model that is made of DC current source was used instead of real BESS model. Specification of the modeled Li-ion battery is shown as Table 2. Li-ion BESS controls not only frequency of microgrid as 60 Hz but also voltage of the microgrid as 380 V. Structure and control block diagram of simplified Li-ion BESS is presented in Fig. 3. Frequency of the microgrid is controlled by a d-axis current control, the voltage of the microgrid is controlled by q-axis current control. Through dq reverse transformation, each of 3 DC current sources produces current to maintain frequency and voltage of the microgrid properly.

Table 2. Specification of battery stack for BESS

Parameter	Value	
Type of battery	Li-ion	
Capacity	70 kW / 140 kWh	
Series number of battery	125 EA	
Parallel number of battery	20 EA	
Rated voltage	Cell	Stack
	3.7 V	462.5 V

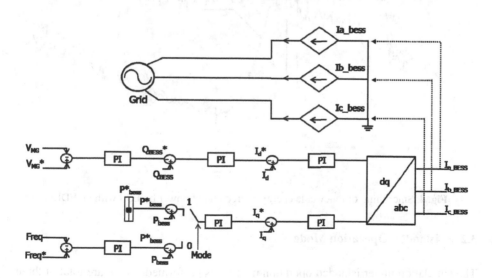

Fig. 3. Structure and block diagram of simplified Li-ion BESS

2.5   Diesel Power Generation System Modeling

The modeled diesel power generation system consists of diesel generator, governor and exciter. Diesel power generation system was modeled using components in RSCAD/RTDS.

Capacity of each system in the modeled microgrid is given in Table 3.

Table 3. Capacity of each system in the modeled microgrid

System	PV array	Wind turbine	Diesel engine	ESS with an EDLC	Li-ion BESS
Capacity	20 kW	30 kW	50 kW	30 kW/ 4.5 MJ	70 kW/ 140 kWh

3   Simulation Results

3.1   Grid-Connected Operation Mode

As shown in Fig. 4, output power oscillation of renewable energy sources is stabilized by charge or discharge of ESS with an EDLC.

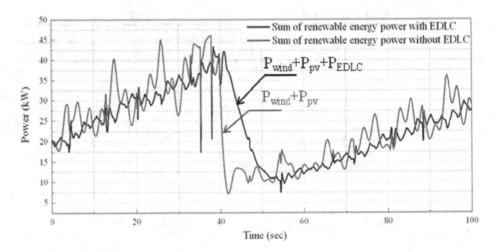

Fig. 4. Smoothing of renewable energy source output power by ESS with an EDLC

3.2   Islanded Operation Mode

The simulation under islanded operation mode was performed. There are total of three cases. The conditions and the output of each system in each case are described in detail in Table 4.

Table 4. Condition of islanded operation mode simulation

	Wind speed (m/s)	Irradiation (W/m²)	Diesel generator output (kW)	Load Capacity (kW)	Operation mode	Li-ion BESS
Case1	6~16	300~1000	35	50	Grid-connected	Connected
Case2	10	600	35	50→20	Grid-connected →Islanded	Connected
Case3	10	600	35	50	Islanded	Disconnected

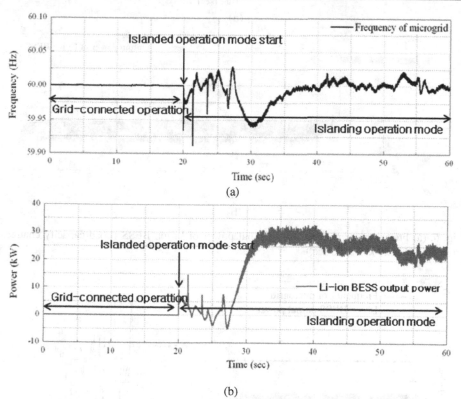

(a)

(b)

Fig. 5. (a) Frequency of microgrid (b) Output power of Li-ion BESS (Microgrid is detached from main grid at 20 sec)

Fig. 5 shows that frequency of microgrid and output power of Li-ion BESS when the operation mode converters grid-connected operation mode into islanded operation mode. Microgrid is separated from main grid at 20 sec. Because renewable energy source power fluctuate, frequency of microgrid fluctuate the moment microgrid is disconnected from main grid.. After 35 sec, frequency of microgrid is maintained by charge and discharge operation of Li-ion BESS.

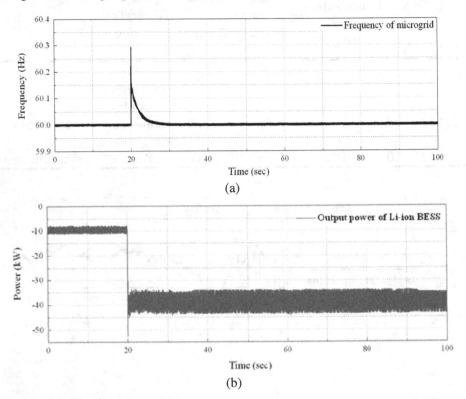

Fig. 6. (a) Frequency of microgird (b) Output power of Li-ion BESS (Load capacity changes from 50 kW to 20 kW at 20 sec.)

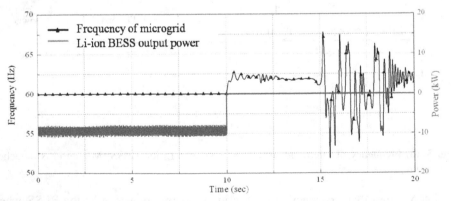

Fig. 7. Frequency of microgird and Output power of Li-ion BESS (Li-ion BESS is eliminated from microgrid at 10 sec)

Fig. 6 indicates frequency of microgrid and output power of Li-ion BESS when load capacity decreases from 50 kW to 20 kW under islanded operation mode. Load capacity decreases at 20 sec. Frequency of microgrid increases in an instant. After 25 sec, frequency of microgrid is became 60 Hz, because Li-ion BESS absorbs the electric power. Fig.7 shows frequency of microgrid and output power of Li-ion BESS when Li-ion BESS is eliminated from microgrid at 10 sec. Frequency of microgrid fluctuate. Microgrid becomes unstable due to Li-ion BESS absence.

4   Conclusion

This paper presents the analysis results of a renewable energy based microgrid. Microgrid having PMSG type wind power generation system, PV power generation system, diesel power generation system, ESS with an EDLC, Li-ion BESS and loads was modeled using RTDS. Output power of renewable energy sources changes according to weather and time. Fluctuation of output power causes an oscillation of frequency. It has a bad effect on electric power quality. ESS is used to solve this problem. Output power fluctuation of renewable energy sources is smoothed by ESS with EDLC. When the modeled microgrid operates islanded operation mode, frequency of microgrid is maintained 60 Hz by Li-ion BESS. The developed microgrid model can be used to develop the protection system and management system for microgrid.

Acknowledgment. This work was supported by the Power Generation & Electricity Delivery of the Korea Institute of Energy Technology Evaluation and Planning (KETEP) grant funded by the Korea government Ministry of Knowledge Economy. (*No. 20111020400220*).

References

1. Lasseter, R.H.: Microgrid. IEEE PES Winter Meeting (January 2002)
2. Lasseter, R.H., Piagi, P.: Control and Design of Microgird Components. PSERC Publication (2006)
3. Peças Lopes, J.A., Moreira, C.L., Madureira, A.G.: Defining control strategies for microgrids islanded operation. IEEE Transactions on Power Systems 21, 916–924 (2006)
4. Tan, K.T., So, P.L., Chu, Y.C.: Control of Parallel Inverter–interfaced distributed generation systems in microgrid for islanded operation. In: International Conference on Probabilistic Methods Applied to Power Systems (PMAPS), pp. 1–5 (2010)
5. Wei, H., Xin, W., Jiahuan, G., Jianhua, Z., Jingyan, Y.: Discussion on Application of Super Capacitor Energy Storage System in Microgrid. In: International Conference on SUPERGEN 2009, pp. 1–4 (2009)

PMSG Type Wind Power Generation System Connected with EDLC in DC-Link

Gyeong-Hun Kim[1], Minwon Park[1], In-Keun Yu[1],
Jin-Hong Jeon[2], and Jong-Bo Ahn[2]

[1] Dept. of Electrical Engineering, Univ. of Changwon, Korea
paku@changwon.ac.kr
[2] Dept. of Renewable Energy System,
Korea Electrotechnology Research Institute, Korea

Abstract. Wind power generation system (WPGS) is the fasest increasing renewable enerngy source techology nowadays. However, output ppower fluctuation of the WPGS due to variation of wind speed casues a problem of low or some high frequency oscillation in power system. Electric double layer capacitor (EDLC) is used to overcome power quality problem caused by output power oscillation of wind turbines. A new connection scheme of EDLC to WPGS is proposed in which the EDLC is directly connected to DC-link of WPGS with permanent magnet synchronous generator. The structure of the proposed system is cost-effective and efficient. The proposed system including an EDLC is modeled and analyzed by PSCAD/EMTDC. The simulation results show the effectiveness and major features of the proposed system.

Keywords: electric double layer capacitor, PSCAD/EMTDC, wind power generation system.

1 Introduction

Wind power generation system (WPGS) is the fastest increasing renewable energy source technology nowadays. However, output power fluctuation of the WPGS due to variation of wind speed causes a problem of low or some high frequency oscillation in Power system such as microgrid.

An energy storage system (ESS) is connected to WPGS through a power converter for overcoming this problem. The conventional ESS with an EDLC consists of a bidirectional DC/DC converter using insulated gate bipolar transistor (IGBT) and a six-pulse width modulation inverter using IGBT as in Fig. 1 [1]. The ESS without the inverter as shown in Fig. 2 is reported for reducing the power converter losses [2].

In this paper, a new connection scheme of electric double layer capacitor (EDLC) to WPGS is proposed in which the EDLC is directly connected to DC-link of WPGS with permanent magnet synchronous generator (PMSG).

The proposed system is modeled and analyzed by PSCAD/ EMTDC. The simulation results show the effective operation of the proposed system to smooth output power fluctuation of WPGS. Finally, the major features of the proposed system are discussed.

T.-h. Kim et al. (Eds.): CA/CES[3] 2011, CCIS 256, pp. 276–281, 2011.
© Springer-Verlag Berlin Heidelberg 2011

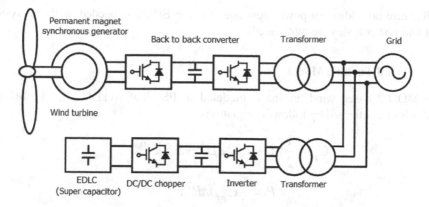

Fig. 1. Conventional energy storage system with an electric double layer capacitor

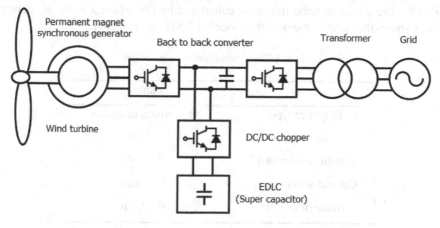

Fig. 2. Energy storage system without an inverter

2   Modeling of the Proposed System

The configuration of the proposed system is shown in Fig. 3, in which an EDLC is connected to DC-link of WPGS with PMSG.

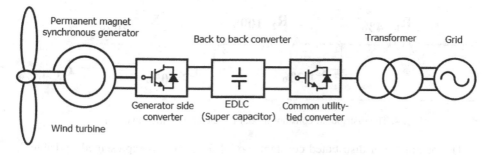

Fig. 3. The configuration of the proposed system

Because no additional power converter for the EDLC is needed, both the system cost and power losses are minimized.

2.1   Wind Turbine Model

The MOD-2 based wind turbine is modeled in PSCAD/EMTDC [3]. The MOD-2 model is characterized by following equations.

$$C_p = \frac{1}{2}\left(\lambda - 0.022\beta^2 - 5.8\right)e^{-0.17\lambda} \tag{1}$$

$$P = \frac{1}{2}C_p\rho\pi R^2 v^3 \tag{2}$$

where, Power coefficient (C_p) is calculated by tip speed ratio (λ) and the blade pitch angle (β). The torque of wind turbine is calculated by (2), where λ is the air density. Table 1 shows the specifications of the modeled 3 MW wind turbine.

Table 1. MOD-2 wind turbine parameters

Items	Value
Propeller type	Horizontal propeller
Rated power	3 MW
Cut-in wind speed	5.8 m/s
Cut-out wind speed	11.8 m/s
Blade diameter	91.43 m

2.2   Electric Double Layer Capacitor Model

An EDLC has many advantageous including high efficiency, high response speed and millions of times of electrical charge and discharge. As shown in Fig. 4, the distributed constant model for EDLC is used [4].

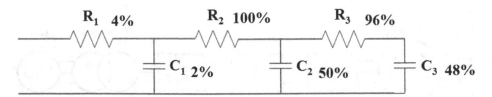

Fig. 4. The distributed constant model for electric double layer capacitor

The parameter of distributed constant model for EDLC is represented in Table 2. Total storage energy of EDLC is 2.5 MJ, and rated voltage is 2.5 kV.

Table 2. Distributed constant parameter

Items	Value
Rated voltage	2500 V
Storage energy	2.5 MJ
C_1	60 F
C_2	1500 F
C_3	1440 F
R_1	0.36 mΩ
R_2	9.0 mΩ
R_E	8.64 mΩ

2.3   Control Design of Power Converter

The maximum power from wind turbine is extracted by a generator side converter (GSC). The maximum power of wind turbine is given by (3).

$$P_{max} = \frac{1}{2} \frac{\rho \pi R^5 C_{p\_max}}{\lambda_{opt}^3} \omega^3 \tag{3}$$

where P_{max} is the power reference of GSC.

Fig. 5 shows the controller of GSC. The active power of the generator is controlled by the q-axis current of generator (i_{qr}).

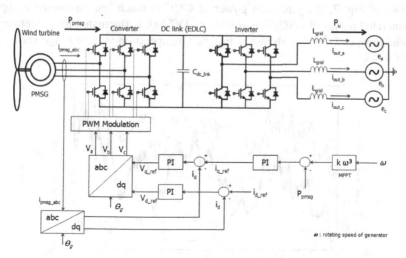

Fig. 5. The control block diagram of generator side converter

The d-axis current is linked to the reactive power. Reference currents of dq-axis are controlled by the PC controller, which generates the voltage reference and PWM for GSC.

A common utility-tied converter (CUC) smoothen the power fluctuation of generator side converter. The control block diagram of CUC is shown in the Fig. 6. Power reference of CUC is limited by EDLC voltage and current limiter as indicated in Fig. 6. The structure of power and current controller is the same as GSC.

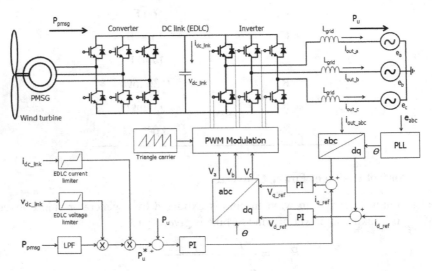

Fig. 6. The control block diagram of grid side converter controller

3   Simulation Results

As shown in Fig. 7, the generated power of CUC is much less fluctuated compared with generated power of GSC. The voltage of DC link is fluctuated for smoothing the generated power of CUC as shown in Fig. 8. The operation voltage range varies from 2.75 kV to 4 kV.

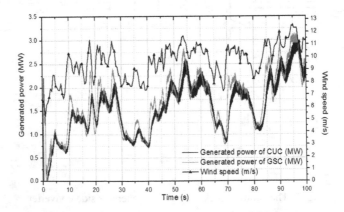

Fig. 7. Wind speed and generated power of the system

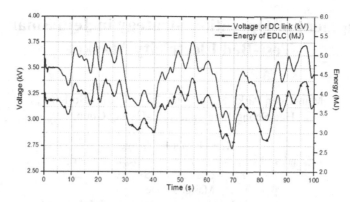

Fig. 8. Voltage and stored energy of EDLC

4   Conclusion

The paper presents a novel EDLC application scheme for PMSG type WPGS. The proposed system mitigates the fluctuation of generated power without an additional inverter or converter. Hence, the system cost and power losses can be reduced. In this system, EDLC operation voltage is limited. However, energy density of the EDLC at low voltage is low. The 5 MJ EDLC and 3 MW wind turbine are modeled and analyzed by PSCAD/EMTDC for demonstrating the effectiveness of the proposed system.

Acknowledgment. This work was supported by the Power Generation & Electricity Delivery of the Korea Institute of Energy Technology Evaluation and Planning(KETEP) grant funded by the Korea government Ministry of Knowledge Economy. (*No. 20111020400220*).

References

1. Li, G., Liu, J., Li, X., Yang, L., Wang, Z., Yang, D.: Wind farm output power regulation based on EDLC energy storage technology. In: International Conference on Power System Technology, pp. 1–5 (2010)
2. Nakanani, M., Muyeen, S.M., Takahashi, R., Tamura, J.: New ESS connection scheme in wind generator output smoothing control. In: International Conference on ICEM 2010, pp. 616–621 (2010)
3. Anderson, P.M., Bose, A.: Stability simulation of wind turbine systems. IEEE Trans. Power Apparatus and System PAS-102(12), 3791–3795 (1983)
4. Kinjo, T., Seniyu, T.: Output leveling of renewable energy by electric double-layer capacitor applied for energy storage system. IEEE Trans. Energy Conversion 21(1), 221–227 (2006)

Development of Operation Strategy in Jeju Smart Grid Test-Bed Electricity Market

Man-Guen Park[1], Seong-Bin Cho[1], Kwang-Ho Kim[1],
Hae-Seong Jung[2], and Koo-Hyung Chung[3]

[1] Korea Power Exchange
miso@kpx.or.kr, sbcho@kpx.or.kr,
bigtiger@kpx.or.kr
[2] Master's Space
econohs@masterspace.co.kr
[3] Korea Electrotechnology Research Institute
kchung@keri.re.kr

Abstract. During several decades, supply-demand balancing problems has been solved by the supply side management expanding generation and transmission capacities. However, recent energy crisis worldwide and spotlight on environmental issues stress the need for developing new strategies managing demand side resources. Smart grid is an alternative for this paradigm shift in the electricity industry. In this paper, we propose operation strategies for demand side resources in the electricity market of Jeju smart grid test-bed.

Keywords: smart grid, demand side resources, electricity market, Jeju test-bed.

1 Introduction

Korea, as a leading country for smart grid deployment, has built the world's largest and most advanced smart grid test-bed in Jeju in order to create and commercialize new business models associated with smart electricity services. As a part of this program, the test-bed electricity market is operated with 10 consortiums in 3 categories: Smart Place (SP), Smart Transportation (ST), and Smart Renewable (SR). Through this electricity market, we develop operation strategies for the application of demand side resources and verify its validity. In this paper, we describe the operation scheme for demand side resources in the electricity market of Jeju smart grid test-bed.

2 Principles of Market Design

In Jeju smart grid test-bed electricity market, customers can participate in price-determination process by submitting their demand bids. This demand side bidding and the following price signal are expected for customers to more use their electricity more rationally. In addition, the concept of virtual power plant (VPP) aggregating various demand side resources by communication networks is introduced to demonstrate its

T.-h. Kim et al. (Eds.): CA/CES³ 2011, CCIS 256, pp. 282–288, 2011.
© Springer-Verlag Berlin Heidelberg 2011

availability. Since Jeju smart grid test-bed project aims to verify the export potential of developed technologies and business models, the test-bed electricity market is formed similar to advanced overseas markets. This electricity market has two-settlement system including a day-ahead market and a real-time market.

Price determination in this test-bed electricity market is based on bidding of market participants in consideration with real power system operating conditions. This aims to analyze overall impacts related to demand side resource applications in preparation for smart grid deployment. This market allows two-way bidding at supply and demand side. Demand side bidding includes three types of resources: normal demand bidding, demand reduction bidding, and demand side generation bidding. Demand reduction and demand side generation bidding also has two types of bidding according to its dispatchablity. Table 1 shows five types of demand side bidding in the test-bed electricity market.

Table 1. Types of demand side bidding

Bidding	Description
Normal demand (ND)	Purchase energy at prices for consumption
Dispatchable demand reduction (DDR)	Demand reduction being able to respond with dispatch orders
Non-dispatchable demand reduction (NDDR)	Demand reduction without dispatch orders
Dispatchable demand side generation (DG)	Generation being able to respond with dispatch orders
Non-dispatchable demand side generation (NDG)	Self-scheduled generation

3   Market Participation by Demand Side Resources

3.1   Categorization of Demand Side Bidding by Consortium

Demand side bidding can be categorized by controllability, VPP configuration, and technical characteristic of a corresponding resource shown as Table 2.

3.2   Bidding Rules by Demand Side Resources

Market buyers may submit hourly demand quantities for which it commits to purchase energy at day-ahead prices for consumption. Each normal demand bid consists of up to 10 blocks with price-descending order. Normal demand bids are only valid in the day-ahead market.

Each non-dispatchable demand reduction offer consisting of up to 10 blocks with price-ascending order should be submitted with its customer baseline load (CBL). Non-dispatchable demand reduction offers cannot be revised in the real-time energy market since these resources cannot respond to the real-time dispatch order.

Table 2. Example of demand side bidding by consortiums

Bidding		SP	ST	SR
ND		Demand for end-users	Battery charging demand	Battery charging demand
DR	NDDR	Reduction of normal demand		
DR	DDR	Reduction of battery charging demand, smart appliances and buildings etc.	Reduction of battery charging demand	
DG	NDG	Single generation of small-size renewable generating units		Single generation of renewable generating units
DG	DG	Integrated operating of small-size renewable generating units and batteries, and microgrids etc.	V2G	Integrated operating of renewable generating units and batteries

Each dispatchable demand reduction offer consisting of up to 10 blocks with price-ascending order should be submitted with its technical specification data due to its availability in the real-time power system operation. Each dispatchable demand reduction resource can also provide ancillary services such as standby reserve in the day-ahead market and/or regulation (AGC) in the real-time energy market through declaration in this offer. Each dispatchable demand reduction offer should include its dispatchable base-point. These offers can be revised in the real-time energy market.

Each non-dispatchable demand side generation resource only offers what it expects to generate into the day-ahead market. These offers should not be revised in the real-time market.

Dispatchable demand side generation resources submit their availability with offer prices. Each dispatchable demand side generation offer should include its technical specification data to be applied in the real-time power system operation. These offers can be revised in the real-time energy market.

3.3   Scaling Up Demand Side Resources to National Level

Scaling factors by demand side resources are used to expand demand side bids of consortiums to national level. This is the reason that demand side bids in the test-bed electricity market can be reflected in the price determination. For normal demands, about 7.5% of forecasted demands in CBP market are assumed as the price sensitive load dynamically varying according to normal demand bids in the test-bed electricity market. Scaling factors for demand reduction resources and demand side generation resources are set as total capacity of respective resources in Jeju smart grid test-bed is expanded to load management target amounts and renewable capacity targets in the 5th Basic Plan of Long Term Electricity Supply and Demand respectively.

Table 3. Description of demand side bidding in the test-bed electricity market

Bidding		ND	NDDR	DDR	NDG	DG
Day-ahead market		O	O	O	O	O
Real-time market		X	X	O	X	X
Bidding blocks		up to 10	up to 10	up to 10	single	up to 10
Capacity payment		X	X	O	X	O
AS	Regulation	X	X	O	X	O
	Standby reserve	X	O	O	X	O
Requirement		metering	CBL	metering & monitoring	metering	metering & monitoring
Resource type		aggregated normal demand	aggregated demand reduction	battery charging demand	renewable generation unit	renewable generation unit + battery

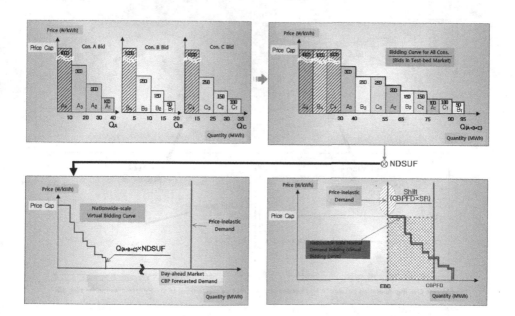

Fig. 1. Scaling-up scheme for normal demand bids

4   Price Determination Process

In the day-ahead market, offers of supply side CBP generators are determined using price-conversion tables based on available capacity offers and cost factors for CBP market. Unit commitment (UC) is scheduled based on average costs for generators while price clearing and economic dispatch (ED) are performed based on offer prices of generators conversed from incremental costs. Reserve requirement for standby reserve is co-optimized with the energy balance of hourly demand and supply. The day-ahead market price is cleared at the point that supply meets demand considering the forecasted demand in CBP market and demand side bids expanded to the nationwide scale.

The real-time market price cleared every 5 minutes is based on 5 minute load forecasting, revised bids for demand side dispatchable resources in the test-bed, and revised offers in CBP market with the regulation requirement. This regulation price is varied with the real-time energy market price and available regulation level. When total available capacity is less than the sum of demand and 400 million kW of reserve requirement, scaricity pricing is applied to provide market participants with strong price signal.

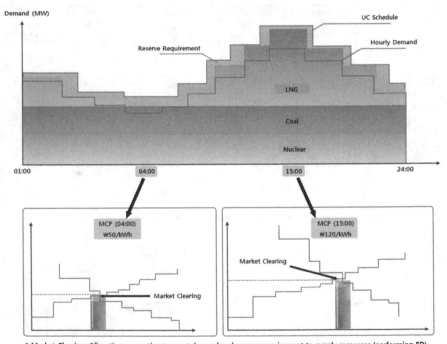

* Market Clearing: Allocating generation to meet demand and reserve requirement to supply resources (performing ED)

Fig. 2. Price determination scheme in the day-ahead market

5   Settlement for Demand Side Resources

Jeju smart grid test electricity market settles for energy, demand reduction, capacity, standby reserve, and regulation respectively. For the energy market, it adopts two-settlement system separating settlements performed for day-ahead market and real-time market. Day-ahead market settlement is financially binding for scheduled hourly quantities and day-ahead hourly market price while real-time market settlement is based on actual hourly quantity deviation from day-ahead schedule hourly quantities priced at real-time market price. Demand reductions are settled for their negative kW provisions by the same method for generators. Standby reserve settlement is based on scheduled quantities and standby reserve price which are determined by co-optimization for energy and reserve in the day-ahead market. On the other hand, regulation service settlement is based on the real-time dispatch scheduling. Fig. 3 depicts the two-settlement system in Jeju smart grid test-bed electricity market.

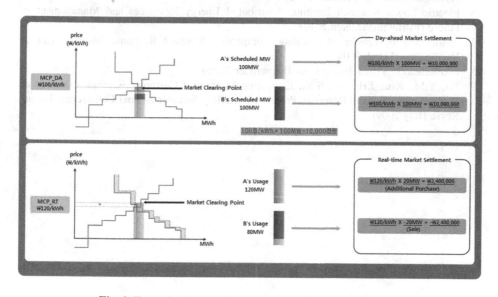

Fig. 3. Example of two-settlement system for normal demand

6   Conclusion

In this paper, we define types of demand side resources in the Jeju smart grid test-bed electricity market and describe the market operating system including bidding, price determination, and settlement. It is expected that the operation scheme for demand side resources demonstrated through the test-bed electricity market operation provides the foundations for paradigm shift in Korean electricity industry. Especially, consortiums aiming to export smart grid technologies and business models can experience the participation in the advanced electricity market through this test-bed electricity market. These experiences may give motivation to promote exports of corresponding technologies for business and get a foothold for sustainable green growth.

References

1. Korea Power eXchange and Korea Electric Power Corporation, Establishment of smart electricity service in Jeju smart grid demonstration test-bed (2009)
2. Brook, A., Lu, E., Reicher, D., Spirakis, C., Weihl, B.: Demand Dispatch. IEEE Power and Energy Magazine 8(3), 20–29 (2010)
3. PJM Member Training Dept, PJM Demand Side Response (January 2009)
4. The Federal Energy Regulatory Commission, National Action Plan on Demand Response (June 2010)
5. The Federal Energy Regulatory Commission, Assessment of Demand Response & Advanced Metering (February 2011)
6. Electric Power Research Institute, Distributed Energy Resources and Management of Future Distribution (March 2010)
7. Association of Edison Illuminating Companies, Demand Response Measurement & Verification (March 2009)
8. PikeResearch, Virtual Power Plant (September 2010)
9. Wi, Y.M., Kim, J.H., Joo, S.K.: Estimating Method of Customer Baseline Load for an Evaluation of Demand Response Program. In: KIEE Summer Annual Conference, Busan, Korea (July 2009)

The Design of CC2420-Based Laboratory Apparatus Monitoring System

ShinHyeong Choi

The Department of Control & Instrumentation Engineering,
Kangwon National University,
1 Joongang-ro Samcheok-si, Gangwondo, Korea
cshinh@kangwon.ac.kr

Abstract. The development of ubiquitous technology makes our lives very comfortable. Services become more varied and will be available and convenient. In this paper, we present the laboratory apparatus monitoring system, which consists of CC2420-based motes, sensor modules, control boards and monitoring server. A sensor node, also known as a mote, is a node in a wireless sensor network that is capable of performing some processing, gathering sensory information and communicating with other connected nodes in the network. Control board make appliances operate. We can check the state of apparatus in real time and prepare for situations of emergency.

Keywords: Ubiquitous, Wireless Sensor Network, Monitoring, Sensor.

1   Introduction

"Ubiquitous computing" technology has started since M. Weiser introduced this new term in his paper [1]. Living space in the ubiquitous can be defined as the environment, in which we can get the information you need from network anywhere, anytime. In the ubiquitous living space, we can acquire information about the change of state of environment and objects in real time. The environment and objects can notice information a person need on their own or take appropriate action. In addition, all objects are intelligent and connected to electronic space, and then ubiquitous space is created and we can exchange information each other. And anytime, anywhere access is achieved without limit. The computer will be placed in the environment and invisible objects, e.g., roads, bridges, tunnels, buildings, ceilings, flower pots, refrigerators, etc. that make up the urban space. This is the connection of physical space and electronic space, infinite space connected is a sensor network.

Sensor network has the distinctive features from the existing network. The primary purpose of the sensor network is to collect automatically the remote information than transfer information with each other.

Each sensor nodes are sensing information around and sensed information is passed to a certain point automatically using wireless communication between sensor nodes. Users remotely collect information around the sensor field and can utilize.

T.-h. Kim et al. (Eds.): CA/CES³ 2011, CCIS 256, pp. 289–295, 2011.

In this paper, as wireless sensor network applications, we propose the environmental information monitoring system based on CC2420 that can monitor the information collected from the sensor in a variety of expensive laboratory apparatus.

2   Related Work

Sensor networks detect and measure the state information of physical space, e.g., light, sound, temperature, moves from sensor nodes, then pass to the central primary node(base station or sink node). Therefore sensor networks consist of many distributed sensor node in the form of multi-hop wireless network. Sensor networks mean wireless sensor networks(WSNs) that the information gathered from sensors deployed in an unspecified area is utilized. The benefit of sensor networks is that can configure the wireless Ad-Hoc networks using low-end hardware. Wireless network technologies such as Bluetooth, WLAN need necessarily the high-end computing device such as computer, PDA, whereas the sensor network node can configure their own network. Wireless sensor networks are now utilized for a variety of distributed sensing purposes; indoor, outdoor, mobile commerce and even body monitoring applications. They are usually made up with wireless sensor nodes; small, cheap, and resource limited devices sensing the environment and communicating with each other. Wireless sensor network systems have been widely adopted for monitoring physical or environmental properties over a large area, e.g., temperature, pressure, notion, luminosity and vibration. In general, WSNs consists of several wireless sensor nodes that send the sensing data to a common base station for further data processing. As most sensor networks are deployed in stringent surroundings, the nodes and the system should be self-powered, self-reconfigured and self-healing. Since the sensor network is usually wide spread and the communication of limited range, multi-hop routing is required[2],[3],[4].

Multi-hop is a technology that makes up the wireless network using fixed or mobile access points. This makes it can expand the range of audible without extending network and act as the base station using the receiving device equipped the wireless repeater. Eventually if there are many nodes in the network that acts as a router, we can form a network that covers a large area with only a relatively small cost. In addition to, Radio Frequency(RF) communication is able to reach farther with the stronger signal strength, on the other hand, if there many middle nodes that act as a router using multi-hop approach, then be able to communicate far enough long distance with a weak signal.

3   The Design of Monitoring System

3.1   The Architecture of System

In this section, we design the monitoring system for apparatus and materials for an experiment and describe each component.

The proposed wireless sensor network consists of two parts mainly: sensor nodes and monitoring server. The block diagram of monitoring system shows as figure 1.

A sensor node is a small computer system with built-in MCU and is the most basic elements that form ubiquitous sensor network(USN). The greatest advantage compared to RFID technology is the ability to configure the optimal network that monitor the environment with sensor nodes and the network you want using the existing wired and wireless communication technology.

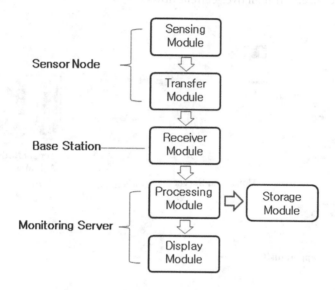

Fig. 1. Block diagram of monitoring system

A sensor node is composed of control, wireless communication, sensor and power supply part. In the application service, a large number of nodes are distributed in a wide range of environments, so low-power, compact and lightweight of sensor node is essential. Sensor nodes can measure environmental information dynamically, generate warning message if abnormal conditions are encounter and able to communicate wirelessly[5],[6]. All sensor nodes send the measured data to base station which is connected to the server via wireless sensor network.

The environmental information such as temperature and humidity data acquired by sensor nodes can be monitored at the server using a real time monitoring system. Administrator can analyze the collected environmental data from the sensor network through the monitoring system based on a high speed network. After the collected environmental data are analyzed and processed, administrator is informed of the result of environmental status inside apparatus and materials for an experiment. Sensor nodes of wireless sensor network are built from hardware of very limited resources. In order to use efficiently the limited resources of the sensor nodes, TinyOS is used as operating system. TinyOS is a free and open source component-based operating system and platform targeting wireless sensor networks. TinyOS is an embedded operating system written in the nesC programming language as a set of cooperating tasks and processes[6].

3.2   Monitoring System

Apparatus and materials for an experiment in the university laboratory are distributed in a specific laboratory depending on the intended use, so manufacturers and hardware specifications are diverse. On one hand, there is a small, simple and inexpensive apparatus, but, on the other hand, most of experiment apparatus have a high price and large size. Therefore the apparatus in the university laboratory has the ability to power itself off if an over-current flows.

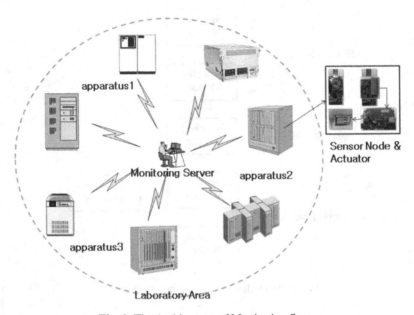

Fig. 2. The Architecture of Monitoring System

The apparatus will sound an alarm if the limit is reached, but there is no response other than to respond to over-current. In other words, to inform real-time an administrator in a remote location whether the current use of apparatus, internal state and the problem occurred are not considered.

In this paper, we propose CC2420-based laboratory apparatus monitoring system, which can identify the state of expensive apparatus from a remote location and take action when the risk arises. The architecture of monitoring system shows as figure 2.

By attaching sensor nodes to collect internal environment information such as temperature and humidity inside all apparatus, we perform monitoring the environmental information inside apparatus. To deliver a variety of environmental information that is collected by sensor nodes to the monitoring server, we use Ad-Hoc communication techniques with respect to location of apparatus and building structures. Features of the system are classified into four categories, Table 1 shows a description of each feature.

Table 1. Composition of Monitoring System

Part	Function	Configuration
Sensing temperature	collect temperature	Sensor module+Mote
Sensing humidity	collect humidity	Sensor module+Mote
Fan actuator	Fan up and stop	DC_BOARD+CON_BOARD +DC_MOTOR
Monitoring server	Real-time monitoring	PC Server

Each system can be made individually, but in this paper, using the sensor module, H-Sensor collects environmental information such as temperature, humidity, illumination. And we can receive simultaneously temperature and humidity by modifying packet.

Temperature and humidity sensing part. Temperature and humidity sensing part consists of sensor module and mote, on one hand, sensor module collects environmental information such as temperature and humidity, on the other hand, mote transmits the collected environmental information to base station through wireless communication. Mote that attaches sensor module uses TI MSP430 microcontroller, which has 10k RAM and 48k flash memory, and transmits the environmental information at 2.4GHz using CC2420 RF Chip for wireless communication. Sensor module and mote shows as figure 3.

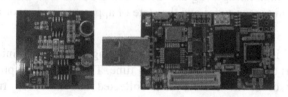

Fig. 3. Sensor Module and Mote

The CC2420 is a true single-chip 2.4 GHz IEEE 802.15.4 compliant RF transceiver designed for low-power and low-voltage wireless applications[8]. Figure 4 depicts the process of packet transmission. Sensor module attached to mote collects temperature and humidity data, and transfers this data to a base station wirelessly, then a base station that connected to monitoring server receive this data.

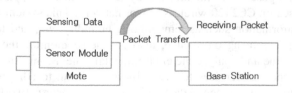

Fig. 4. The Process of Packet Transmission

Fan actuator. Fan actuator can run or stop fan attached to inside apparatus in case of unforeseen circumstances. To achieve this, we attach CON_BOARD(conversion board) to Mote that receives temperature, humidity from sensing parts. CON_BOARD transmits signals that control the fan motor based on received environmental information, and DC_BOARD can operate fan by driving a DC motor connected to the fan. CON_BOARD connected to Mote consists of a total of 10 pins, 10 pins of the top is connected to 40 pins of the back. 40pin connectors attached to mote are connected to each port of the MSP430. If the temperature inside the apparatus reaches the set value, we must operate the fan, so we need 12V DC board to drive fan, this is controlled by relay device. Figure 5 depicts the control flow from mote to fan.

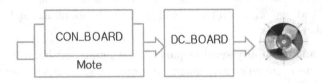

Fig. 5. The Control Flow of Fan Actuator

Monitoring server. If the environmental information is sent to another mote that acts as a base station from sensor nodes attached to the inside apparatus, monitoring server identifies the state of inside apparatus in real time and control a various devices through installed monitoring program. Monitoring Server via the GUI displays the data collected from sensor nodes and the state of apparatus, and records collected data in the file.

As conditions of implementation of the monitoring system, administrators have to monitor the status of inside apparatus in real time. This is done by processing rapidly a large quantity of environmental data collected and analyzed from the sensor network. Based on this information, administrator can maintain optimal status of inside apparatus by taking appropriate action according to set value.

4   Conclusion

Nowadays sensor and wireless communication technologies are rapidly evolving and conquering new application areas in the environment monitoring domain.

This paper proposes the monitoring system of inside apparatus, which is implemented based on CC2420 wireless sensor network. This system can identify the environmental information such as temperature, humidity, etc. and take appropriate action according to sensing data value, also is able to monitor the state of inside apparatus in real time and analyze the environmental state. Monitoring system should provide reliable and fast services for users by transmitting to administrators a large quantity of real-time environmental data collected from sensor network.

References

1. Weise, M.: Hot Topics: Ubiquitous Computing. IEEE Computer (1993)
2. Akyildiz, I.F., Su, W., Sankarasubramaniam, Y., Cayirci, E.: A survey on Sensor networks. IEEE Communications Magazine (August 2002)
3. Karl, H., Willig, A.: A short survey of wireless sensor networks, TKN Technical Report TCK-03-018 (October 2003)
4. Hasenfratz, D., Meier, A., Moser, C., Chen, J.-J., Thiele, L.: Analysis, Comparison, and Optimization of Routing Protocols for Energy Harvesting Wireless Sensor Networks. In: 2010 IEEE International Conference on Sensor Networks, Ubiquitous, and Trustworthy Computing (2010)
5. Lee, D.S., Bhardwaj, S., Alassarela, E., Chung, W.Y.: Evaluation of Detecting QRS-complex Function on Sensor Node for Ubiquitous Healthcare System. In: The 2nd International Symposium on Medical Information and Communication Technology, ISMICT (2007)
6. Shnayder, V., Chen, B.R., Lorincz, K., Fulford-Jones, R.F., Welsh, M.: Sensor Networks for Medical Care, Harvard University Technical Report TR–08–05 (April 2005)
7. http://www.tinyos.net
8. CC2420 Data Sheet,
   http://inst.eecs.berkeley.edu/~cs150/Documents/CC2420.pdf

A Case Study: Online Game Testing
Using Massive Virtual Player

Yeonjun Choi[1], Hangkee Kim[1], Changjoon Park[1], and Seongil Jin[2]

[1] ETRI
[2] Chungname National University,
Yuseonggu, Daejon, Korea
{june,hangkee,chjpark}@etri.re.kr,
sijin@cnu.ac.kr

Abstract. Automated load tests for online games can resduce costs because it doesn't need real players. We will introduce our online game testing tool, EasyQA and show a case study to testing real online game before it is published.

Keywords: Game Testing.

1 Introduction

Recently online game market grows faster than ever. There are many kinds of online games for many users simultaneously. MOGs(Multiplayer Online Game) and MMOGs(Massively Multiplayer Online Game) attract world-wide game users with their rich variety of genres, story, beautiful characters, characters' realistic actions and social networking.

Game servers are developed and managed to accommodate many game players. Stability is one of the most important factors for gam players to play the game long time. So massive tests are performed before official publishment of any online game. It always costs time and people. Test organizers recruit testers and arrange exact time for them to test a game server. But controling testers is difficult because testers are remotely located and their playing does not necessarily match test organizers desires.

Test automation can be a solution of cost reduction[1] and to measure of massive players effect. EasyQA starts from difficulty of online games testing.

1.1 Related Work

LoadRunner[2] provides packet replay-based load testing functionality. It is originally developed for test web sites stability and provides well-known protocols nowadays. But if you want to test this tool to test online games, you should provide exact packet stream data for each users to replay game someone performed priorly. It makes

T.-h. Kim et al. (Eds.): CA/CES[3] 2011, CCIS 256, pp. 296–301, 2011.
© Springer-Verlag Berlin Heidelberg 2011

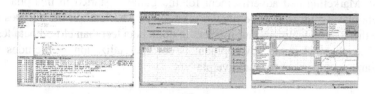

Fig. 1. LoadRunner

difficult to control massive virtual users playing for changeable situations. Definetely, it does not provide any monitoring or chasing of virtual users incluing PC[1] or NPCs[2].

VENUS[3] is used to test online games extensible dummy virtual clients mimicking real gamer's action style. It is whitebox based so we need exact game packets and packet sequences to use it. Besides, testing codes should be embedded in game program source code.

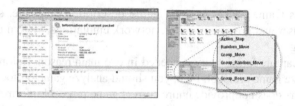

Fig. 2. VENUS

Many changes during development and testing phase also make it difficult to automate game testing. Most of MOGs/MMOGs are complicated application and environment factors like massive users and internet connection quality affect the reliability and tolerance of online game.

1.2   Game Development Process

Game development process has several steps. Even a game is small, the process has 6 steps at least. It starts from game planning, rougph sketch about new game. Game implementation is next phase. Game program codes, PC/NPC and environtal backgrounds, game data are produced in these phases.

Next three phases are related to "test". The third phase is alpha test. It is performed by the game company employees like testing team or secret testers who are recruited for test itself. Next phase is closed beta test. In these phase, the game is shown to general game users for the first time but in restricted manner. Most of important problems should be corrected in this phase and load problem starts to be revealed in this phase. Closed beta tests are performed several times. The last phase of test is open

---

[1] Player Character.
[2] Non-Player Character.

beta test. Marketing and advertisement for the game is started in this phase because open beta players are tend to be regular users of it. And load problem arises seriously because there are much more multiplayers in open beta test than closed beta test.

The last phase of game development is commercialization. It includes upgrades patches and management for massive players.

2   Blackbox Based Online Game Testing Case Study

Blackbox based tesing has benefits on reducing costs[4]. Our system EasyQA is blackbox based online game testing technology.

EasyQA is used to load test for several online games. In this chapter, we show one test case study of MOG.

2.1   EasyQA

EasyQA provides Game packet capture, game description language, scenario based massive virtual user and group controller, network emulations, system usage and user action monitoring.

Game packet capture functionalty is needed in two main reason. Before game testing, you should analyze game protocol. First, you should analyze game protocol before game testing. Developers does not provide entire correct game protocol information for testing in several reason. Second, captured game packets are used to generate virtual user's reaction for environmental change, enemies encounter, looting and so on.

In our system, test automation is achieved through using scenarios. Stress test for server is usually performed through heavy load generation. In game testing, stress is caused by massive multiplayer gaming action. EasyQA virtual users mimic real game player's action and it is achieved through test scenarios.

A test scenario is a sequence of game user's actions. An action is a meaningful user activities like login, enter world and so on. An action is a sequence of game protocols or packets. Figure 3 shows the syntax of game description language[4].

```
Game_Description_Language := (Protocol, Action, Generation_Rules)
    Protocol := (Element)
    Action := (Time_Constraint, Socket, Protocol, Parameter)
    Generation_Rules := (Endianess_Rule, Encryption_Rule,
                         TimeStamp_Rule, HeartBeat_Rule, ...)
    Element := (Name, Type, Length, Byte_string)
```

Fig. 3. Syntax of game description language

Each virtual users can acts individually or grouped together by scenarios. EasyQA controls each virtual user or virtual groups simultaneously.

Network emulation is one of important function. When game companies want to publish their game to abroad, they should go there because networking environment is different to each nation. EasyQA provides various network emulation options to control network situation[5].

During test, system resources availability and events are provided through monitoring functionality.

2.2 Case Study: WORLD FISHING (Moonlight, 淸風明月)

WORLD FISHING is a multiplayer online fishing game[6]. Justnine has been developing it for years and NEOWIZ games[3] publishes it soon.

Fig. 4. Game screen shot

Closed beta test has been performed and open beta test will be on in several months[7]. We've been testing the game server with EasyQA. We tested the game with 34 actions and 19 scenarios. The scenarios are flexible because they are written in game descripting grammar.

2.3 Test Results

During our test, various problem has been revealed and fixed. In first tests, server down bugs were revealed and solved. Most bugs were related data or protocol process.

Load tests are performed as Figure 5.

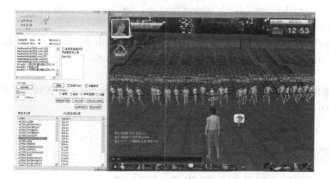

Fig. 5. Load test with EasyQA virtual users

---

[3] One of main Korean online game publisher.

After fixing server down bugs, we have been doing full load test. Figure 5 shows the resource usage result of the first full load test using EasyQA monitor. Test environment was 2 Xeon CPU, 10 groups with 50 virtual users. Two virtual users in a group executes in 1 second. Database server connection daemon, gate server, game servers are in one machine.

The result shows CPU consumption is too much.

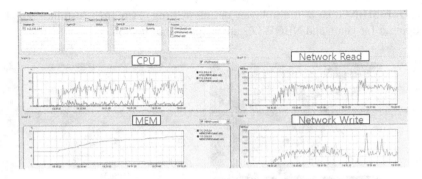

Fig. 6. Resource monitoring

Our monitoring result affected to enlarge system H/W spec, separation of database connection daemon and game server system, database call optimization in orders. Recent full load test was consist of 1,000 virtual users with 200 groups and now we are waiting for next server patch.

3   Conclusion

In this paper, we introduced our EasyQA technology and showed a case study of load testing on online game waiting for publishment. With our approach, we could test online game server with flexible game grammar. We successfully tested more than 10 MOG/MMOG games with various genre like MMORPG, web social game, battle action game, casual game, flash game and so on. Except one case, all tested online games are commercial games.

Future work is planned to improve our system with precise reporting, virtual user intelligence and standard scenario model for online games.

Acknowledgments. This paper is produced during achievemnt under the foundation of Ministry of Knowledge Economy.

References

1. Schultz, C.P., Bryant, R., Langdell, T.: Game Testing All in one, Thomson Course Technology PTR (2005)
2. LoadRunner, http://www.hp.com

3. Lim, B.H., Kim, J.R., Shim, K.H.: A Load Testing Architecture for Network Virtual Environment. In: Proceedings of 8th International Conference on Advanced Communication Technology, pp. 848–852 (2006)
4. Cho, C.-S., Lee, D.-C., Sohn, K.-M., Park, C.-J., Kang, J.-H.: Blackbox and Scenario-Based Testing of Online Games Using Game Description Language. ETRI Journal 33(3), 470–473 (2011)
5. Shin, K., Kim, J., Kim, H., Park, C., Choi, S.: Application Independent User Mode Network Emulator based on Packet Interception from Kernel Mode. In: Modeling and Simulation (2011)
6. Justnine Co. Ltd., http://www.facebook.com/pages/Justnine-CO-LTD/217901281564531?v=info
7. World Fishing (Moonlight), http://cm.pmang.com/

RETRACTED CHAPTER: Characteristics Analysis of the Motor Block Lattice Resistor of a High Speed Train by Structure Improvement

Dae-Dong Lee[1], Jae-Myung Shim[2], and Dong-Seok Hyun[1]

[1] Department of Electrical Engineering, Hanyang University,
Seoul 133-791, Republic of Korea
ldd77@hanbat.ac.kr, dshyun@hanyang.ac.kr
[2] Department of Electrical Engineering, Hanbat National University,
Daejeon 305-719, Republic of Korea
jmshim@hanbat.ac.kr

Abstract. Dynamic braking, which is frequently used in high speed trains, is a function and device that provides braking force using the electricity that is generated from a traction electric motor, and also dissipates heat from the lattice resistor that converts the current from the traction electric motor into heat. The heat from the lattice resistor, which is located in the motor block of a high speed train, damages the resistor wires and induces cracks in the insulators that affect the dynamic choppers, traction inverters, and electric motors during dynamic braking, and makes it difficult to control driving during acceleration or deceleration. In this study, the motor block lattice resistor, which was recently suggested to compensate for these problems, was designed, and experiments were performed on heat analysis simulation and temperature increase. Further field tests were performed to verify the advantages of the motor block lattice resistor.

Keywords: Braking resistor, field test, high speed train, motor block lattice resistor, temperature increase test, total heat flux.

1   Introduction

Technologies on railway vehicles have been enhancing the overall capabilities to design and operate mass transportation systems such as general trains, subway trains, and light rail transit. Korea Train eXpress(KTX), which was recently introduced and operated, has 20 cars per train and currently has 46 trains running, 34 of which are domestically manufactured and the others, imported [1].

The power source of the train is 25kV, single-phase, 60Hz AC, and its traction and braking forces are 13,560 (kW) and 300 (KN), respectively. Its braking methods include regeneration braking, dynamic braking, and air braking. The motor block resistor, which is used in regeneration and dynamic braking, is called the lattice resistor.

The motor block is a key element of the performance enhancement and stability of a train. The electric braking circuit of a high speed train normally secures the braking

This chapter has been retracted due to multiple publications. The erratum to this chapter is available at DOI: 10.1007/978-3-642-26010-0_48

T.-h. Kim et al. (Eds.): CA/CES[3] 2011, CCIS 256, pp. 302–311, 2011.
© Springer-Verlag Berlin Heidelberg 2011

force by controlling the braking chopper according to the amount of regenerated energy. In case of emergency braking or a dead section, however, when the current input to the motor block is above the limit, the circuit activates the dynamic braking, in which the excessive current is discharged as a form of heat through the lattice resistor. The heat from the lattice resistor, however, damages the resistor wires and induces cracks in the insulators that affect the dynamic choppers, inverters, and traction electric motors during dynamic braking, and make it difficult to control driving during acceleration or deceleration.

In this study, the motor block lattice resistor, which was recently suggested to compensate for these problems, was designed, and heat analysis simulation and temperature increase experiments were performed. The advantages of the motor block lattice resistor were verified through further field tests.

2   Motor Block Lattice Resistor

2.1   Structure of the Propulsion System of a High Speed Train

The parts of the motor block of a high speed train are shown in Fig. 1. The motor block has two thyristor converters, one smoothing reactor, two inverters, two three-phase synchronous motors, one chopper, and two Power Factor Correction (PFC) circuits for power factor control and harmonic wave reduction [2].

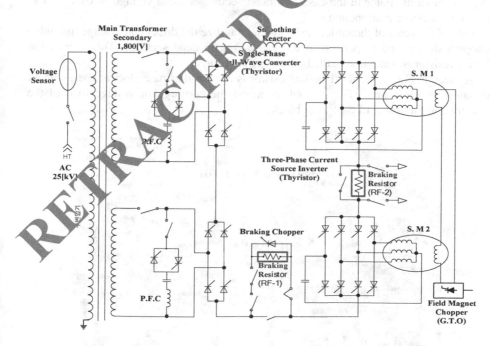

Fig. 1. Circuit of the propulsion control system of a high speed train

The main transformer converts the 25kV cable voltage into 1,800 V, and the two single-phase bridge rectifiers that are serially connected and make up a thyristor perform variable rectification of the transformer's second winding voltage according to the switching degree. The current of the rectified DC source is smoothened by the smoothing reactor and flows into the two traction electric motors, which are composed of two 1,130kW three-phase synchronous motors and two three-phase current-type inverters that control acceleration or deceleration and regeneration [3-5].

The inverter has a forced commutation mode and a natural commutation mode. In the forced commutation mode, the current is rectified by the capacitor and thyristor, and in the natural commutation mode, by the inter-phase voltage generated by the counter-electromotive force of a synchronous motor [6].

2.2   Structure and Role of the Motor Block Lattice Resistor

The motor block lattice resistor is installed at the direct-current link of the input unit of the high speed train's propulsion control system, as shown in Fig. 1. It is called a 'lattice resistor' because the resistors are arranged in the form of a lattice.

The lattice resistor is controlled by the separately excited inverter operation of a converter and composed of two circuits: one for securing the electric braking force in normal operations by controlling the braking chopper according to the amount of the regenerated energy, and the other for dissipating the generated electric energy from the synchronous motor in the case of a dead section, a cable voltage of over 25 kV, and a transformer malfunction.

One of the roles of the lattice resistor is to stabilize the direct end voltage through a chopper device and to perform dynamic braking in dead sections. This is why the lattice resistor is sometimes called a 'braking resistor.'

As seen in Fig. 1, the RF-1 lattice resistor is used to dissipate electric energy under dynamic braking, and RF-2 is used to adjust the cooling fan voltage to cool the resistor and the inside of the motor block.

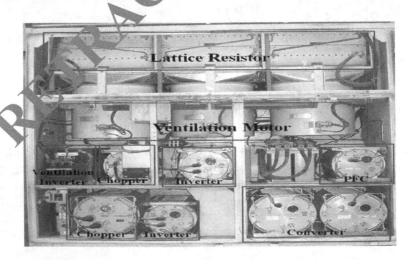

Fig. 2. Structure of the motor block

The lattice resistor, installed in the upper position of the motor block structure as seen in Fig. 2, is cooled by the fan motor located underneath, and the blown heat is discharged through high speed train hood, which is installed on top of the high speed train, as seen in Fig. 3. The damages to the resistor wires due to the heat, as seen in Fig. 4, and the cracks in the insulators, as seen in Fig. 5, affect dynamic braking.

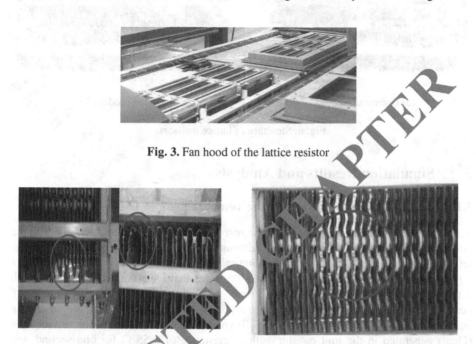

Fig. 3. Fan hood of the lattice resistor

Fig. 4. Damages to resistor wires   **Fig. 5.** Cracks in the insulator

2.3 Suggested Lattice Resistor

As conventional lattice resistors experienced frequent damages to their wires with heat expansion, the recently suggested model reinforced the central part of the resistor, which is the most vulnerable part, with insulators to prevent damage. In addition, considering the temperature increase due to the narrow interval between the lattices, instead of the previous structure of 28 resistors (28S), as seen in Fig. 6 (a), the structure with 30 resistors (30S) was suggested, as seen in Fig. 6 (b).

The components of the conventional resistor wires were Ni/Cr/Fe with the proportions of 48/23/29%, whereas the suggested model excludes the Fe component, which has a low melting point and uses the Ni/Cr alloy at a ratio of 80/20%.

In addition, the suggested lattice resistor model was designed to operate in dead sections when Vacuum Circuit Breaker(VCB) and converter devices have a gate off status, and it also operates when the cable voltage exceeds 2,850 V and when a forced short-circuit or emergency resistor braking is applied.

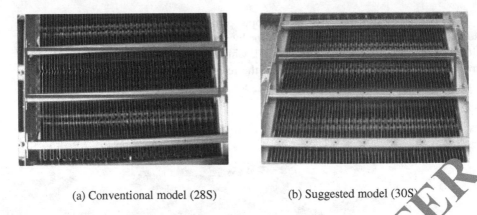

(a) Conventional model (28S)   (b) Suggested model (30S)

Fig. 6. Structure of lattice resistors

3   Simulation Results and Analysis

3.1   Calculation of the Increase in the Temperature of a Lattice Resistor

Temperature increases in the lattice resistors were calculated for both the conventional and suggested models during dynamic braking to consider the temperature increase due to the narrow intervals of the lattices.

The lattice resistor had six units of resistor wires that were serially connected with a resistance of 0.55 Ω per unit and a combined resistance of 3.3 Ω. The operating peak current (I_P) under the combined resistance (R_C) of 3.3 Ω and the operating voltage of 2,850 V was calculated as shown in equation (1). The amount of heat (Qcal) generated in the unit resistor with a resistance of 0.55 Ω for one second was calculated using equation (2) as follows:

$$Ip = V/R_C \tag{1}$$

$$Q_{cal} = 0.24I^2RT \tag{2}$$

Where in the specific heat (C) of the components of the resistor wire were 0.2079 cal/g℃ for Ni, 0.1178 cal/g℃ for Cr, and 0.1070 cal/g℃ for Fe.

The components of the conventional model (28S) were Ni/Cr/Fe with the proportions of 48/23/29%. The total mass (M) was 20.23 kg/m^3, and the components of the suggested model (30S) were Ni/Cr at a ratio of 80/20% and a total mass (M) of 21.08 kg/m^3.

The composite specific heat (Cs) of the conventional model (28S) was 0.1579 cal/g℃, and that of the suggested model (30S) was 0.1899 cal/g℃. The temperature increase (T) was calculated using equation (3).

$$Qcal = C_sMT \tag{3}$$

The calculation with equation (3) resulted in an increase in the final temperature of 30.82 °C/s for the conventional model (28S) and 24.59 °C/s for the suggested model (30S). It was found that the temperature increase was 6.28 °C/s slower in the suggested model than in the conventional model.

3.2   Thermal Energy Distribution in a Lattice Resistor

The temperature increase in the conventional model, under the conditions of no cooling fan and an initial temperature of 11 °C, is shown in Table 1. That of the suggested model is shown in Table 2.

Considering the temperature increase conditions in Table 2, the simulation that was performed with ANSYS, thermal analysis software, resulted in a thermal energy distribution based on the location of the lattice resistor for the conventional model, as seen in Fig. 7 (a), and suggested model, as shown in Fig. 7 (b). The seven thermal energy distributions by location are listed in Table 3. The measured thermal energy distribution was lower in the suggested model, which implies that the thermal characteristics of the suggested model are superior to those of the conventional model.

Table 1. Temperature increase in the conventional model (28S)

Time [sec]	Temperature [°C]
0	11
2	72.64
4	134.28
6	195.92
8	257.56
10	319.20

Table 2. Temperature increase in the suggested model (30S)

Time [sec]	Temperature [°C]
0	11
2	60.18
4	109.36
6	158.54
8	207.72
10	256.90

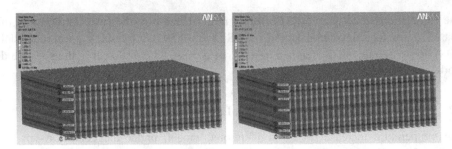

(a) Conventional model (28S)   (b) suggested Model (30S)

Fig. 7. Thermal energy distribution by location in lattice resistors

Table 3. Thermal energy distribution by location

Location	Conventional Model	Suggested Model
①	1.9750e-11	1.5973e-11
②	2.8099e-12	2.7567e-12
③	1.4766e-11	1.1654e-11
④	4.2421e-12	3.4153e-12
⑤	1.4382e-11	1.1812e-11
⑥	2.8163e-12	2.3704e-12
⑦	1.8400e-11	1.5754e-11

4   Experiment Results and Analysis

4.1   Results of the Temperature Increase Experiment

Forced cooling of the lattice resistor was performed with a cooling fan motor with a wind velocity of 2 m/s to keep the experiment conditions identical to those of the field, and the four spots at which the damages to the resistor wire were greatest in the field condition with a surrounding temperature of approximately 11℃ were selected for the temperature measurement, as shown in Fig. 8.

The temperatures were measured with infrared thermometers because attached-type thermometers could not be used due to such harsh field conditions as high voltage, forced cooling, and limited spaces.

The results of the experiments on the conventional and suggested lattice resistors under the same conditions are listed in Tables 4 and 5.

The average temperatures appear to be almost similar, but the smaller temperature increase was measured in the suggested model.

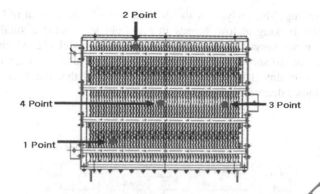

Fig. 8. Temperature measurement points

Table 4. Results of the conventional model experiment

Time (min.)	Measurement Point in the Resistor				
	1	2	3	4	Ave.
15	245	172	216	209	211
20	231	176	196	213	204
25	241	170	212	208	208
30	238	176	208	211	208

Table 5. Results of the suggested model experiment

Time (min.)	Measurement Point in the Resistor				
	1	2	3	4	Ave.
15	245	191	175	215	207
20	242	181	181	206	203
25	244	184	180	212	205
30	244	181	183	213	205

4.2   Field Test Results

The wave forms of the currents during the regeneration braking and dynamic braking that were performed in the field conditions of speed 60km for the conventional lattice resistor and the suggested lattice resistor were compared and analyzed.

A hicorder (HIOKI 8842, 16CH) and a clamp meter (HIOKI 3285, 2,000 A/1V) were used for the measurements, and the braking resistors of RF-1 and RF-2 in a motor block were selected as the measurement points.

Fig. 9 shows the graph of the current wave form of the motor block grid resistor during the regeneration braking of an express train, and Fig. 10 shows the results of the dynamic braking. The analysis of the current wave form, as seen in Fig. 9, shows that regeneration braking at low speeds in the field test yields a small amount of currents that are not very different with conventional Model (42 A) and suggested Model (40 A). Fig. 10 shows that the currents generated during dynamic braking in the field test were almost identical, and it is estimated that the two models have similar performance degrees with 120 A.

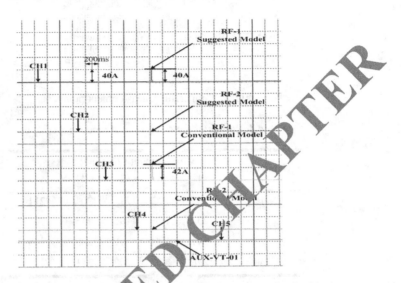

Fig. 9. Current wave graph in a lattice resistor during regeneration braking

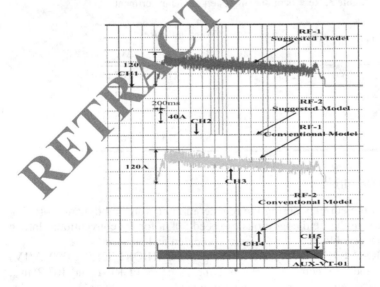

Fig. 10. Current wave graph in a lattice resistor during dynamic braking

5   Conclusion

In this study, a new suggested model for a motor block lattice resistor was suggested to prevent damages to the resistor wires due to the thermal expansion during regeneration braking in a high speed train. Resistors and insulators were added to the new lattice resistor after considering the temperature increase in the conventional models due to the narrow lattice intervals, and the resistor temperature estimation through a component analysis confirmed that the temperature increase was less in the suggested model than in the conventional model. Moreover, the outstanding performance of the suggested model was confirmed via the temperature increase experiment.

The current measurements in the field test also showed that the suggested model is superior to the conventional model during regeneration braking and its performance is similar to that of the conventional model during dynamic braking.

In addition, it was found that the new suggested lattice resistor, which was suggested to maintain the proper temperatures, reduced the damages to the resistors and the cracks in the insulators during the operation of a high speed train, and thus helped secure the stability of the products and reduce the temperature inside a motor block. It is believed that the new suggested model will contribute to the best performance of the peripherals in a motor block, which include the inverter, chopper and converter, etc.

References

1. Lee, W.-K., Park, K.-B.: A Study On Design of propulsion and control system for Korean High Speed Train. In: Spring Conference Proceedings on Korean Society for Railway, pp. 576–588 (2000)
2. Lee, E.-K., Lee, Y.-H., Song, J.-S., Kwon, S.-B.: Study power conversion unit for propulsion system of the Korea Train eXpress (KTX). In: Fall Conference Proceedings on Korean Society for Railway, pp. 2338–2345 (2009)
3. Han, Y.-J., Kim, S.-W., Choi, K.-Y., Cho, M.-S., Choi, S.-K., Choi, J.-S., Kim, J.-S.: A Study on Traction Characteristics of KTX. In: Fall Conference Proceedings on Korean Society for Railway, pp. 175–180 (2003)
4. Kim, Y.-J., Kim, D.-S., Lee, H.-W., Seo, K.-D., Kim, N.-H.: Main Power Conversion Device Development. Journal of Power Electronics 2(4), 21–28 (1997)
5. Ryoo, A.-S., Chung, E.-S., Hwang, K.-C., Choi, J.-M., Ryoo, H.-J., Kim, Y.-J.: Development and Combined test of Traction system for the Korean High Speed Train. In: Fall Conference Proceedings on Korean Society for Railway, pp. 1013–1018 (2002)
6. Bose, B.K.: Power Electronics and Drives (1986)

RETRACTED CHAPTER: Estimation of Deterioration Degree in Overhead Transmission Lines by Tension Load Analysis

Dae-Dong Lee[1], Jae-Myung Shim[2], Young-Dal Kim[2], and Dong-Seok Hyun[1]

[1] Department of Electrical Engineering, Hanyang University,
Seoul 133-791, Republic of Korea
ldd77@hanbat.ac.kr, dshyun@hanyang.ac.kr
[2] Department of Electrical Engineering, Hanbat National University,
Daejeon 305-719, Republic of Korea
{jmshim,zeromoon}@hanbat.ac.kr

Abstract. When a forest fire hits a mountainous area, the life of an overhead transmission line is affected by the heat, extinguishing water, chemicals, and dust. The life of a wire depends on the combination of these elements. Generally, how a conductor wire is affected by forest fire can be analyzed only when the forest fire is accurately modeled and its effects identified. In Korea, however, there are few studies that were conducted based on a forest fire model for transmission lines. There have not been any result from analyzing actual test specimens that were exposed to forest fire. In this study, an artificial dust experiment device was designed and used in the tests because the deterioration characteristics from a forest fire and dust cannot be directly analyzed. The device is set to show field conditions. ACSR 410 mm^2 were used as test specimens. These wires are commonly used for overhead transmission lines in Korea and now are used to analyze tensile strength. In addition, the transmission line samples were collected from the field where a forest fire occurred. They were then compared with the experiment data to estimate their degree of deterioration.

Keywords: ACSR, overhead transmission lines, estimation of deterioration degree, tension load, artificial flame, forest fire.

1   Introduction

The deterioration of the aluminum stranded conductors steel reinforced (ACSR) wire progresses according to the interactions among various factors including the wire material, manufacturing method, wiring condition and the surroundings [1-2]. The ACSR is usually employed in extra-high voltage overhead distribution and transmission lines.

Overhead transmission lines in Korea are mostly located in the mountainous areas. When a forest hits a mountainous area, galvanized steel wires and aluminum stranded wires in the transmission lines directly or indirectly exposed to fire will deteriorate due to the flame and heat, which may cause line-to-line or grounding faults [3-6].

This chapter has been retracted as it is a duplicate of the chapter starting on page 86. The erratum to this chapter is available at DOI: 10.1007/978-3-642-26010-0_48

Accordingly, the forest fire significantly reduces the life of the wire because the overall tension load of a wire can decrease according to diverse corrosion types caused by flames. It is necessary to analyze how much overhead transmission lines deteriorated from the forest fire.

Because the characteristics of the ACSR change when it is affected by fire, the wire must be replaced or reinforced. There are, however, just a few studies worldwide on the degree of wire deterioration. No precise replacement standard exists. Therefore, further studies on this sector are urgently needed [7].

As it is difficult to analyze wire characteristics after the flame and dust from forest fire have affected the wires, an environment that was similar to the actual field situation was assumed in this study. Dusts were deposited on the new 410 mm² ACSR sample wire using an artificial dust experiment device at different distances and temperatures. This was done to analyze the tensile strength of the ACSR conductor based on temperature.

In addition, the transmission line samples were collected from the field in Korea where forest fires have actually occurred. They were then compared with the experiment data to estimate the degree of deterioration.

2   Structure and Experiment Method of an ACSR

2.1   Structure and Corrosion of ACSR

As shown in Fig. 1 the ACSR 410 mm² used in the experiment had an inner layer of 7 galvanized steel wire strands and two layers of 26 light aluminum element wires. The latter two layers carried the current and the seven former layers bore the mechanical tension [8]. The zinc layer that covers the galvanized steel wire is melted by heat, and this accelerates the atmospheric corrosion of the steel wire. The aluminum element wire is also corroded because of galvanic corrosion from the contact of the steel wire without the zinc layer with the aluminum wire. The galvanic corrosion occurs inside the ACSR, and its resultant defects cannot be detected visually.

Due to the galvanic corrosion inside the ACSR, however, the cross-section of the aluminum element wires decreases. Consequently, several types of corrosion by exposure to flames reduce the overall tension load of the ACSR and also greatly reduce its life and increase the power loss in the transmission lines [9-10].

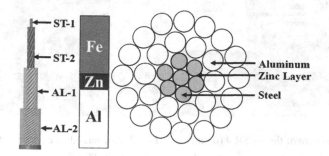

Fig. 1. Structure of the ACSR 410 mm²

2.2   Experiment Method

Using conductors that had been installed and used for a certain time to verify the changes in the mechanical characteristics of ACSR 410 mm² power transmission cables due to forest fire would not yield accurate reference data, since complex corrosion would have already progressed to some extent on the collected cable.

There are no standards for forest fire models or simulations at present. In this study, an artificial dust experiment device was designed and manufactured, as shown in Fig. 2, Oak trees 5 kg, which are common in Korea and 50 cm ACSR used for the experiment. Wire-dust distances were set at 20 cm, 40 cm, 60 cm, and 80 cm. As an additional experiment, ambient temperature was kept constant at 500°C for 15 min, and the tension characteristic was analyzed using the experiment data.

As shown in Fig. 3 it was verified with the naked eye that the specimens were damaged by flame and dust. The specimens were then cooled at normal temperature.

The ambient temperature was measured with four clearance length that ranged from 20 cm to 80 cm, at 20cm intervals. The temperature measurements were conducted at ST-2, the area between ST-2 and AL-1, and at AL-2. The measured temperature data were monitored and collected using a notebook via a data collection device.

To check the mechanical characteristics of the specimen, tension test were conducted according to the Korean (Industrial) Standards. Average data were obtained from the tests with five specimens, and used for the results analysis. For ST-1, which was the innermost spot, average values were not obtained, as there was only one specimen, and the value was not used in this test.

The small wires were identified as follows. ST-1: galvanized steel wire, ST-2: galvanized steel stranded wire, AL-1: inner aluminum stranded wire layer and AL-2: outermost aluminum stranded wire layer.

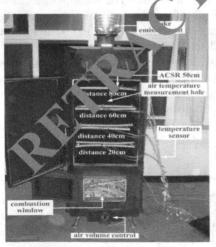

Fig. 2. Structure of the ACSR 410 mm²

Fig. 3. Artificial dust experiment device (after experimental)

2.3   Experiment Method for the Specimens Affected by Forest Fire

To analyze the tension load characteristic of 410 mm^2 ACSR affected by forest fire, as the overhead line conductor, the wires that deteriorated from the flames were collected from three sections and cut into five pieces with a length of 50 cm. The tension test was conducted according to the Korean (Industrial) Standards in the same manner as with the new wire to analyze its mechanical characteristics. An average value was obtained from the tension tests for fifteen specimens.

To reduce errors in the test data, the average value of five measurements in the same condition were used as the mechanical characteristic of the wire was analyzed. The aluminum wires (AL-1 and AL-2), which were directly affected by the flames as they were positioned in the outer layers, were excluded from the test, and the tension characteristic of only the galvanized steel wire (ST-2), which supplied tension load, was analyzed. For the galvanized steel core (ST-1), which was the innermost spot, average values were not obtained as there was only one specimen. The value was not used in this test.

3   Experiment Results and Analysis

3.1   Temperature Test Results Analysis

Fig. 4-7 show the temperature data with reference to the wire-dust clearances of 20 cm, 40 cm, 60 cm, and 80 cm when the 5 kg Oak tree was burnt using the artificial experiment device. These figures show the temperature data scanned in real time with 10 seconds as one interval. In the figures, 20, 40, 60, and 80 represent the clearances of 20 cm, 40 cm, 60 cm, and 80 cm, respectively. The ambient and surface temperatures of the wire are also shown.

In the representation of the surface temperature, ST-2/AL-1 represents the area between the galvanized steel wire (ST-2) and the inner aluminum stranded wire (AL-1); AL-1/AL-2, the area between the inner aluminum stranded wire (AL-1) and the outer aluminum stranded wire (AL-2); and AL-2, the outer aluminum stranded wire (AL-2).

From the temperature data in Fig. 4−7 the analysis results of the temperature data showed that the ambient temperature started to increase from about 250 sec and continued until it reached 720 sec, and then gradually decreased. The wire surface temperature started to increase from 500 sec to 1,000 sec, and then gradually decreased.

The ambient temperature and wire surface temperature fell below 100°C after about 4,500 sec. This seems to have been because the ambient temperature increase preceded the wire surface temperature increase due to the convection heat in the artificial dust experiment device, whereas the flame and dust gradually transferred heat to the wire surface.

The highest ambient temperature according to the diverse wire-flame distances was about 699°C. At a wire-flame distance of 20 cm, as shown in Fig. 4 the highest wire surface temperature was 480°C for ST-2/AL-1, 510°C for AL-1/AL-2, and 505°C for

AL-2. At a wire-flame distance of 40 cm, as shown in Fig. 5 the highest wire surface temperature was 439°C for ST-2/AL-1, 378°C for AL-1/AL-2, and 453°C for AL-2.

At a wire-flame distance of 60 cm, as shown in Fig. 6 the highest wire surface temperature was 403°C for ST-2/AL-1, 418°C for AL-1/AL-2, and 428°C for AL-2.

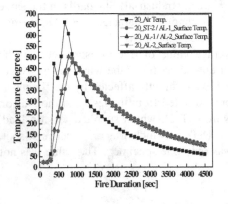

Fig. 4. Temperature data by 20 cm distance

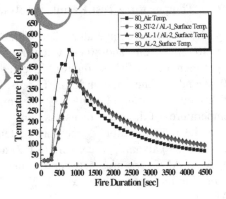

Fig. 5. Temperature data by 40 cm distance

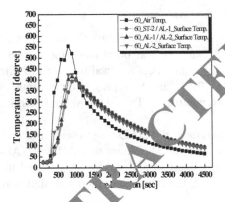

Fig. 6. Temperature data by 60 cm distance

Fig. 7. Temperature data by 80 cm distance

At a wire-flame distance of 80 cm, as shown in Fig. 7 the highest wire surface temperature was 444°C for ST-2/AL-1, 387°C for AL-1/AL-2, and 401°C for AL-2.

These data indicate that a wire deteriorated more as the flames came closer to the wire, and deteriorated less as the flames went farther. In Fig. 7 however, the surface temperature on ST-2/AL-1 with a clearance of 80 cm was slightly higher than those on other wires even though its clearance was longest. This seems to have been caused by the error from the un-uniform shape of the flames.

Fig. 8-11 show the temperature data with reference to the clearances of 20 cm, 40 cm, 60 cm, and 80 cm when the oak tree was burned using the artificial experiment device. Ambient temperature was kept constant at 500°C for 15 min.

The ambient temperature with reference to the clearance was kept almost constant at 500°C for 900 sec, but the highest temperature on the wire surface significantly varied.

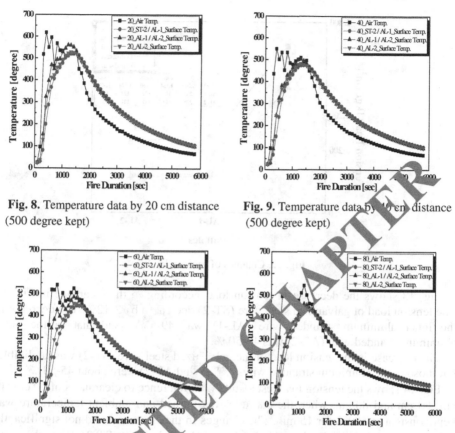

Fig. 8. Temperature data by 20 cm distance (500 degree kept)

Fig. 9. Temperature data by 40 cm distance (500 degree kept)

Fig. 10. Temperature data by 60 cm distance (500 degree kept)

Fig. 11. Temperature data by 80 cm distance (500 degree kept)

As shown in Fig. 4-7 show the highest temperature on the wire surface was 532°C for 20 cm, 486°C for 40 cm, 456°C for 60 cm, and 452°C for 80 cm, which showed that the highest temperature on the wire surface was inversely proportional to the clearance.

In addition, the highest surface temperatures of AL-1 spots were slightly higher than those of AL-2, though all of them were positioned in the inner layer. This seems to have been caused by heat that was slowly emitted in the air due to the deterioration over a long time. The temperature data, however, were negligible because they were not significant.

3.2   Mechanical Characteristics and Analysis

Fig. 12 shows the tension load test results with reference to clearances of 20 cm, 40 cm, 60 cm and 80 cm, When the 5 kg oak tree was burned the changes in the clearances did not significantly influence the tension load of the galvanized steel wire (ST-2), but significantly influenced those of the aluminum stranded wires (AL-1 and AL-2).

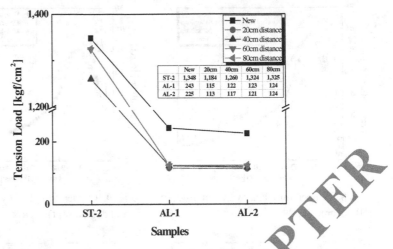

Fig. 12. Changes of tension load

Fig. 13 shows the decrease in tension load according to the clearance in Fig. 12 The tension load of galvanized steel wire (ST-2) decreased by 2-12%. The decrease in the inner aluminum stranded wire (AL-1) was 49-53%, and that in the outer aluminum stranded wire (AL-2) was 45-50 %.

The decrease in the tension load of the galvanized steel wire (ST-2) was negligible, but those in the aluminum stranded wires (AL-1 and AL-2) were about 45-53 %.

Fig. 14 shows the tension load test results with reference to clearances of 20 cm, 40 cm, 60 cm and 80 cm, when the oak tree was burned and ambient temperature was kept constant at 500°C for 15 min. The changes in the clearances did not significantly influence the tension load of the galvanized steel wire (ST-2) (Fig. 12), but significantly influenced those of the aluminum stranded wires (AL-1 and AL-2).

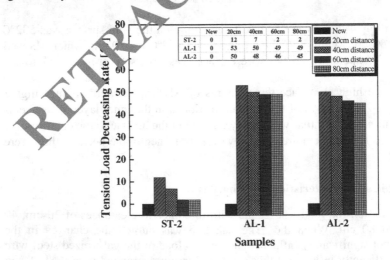

Fig. 13. Decreasing rate of tension load

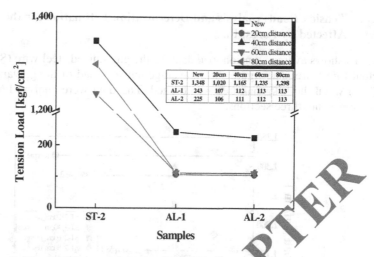

Fig. 14. Changes of tension load (500 degree kept)

Fig. 15 shows the decrease in tension load according to the clearances in Fig. 14. The tension load of galvanized steel wire (ST-2) decreases by 4-24%. The decrease in the inner aluminum stranded wire (AL-1) was 53-56%, and that in the outer aluminum stranded wire (AL-2) was 50-53%.

If tension load decreases by 20%, it represents the life limit. From Fig. 12-15 the test results indicate that the galvanized steel wire (ST-2) was not significantly damaged by the artificial dust because it was located in the innermost layer of the wire. The aluminum stranded wire (AL-1 and AL-2) were significantly damaged because they were located in the outer layers. Besides, the aluminum stranded wires (AL-1 and AL-2) must be replaced as their life limit had already exceeded.

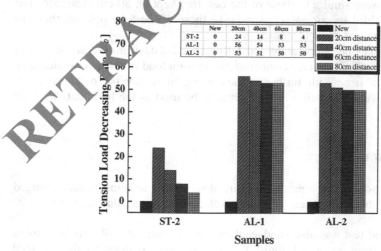

Fig. 15. Decreasing rate of tension load (500 degree kept)

3.3   Tension Load Analysis and Deterioration Estimation for the Specimen Affected by Forest Fire

Fig. 16 shows average tension load data for the galvanized steel wire (ST-2) during an actual forest fire. The figure shows average tension load of the galvanized steel wire (ST-2) when the 5 kg oak tree was burned. The data were analyzed by dividing the specimens into three sections.

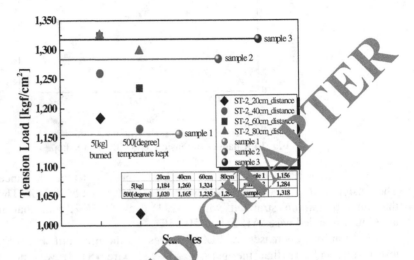

Fig. 16. Flame suppositions of forest fire samples

As shown in Fig. 16, the test result of the first specimen was similar to that of the oak tree that was kept at 500°C with a 40 cm clearance, and the test results of the second specimen were similar to those of the oak tree kept an 80 cm clearance. The test results of the third specimen were similar to those of the 5 kg oak tree that was burned with a 60 cm and 80 cm clearance.

It is expected that the temperature and tension load data from the artificial dust experiment can be used as data for estimating the tension load of the deteriorated wire in an actual forest fire. With further studies using more diverse parameters and specimens from actual forest fires, these data may be used as the basic data for wire life estimation.

4   Conclusion

In this study, the sound 410 mm² ACSR wire deteriorated as temperatures changed using an artificial dust experiment device to collect temperature data and analyze its tension characteristics.

The tension load test was also conducted on the 410 mm² ACSR wire specimens that deteriorated from an actual forest fire in the same manner as the artificial deterioration test. The results were comparatively analyzed.

The measurement of the data that examined the tension load characteristics of the ACSR wire exposed to artificial dust and flames showed that there was almost no change in the tension load of the galvanized steel wire (ST-2) because it existed inside and was not exposed to flame and dust. The tension load of the aluminum stranded wires (AL-1 and AL-2), however, significantly decreased according to the wire-flame clearances.

In addition, specimens from the actual forest fire field were compared with the laboratory data to estimate the degree of deterioration of specimens.

It is expected that the resulting analysis data may be used as data for estimating refurbishment life of deteriorated ACSR wires.

References

1. A selection of project Power distribution administration, Korea Electric Power Research Institute, KRC-92D-001 (1992)
2. Influence of Air pollution on Power System, Korea Electric Power Research Institute, KRC-92C-S05 (1993)
3. Electric Power Research Institute, Transmission Line Reference Book, 345 kV and Above/Second Edition (1989)
4. West, H.J., Mcmullan, D.W.: Fire Induced Flashovers of EHV Transmission Lines. In: IEEE-PES Winter Meeting, New York, Paper A73047-2 (February 1978)
5. Kim, S.-D.: An Experimental Study on a Solenoid Eddy Current Sensor to Inspect Deteriorations in Overhead Distribution Lines. Journal of the Korean Institute of Illuminating and Electrical Installation Engineers 13(1), 77–85 (1999)
6. Kim, Y.-K., Chang, S.-K., Cho, J.-I.: Effects of Corrosion Environment on Mechanical Properties of Catenary Wires. Korean Society for Railway 5(1), 32–39 (2002)
7. Kojima, Y., Fukuda, J., Kumec, T., Iinuma, J., Endo, M.: Corrosion Detector Robot for Overhead Transmission Line. Fujikura Technical Review (21), 74–83 (1992)
8. Jeong, J.-K., Kang, J.-W., Kang, Y.-W., Shim, E.-B., Kim, J.-B.: Experimental Detections of the Aluminum Layer Corrosions for ACSR Transmission Ground Wires. Journal of the Korean Institute of Electrical Engineers 46(7), 1102–1108 (1997)
9. Influence of Air pollution on Power System, Korea Electric Power Research Institute, KRC-92C-S05 (1993)
10. The Development of System for ACSR Life-Time Estimation, KEPRI, TR.97EJ02.2000.16 (2000)

RETRACTED CHAPTER: Structure Vibration Analysis and Active Noise Control of a Power Transformer by Mobility Measurement

Young-Dal Kim[1], Jae-Myung Shim[1], Keun-Seok Park[1],
Yun-Mi Jeong[1], and Dae-Dong Lee[2]

[1] Department of Electrical Engineering, Hanbat National University,
Daejeon, Republic of Korea
{zeromoon,jmshim,jym0809}@hanbat.ac.kr,
smg-park@nate.com
[2] Department of Electrical Engineering, Hanyang University,
Seoul, Republic of Korea
1dd77@hanbat.ac.kr

Abstract. Most cases of power transformer failure are caused by physical factors linked to the transient vibrations of multiple 120 Hz combinations. In addition, the noise generated in the transformer from this vibration not only directly contributes to the worsening of the work environment but also causes psychological stress, resulting in the worsening of the workers' efficiency and of the living environment of the inhabitants around the power plant. Thus, to remedy these problems, the mechanical-excitation forces working on a power transformer were categorized in this study, and the mechanical-damage mechanism was identified through the vibration transfer paths acting on machines or structures. In addition, a study on active noise cancellation in a transformer using the FXLMS algorithm was conducted to develop a system that is capable of multiple-sound/channel control, which resulted in the active noise reduction effect when applied on the field.

Keywords: Active Noise Control, Filtered-XLMS, Power Transformer, Structure Vibration Analysis.

1 Introduction

In transformers, a multiple combination of 120 Hz electrical frequencies is generated by the magnetostriction in the internal iron core which is emitted externally through the transformer tank's outer wall. Here, the resonance greatly increases if the transformer tank's resonant frequency is the same as the frequency of the magnetostriction which is caused by the transformer's internal magnetic field. To prevent such a resonance phenomenon, forced dampening can be added to the tank system, or the resonance can be controlled by adjusting rigidity and mass.

Adding damping to a large structure, however, such as a transformer tank, is difficult from the viewpoint of cost and manufacturing, and therefore, mass and rigidity adjustment is performed on the tank's mass, and soundproof walls have been installed recently.

This chapter has been retracted due to multiple publications. The erratum to this chapter is available at DOI: 10.1007/978-3-642-26010-0_48

T.-h. Kim et al. (Eds.): CA/CES³ 2011, CCIS 256, pp. 322–332, 2011.
© Springer-Verlag Berlin Heidelberg 2011

Such methods are feasible for high-frequency noises but cause a huge economic burden on blocking low-frequency noise. Thus, much effort is being done internationally to put a newly proposed method called Active Noise Control (ANC) to practical use [1-3]. Here, Ross [4] researched on the control of the transformer noise in the transformer room while Morgan studied how to perform active noise control in a three-dimensional space [5].

Currently, while noise cannot be removed within the entire space, it is possible to establish local silence areas [6]. Here, much effort is being done to implement active noise control with a single system while avoiding a complicated acoustic system [7-9].

Therefore, through this study, we intend to contribute to the noise reduction in large transformers by analyzing the type of vibration in the transformer tank via mode analysis and developing the ANC system for application in field transformers.

2   Power Transformer Structure Vibration Analysis and ANC Algorithm

2.1   FEM on ANSYS

In the ANSYS/SOLID187 Used in this study, the prism/tetrahedral element was not used. The boundary condition of Young's modulus was 200 GPa (based on cast carbon steel), density was 7,800 kg/m^2, and the Poisson's ratio was set at 0.32. The node size for using Block Lanczos as a mode method was 173,249, and the element size was set at 87,016. ANSYS was used as the analysis tool while using a tetrahedron forming a mesh.

A free mesh is advantageous in forming an irregular-type mesh on a complex form, such as a transformer tank. In addition, by adding a shape-dependent mesh (smart-sized mesh), the no. of meshes of the entire model was set. By using the finite-element model (FEM) in Fig. 1(a), the mesh shape in Fig. 1(b) was obtained. As shown in Fig. 1(a), the part contacting the ground surface through the entire transformer tank's weight showed almost no vibration-related displacement and thus assigned a fully fixed constraint while excluding the influence of insulator oil.

Fig. 2(a) was analyzed at the natural-mode shape of 118.1 Hz, where the resonance condition was local and did not affect the transformer. Fig. 2(b) was analyzed, however, at the natural-mode shape of 121.3 Hz, where the transformer was not greatly affected, and it was found that vibrations could be induced at the bushings.

Fig. 2(c) was analyzed at the natural-mode shape of 238.2 Hz, where the resonance condition was local and did not affect the transformer. Fig. 2(d) was analyzed at a natural-mode shape of 241.1 Hz, where resonance occurred at the transformer's upper side.

It was found that there is a possibility of large vibration in various bushing areas. The analysis of the transformer's structural and dynamic-response characteristics, which was done at the natural mode, resulted in the detection of resonant frequencies near 120 and 240 Hz. It is thus concluded that there is a possibility of induced vibrations.

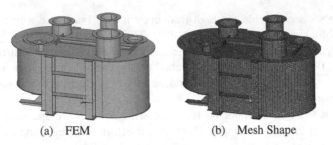

(a) FEM   (b) Mesh Shape

Fig. 1. Shape of power transformer

(a) 118.1 Hz   (b) 121.3 Hz

(c) 236.2 Hz   (d) 241.1 Hz

Fig. 2. Shape of natural mode

2.2   Filtered-X LMS Algorithm

For active control of the noise generated by large transformers, methods such as the feedback and feed forward control algorithm are used as well as hybrid control algorithms that improve the stability and control performance by combining the advantages of the two. In the noise produced by large transformers, the flux changes 120 times per second according to the 60 Hz frequency signal, and the noise is caused by the core and coil. In addition, as the noise transfer path is time-varying according to various factors, such as temperature, moisture, and obstacles, accurate modeling is difficult. The reference signal, however, can be easily measured from the transformer's vibrations or current, and control of complex structures is possible using such reference signal. In addition, it is recommended that control be performed using the effective feed forward method.

In the LMS algorithm, the control output is directly sensed by a sensor measuring the error signal. Thus, the sensor has to be at the same location as the exciter. However, the LMS algorithm cannot be directly applied in most cases because the additional exciter and the sensor are at different locations.

In this study, control was performed using the filtered-X LMS algorithm, which is based on the LMS method that is frequently used for reducing the noise and vibration of large transformers. Assuming that a system from the control output to the sensor exists, a modified filtered-X LMS algorithm was applied considering this. Its block diagram is as shown in Fig. 3.

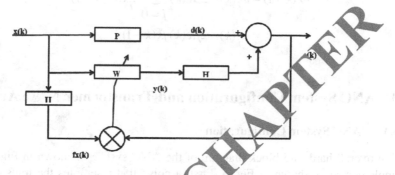

Fig. 3. Block diagram of the FXLMS algorithm

$\hat{H}$ is the model of the error system, which is assumed to be an FIR filter with a length of LK +1 As in the LMS method, the FXLMS algorithm uses the steepest-descent method to minimize the square of the instantaneous error e2(k). The input of the controller W is the x(k) signal, and the output is y(k). Assuming that the error system model and the error system are the same as in the LMS method, the error signal is expressed as in Eq. (1)

$$e(k) = d(k) + \sum_{j=0}^{L_k} h_i\, y(k-j)$$

$$= d(k) + \sum_{i=0}^{L} \sum_{j=0}^{L_k} h_i w_i(k-j)\, x(k-i-j) \tag{1}$$

Meanwhile, the coefficient of the applied filter can be derived using Eq. (2).

$$\omega_i(k+1) = \omega_i(k) - \mu\nabla_i(k) \tag{2}$$

If it is assumed that $\omega_i(k) \square \omega_i(k-1) \square \cdots \square \omega_i(k-L_h)$ is satisfied, that is, that the coefficient changes slowly, the instantaneous slope is calculated as in Eq. (3).

$$\nabla_i(k) = \frac{\partial e^2(k)}{\partial \omega_i(k)} = -2e(k) \sum_{j=0}^{Lk} h_i x(k-i-j) \tag{3}$$

Thus, the equation with the updated filter coefficient is given as in Eq. (4). Here, $fx(k)$ is the reference signal that passed the error system model.

$$\omega_i(k+1) = \omega_i(k) - 2\mu e(k) \sum_{j=0}^{L_k} h_i x(k-i-j)$$
$$= \omega_i(k) - 2\mu e(k) fx(k-1) \tag{4}$$

3   ANC System Configuration and Transformer Noise Analysis

3.1   ANC System Configuration

The overall hardware block diagram of the ANC system is shown in Fig. 4 and was implemented as shown in Fig. 5. First, a noise that resembles the transformer noise source was generated in the lab, and then ANC was applied to observe the noise cancellation effect according to the control output and location of the error microphone. In addition, for the field experiment, a system supporting up to 20 channels was built as shown in Fig. 6. A test was then performed by applying up to 15 channels on a currently operating 154(k) 60(MVA) 3 phase transformer. In addition, to measure and analyze the noise of the large-scale transformer, measurement was performed at the error microphone located at the right side, as shown in Fig. 6.

The noise map for each frequency is shown in Fig. 7. The measurement results showed the following maximum values at each frequency: 20 Hz - 95.55 dB, 240 Hz - 82.59 dB, 360 Hz - 84.07 dB, 480 Hz - 80.62 dB, 600 Hz - 75.05 dB and 720 Hz - 72.56 dB.

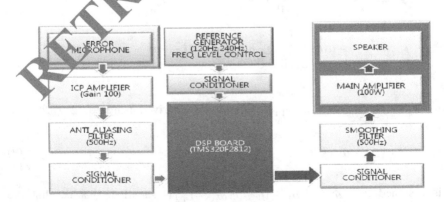

Fig. 4. ANC system diagram

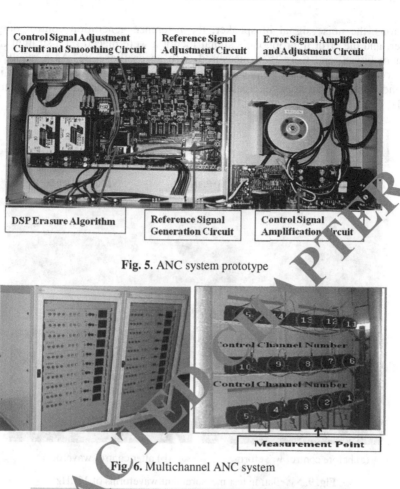

Fig. 5. ANC system prototype

Fig. 6. Multichannel ANC system

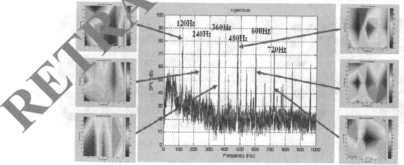

Fig. 7. Relationship between the transformer noise map and frequency

3.2   Simulation Test Measurement and Analysis

The simulation test conditions were divided into two types, according to the noise, control output, and location of the error microphone, and the data were measured for the single-tone control frequencies of 120 and 240 Hz. First, for the simulation test conditions, the noise signal of speaker, the reference generation control output of speaker, and the error microphone's signal location were placed on a straight line, as shown in Fig. 8, and were then measured with an oscilloscope. As a result, at the single-tone frequencies of 120 and 240 Hz, the measurements were as shown in Fig. 9-10 and Table 1. The noise decreased by microphone output waveform the most at 240 Hz, up to 22.3 dB, as shown in Fig. 10.

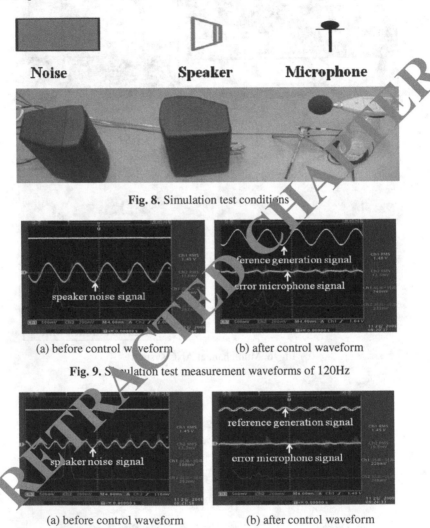

Noise   **Speaker**   **Microphone**

Fig. 8. Simulation test conditions

(a) before control waveform   (b) after control waveform

Fig. 9. Simulation test measurement waveforms of 120Hz

(a) before control waveform   (b) after control waveform

Fig. 10. Simulation test measurement waveforms of 240Hz

Table 1. Measurement results at the simulation test conditions

control conditions	before control	after control	decrement
120 Hz	80.8 dB	69.7 dB	11.1 dB
240 Hz	80.8 dB	58.5 dB	22.3 dB

3.3   Field Experiment Measurement and Analysis

The field test conditions were as shown in Table 2. As can be seen at the right side of Fig. 6, control was performed at 15 locations, while the noise was measured at four points, as shown at the right and left sides of Fig. 6. The data measurement results for the single-tone control frequencies of 120 and 240 Hz are shown in Fig. 11-14 and Table 3. As can be seen in Fig. 12(a), the noise was greatly reduced to ca. 13.0 dB at measurement point -1 at 120 Hz, while as can be seen in Fig. 14(b), it decreased by ca. 25.1 dB at measurement point -2 at 240 Hz.

Table 2. Field experiment conditions

control items	control conditions
shutter door conditions	closed
control frequency	120 Hz and 240 Hz
main AMP gain	0 %
reference signal frequency level	120 Hz and 240 Hz = 80 %
reference signal total level	80 %

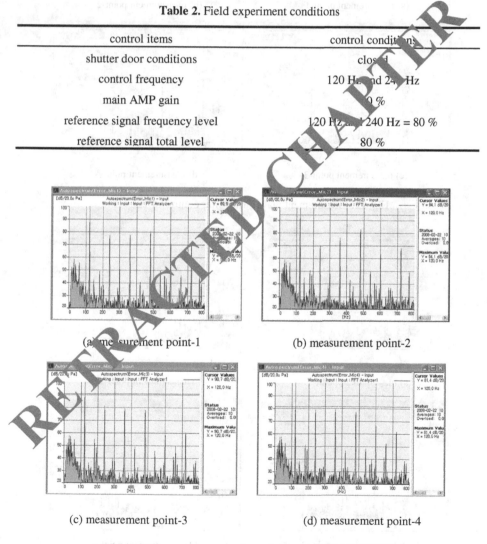

(a) measurement point-1

(b) measurement point-2

(c) measurement point-3

(d) measurement point-4

Fig. 11. Measurement waveforms before control of 120 Hz

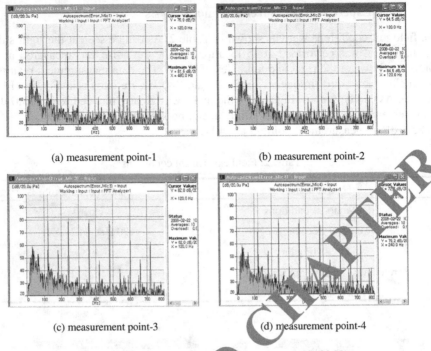

(a) measurement point-1

(b) measurement point-2

(c) measurement point-3

(d) measurement point-4

Fig. 12. Measurement waveforms after control of 120 Hz

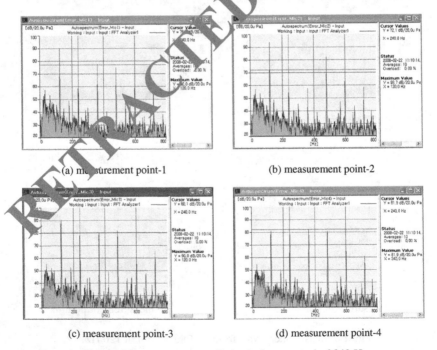

(a) measurement point-1

(b) measurement point-2

(c) measurement point-3

(d) measurement point-4

Fig. 13. Measurement waveforms before control of 240 Hz

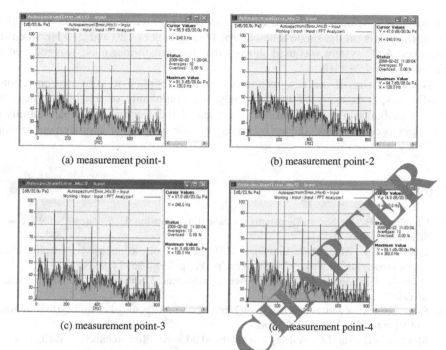

(a) measurement point-1

(b) measurement point-2

(c) measurement point-3

(d) measurement point-4

Fig. 14. Measurement waveforms after control of 240 Hz

Table 3. Measurement results under the field test

control conditions	controls	Measurement Point / Noise (dB)				
		1	2	3	4	average
120 Hz	before control	89.9	94.1	90.7	81.4	89.0
	after control	76.9	84.5	82.0	72.2	78.9
	decrement	13.0	9.6	8.7	9.2	10.1
240 Hz	before control	76.8	72.1	80.1	81.9	77.7
	after control	55.9	47.0	67.0	74.9	61.2
	decrement	20.9	25.1	13.1	7.0	16.5

4   Conclusion

In this thesis, the structural vibration of a single-phase transformer was analyzed through mobility measurement while performing simulated and field experiments on transformer noise reduction during operation, using an active noise control system on which the FXLMS algorithm was applied. As for the transformer's resonance test results, the natural mode analysis of the transformer's structural and dynamic-response characteristics revealed resonant frequencies near 120 and 240 Hz. It is thus concluded that vibrations may be caused. In addition, the measurement of the field transformer data on the single-tone control frequencies of 120 and 240 Hz when the developed ANC system was used showed that the transformer noise was reduced by at least 13.0 and 25.1 dB.

As shown here, if the new technology will be applied to currently operational transformers, it is expected that not only the complaints of inhabitants near the substations but also the occupational diseases of the workers in the substations or power plants can be reduced, thereby greatly contributing to the improvement of work efficiency

References

1. Chaplin, G.B.: Method and apparatus for canceling vibration. U. S. Patent No. 4, pp. 441–489 (1984)
2. Eriksson, L.J., Allie, M.C., Bremigan, C.D.: Active noise control using adaptive digital signal processing. In: Proc. ICASSP, New York, pp. 2594–2597 (1988)
3. Warnaka, G.E., Poole, L., Tichy, J.: Active attenuator. US Patent 473. 906, September 25 (1984)
4. Ross, C.F.: An algorithm for designing a broadband active sound control system. J. Sound and Vibration 80(3), 373–380 (1982)
5. Morgan, D.R., Thi, J.C.: A delay less sub band adaptive filter architecture. IEEE Trans. on Signal Proc. 43(8), 1819–1830 (1995)
6. Tokhi, M.O., Leitch, R.R.: Active Noise Control. Clarendon Press, Oxford (1992)
7. Efron, A.J., Han, L.C.: Wide-area adaptive active noise cancellation. IEEE Trans. on Circuits and System-II: Analog and Digital Proc. 41(6), 405–409 (1994)
8. Graupe, D., Efron, A.J.: A Output-Whitening Approach to Adaptive Active Noise Cancellation. IEEE Trans. on Circuits and Systems 38(11), 1306–1313 (1991)
9. Oppenheim, A.V., Zangi, K.C., Gaupe, D.: Single-Sensor Active Noise Cancellation. IEEE Transactions on Speech and Processing 2(2), 285–290 (1994)

Complexity Adaptive Branch Predictor
for Thermal-Aware 3D Multi-core Processors

Jin Woo Ahn[1], Dong Oh Son[1], Hyung Gyu Jeon[1],
Jong Myon Kim[2], and Cheol Hong Kim[1,*]

[1] School of Electronics and Computer Engineering,
Chonnam National University,
Gwangju, 500-757 Korea
[2] School of Electrical Engineering, University of Ulsan,
Ulsan, 680-749 Korea
{ajw0411,sdo1127,hggodman,jongmyon.kim}@gmail.com,
chkim22@chonnam.ac.kr

Abstract. High-performance processors usually perform speculative executions for improving the instruction-level parallelism. In the speculative executions, the most important factor determining the performance is the accuracy of the branch predictor. As this accuracy becomes higher, thereby enhancing the instruction-level parallelism, the hardware complexity of the branch prediction logic increases. In the conventional 2D multi-core processor, the branch predictor is not classified as the hot unit. However, in the 3D multi-core processor where the power density is substantially high, the temperature of the complicated branch predictor also becomes high, which causes a negative impact on the processor reliability. To reduce the temperature of the branch predictor in the 3D multi-core processor, we propose the thermal management technique which determines the hardware complexity of the branch predictor in each layer by considering the temperature. According to our experimental results, the proposed complexity adaptive branch predictor technique shows a superior thermal efficiency than the conventional dynamic thermal management technique.

Keywords: 3D Multi-core Processor, Branch Predictor, Hotspot, Dynamic Thermal Management.

1 Introduction

Speculative executions have been widely used in high-performance processors to improve the instruction-level parallelism. In determining the efficiency of speculative executions, branch predictor is the most important factor. The branch predictor decides the following path of the instruction stream when the branch instruction is encountered. If the processor predicts the correct path by the accurate branch

---

* Corresponding author.

T.-h. Kim et al. (Eds.): CA/CES[3] 2011, CCIS 256, pp. 333–343, 2011.
© Springer-Verlag Berlin Heidelberg 2011

predictor when the conditional branch instruction is executed, the processor can execute more instructions per cycle, leading to improved performance. Therefore, the instruction-level parallelism in the processor can be improved as the accuracy of the branch predictor improves. For this reason, many studies have focused on the techniques to improve the accuracy of the branch predictor[1-9].

The hardware complexity of recent branch predictors is very high to provide high accuracy, because the accuracy of the branch predictor is usually proportional to the hardware complexity of the branch predictor. Unfortunately, the power consumption in the branch predictor increases as the corresponding hardware complexity becomes high. Increased power consumption in the branch predictor causes harmful effects on the thermal behavior. Especially, the temperature of the complicated branch predictor can be a serious problem in the 3D multi-core processor, whereas it has no problem in the conventional 2D multi-core processor. Previous studies reported that the peak temperature of the 3D multi-core processor is much higher than that of the 2D multi-core processor[13]. High temperature in the processor leads to hot spot problem that can cause timing errors[11] and physical damage[12]. Therefore, it is important to consider the temperature of the branch predictor in the 3D multi-core processor. To improve the performance of the 3D multi-core processor by alleviating the thermal problem in the branch predictor, this paper proposes the hardware complexity adaptive branch predictor, which considers the temperature pattern of each layer in the 3D multi-core processor. We also analyze the thermal behavior, power consumption and performance of 3D multi-core processors according to the branch prediction technique.

The rest of this paper is organized as follows. Section 2 describes the overview of previous related work. In Section 3, we explain the proposed complexity adaptive branch predictor for thermal-aware 3D multi-core processors. In Section 4 and Section 5, we describe our simulation methodology and detailed experimental results. Finally, we present our conclusions in Section 6.

2   Related Work

2.1   Dynamic Thermal Management

As process technology scales down, single chip can be composed of larger number of transistors. Increased transistors have enabled improving the performance of the processor. However, increased transistors on the chip cause high power density, resulting in thermal hot spots on a chip. Thermal hot spots have negative impact on the reliability and the performance of the processor.

Dynamic thermal management methods such as Dynamic voltage scaling(DVS) and dynamic frequency scaling(DFS), which control the internal operation based on the thermal behavior of the processor, lower the peak temperature or keep the average temperature under a given threshold[14]. However, these techniques degrade the processor performance. For example, dynamic voltage scaling degrades the performance by 3%, and dynamic frequency scaling degrades the performance by 6%[17]. Ideal fetch engine gating scheme also degrades the processor performance by

10%[15]. In the 3D multi-core processor, the thermal problem is a big challenge. Previous studies show that the peak temperature of the 3D multi-core processor can reach to 90°C[16]. Therefore, the dynamic thermal management in the 3D multi-core processor may degrade the performance significantly.

2.2   3D Stacking Technique

In the 2D multi-core processor, a large portion of the total chip area is consumed by the interconnection, resulting in the increased wire length. The increased wire length causes increased delay and performance degradation. To overcome the problems in the 2D multi-core processor, the 3D stacking technique has become one of the efficient solutions in the processor design. However, the 3D stacking technique increases the power density in the chip, resulting in severe thermal problems. For an example, the peak temperature of the 3D multi-core processor is increased by 17~20°C compared to that of the conventional 2D multi-core processor[10]. For this reason, thermal problems should be considered in designing the 3D multi-core processor.

3   Thermal-Aware Branch Predictor

For analyzing the thermal efficiency of the 3D multi-core processor according to the type of the branch predictor, we have simulations with various 3D quad-core processors. In the simulated 3D quad-core processor, each core is modeled as Alpha 21264. The detailed floorplan of each core is shown in Figure 1.

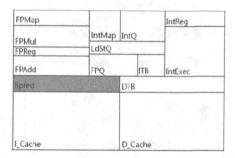

Fig. 1. Alpha21264 Processor Core

To reduce the temperature of the branch predictor in the 3D multi-core processor, we propose the Complexity Adaptive Branch Predictor(CABP) technique. In the CABP, we set five different branch predictors (Level1 to Level5) varying the hardware complexity, where Level5 represents the branch predictor with the lowest complexity and Level1 denotes the branch predictor with the highest hardware complexity.

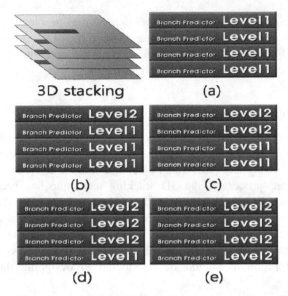

Fig. 2. 3D-Quad-core Processors with Various Combinations of Branch Predictors

The motivation of the CABP technique can be summarized as follow: The cores near the heat sink have higher cooling efficiency than the cores far from the heat sink. Therefore, in the CABP technique, the branch predictor with low hardware complexity is assigned to the cores far from the heat sink. On the other hand, the branch predictor with high hardware complexity is assigned to the cores near the heat sink.

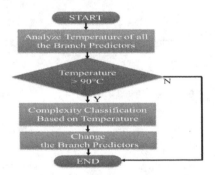

Fig. 3. Block Diagram of the CABP technique

To apply the proposed CABP technique to the 3D quad-core processors, we perform the following steps: 1) analyze the temperature of all the branch predictors in Figure 2. 2) Based on the temperature of the branch predictor in step1 and complexity classification depending on the temperature shown in Table 1, the corresponding branch predictor is assigned to each layer. Initially, the branch predictor of each layer is set to Level1 as shown in Figure 1-(a) to maximize the accuracy of the branch predictor. Then, if the peak temperature of the branch predictor in 4th layer is over

100°C, we assign Level5 branch predictor to 4th layer. If the peak temperature of the branch predictor in 3rd layer is between 95°C and 100°C, we assign Level4 branch predictor to 3rd layer.

Table 1. Complexity Classification Based on Temperature

Temperature(°C)	Complexity
90~95	Level3
95~100	Level4
100~	Level5

4   Experimental Methodology

We use SimpleScalar[18] simulator, which provides a cycle-level modeling of processors. Detailed parameters used in the simulation are shown in Table 2. To obtain the power trace, we use Wattch[19]. We chose mcf application from SPEC2K benchmark[17], because the processor shows the worst thermal efficiency in executing the mcf application in our previous study [15].

Table 2. Processor Parameter

Parameter		Value
Functional Units		4 integer ALUs, 4 FP ALUs, 1 integer multiplier/divider 1 FP multiplier/divider
Frequency / V_{dd}		3.0GHz/1.5V
On-chip caches	L1	32KB, 4-way, 32bytes lines, 1 cycle latency
	L2	512KB, 8-way, 32bytes lines, 12 cycle latency

Modeling parameters of the branch predictor are presented in Table 3. We use combined branch predictor[20], which combines two independent components. In our simulation, the combined branch predictor consists of bimodal branch predictor and gshare branch predictor. It also uses a hardware selector to choose one from two prediction results.

Table 3. Branch Predictor Parameter

Complexity	Bimodal	Gshare	Selector
Level1	4096B	4096B	4096B
Level2	2048B	2048B	2048B
Level3	1024B	1024B	1024B
Level4	512B	512B	512B
Level5	256B	256B	256B

To solve the thermal problem of the branch predictor, we apply the conventional dynamic thermal management and the proposed CABP technique. In the conventional dynamic thermal management technique, if the peak temperature of the branch predictor goes over the thermal threshold, the branch predictor is stalled to reduce the temperature. In order to evaluate the temperature of the simulated 3D quad-core processors, we use HotSpot 5.0 as our thermal modeling tool[21]. HotSpot grid model is capable of modeling the 3D multi-core processors. Thermal modeling parameters of the silicon layer and thermal interface materials are shown in Table 4.

Table 4. Thermal Modeling of 3D Quad-core Processor

Parameters		Heat capacity (J/m³K)	Resistivity (m-K/W)	Thickness (meter)
Layer0	Die	1.75e6	0.01	0.00015
	TIM	4e6	0.25	2.0e-05
Layer1	Die	1.75e6	0.01	0.00015
	TIM	4e6	0.25	2.0e-05
Layer2	Die	1.75e6	0.01	0.00015
	TIM	4e6	0.25	2.0e-05
Layer3	Die	1.75e6	0.01	0.00015
	TIM	4e6	0.25	2.0e-05

We model the 3D quad-core processor as shown in Figure 4. Layer3 denotes the layer near the heat sink while Layer0 represents the layer far from the heat sink.

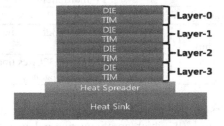

Fig. 4. Hotspot Modeling of Simulated 3D Quad-core processor

5   Experimental Results

In the experimental results, NO-DTM denotes the results of the models without any thermal-aware methods. DTM represents the results of the models with the conventional dynamic thermal management technique. CABP denotes the results of the models with the proposed CABP technique.

In order to apply the CABP technique to the 3D multi-core processor, we analyze the peak temperature of the branch predictors according to the vertical location of the branch predictor, as shown in Table 5. Based on the temperature results, we determine the hardware complexity of the branch predictor, as explained in Section 3.

Table 5. Peak Temperature of 3D Quad-core Processor

Temp(°C)	(a)	(b)	(c)	(d)	(e)
Layer0	107.36	105.12	103.79	103.01	102.66
Layer1	103.68	102.35	100.66	99.72	99.3
Layer2	96.08	95.3	94.36	92.99	92.4
Layer3	83.9	83.51	83.05	82.43	81.46

For an example, in the (a)-type architecture, the peak temperature of Layer0 and Layer1 is over 100°C. Therefore, we assign Level5 complexity branch predictors to both layers. Because the peak temperature of Layer2 and Layer3 is 96.08°C and 83.9°C, we assign Level4 and Level1 complexity branch predictors to each layer, respectively. By using this process, we assign thermal-aware complexity branch predictors to each layer as shown in Figure 5 from the branch predictors in Figure 2.

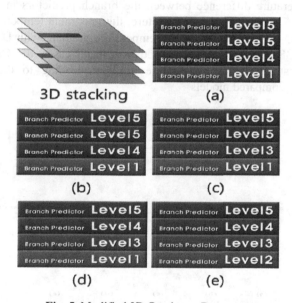

Fig. 5. Modified 3D Quad-core Processor

5.1   Temperature Analysis

Figure 6 shows the peak temperature according to each model. In the (a)-type architecture, the peak temperature of the branch predictor with NO-DTM is 107.36°C. DTM and CABP technique reduce the peak temperature of the branch predictor to 97.72°C and 88.19°C, respectively. Average peak temperature of five architectures with the CABP technique is 89.66°C, while that with NO-DTM and DTM is 104.39°C and 90.19°C, respectively. Our results prove that the proposed CABP technique can reduce the peak temperature of the branch predictor more effectively than the conventional DTM technique.

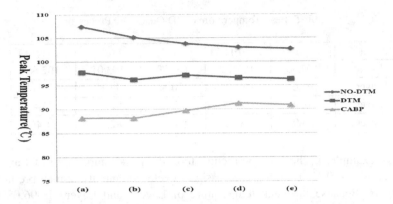

Fig. 6. Peak temperature of 3D Quad-core Processors

We also analyze the maximum temperature gradient of the branch predictor, which means the temperature difference between the branch predictors in stacked layers, shown in Figure 7. In the (a)-type architecture, the maximum temperature gradient is 23.36°C with NO-DTM. The maximum temperature gradient with DTM and CABP technique is 18.38°C and 10.46°C, respectively. In all cases, the CABP technique shows the lowest maximum temperature gradient, leading to the best thermal efficiency among compared models.

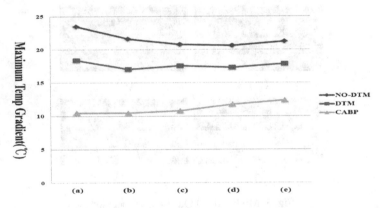

Fig. 7. Maximum Temperature Gradient of 3D Quad-core Processors

5.2   Power Consumption Analysis

Figure 8 shows the normalized average power consumption of the branch predictor according to the thermal management techniques. In the (a)-type architecture, the conventional DTM reduces the average power consumption by 0.37%, while the proposed CABP technique reduces the average power consumption by 53.85%. For the other architectures, the DTM reduces the average power consumption by 0.36%, 0.31%, 0.30%, and 0.28%, respectively, while the proposed CABP technique reduces the average power consumption by 51.7%, 39.9%, 32.12%, and 33.86%, respectively.

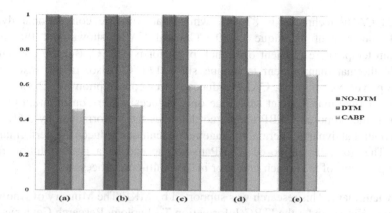

Fig. 8. Normalized Average Power Consumption of 3D Quad-core Processors

5.3   Performance Analysis

Figure 9 shows the normalized performance of the processor according to the branch predictor model. In the (a)-type architecture, the conventional DTM reduces the performance by 30%, while the proposed CABP technique reduces the performance by 4.53%. For the other architectures, the DTM reduces the performance by 28.99%, 27.98%, 26.81%, and 24.53%, respectively, while the CABP technique degrades the performance by 4.47%, 3.79%, 2.62%, and 2.63%, respectively.

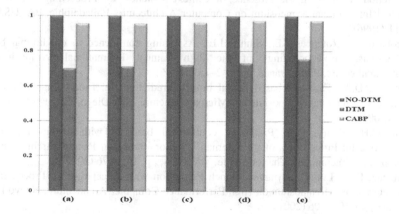

Fig. 9. Normalized Performance of 3D Quad-core Processors

6   Conclusions

In the 3D multi-core processor, increased power density of the branch predictor causes thermal problems. To solve the thermal problem in the branch predictor for the 3D multi-core processor, we propose the Complexity Adaptive Branch Predictor(CABP) technique. The average temperature of the branch predictor with the proposed CABP technique is 87.7°C, while that with the conventional dynamic thermal management technique is 89.7°C. And CABP shows that the average maximum temperature gradient of branch predictor is 11.2°C. But the conventional dynamic thermal management technique show 17.6°C. Also, in the result of the average power consumption, CABP reduces power consumption by 42.3%. But the dynamic thermal management technique only reduces power consumption by 0.3%. Moreover, the proposed CABP technique degrades the performance by 3.6%, while the conventional dynamic thermal management technique reduces the performance by 27.6%. Therefore, the proposed CABP technique can be a good solution for the thermal problems of the branch predictor in 3D multi-core processors.

Acknowledgment. This research was supported by MKE(The Ministry of Knowledge Economy), Korea, under the ITRC(Information Technology Research Center) support program supervised by the NIPA(National IT Industry Promotion Agency) (NIPA-2011-C1090-1111-0008).

References

1. Falcon, A., Stark, J.: Prophet/Critic Hybrid Branch Predictor. In: Proceedings of the 31st Annual International Symposium on Computer Architecture, Munchen, Germany, pp. 250–262 (2004)
2. Evers, M., Chang, P.Y., Patt, Y.N.: Using hybrid branch predictors to improve branch prediction accuracy in the presence of context switches. In: Proceedings of the 23rd Annual International Symposium on Computer Architecture, Philadelphia, PA, USA, pp. 3–11 (1996)
3. Jacobsen, E., Rotenberg, E., Smith, J.E.: Assigning confidence to conditional branch predictions. In: Proceedings of the 29th Annual International Symposium on Microarchitecture, Paris, France, pp. 142–152 (1996)
4. Jimenez, D.A.: Fast path-based neural branch prediction. In: Proceedings of the 36th Annual International Symposium on Microarchitecture, San Diego, CA, USA, pp. 243–252 (2003)
5. Loh, G.H., Henry, D.S.: Predicting conditional branches with fusion-based hybrid predictors. In: Proceedings of the International Conference on Parallel Architecture and Compilation Techniques, Charlottesville, VA, USA, pp. 165–176 (2002)
6. Jimenez, D.A., Lin, C.: Dynamic Branch Prediction with Perceptron. In: Proceedings of the International Symposium on High Performance Computer Architecture, Nuevo Leone, Mexico, pp. 197–206 (2001)
7. Kwak, J.W., Jhon, C.S.: High-performance embedded branch predictor by combining branch direction history and global branch history. Journal of Computers & Digital Techniques 2(2), 142–254 (2008)
8. Simon, B., Calder, B., Ferrante, J.: Incorporating predicate information into branch predictors. In: Proceedings of the International Symposium on High Performance Computer Architecture, Anaheim, California, USA, pp. 53–64 (2003)
9. Kise, K., Katagiri, T., Honda, H., Yuda, T.: The bimode++ branch predictor. In: Proceedings of Innovative Architecture for Future Generation High-Performance Processors and Systems, Maryland, USA, pp. 17–25 (2005)

10. Torregiani, C., Oprins, H., Vandevelde, B., Beyen, E., De Wolf, I.: Compact Thermal Modeling of Hot spots in Advanced 3D-Stacked ICs. In: Proceedings of Electronics Packaging Technology Conference, Singapore, pp. 131–136 (2009)
11. Joyner, J.W., Zarkesh-Ha, P., Meindl, J.D.: A Stochastic Global Net-length Distribution for a Three-Dimensional System on Chip (3D-SoC). In: Proceedings of the 14th IEEE International ASIC/SOC Conference, Arlington, VA, USA, pp. 147–151 (2001)
12. Puttaswamy, K., Loh, G.H.: Thermal Analysis of a 3D Die Stacked High Performance Microprocessor. In: Proceedings of ACM Great Lakes Symposium on VLSI, Philadelphia, USA, pp. 19–24 (2006)
13. Xie, Y., et al.: Design Space Exploration for 3D Architecture. ACM Journal of Emerging Technologies for Computer Systems 2(2), 65–103 (2006)
14. Donald, J., Martonosi, M.: Techniques for multicore thermal management: Classification and new exploration. In: Proceedings of 33rd International Symposium on Computer Architecture, Bostone, MA, USA, pp. 78–88 (2006)
15. Lee, C.J., Kim, H., Mutlu, O., Patt, Y.N.: Performance-Aware Speculation Control using Wrong Path Usefulness Prediction. In: Proceedings of the International Symposium on High Performance Computer Architecture, Salt Lake City, UT, USA, pp. 39–49 (2008)
16. Coskun, A.K., Kahng, A.B., Rosing, T.S.: Temperature- and Cost-Aware Design of 3D Multiprocessor Architectures. In: Proceedings of 12th Euromicro Conference on Digital System Design and Architectures, Methods and Tools, Patras, Greece, pp. 183–190 (2009)
17. SPEC CPU2000 Benchmarks, http://www.specbench.org
18. Burger, D.C., Austin, T.M.: The SimpleScalar tool set, version 2.0. ACM SIGARCH CAN 25(3), 13–25 (1997)
19. Brooks, D., Tiwari, V., Martonosi, M.: Wattch: a framework for architectural-level power analysis and optimizations. In: Proc. of the 27th International Symposium on Computer Architecture, Vancouver, pp. 83–94 (2000)
20. McFarling, S.: Combining branch predictors. Technical Report TN-36, Compaq Western Research Lab. (1993)
21. Skadron, K., Stan, M.R., Huang, W., Velusamy, S., Sankaranarayanan, K., Tarjan, D.: Temperature-Aware Microarchitecture. In: Proceedings of the 30th International Symposium on Computer Architecture, San Diego, CA, USA, pp. 2–13 (2003)

Convenient Way for Detecting Check Bits
in Hamming Code

Rahat Ullah, Jahangir Khan, Shahid Latif, and Inayat Ullah

Department of Computer Science and IT,
Sarhad University of Science and Information Technology (SUIT),
Peshawar 25000 Pakistan
{rahat.csit,jahangir.csit,shahid.csit,inayat.csit}@suit.edu.pk

Abstract. When the data is transmitted through the channel, error mostly occurs in data which can be detected and corrected at the receiver side by using Hamming code. This technique is used now days in Wireless communication, in deep space communication etc, e.g. Fixed wireless broadband with high error rate where there is need of correction not only detection in the data. In this coding scheme the detection of data depend on the check/parity bits, these bits play a vital role in hamming code because they locate the position where the error has been occurred. These check bits are inserted into the data at specified position at the transmitter side.. But for the correction of data at receiver side without any need of retransmission, we need to find the value of check bits. And to find theses bits we design a matrix which gives us the values of check bits (0.1) with the help of data bits. Normally these bits can be found by using Ex-Or gate[16]. In this paper I have found these bits using another logic that is AND-OR logic., for the sake of convenience and knowledge. When the data is received at the receiver side and suppose error is occurred than at the receiver side again we need to find the check bits by repeating the process at transmitter side. Than will compare the check bits at transmitter and receiver side using a new logic, that is AND-OR logic, which will locate the position of error. And the data can be recovered easily without need of retransmission of data.

Keywords: Coding, Parity/Check Bits, Error Detection/Correction.

1   Introduction

Coding theory is concerned with consistency of communication over noisy channels. The following application areas are included: deep space communication, satellite communication, data transmission, data storage, mobile communication, file transfer, and digital audio/video transmission. Error correcting codes are used in a wide range of communication systems from deep space communication, to quality of sound in compact disks and wireless phones. If we generally discuss The main method used to recover messages that might be distorted during transmission over a noisy channel is to inhabit redundancy. We make use of redundancy present in human languages to

T.-h. Kim et al. (Eds.): CA/CES³ 2011, CCIS 256, pp. 344–356, 2011.
© Springer-Verlag Berlin Heidelberg 2011

detect and than correct errors. This happens in both oral and written communication. For example, if you read the sentence "Health is mealth" you can tell that something is wrong. So we can detect an error. Moreover we can even correct it. We are doing two things here: error detection and error correction. What are the principles that we are using to achieve these goals? First, because the string "miscake" is not a valid word in English, we know that there is an error. Here, the redundancy manifests itself in the form of the fact that not every possible string is a valid word in the language. Secondly, the word "miscake" is closest to the valid word "mistake" in the language, so we conclude that it is the most likely word intended. Of course we can also use the context and meaning to detect and/or correct errors but that is an additional feature, not available to computers. When I enter the string "mistaky" to Merriam-Webster online dictionary (http://www.m-w.com), no entry can be found for it, however, the computer comes up with a list of suggested words, the first of which is "mistake". So, the computer is telling me that "mistake" is the most likely word to be intended, because it is closest to the given string. This is called the maximum likelihood principle. As I typed this article on my computer I witnessed many instances of this principle used by my word processor. For instance, when I mistakenly typed "fisrt" it automatically corrected it to "first". There are also other ways redundancy is used in natural languages. As already pointed out, Redundancy in context often enables us to detect and correct errors, vagueness, and ambiguities. When humans communicate, redundancy, either explicitly introduced by the speaker/author or built into the language, comes into play to help the audience understand the message better by overcoming such obstacles as noise, accent, hearing difficulties etc.

Wireless communication is a field that has been in existence for over 100 years, as far back as Marconi's trans-Atlantic wireless telegraph in 1896 [1]. The foundations of wireless communication were formally established by Claude E. Shannon in 1948 [2]. In his landmark paper, Shannon asserted that by proper encoding of information, error induced by a noisy channel or storage medium can be reduced to any desired level when the data rate is bounded by channel capacity. Since then, many coding techniques have been developed for wireless communication systems to achieve channel capacity.. In 1950, Richard W. Hamming discovered the first class of linear block codes for error correction, only two years after Shannon's theory. Hamming codes are 1-error-correcting codes and are capable of correcting any single error over the span of the code block length [3]. Hamming codes are perfect codes and can be decoded easily with a look-up-table [4].

Hamming codes and shortened Hamming codes have been widely applied in digital communication and data storage system over the years owing to the high data rate and decoding simplicity.

Actually Coding theory is the branch of mathematics concerned with accurate and efficient transfer of data across noisy channels as the theory of message sent. A transmission channel is the physical medium through which the information is transmitted, such as telephone lines, or atmosphere in the case of wireless communication. Undesirable disturbance (noise) can occur across the communication channel, causing the received information to be different from the original information sent [5]. Another prominent example is the ubiquitous CD: a scratch on a music CD has no effect on sound quality, completely unlike phonograph records. Coding theory deals with detection and correction of transmission errors caused by noise in the channel. The primary goal of coding theory is efficient encoding of information, easy transmission of encoded messages, fast decoding of received information and correction of errors introduced in the channel [6]. Coding theory is used all the time: in reading CDs, receiving transmissions from satellites, or in cell phones [7]. So as my paper is about hamming code, so will discuss that this technique is used to detect single bit error. And will use check bits for the detection of error, on receiver as well as on transmitter side. I have found these check bits by using Ex-OR logic as well as AND-OR logic.

This paper is organized in such away that the first portion explains the brief introduction about occurring of errors in the information and that how the concept of information theory and than coding techniques came into being, the second portion contains information about types of errors, third portion is about different types of error detecting techniques and its failure, in the last section I have discussed hamming code in fully detailed by using two logical circuits.

2   Types of Errors

When binary data is transmitted and processed from source to destination, it is –as are all electrical signals—susceptible to noise that can alter or distort its content. 1s may be effectively changed to 0s and 0s to 1s [8]. Two types of errors could be possible. Single bit error and a burst error [9]. For example, at the transmitter side the data was 001100, and at the receiver side it is 001110, so as we seen the second bit from the right side is changed, this is type of single bit error [9]. When more than one bit changes in the data, that type of error is called burst error [9].

3   Error Detection

When we know what type of error can occur in the data, will we be able to recognize one when we see it? If we have a copy of the intended message for transmission, than of course we will be able to detect. But if we have no copy than we will be unable to find the error, until we decode the data and find that it is of no worth, by making no sense. If we use this concept in the machine than it will be so costly, slow of questionable value. We don't need a system than decode whatever comes in, then sit around trying to decide if the engine really intended to use the word chiadfh in the middle of an array of whether statistics. What we need is a mechanism that is simple and entirely objective.

3.1   Redundancy

Error detection uses the process of redundancy, which means adding extra bits with the data for detecting error at the destination point. The following figure.1 shows that how the extra bits were added to the information to check the accuracy in the information at the receiving side. Once the data stream has been generated, it passes through a device that analyses it and the redundant bit are appropriately generates. The data is know enlarged by adding redundant check, and travels to the receiver. The receiver puts the entire stream to the checking function. If the received bit stream passes the checking criteria, the data portion of the data unit is accepted and the redundant bits are discarded [9].

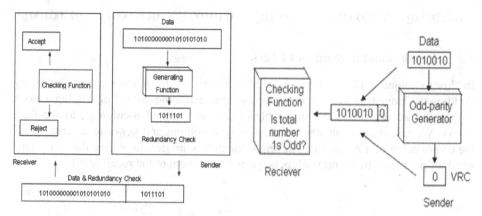

Fig. 1. Process of Using Redundant Bits   **Fig. 2.** Adding Parity bit with the Information

3.2   Vertical Redundancy Check

Vertical redundancy check is also called parity check. In this technique a parity bit (redundant check) is appended to every data unit. There are two types of parity bits, Odd and Even parity. For even parity, the number of 1's in the code word including parity bit should be Even[9,10,11]. Similarly for Odd parity the number of 1's in the code word including parity bit should be equal to Odd [9,10,11]. The principal for both the techniques (Odd/Even parity) is same, the calculation is different. I will use use Odd parity over here. Suppose we want to transmit the binary unit 1010010 [ASCIII R (82)]; See the below fig. 2. Adding together all the 1s gives us 3, an Odd number. Before transmitting the data, we pass it through the parity generator. The parity generator counts the number of 1s in the data and tag on 0 to the end in this case. The message will be enlarge by one bit that is 10100100, total eight bits including parity bit. The message will be transmitted across the network link. When it reaches to the destination, the receiver will put all bits in the Odd parity checking function. The number of ones will be counted; if the messages receive is 10100100, than the data will be accepted. But if the data receives is 10101100, than the parity checker will detect that error has been occurred in the message, and it will be reject the whole segment of data. When we use Even parity generator it will keep the number of ones even.

Imagine we want to transmit the word "Sarhad". In ASCII the six characters are coded as [3], using Even parity generator.

01010011	01100001	01110010	01101000	01100001	01100100
S	a	r	h	a	d

Each of the 2nd 4th 5th and 6th character has Odd number of 1s, so the parity bit is 1. and as the 1st and 3rd character has Even number of 1s, so the parity is 0. the following figure shows the actual number sent, with underlined parity bits.

010100110   011000011   011100100   011010001   011000011   011001001

3.3   Longitudinal Redundancy Check

In this technique a block of bits is organized in a table of rows and columns, by dividing the long stream of bits in sub-groups. For Example instead of sending a block of 32 bits, we organize them in a table of 4-rows and and 8-columns, as the fig.3 shows. We calculate the number of ones in each column and generate a parity bit, at the end of column; it means that total eight parity bits are generated. We then attach the block of parity bits to the original message and send them to the receiver [9].

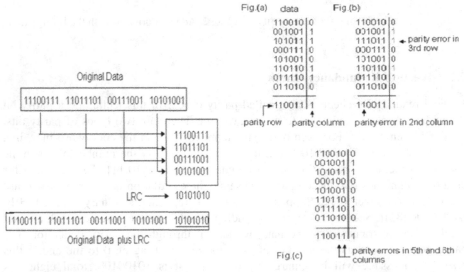

Fig. 3. Organizing Data in LRC   **Fig. 4.** Block Parity

3.4   Block Parity

When several binary words are transmitted or stored in succession, the resulting collection of bits can be regarded as a *Block* of data, having rows and columns. For example, eight 6-bit words in succession form an 8*6 block. Parity bits can than be assigned to both rows and columns, as illustrated in fig.4(a). this scheme makes it possible to correct any single error occurring in a data word and to detect any two errors in a word. For Example, as shown in fig.4(b), suppose the second bit in the third data word is in error, having been changed from 0 to 1. then the number of 1s in the second column is even, and the number of 1s in the third row is even. Therefore, the (odd) parity bits in the second column and third row both detect the error, and we know that the second bit in the third word must be change from 1 to 0[12].

Fig.4(c) shows how two errors in one data word are changed, transforming 000111 to 000100. Since the total number of 1s is still odd, the parity bit in the fourth row does not detect the error. How ever the parity bit in the fifth and sixth columns do detect the error. We are not able to correct the error in this case because there is no information revealing the row where the error occurred. The parity row is often called a parityword, and the block parity technique, also called word parity is widely used for data stored on magnetic tape[12].

3.5   Checksum

A checksum is a simple type of redundancy check that is used to detect errors in data. Errors frequently occur in data when it is written to a disk, transmitted across a network or otherwise manipulated. The errors are typically very small, for example, a single incorrect bit, but even such small errors can really affect the superiority of data, and even make it useless. In its simplest form, a checksum is produced by calculating the binary values in a packet or other block of data using some algorithm and storing the results with the data. When the data is retrieved from memory or received at the other end of a network, a new checksum is calculated and compared with the existing checksum. A non-match indicates an error; a match does not necessarily mean the absence of errors, but only that the simple algorithm was not able to detect any. Among the types of errors that cannot be detected by simple checksum algorithms are reordering of the bytes, inserting or deleting zero-valued bytes and multiple errors that cancel each other out. Fortunately, however, these errors can be detected with more sophisticated methods, such as *cyclic redundancy checks* (CRC). Although such techniques have the disadvantage of requiring greater system resources (in the form of processor time and bandwidth), this has become an more and more insignificant consideration in recent years as a result of the continued increases in processor speed and bandwidth[13]. Suppose we have a fairly long message, which can logically be divided into shorter words (a 128 byte message, for instance). We can introduce an accumulator with the same width as a word (one byte, for instance), and as each word comes in, add it to the accumulator. When the last word has been added, the contents of the accumulator are appended to the message (as a 129th byte, in this case). The added word is called a checksum [13, 14]. Now, the receiver performs the same operation, and checks the checksum. If the checksums agree, we assume the message was sent without error. A related approach would be, instead of performing an actual addition, we can just do a bitwise exclusive-or of the new word with the accumulator. If we do this, we calculate a *vertical parity* on the data. Notice that in the special case of a one-bit word, this is equivalent to calculating the parity of the buffer! Performing a vertical parity has two advantages over a real checksum: it can be performed with less hardware if the data is serial, and it will lead us into performing a CRC. To see how a vertical parity can be performed with less hardware than a checksum, take a look at the next figure.

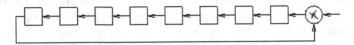

This figure shows an eight bit shift register and an exclusive-or gate. Initially, the shift register is filled with 0's. As each bit is put into it, the new bit is exclusive-ored with the contents of the eighth cell in the register. When the entire message has been passed through the shift register, it contains the vertical parity.

Here's an example of passing a 32 bit message through the unit:

```
00000000 11010110101010010100011101101010
(as we start, the shift register is empty
00000001 1010110101010010100011101101010
00000011 010110101010010100011101101010
00000110 10110101010010100011101101010
00001101 0110101010010100011101101010
00011010 110101010010100011101101010
00110101 10101010010100011101101010
01101011 0101010010100011101101010
11010110 101010010100011101101010
(at this point, the shift register contains the first byte of the message
10101100 01010010100011101101010
01011001 1010010100011101101010
10110011 010010100011101101010
01100111 10010100011101101010
11001111 0010100011101101010
10011111 010100011101101010
00111111 10100011101101010
01111111 0100011101101010
(it now contains the vertical parity of the first two bytes of the message)
11111110 100011101101010
11111100 00011101101010
11111001 0011101101010
11110011 011101101010
11100111 11101101010
11001110 1101101010
10011100 101101010
00111000 01101010
(first three bytes)
```

```
01110000 1101010
11100001 101010
11000010 01010
10000101 1010
00001010 010
00010100 10
00101001 0
01010010
```
(and the vertical parity of the whole 32 bit message)

Notice that a checksum or a vertical parity is very efficient, but it isn't capable of correcting errors.The problem with checksums is that a 1-bit error turns into a 1-bit code. If you have a burst of noise, the odds are far too good that you'll end up with something that still looks correct, even though it isn't.

3.6   Cyclic Redundancy Check

The cyclic redundancy check, or CRC, is a technique for detecting errors in digital data, but not for making corrections when errors are detected. It is used primarily in data transmission. In the CRC method, a certain number of check bits, often called a checksum, are appended to the message being transmitted. The receiver can determine whether or not the check bits agree with the data, to ascertain with a certain degree of probability whether or not an error occurred in transmission. If an error occurred, the receiver sends a "negative acknowledgement" (NAK) back to the sender, requesting that the message be retransmitted[15]. The technique is also sometimes applied to data storage devices, such as a disk drive. In this situation each block on the disk would have check bits, and the hardware might automatically initiate a reread of the block when an error is detected, or it might report the error to software. The material that follows speaks in terms of a "sender" and a "receiver" of a "message," but it should be understood that it applies to storage writing and reading as well[9, 14].

4   Hamming Code

Messages that are transmitted over a communication channel can be damaged; their bits can be masked or inverted by noise. Detecting and correcting these errors is important. Some simple codes can detect but not correct errors[8,9]; others can detect and correct one or more errors[3]. This paper addresses one Hamming code that can correct a single-bit error which is detected with the help of parity/check bits using two logics. Other Hamming codes are more powerful, but beyond the scope of this paper.

The Hamming single-bit correction code is implemented by adding check bits also called parity bits to the output message according to the following pattern:

i) The message bits are numbered from left to right, starting at 1.
ii) Every bit whose number is a power of 2 (bits 1, 2, 4, 8,...) is a check bit[8].
iii) The other are the output message bits (bits 3, 5, 6, 7, 9,...) contain the data bits, in order.

Each check bit establishes even parity over itself and a group of data bits and can be fine with the help of Ex-OR gate[16] or also by using AND-OR logic because both the circuits have same performance[17], fig.16. A data bit is in a check bit's group if the binary representation of the data bit's number contains a 1 in the position of the check bit's weight. For instance, the data bits associated with check bit 2 are all those with a 1 in the 2's position of their binary bit number—bits 2, 3, 6, 7, and so forth. Fig.5 shows an 8-bit data message. It shows the assignment of data bits and check bits to the bits of a12-bit output message. The horizontal lines below the output message box have dots to indicate the assignment of output bits to check groups. Each check group has a ones count box, with a parity bit that is inserted into the output message.

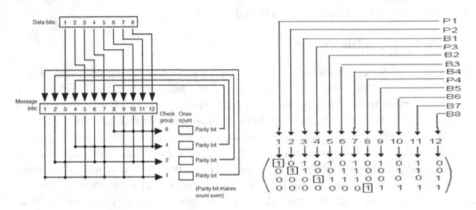

Fig. 5. Designing Matrix for Parity bits   **Fig. 6.** Indicating Positions for Parity bits

To find the value of check/parity bit, that which parity should be zero and which should be one, we will design a matrix having columns equal to the bits contained in the whole stream of data including parity bits according to the order given in the given figure. And will have rows equal to the number of parity bits used in the data, for example if we have used four parity bits, than it will have four rows, for five parity bits it will have five rows and so on.Fig.6 shows.

Inbox bits in Fig.6 are the starting bits for P1, P2, P3, P4. For P1 we have used 1010101....., for P2, 1100110011....., for P3, 11110000111100....., for P4, 111111110000000001111111100...., and so on[16].

Now to calculate the values of P1, P2, P3, P4 from the matrix by Ex-OR or by using another logic AND-OR, which is the main target of the paper. Because as the figure.7 shows the outputs of both the circuits are same.

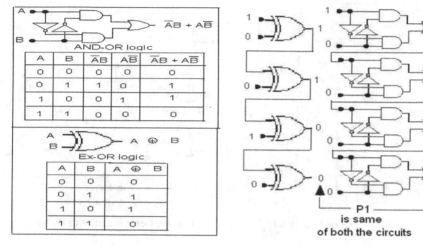

Fig. 7. Showing the Two equivalent logics

Fig. 8. Detection of First Parity bit

For parity one, from the matrix, we get the following information about the bits

$$P1=3 \oplus 5 \oplus 7 \oplus 9 \oplus 11$$

$$=B1 \oplus B2 \oplus B4 \oplus B5 \oplus B7$$

$$=1 \oplus 0 \oplus 0 \oplus 1 \oplus 0$$

As the fig.8 shows that when we implement the given logic by Ex-OR & AND-OR logic, we get the same parity, 0.

For parity two, from the matrix, we get the following information about the bits.

$$P2=3 \oplus 6 \oplus 7 \oplus 10 \oplus 11$$

$$=B1 \oplus B3 \oplus B4 \oplus B6 \oplus B7$$

$$=1 \oplus 1 \oplus 0 \oplus 1 \oplus 0$$

As the fig.9 shows that when we implement the given logic by Ex-OR & AND-OR logic, we get the same parity, 1.

For parity three, from the matrix, we get the following information about the bits.

$$P3=5 \oplus 6 \oplus 7 \oplus 12$$

$$=B2 \oplus B3 \oplus B4 \oplus B8$$

$$=0 \oplus 1 \oplus 0 \oplus 1$$

Fig.10 shows that by implementing the two logics we received the parity '0'.

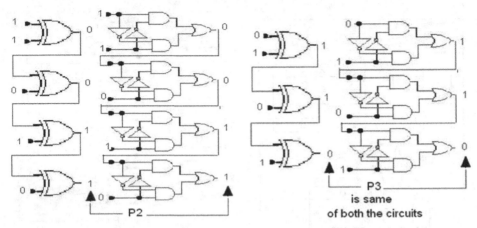

Fig. 9. Detection of second Parity bit   **Fig. 10.** Detection of third Parity

For the 4th parity/check bit we get the following information.

$$P4=5 \oplus 6 \oplus 7 \oplus 8$$

$$=B5 \oplus B6 \oplus B7 \oplus B8$$

$$=1 \oplus 1 \oplus 0 \oplus 1$$

Fig.11 shows the value of parity four, '1'.

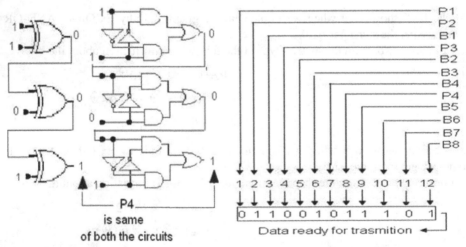

Fig. 11. Detection of 4th Parity   **Fig. 12.** Parity bits are inserted in the Data

Now we are ready to send our data, but first we need to insert the parity bits in the data at specified positions, as (bits 1, 2, 4, 8), fig.12. The data becomes: 0 1 1 0 0 1 0 1 1 1 0 1.

When the message reaches the destination, we know the parity position, so the data is collected from positions 3, 5, 6 ,7 ,9 ,10 ,11 ,12. Suppose the received message is 0 1 1 0 0 0 0 1 1 1 0 1, as the parity bits are at positions 1,2,4, and at 8 from left to right, so collect the data bits for decoding process, which is 10001101. The same process will be repeated, the matrix will be design, and than will find a parity bits at receiving side.As we have already did these things at transmitter side, we will find the parity bits by putting the received data bits. Which given below, in gif.12.

$P1 = 3 \oplus 5 \oplus 7 \oplus 9 \oplus 11,$ $P2 = 3 \oplus 6 \oplus 7 \oplus 10 \oplus 11,$ $P3 = 5 \oplus 6 \oplus 7 \oplus 12$ $P4 = 5 \oplus 6 \oplus 7 \oplus 8$
$= B1 \oplus B2 \oplus B4 \oplus B5 \oplus B7$ $= B1 \oplus B3 \oplus B4 \oplus B6 \oplus B7$ $= B2 \oplus B3 \oplus B4 \oplus B8$ $= B5 \oplus B6 \oplus B7 \oplus B8$
$= 1 \oplus 0 \oplus 0 \oplus 1 \oplus 0$ $= 1 \oplus 0 \oplus 0 \oplus 1 \oplus 0$ $= 0 \oplus 0 \oplus 0 \oplus 1$ $= 1 \oplus 1 \oplus 0 \oplus 1$
$= 0$ $= 0$ $= 1$ $= 1$

To check error in the data through the channel, we will compare the parity bits at receiver and transmitter ends, that we have at the source and destination, if it gives the answer zero, that received data is error free, otherwise it will locate the poison.

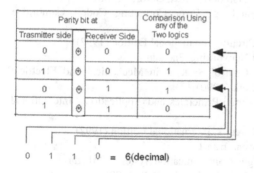

Parity bit at		Comparison Using any of the Two logics
Trasmitter side	Receiver Side	
0	⊕ 0	0
1	⊕ 0	1
0	⊕ 1	1
1	⊕ 1	0

0   1   1   0 = 6(decimal)

Fig. 13. Detecting the location of error

Error at position 6th in the received message

| 0 | 1 | 1 | 0 | 0 | 0 | 0 | 1 | 1 | 1 | 0 | 1 |

| 0 | 1 | 1 | 0 | 0 | 1 | 0 | 1 | 1 | 1 | 0 | 1 |

Error corrected

Fig. 14. Received message is corrected

Fig.13 shows that the error was occurred at position 6, and was corrected. As shown in figure. 14.

5   Conclusion

At the birth of Information theory the hot issue was to send the information in an understandable formate. Coding concept was introduced that the data can be send in the coded form, such that it gives us information about the state of data. At initial levels single parity bits were used for the detection of error in the information, than multiple bits were used. But the problem was the retransmission of information in case of any error occurrence in the data, so hamming introduced a coding technique for the error detection as well as correction of that error at the receiver side. In this technique hamming added some extra bits at some specific position called parity/check bits, but for the detection of those parity bits Ex-OR logic was primarily used. The main task of the paper is to introduce a new logic for the detection of the same parity bits with a new logic, that is AND-OR logic, which is for the sake of convenience and knowledge in digital communication.

References

[1] Belrose, J.: Fessenden and Marconi: Their Differing Technologies and Transatlantic Experiments During the First Decade of this Century. In: International Conference on 100 Years of Radio, London, UK, pp. 32–43 (September 1995)

[2] Shannon, C.E.: A Mathematical Theory of Communication. Bell System Technical Journal, 379–423, 623–656 (July, August 1948)

[3] Hamming, R.: Error Detecting and Error Correcting Codes. Bell System Technical Journal, 147–160 (April 1950)

[4] Lin, S., Costello, D.J.: Error Control Coding: Fundamentals and Application. Prentice Hall (April 2004)

[5] Shannon, C.E.: A mathematical theory of communication. Bell Syst. T. J. 27, 379–423 (1948)

[6] Hill, R.: A first course in coding theory. Clarendon Press, Oxford (1986)

[7] Huffman, W.C., Pless, V.: Fundamentals of Error Correcting Codes. Cambridge University Press (2003)

[8] Bogart Jr, T.F.: Introduction to Digital Circuits, International Edition (1992)

[9] Forouzan, B.: Data Communication and Networking, 2nd edn.

[10] Bolton, W.: Mechatronics: Electronic Control Systems in Mechanical and Electrical Engineering, 2nd edn. Longman, New York (1990)

[11] Tocci, R.J., Widmer, N.S.: Digital systems, Principles and Applications, International Edition-7th

[12] Bogart Jr, T.F.: Introduction to Digital Circuits, International Edition (1992)

[13] http://www.linfo.org/checksum.html

[14] Lathi, B.P.: Modern Digitasl and Analogue Communication Systems, 3rd edn.

[15] Tanenbaum, A.S.: Computer Networks, 2nd edn. Prentice Hall (1988)

[16] Wells, R.B.: Applied Coding and Information Theory for Engineers, Published by Dorling Kindersley (India)

[17] Floyd, T.L., Jain, R.P.: Digital Fundamentals, 7th/8th edn.

Motion Vector Refinement Algorithm for the High Definition Video Coding

Le Thanh Ha[1], Seung-Won Jung[2], The Duy Bui[1],
Dinh Trieu Duong[1], and Sung-Jea Ko[2]

[1] University of Engineering and Technology,
Vietnam National University, Hanoi, Vietnam
[2] Department of Electronics Engineering, School of Electrical Engineering, Korea
University, Seoul, Korea

Abstract. In H.264/AVC, simplified rate distortion optimisation (RDO) is performed to estimate the motion vector (MV). As a result, the estimated MV is often suboptimal since the residual bitrate is not considered, which results in the deterioration of the coding efficiency. In this paper, we propose an MV refinement algorithm in which the final MV is selected from a set of candidate MVs by using the RDO including the residual bitrate. To further improve the performance of optimal MV selection, the RD calculation method in the RDO is modified using the deblocking filters. Experimental results show that the proposed algorithm outperforms the conventional H.264 in terms of coding efficiency.

Keywords: H.264, RDO, Coding Efficiency, HDTV.

The increasing popularity of the high definition television (HDTV) requires a higher compression efficiency. Therefore, a lot of endeavors to improve the coding efficiency of the state-of-the-art video coding standard, H.264/AVC [1], have been reported in the literature. Among many techniques adopted in H.264/AVC, the rate distortion optimisation (RDO) is a key component for the coding efficiency. Two different RDOs are performed for motion estimation and mode decision, respectively. For the estimation of motion vector (MV), a simplified RDO which does not consider the residual bitrate is utilised. In order to select the best encoding mode, a complicated RDO including the residual bitrate is performed on the estimated MV. Because the the estimated MV is often suboptimal due to the simplification of RDO in motion estimation, the coding efficiency can be deteriorated.

In order to increase the probability that the optimal MV is selected, in this paper, we extend the complicated RDO so that it is performed on a set of candidate MVs instead of a single MV. The set of candidate MVs is formed by the estimated MV and neighboring previously coded MVs. In addition, because deblocking artifacts appear in the decoded blocks, they can reduce the accuracy of RD calculation and deteriorate the performance of selection of the encoding modes and MVs in the complicated RDO. Therefore, we apply deblocking filters to remove blocking artifacts out of the decoded block before RD calculation to obtain more accurate MVs and better encoding modes.

T.-h. Kim et al. (Eds.): CA/CES^3 2011, CCIS 256, pp. 357–363, 2011.
© Springer-Verlag Berlin Heidelberg 2011

The remainder of this paper is organised as follows. In Section 1, we present an overview of RDOs for motion estimation and mode selection. The details of our proposed method are presented in Section 2. Several experimental results demonstrating our method's performance are in Section 3. Finally, Section 4 summarizes and concludes the paper.

1 Rate-Distortion Optimisation Model

In the inter coding of H.264/AVC, the Lagrangian method is used to find the MV and encoding modes. First, the estimated MV, emv, is obtained as follows:

$$
\begin{aligned}
emv &= \arg\min_{mv} J_{\text{MV}}(mv|\lambda_{\text{MV}}) \\
&= \arg\min_{mv}(D(\text{X}, \text{P}(mv)) \\
&\quad + \lambda_{\text{MV}} \cdot R_{\text{MV}}(mv - pmv)),
\end{aligned}
\tag{1}
$$

where $\text{P}(mv)$ is the reference block, $D(\text{X}, \text{P}(mv))$ is the sum of absolute differences (SAD) between the original block X and the reference block $\text{P}(mv)$, pmv is the predicted motion vector (PMV) which is formed by using the previously coded MVs, and $R_{\text{MV}}(mv - pmv)$ is the bitrate required for encoding the difference between mv and pmv. The Lagrange multiplier λ_{MV} associated with the rate is defined in [1]. Here, it should be noted that the bitrate required for encoding the residual block is neglected. Therefore, this simplified RDO can produce the suboptimal MV.

Once the MVs for all encoding modes are estimated, the best encoding mode M is selected by:

$$
\begin{aligned}
M &= \arg\min_{m} J_M(m|QP, \lambda_{\text{MO}}, emv) \\
&= \arg\min_{m}(D(\text{X}, \overline{\text{X}}|QP, emv) + \lambda_{\text{MO}} \cdot R),
\end{aligned}
\tag{2}
$$

in which

$$
R = R_{\text{MV}}(emv - pmv) + R_{\text{RE}}(m|QP, emv).
\tag{3}
$$

where $D(\text{X}, \overline{\text{X}}|QP, emv)$ is the SAD between the original block X and the reconstructed block $\overline{\text{X}}$, QP is the quantisation parameter, and R_{RE} is the bitrate required to encode the residuals. The Lagrange multiplier λ_{MODE} associated with the rate is defined in [1].

2 Proposed Method

Suppose that the optimal MV is estimated by applying the complicated RDO as follows:

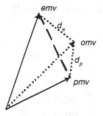

Fig. 1. Example of predicted, estimated, and optimal MVs

$$
\begin{aligned}
omv &= \arg\min_{mv\in\psi} J_{M-MV}(mv) \\
&= \arg\min_{mv\in\psi} J_M(M|QP, \lambda_{MO}, mv),
\end{aligned}
\tag{4}
$$

where ψ is a set of candidate searching positions. For the general case, all positions in the motion search range are included in this set. In this work, we use the candidate set consisting of a small number of positions based on emv and pmv to estimate the optimal MV.

Figure 1 visualises an example of MVs in which emv and pmv are known and the optimal MV omv is needed to be estimated. To estimate the position of omv, we assume that the distances from omv to emv and to pmv have zero mean Laplacian distributions. Then, the probability of d being the distance from omv to emv can be written as:

$$
P_e(d) = \frac{\alpha}{2}e^{-\alpha d}
\tag{5}
$$

and to pmv as

$$
P_p(d) = \frac{\beta}{2}e^{-\beta d},
\tag{6}
$$

where the parameters α and β are positive. Since the distance from omv to emv and to pmv can be assumed to be independent, the probability of omv can be obtained by:

$$
\begin{aligned}
P_o(d_e, d_p) &= P_e(d_e) \cdot P_p(d_p) \\
&= \frac{\alpha}{2}e^{-\alpha d} \cdot \frac{\beta}{2}e^{-\beta d} \\
&= \frac{\alpha \cdot \beta}{4} \cdot e^{-(\alpha d_e + \beta d_p)},
\end{aligned}
\tag{7}
$$

where d_e and d_p are the distance from omv to emv and to pmv, respectively. It is straightforward to see that maximising $P_o(d_e, d_p)$ in (7) is equivalent to find d_e and d_p by:

$$
\begin{aligned}
&\arg\min_{d_e, d_p} \; \alpha d_e + \beta d_p \\
&\text{subject to } d_e + d_p \geq D, d_e \geq 0, d_p \geq 0,
\end{aligned}
\tag{8}
$$

The solutions of (8) are given in three cases. If $\beta > \alpha$, we have:

$$\alpha d_e + \beta d_p = \alpha(d_e + d_p) + (\beta - \alpha)d_p$$
$$\geq \alpha D. \tag{9}$$

Equality holds when $d_e + d_p = D$ and $d_p = 0$ which means $d_e = D$ and the estimated optimal MV $\widehat{omv}$ equals pmv. If $\beta < \alpha$, we have:

$$\alpha d_e + \beta d_p = \beta(d_e + d_p) + (\alpha - \beta)d_e$$
$$\geq \beta D, \tag{10}$$

Equality holds when $d_e + d_p = D$ and $d_e = 0$ which means $d_p = D$ and the estimated optimal MV $\widehat{omv}$ equals emv. If $\alpha = \beta$, we have:

$$\alpha d_e + \beta d_p = \alpha(d_e + d_p)$$
$$\geq \alpha D, \tag{11}$$

Equality holds when $d_e + d_p = D$. It means that $\widehat{omv}$ can lie anywhere between emv and pmv. From this analysis, although the typical values of α and β are unknown, we can assume that the estimated optimal MV is equal to emv or pmv with a high probability.

In order to validate the above assumption, we measure the distribution of $\widehat{omv}$ by encoding the 720p sequences *CityCorr* and *Crew* with 100 P-frames and the average probability of $\widehat{omv}$ is presented in Table 1. We can see that $P[\widehat{omv} = emv]$ and $P[\widehat{omv} = pmv]$ are much higher than the others in all tested values of QP. Therefore, we use the MV candidate set consisting of emv and pmv. Then, Eq. (4) can be simplified to:

$$\widehat{omv} = \begin{cases} emv, \text{if } J_{M-MV}(emv) < J_{M-MV}(pmv), \\ pmv, \text{otherwise.} \end{cases} \tag{12}$$

In H.264/AVC, pmv is the median vector of the previously calculated MVs. To improve the accuracy of the MV prediction, a method called competitive spatio-temporal scheme (CSTS) was proposed in [2]. This scheme gathers additional PMVs for the current MV from spatially neighboring and temporally collocated blocks. Then, the best PMV index, I, is obtained by:

$$I = \arg \min_i J_{\text{PMV}}(pmv_i | mv)$$
$$= \arg \min_i R_{\text{MV}}(mv - pmv_i) + R_M(i), \tag{13}$$

where pmv_i is the ith PMV, and $R_M(i)$ is the bitrate required to encode the index i. When the CS is combined with the proposed method, pmv in Eq. (12) is replaced by pmv_I.

Table 1. MV candidate distributions

QP	23	28	33	38
$P[\widehat{omv} = emv]$	0.84	0.85	0.87	0.86
$P[\widehat{omv} = pmv]$	0.09	0.10	0.09	0.11
$P[\widehat{omv} \neq emv \cap \widehat{omv} \neq pmv]$	0.07	0.05	0.04	0.03

Table 2. Simulation conditions

Reference software	KTA2.3 [5]
Sequence resolution	720p, 1080p
Number of frames	150 (720p), 125 (1080p)
Frame rate (Hz)	60 (720p), 25 (1080p)
Number of references	4
MV search range	±64
MV estimation method	EPZS
GOP structure	IPPP (High profile)
Entropy coding method	CABAC
CSTS	Enabled
QP	22/27/32/37 for I-frames 23/28/33/38 for P-frames

Both the mode decision and the proposed MV selection compute SAD between the original block X and the decoded block $\overline{X}$ based on the complicated RDO in (4). However, the blocking artifacts appearing in the decoded blocks can deteriorate the accuracy of SAD calculation [4]. Therefore, removing the blocking artifacts out of the decoded blocks before calculating SAD is advantageous to obtain better encoding modes and more accurate MVs. To this end, we perform the adaptive deblocking filter [3] to every 4×4 block edges of the decoded MB in the mode decision stage, so called MB adaptive deblocking filtering (MADF). Here, the filter coefficients are determined using the boundary strength and pixel values across the block edges. Then, the distortion is obtained by calculating the SAD between the original block X and the filtered version of $\overline{X}$. By using the proposed distortion measurement, the RD cost can be more precisely measured so that the more accurate MVs can be obtained.

3   Experiment Results

The simulation conditions are given in Table 2. Several sequences with various resolution, frame rate, and number of encoded frames were tested. In our simulations, group of picture (GOP) structure of IPPP is used, CABAC is used for entropy coding, and all intra/inter encoding modes are enabled to evaluate the performance of the proposed methods. The experimental results for several HD sequences are presented in Table 3 and those for the same sequences are presented in Table 4. The Bjøntegaard delta bitrate (ΔBR) and PSNR (ΔPSNR)

Table 3. Performance comparison with conventional H.264/AVC

Sequence	Prop		Prop&MADF	
	ΔBR (%)	ΔPSNR (dB)	ΔBR (%)	ΔPSNR (dB)
720p				
1. Crew	-1.12	0.031	-2.02	0.053
2. Cyclists	-1.59	0.046	-2.08	0.060
3. Optis	-1.76	0.048	-2.20	0.060
4. Raven	-1.49	0.054	-1.94	0.071
1080p				
5. CrowdRun	-0.88	0.039	-1.24	0.055
6. Toys&Calendar	-0.81	0.028	-1.56	0.047
7. VintageCar	-0.98	0.031	-2.01	0.046
8. WalkingCouple	-1.36	0.040	-1.84	0.052

Table 4. Performance comparison with conventional H.264/AVC when combining with CSTS

Seq.	CSTS		Prop&CSTS		Prop&CSTS &MADF	
	ΔBR (%)	ΔPSNR (dB)	ΔBR (%)	ΔPSNR (dB)	ΔBR (%)	ΔPSNR (dB)
1.	-3.31	0.081	-5.06	0.126	-5.89	0.149
2.	-10.18	0.269	-11.35	0.298	-11.80	0.315
3.	-3.91	0.104	-5.72	0.150	-6.27	0.166
4.	-10.10	0.327	-11.46	0.376	-11.62	0.388
5.	-1.85	0.081	-1.87	0.081	-2.26	0.099
6.	-12.09	0.287	-13.37	0.318	-13.99	0.335
7.	-5.03	0.106	-6.30	0.132	-7.58	0.156
8.	-1.82	0.051	-3.32	0.091	-3.81	0.106

[6] were used to evaluate the performance. It can be seen that our proposed method improves the RD performances of all tested sequences. The performance comparison of our proposed method with conventional H.264/AVC is presented in Table 3, in which the bitrate is reduced by 1.76% at *Optis*. When MADF is applied, the bitrate is further reduced by 1.01% at *VintageCar*. As can be seen in Table 4, the combination of the proposed method with the CSTS can further reduce the bitrate where 1.75% and 1.50% additional bit savings are observed in *Crew* (720p) and *WalkingCouple* (1080p), respectively. In addition, the average bitrate further reduced by MADF method is about 0.47%.

4   Conclusion

We have presented an algorithm for improving the performance of RDO to choose the encoding MVs. Firstly, a set of candidate MVs is formed from the estimated

MV and the neighboring previously encoded MVs. Then, the final MV is selected from the set by using the RDO including the residual bitrate. We also combined an effective method for RD cost calculation using the deblocking filters to the proposed method. Experimental results show that the proposed algorithm is suitable to the HD video coding applications.

Acknowledgments. This research was supported by Project No:CN.11.01 of University of Engineering and Technology, Vietnam National University, Hanoi.

References

1. Joint Video Team (JVT) of ISO/IEC MPEG & ITU-T VCEG. Draft ITU-T recommendation and final draft international standard of joint video specification (ITU-T rec. H.264—ISO/IEF 14496-10 AVC), JVT-G050 (2003)
2. Jung, J., Laroche, G.: Competition-Based Scheme for Motion Vector Selection and Coding. Doc. VCEG-AC06 (2006)
3. List, P., Joch, A., Lainema, J., Bjøntegaard, G., Karczewicz, M.: Adaptive Deblocking filter. IEEE Trans. on Circuits Syst. Video Technol. 13, 614–619 (2005)
4. Le, T.H., Jung, S.W., Park, C.S., Ko, S.J.: Macroblock-Level Deblocking Method to Improve Coding Efficiency for H.264/AVC. ETRI J. 32(2), 336–338 (2010)
5. Joint Video Team (JVT), KTA software version 2.3,
   http://iphome.hhi.de/suehring/tml/download/KTA/
6. Bjøntegaard, G.: Calculation of Average PSNR Differences between RD-Curves. Doc. VCEG-M33, 13th Meeting (2001)

Novel Low-Voltage Small-Area I/O Buffer
for Mixed-Voltage Application

Young-Wook Kim[1,2], Joung-Yeal Kim[1,2], Young-Hyun Jun[2], and Bai-Sun Kong[1]

[1] School of Information and Communication Engineering, Sungkyunkwan University,
Suwon, 440-746, Korea
[2] Memory Division, Samsung Electronics,
Hwasung, 445-701, Korea
sfturtle@naver.com

Abstract. Novel mixed-voltage I/O buffer with fast low-voltage operation and small-area realization is proposed. The I/O buffer provides reduced latency at low supply voltages by eliminating the voltage swing degradation at timing-critical nets. The buffer also provides smaller layout area by avoiding dedicated bulky circuits like dynamic gate-bias circuit (DGBC) and hot-carrier prevention circuit (HCPC). Evaluation results in 130-nm CMOS process indicated that the proposed mixed-voltage I/O buffer achieves up to 52% reduction on latency and up to 39% reduction on layout area as compared to conventional mixed-voltage I/O buffers.

Keywords: I/O buffer, mixed-voltage, hot-carrier injection, low voltage, area reduction.

1   Introduction

In microelectronic systems composed of ICs powered by different supply voltages, the use of conventional non-mixed-voltage I/O buffers causes serious problems such as undesirable short-circuit current, junction leakage, and gate-oxide reliability [1]. A substantial amount of the short-circuit current can flow from an I/O pad to the power supply in the case that the signal voltage of the I/O pad driven externally is higher than the supply voltage of the IC. The junction-leakage current can also occur at the drain-well junction of the pull-up PMOS driver transistor in the buffer when a signal voltage driven externally is higher than the well bias. The gate-oxide reliability issue induced by hot-carrier injection can occur when any transistor in the buffer is turned on with too large voltage difference between the drain and source or between the gate and source.

For overcoming these problems, several mixed-voltage I/O buffers have been proposed [1]-[3]. To eliminate undesirable short-circuit current and junction leakage, a mixed-voltage I/O buffer adopting a gate-voltage tracking and a dynamic n-well biasing techniques has been proposed [1]. In this I/O buffer, the gate voltage of the driver pull-up transistor is properly tracked to eliminate the short-circuit current from the I/O pad to the power supply. The n-well for the transistor is also biased

T.-h. Kim et al. (Eds.): CA/CES[3] 2011, CCIS 256, pp. 364–370, 2011.
© Springer-Verlag Berlin Heidelberg 2011

dynamically to eliminate the junction leakage through the well. However, the buffer requires many extra transistors having complicated connections, resulting in an increased design cost and layout area. To avoid the gate-oxide reliability problem, a mixed-voltage I/O buffer with NMOS blocking technique has been proposed [2]. The buffer has a dynamic gate-bias circuit (DGBC) to prevent the gate-oxide reliability issue by properly forcing the gate of the blocking transistor. But, operated at ultra-low voltage region, the use of these techniques can limit the voltage swing of received inputs, degrading the receiving speed. Moreover, they still suffer from the gate-oxide reliability problem during transition intervals from a receive mode to a transmit mode. For avoiding this problem during transition intervals, a mixed-voltage I/O buffer having hot-carrier prevention circuits (HCPCs) has been proposed [3]. HCPCs in the buffer have an important role of transferring charges deposited at nodes vulnerable to hot-carrier effect to the supply rail for preventing the gate-oxide reliability problem. But, this circuit still has a large area penalty and severe speed degradation at low supply voltage. In this paper, a novel mixed-voltage I/O buffer is proposed to provide a reliable and fast operation at ultra-low supply region with significantly reduced area penalty.

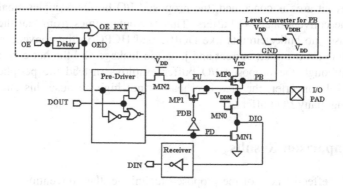

Fig. 1. Proposed low-voltage small-area mixed-voltage I/O buffer

2   Proposed Mixed-Voltage I/O Buffer

The proposed mixed-voltage I/O buffer is shown in Fig. 1. The buffer consists of a pre-driver, a main driver, a receiver, and a peripheral circuit (shown in the dotted box). PB, the substrate of MP0 and MP1, is driven by a level converter shifting the signal levels of an inverted OE_EXT from GND to VDD and from VDD to VDDH (2VDD). PU, the gate of MP0, is driven by the pre-driver via MN2, while PD, the gate of MN1, is directly driven by the pre-driver. Although PU is also connected to PB via MP1, signal fighting between the pre-driver output and PB does not occur since MP1 is turned on only when PU is at logic high. The gate of stacked NMOS transistor MN0 is connected to VDDM. In the transmit mode, OE becomes high, and both PU and PD go high or low depending on the logic value at DOUT, turning either MP0 or MN1 on for driving the I/O pad. During this mode, the voltage of PB stays at

VDD for avoiding the body effect of MP0. In the receive mode, PU and PD stay at VDDH and GND, respectively, turning MP0 and MN1 off. Note that the logic high of DIO reaches up to full VDD for incoming high data since the gate of MN0 is biased at VDDM. The voltage of PB stays at VDDH during this mode for preventing undesirable drain-well junction-leakage current of MP0. During the transition period from a receive mode to a transmit mode, in which OE is enabled and the pre-driver is not yet activated, residue charges deposited at PU and the I/O pad due to previous incoming high data are eliminated and their voltages settle at VDD and VDD+VTH, respectively. Although the settling voltage of I/O pad is somewhat higher than VDD, the drain-source voltage of MN0 during the transmit mode never exceeds VDD since the gate of this transistor is biased at VDDM and the source of this transistor does not abruptly go GND, resulting in no hot-carrier injection.

The proposed mixed-voltage I/O buffer has several advantages as compared to conventional mixed-voltage I/O buffers. As seen by the operation of the proposed buffer, the logic high of the received signal at DIO always reaches at VDD, allowing the voltage swing to be larger by VTH than those of the conventional I/O buffers. The full swing at DIO relieves an increase of receiver latency at scaled supply voltages, allowing for a faster operation of the proposed I/O buffer at ultra-low-voltage region. As far as layout area is concerned, the proposed I/O buffer occupies smaller silicon area than the conventional I/O buffers. This attribute comes from that the proposed I/O buffer uses no bulky circuits like DGBC and HCPC in the conventional buffers for eliminating short-circuit current and junction leakage and the hot-carrier injection problem. Although the proposed I/O buffer employs instead the peripheral circuit having a level converter, the area overhead is not high because this circuit can be shared among many I/O buffers.

3   Comparison Results

To verify the effectiveness of the proposed technique, the conventional [2], [3], and the proposed mixed-voltage I/O buffers all having 4 I/O pads have been designed in 130-nm CMOS process. With a supply voltage of 1.2 V, the voltage levels for VDDM and VDDH are set to be at 1.5 V (VDD + 0.3 V) and 2.4 V (2VDD), respectively. In the conventional I/O buffer in [2], the HCPC with shared level converter is used for eliminating hot-carrier injection.

Fig. 2 shows the simulated waveforms of the conventional and proposed mixed-voltage I/O buffers operating at 0.6 V. Fig. 2(a) depicts the waveforms during a receive mode in which the data is received from the I/O PAD. In this case, the rising slopes of DIO's in conventional I/O buffers are distorted at a voltage around 0.3 V since the I/O PAD ceases to drive the nodes at above this signal level. Hence, the latencies from DIO's to DIN's of the conventional I/O buffers are significantly increased. Meanwhile, the proposed I/O buffer has no such distortion at DIO, providing a far reduced latency. Numerically, the latency from DIO to DIN of the proposed mixed-voltage I/O buffer is shown to be 52% and 42% smaller than those of the conventional mixed-voltage I/O buffers in [2] and [3], respectively. Fig. 2(b) shows the simulated waveforms of mixed-voltage I/O buffers during a transmit mode in which the data is transmitted to the I/O PAD. The voltage level of I/O PAD driven by the conventional I/O buffer in [2] temporarily stops rising near 0.3 V, resulting in a severe distortion on the waveform of the I/O PAD. This is because the DGBC in the buffer is slower than the driver pull-up transistor. The waveforms at the I/O PAD's of the conventional I/O buffer in [3] and the proposed I/O buffer have no such distortion, and are very similar to each other. The latency of the proposed I/O buffer is slightly lower than those of the conventional I/O buffers.

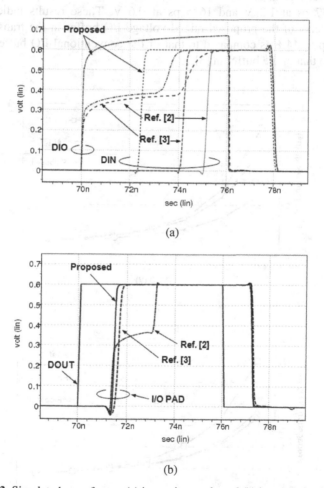

Fig. 2. Simulated waveforms: (a) in receive mode and (b) in transmit mode

For evaluating the speed performance of mixed-voltage I/O buffers depending on the change of supply voltage, simulated propagation delays for the receive and transmit modes for supply voltages ranging from 0.6 V to 1.2 V are simulated and compared in Fig. 3. The propagation delay from the I/O PAD to DIN for receiving a high data in the receive mode are depicted in Fig. 3(a). The receive delays of the conventional I/O buffers in [2] and [3] are 580 ps and 570 ps at 1.2 V, and go up to 5090 ps and 4200 ps at 0.6 V, respectively. The receive delays of the proposed I/O buffer are 520 ps at 1.2 V and 2440 ps at 0.6 V. These results indicate that the proposed mixed-voltage I/O buffer achieves up to 52% improvement in terms of receive delay. Fig. 3(b) depicts the simulated propagation delay from DOUT to I/O PAD for transmitting the data in the transmit mode. The transmit delays of the conventional I/O buffers in [2] and [3] are 359 ps and 378 ps at 1.2 V, and go up to 3008 ps and 1837 ps at 0.6 V, respectively. The transmit delays of the proposed I/O buffer are 377 ps at 1.2 V and 1675 ps at 0.6 V. These results indicate that the propagation delay of the proposed mixed-voltage I/O buffer in the transmit mode is reduced by up to 44% as compared to that of the conventional I/O buffer in [2], and comparable to that of the buffer in [3].

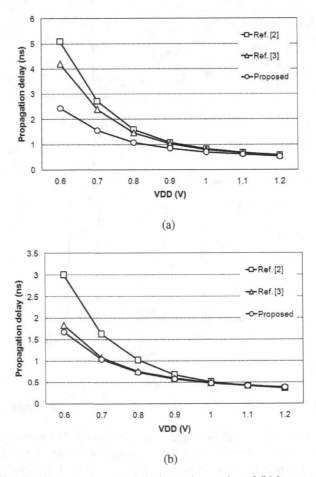

(a)

(b)

Fig. 3. Simulated propagation delay: (a) in receive mode and (b) in transmit mode

To evaluate the performance of mixed-voltage I/O buffers in terms of silicon area, the layout size occupied by each I/O buffer are compared in Fig. 4. For a fair comparison for the buffer size, the layout area of the I/O pad is excluded. In Fig. 4, 'Driver/Receiver' denotes the area occupied by the driver and receiver in each buffer dedicated to each I/O bit. 'Shared peripheral' means the area occupied by the peripheral circuit shared among four I/O bits, which is one-fourth of the actual layout size. 'DGBC' and "HCPC" indicate the area occupied by the dynamic gate-bias circuit and the hot-carrier prevention circuits used in the conventional mixed-voltage I/O buffers, respectively. Whereas the area of the conventional I/O buffers in [2] and [3] are 31475 um^2 and 31223 um^2, respectively, that of the proposed I/O buffer is as small as 19079 um^2, which indicates up to 39% reduction on silicon area. The area reduction of the proposed I/O buffer is mainly achieved by avoiding the use of bulky circuits like HCPC and DGBC.

To evaluate the immunity to the gate-oxide reliability problem due to hot-carrier injection, the dependency of the peak drain-source voltage of relevant transistors in each mixed-voltage I/O buffer on supply voltage is compared in Fig. 5. The peak drain-source voltage is measured during the transition period from a receive mode to a transmit mode. The range of the supply voltage in this comparison is from 0.6 V to 1.2 V. As shown in Fig. 5, the conventional mixed-voltage I/O buffer in [2] reveals peak drain-source voltages of 0.96 V at a 0.6 V supply and of 1.71 V at a 1.2 V supply, indicating that the buffer suffers from a severer hot-carrier injection as the supply voltage goes higher. For the conventional I/O buffer in [3], the peak drain-source voltage reaches up to 1.25 V at a 1.2 V supply, still suffering from the hot-carrier injection problem. Meanwhile, the peak drain-source voltage of the proposed mixed-voltage I/O buffer maintains to be less than 1 V at all supply voltages, and goes just around 0.95 V even at the maximum supply voltage of 1.2 V. These results indicate the the proposed mixed-voltage I/O buffer achieves up to 44% reduction on the peak drain-source voltage in the circuit, implying that it has far better immunity to the gate-oxide reliability problem.

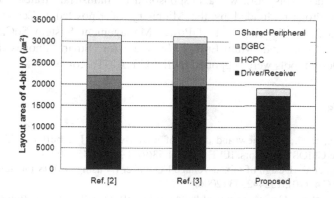

Fig. 4. Area comparison for mixed-voltage I/O buffers

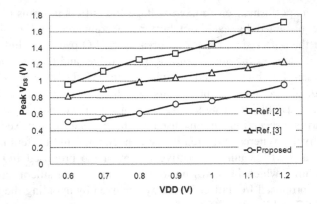

Fig. 5. Comparison for the peak drain-source voltages of mixed-voltage I/O buffers

4   Conclusion

In this paper, a novel low-voltage small-area mixed-voltage I/O buffer is proposed and evaluated. The proposed I/O buffer provides lower latency and smaller layout area than conventional I/O buffers. The conventional and proposed mixed-voltage I/O buffers are designed in a 130-nm CMOS process, whose evaluation results indicate that the proposed I/O buffer achieves up to 52% reduction on propagation delay. They also indicate that the proposed I/O buffer achieves up to 39% reduction on silicon area as compared to conventional mixed-voltage I/O buffers.

Acknowledgement. This work was supported by Korea Science and Engineering Foundation (R01-2006-11296-0). This work was also sponsored by ETRI System Semiconductor Industry Promotion Center, Human Resource Development Project for SoC Convergence. This work was also sponsored by Industrial Strategic Technology Development Program funded by the Minnistry of Knowledge Economy (MKE, Korea) (10039239, "Development of Power Management System SoC Supporting Multi-Battery Cells and Multi-Energy Sources for Smart Phones and Smart Devices"). Design tools were supported by IDEC KAIST, Korea.

References

1. Ker, M.D., et al.: Overview and design of mixed-voltage I/O buffers with low-voltage thin-oxide CMOS transistors. IEEE TCAS-I 53(9), 1934–1945 (2006)
2. Ker, M.D., et al.: Design of mixed-voltage I/O buffer by using NMOS-blocking technique. IEEE JSSC 41(10), 2324–2333 (2006)
3. Ker, M.D., et al.: Design on mixed-voltage I/O buffers with consideration of hot-carrier reliability. In: International Symposium on VLSI Design, Automation and Test, pp. 1–4 (April 2007)

Study for the Improvement of the Energy Storage System Efficiency Using Auto Level-Tuning Algorithm

Won Seok Choi[2,*], Kyoung-Bok Lee[1], Seounng-Gil Baek[1],
Gil-Dong Kim[2], Han-Min Lee[2], and Kyu-Joong Kim[1]

[1] Kyoung-Bok Lee, Daejeon Metropolitan Express Transit Corporation,
110 Samjeong-Dong Dong-gu, Daejeon 300-738, Korea
[2] Department of Electrical Engineering, Hanbat National University, Daejeon Korea
{bjhlkb,baeker,1122kjw}@hanmail.net, {gdkim,hanmin}@krri.re.kr,
wschoi@hanbat.ac.kr

Abstract. This paper is about control algorithms that bi-direction DC-DC Converter using Super Capacitor and regenerative power from DC feeding system in electrical train. In order to take advantage of regenerative energy efficient, charge and discharge level value of energy storage system serve as an important factor. Respect to output fluctuations of the substation and catenary voltage changing, we offers Charge-Discharge Auto Level Tuning Algorithms to improve system following of Energy Storage System.

Keywords: Bi-direction DC-DC converter, Energy storage system(ESS), Auto Level Tuning.

1   Introduction

The development of renewable energy for controlling the CO_2 emission as an urgent issue is rising as Tokyo Protocol takes effect in order to prevent global warming due to the energy depletion and the environmental pollution with facing the environmental crisis represented by climatic change and the resource crisis represented by high oil prices at the same time.

While an urban railway subway train runs, the energy storage system runs after it saves in energy storage equipment without wasting regenerative energy disappeared in the air. It can contribute to preventing of regeneration canceled, energy conservation, eco-friendly and efficient usage of electric power, effect of CO_2 reduction as well as reduction of electric energy consumption with a reusing system while the train is operating (powering).

In order to utilize regenerative energy efficiently, the charge-discharge level value of energy saving system have to play a major role. However, the change of catenary voltage according to operating trains and the change of substation's output voltage have made it difficult to use this system effectively.

---

* Corresponding author.

T.-h. Kim et al. (Eds.): CA/CES³ 2011, CCIS 256, pp. 371–380, 2011.
© Springer-Verlag Berlin Heidelberg 2011

This paper shows the optimized method of energy storage system by applying a charge-discharge Auto Level Tuning algorithm to raise the reduction amount of power and suitableness of a system with the change of catenary voltage according to operating trains and the change of substation's output voltage and a control algorithm of DC-DC converter controlling regenerative power for usage of the regenerative power produced in power supply system of DC subway.

2   Catenary Voltage Change of DC Substation

2.1   Power Supply System of DC Subway

Substation facilities are composed of 2500[kW], 12pulse rectifier and 2500[kW] rectifier has an ability to convert AC into DC. The following Table 1 shows the rectifier rating of substation facilities.

Table 1. Rectifier Rating

Item	Voltage
Rated DC Voltage	1500[V]
Secondary voltage of transformer	600[V]
Voltage ratio	1.35
Secondary voltage of rectifier	810[V]
Secondary voltage of rectifier 12pulse	1620[V]

2.2   Analysis of Catenary Voltage Change of DC Substation

In DC feeding system of train, bus power through transformer and rectifier are decided by the power supply change of Korea Electric Power Corporation(KEPCO).

The power supply change of KEPCO is permitted up to ±3 [%], and we found that catenary voltage of a bottom part of the rectifier as the result of actual measurement was fluctuated from 1612 to 1640[V] by 1625[V] standard without a regular pattern.

Fig. 1 is a result of measuring one wire of a bottom part of the rectifier with DCPT while a train operating and we can realize that catenary voltage is wavering with thick outline measured regardless of operating a train. Here, sharply shaped measured voltage is generated as the train powering and regenerative braking.

The energy storage system(ESS) used in public is set up to charge-discharge the energy storage system when certain voltage becomes higher or lower than catenary voltage under the premise that catenary voltage is regular. However, according to expand substation capacity, it is difficult to set up the voltage starting energy storage devices discharge as certain voltage in the situation that a drop of electric pressure made at the moment that train powering is very small.

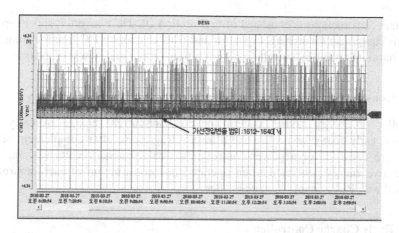

Fig. 1. Analysis of catenary voltage change (Recorder scale 300:1[V])

Also, while a drop of electric pressure made with other problems at the moment that train powering is below 15[V]. it might not enable the performance of charge-discharge of actual energy saving system to go on smoothly because the catenary voltage has a range above 30[V]. For these reason, it needs to be changed the maintaining and starting the charge-discharge voltage of energy storage system according to change of catenary voltage. However, it is very hard to track the change of catenary voltage because the change of catenary voltage is not to have a regular pattern by a train operation pattern or certain time.

3   Construction of Energy Storage System

3.1   Construction of Bi-direction DC-DC Converter

Power converter device of energy storage system is consisted to charge-discharge energy bi-directionally by duty ratio with applying bi-direction DC-DC converter as you see Fig. 2.

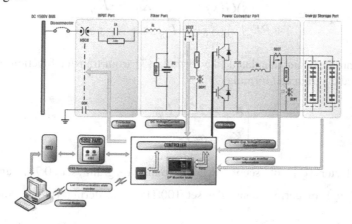

Fig. 2. Block diagram of energy storage system

System constructions is consisted of bi-direction DC-DC converter, super capacitor which is equipment for storing, capacitor and filter reactor on DC-link for eliminating higher harmonic wave by switching between transformer and power of catenary.

3.2   Construction of System Controller

Controller of energy saving system for constant-current charge of early super capacitor, early charge controller and a train retrogressive after complement of early charge are consisted of a power controller to make catenary voltage stable using regenerative energy generated when operated and construction of each controller is designed with PI-PI double loop controller.

3.3   Early Charge Controller

Early charge controller to charge early super capacitor and consisted of soft start controller for prevention of rush current by dv/dt, current controller for constant current and voltage controller for controlling duty ratio according to output value of current controller when super capacitor is totally discharged.

Real soft start controller controls system for 1.2[sec] after converter operation and the rest parts are controlled by double loop controller for constant current control.

System transfer function $G(s)$ is calculated by bi-direction DC-DC converter like formula (1).

$$G(s) = \frac{I_{sc}(s)}{V_{BL}(s)} = \frac{1}{sL_{BL}} \tag{1}$$

Close system transfer function $H(s)$ from calculated system transfer function of second-degree round diagram and formula (2)

$$H(s) = \frac{PI_{cc}(s)G(s)}{1 + PI_{cc}(s)G(s)} = \frac{K_{Ip}s + K_{Ii}}{L_{BL}s^2 + K_{Ip}s + K_{Ii}} \tag{2}$$

Current controller gain calculated like formula (3) from transfer function of second-degree round diagram and formula (2).

$$\begin{cases} K_{Ip} = 2\xi\omega_n L_{BL} \\ K_{Ii} = \omega_n^2 L_{BL} \end{cases} \tag{3}$$

Damping factor (ξ) of second-degree round diagram set 0.707 and corner frequency (ω_n) of current controller set 100[Hz] considering voltage controller of inner loop.

System transfer function $G(s)$ are described like formula (4) from current equation flowing super capacitor in voltage controller of inner loop.

$$G(s) = \frac{V_{sc}(s)}{I_{sc}(s)} = \frac{1}{sC_{sc}} \tag{4}$$

Close system transfer function $H(s)$ from calculated system transfer function derive from formula (5).

$$H(s) = \frac{PI_{vc}(s)G(s)}{1 + PI_{vc}(s)G(s)} = \frac{K_{Vp}s + K_{Vi}}{C_{sc}s^2 + K_{Vp}s + K_{Vi}} \tag{5}$$

Gain selection of voltage controller calculated like formula (6) in the same way as current controller from transfer function of second-degree round diagram.

$$\begin{cases} K_{Vp} = 2\xi\omega_n C_{sc} \\ K_{Vi} = \omega_n^2 C_{sc} \end{cases} \tag{6}$$

Corner frequency set 1[kHz] considering response speed and switching frequency for current controller of external loop in this system.

3.4 Power Mode Controller

Fig. 3 is an abbreviated composition diagram of power mode controller applied to a test. When it is power mode, a current controller as an inner loop has faster corner frequency than power controller's as an external loop is located in inner loop unlike an early charging mode.

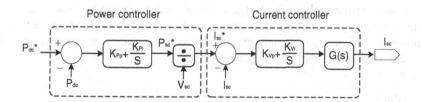

Fig. 3. Composition of power control mode

Power controller, external loop, is controlling power of DC link on power mode. So, impedance of DC link estimate value and actual value are always same. Finally, it becomes calculated on the same as error value compensated by V_{dc}^2.

System transfer function $G(s)$ in power controller is calculated by a relationship of formula (7) as system transfer function like formula (8).

$$P_{dc} \cong P_{sc} = \frac{1}{2}C_{sc}V_{sc}^2 = V_{sc}I_{sc} \tag{7}$$

$$G(s) = \frac{P_{dc}(s)}{I_{sc}(s)} = V_{sc}(s) = \frac{1}{sC_{sc}} \tag{8}$$

3.5   Charge-Discharge Auto Level Tuning Algorithm

Energy storage system construction and controller design are planned from the supposition that catenary voltage is in the steady condition. However, ideal catenary voltage like this is not only existed in the country but also all over the world actually.

In other words, as points must be considered when charge and discharge are started the range of catenary voltage fluctuation, starting to charge and discharge accordingly, and change of maintain voltage are required.

Energy storage system must be not charged with substation power when the system is charged by analyzing movement of a rectifier's output power in substation, don't have to set as a constant discharge system with choosing too high discharge starting voltage. Therefore, if charge-discharge starting voltage of energy storage system is fixed, energy saving rate cannot help falling owing to staying on the over charge and the over discharge with a result that super capacitor has much discharging conditions than charging' or much charging conditions than discharging' according to change of the substation power and a train operation.

The following shows charge-discharge control block diagram of energy storage system applied Auto Level Tuning Algorithm.

Fig. 4 is as the flow chart of charge-discharge Auto Level Tuning shows, unless charge or discharge is started for a period of time on the over discharge or over charge of super capacitor with changing power of a main line, upon predicting and deciding that catenary normal voltage is changed, charge and discharge becomes started with raising or lowering charge-discharge starting voltage step by step. As a result, we can maximize the efficiency of system by raising the using rate of energy storage system with increasing the number of charge or discharge.

4   Test

4.1   Test Conditions

Table 2. shows charge-discharge conditions of energy storage system applied to the test and limited charge-discharge capacity of super capacitor, and current able to flow through super capacitor is limited to 200[A].

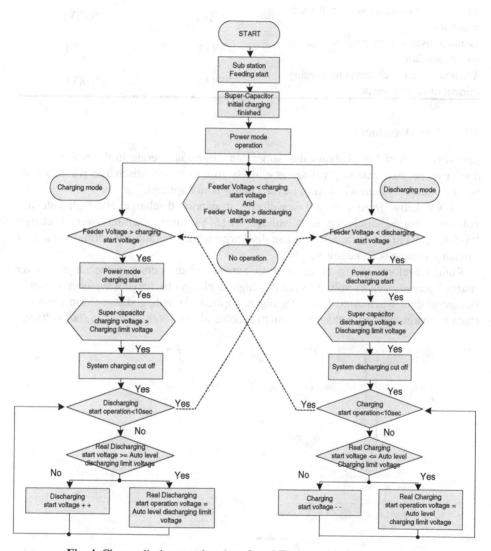

Fig. 4. Charge-discharge value Auto Level Tuning control block diagram

Table 2. Energy storage system charge-discharge conditions

Item	Normal set	Auto Level Tuning set
Charging start voltage	1660[V]	1645[V]~1660[V]
Discharging start voltage	1615[V]	1615[V]~1624[V]
Limited over charging voltage of super capacitor	1050[V]	1050[V]
Limited over discharging voltage of super capacitor	450[V]	450[V]
Limited over discharging/charging current of super capacitor	200[A]	200[V]

4.2   Test Waveform

Left waveform of Fig. 5 shows that super capacitor can operate in the range of over discharge because catenary voltage is entirely low as charge-discharge waveform of energy storage system when Auto Level Tuning is not applied.

As we know from enlarged waveform, it cannot discharge although catenary voltage becomes discharge start voltage 1615[V] after reaching over discharge level(450[V]) of super capacitor. It can discharge while operating at normal voltage of catenary voltage become lower.

Right waveform of Fig. 5 shows super capacitor can operate in the range of over charge because catenary voltage is entirely high as charge-discharge waveform of energy storage system when Auto Level Tuning is applied. As enlarged waveform shows, it starts to charge catenary voltage is about to become above 1660[V], charge start voltage.

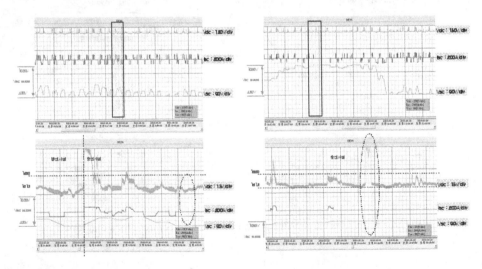

Fig. 5. Operation test waveform of over discharge/charge when Auto Tuning is not applied

However, because normal voltage of catenary voltage had been high, when a train runs back after reaching over charge level(1050[V]) of super capacitor, it cannot discharge because catenary voltage cannot go down below discharge start voltage 1615[V].

Therefore, it cannot be charged up although regenerative power is generated before catenary voltage goes down below discharge start voltage according to train operations and change of substation output.

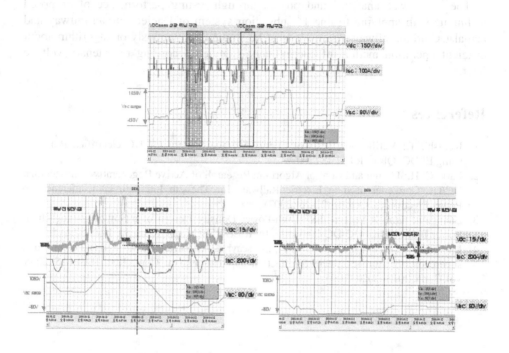

Fig. 6. Test waveform applying Auto Level Tuning algorithm

Fig. 6 is test waveforms applied charge-discharge Auto Level Tuning algorithms. As an enlarged waveform shows, it must be started to charge by increasing charge starting voltage step by step with deciding that catenary normal voltage gets lower if it is not a charge operation for a period of time on the over discharge of super capacitor according to a train operation and an output change of substation.

Also, it must be started to discharge by increasing discharge starting voltage step by step with deciding that catenary normal voltage gets higher unless it is a discharge operation for a period of time on the over discharge.

5   Conclusion

Energy saving system can improve the effect on reducing electricity cost through reusing regenerative energy generated when a train operates, and can be expected the effect on reduction of CO_2 emission reduction of peak power, stabilization of catenary voltage and substation facility of urban railway organization in the era of high oil price.

This paper suggests charge and discharge Auto Level Tuning algorithm can get effect on reduction of optimal energy with bi-direction DC-DC converter able to realize stabilization of catenary voltage and use regenerative energy of DC urban railway efficiently.

The effect was analyzed and proved through testing performance of proposed technique with applying to line 1st substation system of Daejeon urban railway and actual DC urban railway system. It must be studied continuously on algorithm about efficient operation method of energy saving device according to catenary voltage later.

References

1. Konishi, T.: Verification Tests of Energy Storage System for DC electrified Railways using ELDC. QR of RTRI 48 (2007)
2. Park, C.-H.: Design and Control Algorithm Research of Active Regenerative Bidirectional DC/DC Converter used in Electric Railway. In: The 7th International Conference on Power Electronics, October 22-26 (2007)
3. Zhang, J., Kim, R.Y., Lai, J.S.: High-Power Density Design of a Soft-Switching High-Power Bidirectional DC-DC Converter. In: IEEE PESC Conf. Rec., pp. 1–7 (2006)
4. Lhomme, W., Delarue, P., Barrade, P., Bouscayrol, A., Ruffer, A.: Design and control of a supercapacitor storage system for traction applications. In: Conf. Rec. IEEEIAS 2005, vol. 3, pp. 2013–2020 (2005)

Development of Strain Sensor Using Aligned Carbon Nanotubes

Yongho Choi[1], Seok-Mo Hong[1], and Byungjoo Park[2,*]

[1] Department of Materials Science and Engineering, Jungwon University
Goesan-eup, Goesan-Gun, Chungcheongbuk-do, 367-805, Korea
yhchoi@jwu.ac.kr, sgkim@hnu.kr
[2] Department of Multimedia Engineering, Hannam University
133 Ojeong-dong, Daeduk-gu, Daejeon, Korea
bjpark@hnu.kr

Abstract. Carbon nanotube has received great research attentions as a next generation material due to its superior electrical, mechanical and chemical properties. Using the properties, carbon nanotube is able to improve the sensitivity of bio sensors, gas sensors and mechanicals sensor. When a single walled carbon nanotube is adapted for the mechanical sensor, a mechanical force deforms the single walled carbon nanotube and changes its electrical properties. The electrical change is due to the change of energy band gap of the single walled carbon nanotube. In this study, we demonstrate an efficient structure of the strain sensor to raise its sensitivity using aligned and multiple numbers of single walled carbon nanotubes. The structure of strain sensor demonstrated in this study is much reliable and efficient compared to the sensor with individual single walled carbon nanotube.

Keywords: MIPv6, HMIPv6, Reverse Binding, Look-Up.

1 Introduction

Carbon nanotube (CNT) shows excellent electrical, mechanical, chemical, and physical properties and receives a many interest for various applications.[1-7] The CNT has a higher heat conductivity compared to a diamond and has a great tensile strength as young's modulus of 4.5 x 1010 Pa.[1] Also the CNT has a high specific surface area due to its small dimension and shows active absorption behavior with other chemical species at the surface. Moreover, it permits higher current density than copper and shows a big possibility of using it as electrical conductors. Single walled carbon nanotube (SWNT) can be either metallic or semiconducting material depending on its geometry.[6] During a past decade, the CNT has been a very interesting subject in science and engineering fields and researched to utilize it in electrical, physical and chemical applications.[5, 8, 9]

The SWNT has a high surface aspect ratio which gives high sensitivity when it is used in bio or chemical sensors. However, the nano-scale dimension of SWNT is an

---

* Corresponding author.

T.-h. Kim et al. (Eds.): CA/CES³ 2011, CCIS 256, pp. 381–386, 2011.
© Springer-Verlag Berlin Heidelberg 2011

obstacle for device fabrication and the difficulty of modulation its geometry slows the development in applications.[2, 10-13]

In this research, we fabricate mechanical strain sensor using aligned and multiple numbers of SWNTs. In previous studies, an individual semiconducting SWNT was investigated under mechanical stress.[14, 15] The multiple numbers of SWNTs in our device is able to improve a detection limit of the sensor and also provides higher sensitivity compared to individual SWNT sensor. Therefore, the strain sensor demonstrated in this study is much practical and closer to commercialization.

2   Experiment and Discussion

Figure 1 shows the fabrication procedures of catalysts for SWNTs growth. Firstly, SiO2 was thermally grown on Si substrate. In order to create metal electrodes on the SiO2 substrate, photoresist (S1813) was spin coated and patterned by photolithography as shown in figure 1(a) and figure 1(b).

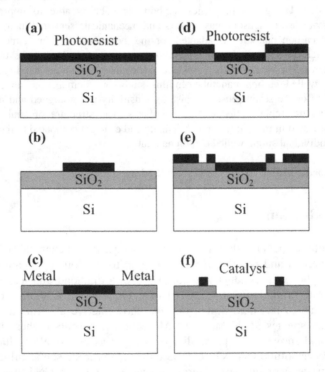

Fig. 1. Catalyst preparation for electric field assisted SWNTs growth

A metal, Mo, was electron-beam evaporated under vacuum on the sample and the photoresist remained on the substrate were removed by lift-off process with Acetone with a short period sonication, see figure 1(c). We conducted a patterning of catalyst to synthesis the SWNTs at desired locations. Before the deposition of catalysts, photoresist was spin coated and then patterned by photolithography as shown in figure 1(d) and figure 1(e). Finally catalyst nano particles were spin coated on the whole substrate and the remained photoresist was removed by lift-off process, see figure 1 (f). The sample was then moved to the growth system for SWNTs growth.

Figure 2 shows the electric field assisted chemical vapor deposition system. The sample was put inside of 1 inch quartz tube and each Mo electrodes on the substrate were separately connected to positive and negative terminal of power supply which was outside of the quartz tube. The applied voltage 10V from the positive terminar. The flow rate of 200 sccm of Ar and 200 sccm of H2 gases were introduced in the tube and the temperature of the furnace was increased to 900oC. When the temperature reached to 900oC, Ar flow was stopped and introduced CH4 gas with flow rate of 200 sccm in the tube for 10 mins to synthesis the SWNTs. Finally, CH4 flow was stopped and Ar gas with flow rate of 200 sccm was introduced in the tube and the temperature of the furnace was decreased. When the temperature was decreased to room temperature, the sample was taken out and characterized by atomic force microscopy.

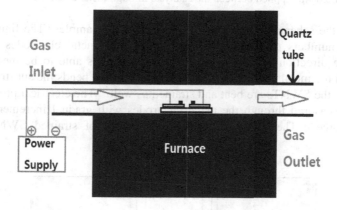

Fig. 2. Schematic diagram of electric field assisted chemical vapor deposition system

Figure 3 is the schematic diagram of the fabricated sample which used for the growth process. During the growth period, electric field was applied between the catalysts through metal electrodes. The main reason for applying electric field is to improve directionally of the growing SWNTs.[16] The SWNTs are aligned in one direction following the direction of electric field. The CNTs grown by chemical deposition system without electric field are mostly oriented in random directions and which decreases the sensitivity of the strain sensor.[17, 18] Consequently, the SWNTs aligned in one direction are able to improve the sensitivity and reliability of the strain sensor.

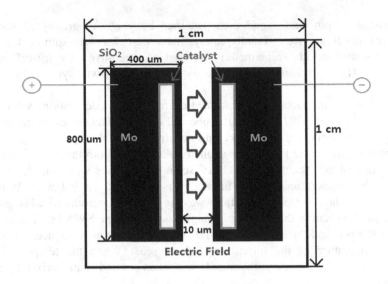

Fig. 3. Schematic diagram of fabricated sample used for SWNTs growth. During the growth period, electric field was applied between the catalysts through metal electrodes.

Figure 4 is the schematic diagram of final state of the sample. The figure shows that multiple numbers of SWNTs are connecting two metal electrodes and well aligned in one direction. The property of strain sensor is able to be measured by pressing down the metal electrodes. The mechanical force bends the substrate and at the same time, the SWNTs are bent and strained as well. The electrical properties of SWNTs are measured through the metal electrodes with gradual increments of the mechanical force. The study of electrical properties of strained SWNTs is in progress.

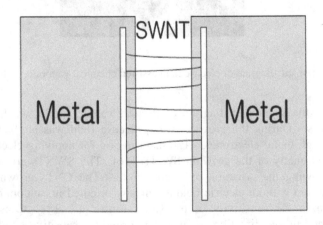

Fig. 4. Schematic Diagram of Final State of Sample

Figure 5 is the atomic force microscopy image of electric field assisted grown SWNTs. As shown in the figure, the SWNTs are well aligned in one direction. Some SWNTs are not connecting the metal electrodes and the length of SWNTs is quite rely on the duration of growth. The growth time in our experiments was ~10 mins and it should be longer for higher yield of SWNTs connections which improves the sensitivity and reliability of the strain sensor.

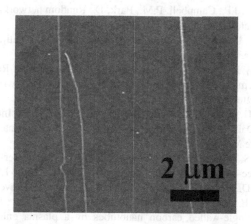

Fig. 5. Atomic force microscopy image of electric field assisted grown SWNTs

3   Conclusion

The efficient structure of the strain sensor using SWNTs was demonstrated. The SWNTs were grown with electric field and the electric fiend improved the directionality of SWNTs. The multiple numbers of SWNTs and well aligned SWNTs in the strain sensor structure are able to raise the sensitivity and reliability of the strain sensor compared to the sensor with individual SWNT and/or randomly oriented SWNTs.

Acknowledgments. This research was supported by Basic Science Research Program through the National Research Foundation of Korea (NRF) funded by the Ministry of Education, Science and Technology (2011-0015131).

References

1. Dresselhaus, M., Dresselhaus, G., Avouris, P.: Carbon Nanotubes: Synthesis, Structure, Properties and Applications. Springer, Heidelberg (2001)
2. Javey, A., Wang, Q., Ural, A., Li, Y.M., Dai, H.J.: Carbon nanotube transistor arrays for multistage complementary logic and ring oscillators. Nano Letters 2(9) (2002)
3. Aguirre, C.M., Auvray, S., Pigeon, S., Izquierdo, R., Desjardins, P., Martel, R.: Carbon nanotube sheets as electrodes in organic light-emitting diodes. Applied Physics Letters 88(18) (2006)

4. Appenzeller, J., Knoch, J., Martel, R., Derycke, V., Wind, S.J., Avouris, P.: Carbon nanotube electronics. IEEE Transactions on Nanotechnology 1(4) (2002)
5. Bradley, K., Gabriel, J.C.P., Gruner, G.: Flexible nanotube electronics. Nano Letters 3(10) (2003)
6. Dresselhaus, M.S., Dresselhaus, G., Eklund, P.C.: Science of fullerenes and carbon nanotubes. Academic Press, San Diego (1996)
7. Kim, P., Lieber, C.M.: Nanotube nanotweezers. Science 286(5447) (1999)
8. Snow, E.S., Novak, J.P., Campbell, P.M., Park, D.: Random networks of carbon nanotubes as an electronic material. Applied Physics Letters 82(13) (2003)
9. Ozel, T., Gaur, A., Rogers, J.A., Shim, M.: Polymer electrolyte gating of carbon nanotube network transistors. Nano Letters 5(5) (2005)
10. Fan, Z., Ho, J.C., Jacobson, Z.A., Yerushalmi, R., Alley, R.L., Razavi, H., Javey, A.: Wafer-Scale Assembly of Highly Ordered Semiconductor Nanowire Arrays by Contact Printing. Nano Letters (2007)
11. Javey, A., Kim, H., Brink, M., Wang, Q., Ural, A., Guo, J., McIntyre, P., McEuen, P., Lundstrom, M., Dai, H.: High- k dielectrics for advanced carbon-nanotube transistors and logic gates. Nature Materials 1(4) (2002)
12. Javey, A., Nam, S., Friedman, R.S., Yan, H., Lieber, C.M.: Layer-by-layer assembly of nanowires for three-dimensional, multifunctional electronics. Nano Letters 7(3) (2007)
13. Li, Y.M., Mann, D., Rolandi, M., Kim, W., Ural, A., Hung, S., Javey, A., Cao, J., Wang, D.W., Yenilmez, E., Wang, Q., Gibbons, J.F., Nishi, Y., Dai, H.J.: Preferential growth of semiconducting single-walled carbon nanotubes by a plasma enhanced CVD method. Nano Letters 4(2) (2004)
14. Minot, E.D., Yaish, Y., Sazonova, V., Park, J.-Y., Brink, M., McEuen, P.L.: Tuning Carbon Nanotube Band Gaps with Strain. Physical Review Letters 90(15) (2003)
15. Yamada, T., Hayamizu, Y., Yamamoto, Y., Yomogida, Y., Izadi-Najafabadi, A., Futaba, D.N., Hata, K.: A stretchable carbon nanotube strain sensor for human-motion detection. Nat. Nano 6(5)
16. Ural, A., Li, Y.M., Dai, H.J.: Electric-field-aligned growth of single-walled carbon nanotubes on surfaces. Applied Physics Letters 81(18) (2002)
17. Adhikari, A.R., Huang, M.B., Wu, D., Dovidenko, K., Wei, B.Q., Vajtai, R., Ajayan, P.M.: Ion-implantation-prepared catalyst nanoparticles for growth of carbon nanotubes. Applied Physics Letters 86(5) (2005)
18. Peng, H.B., Ristroph, T.G., Schurmann, G.M., King, G.M., Yoon, J., Narayanamurti, V., Golovchenko, J.A.: Patterned growth of single-walled carbon nanotube arrays from a vapor-deposited Fe catalyst. Applied Physics Letters 83(20) (2003)

Design of a High Voltage Acceleration Power Supply for a Neutral Beam Injection System

Jeong-Tae Jin, Seung-Ho Jeong, Kwang-Won Lee, Dae-Sik Chang,
Doo-Hee Chang, and Byung-Hoon Oh

Korea Atomic Energy Research Institute,
1045 Daedeok-daero, yuseong-gu, Daejeon, 305-353
jtjin@kaeri.re.kr

Abstract. An improved design of a 120 kV, 70 A DC power supply for accelerating the ions produced by the ion source of the neutral beam injection system at the Korea Atomic Energy Research Institute (KAERI) is presented. The power supply consists of 4 sets of fixed 22 kV DC power modules, 1 set of 11 kV DC power module, and 40 sets of 800 V DC power modules. It is controlled through a type of step pulse modulation with different step voltages, that is, 22 kV and 11 kV DC voltages controlled by gas insulated switch gears and 800 V DC voltages controlled by IGBT switches.

Keywords: neutral beam, acceleration power supply, high voltage, high power.

1   Introduction

To deliver sufficient heating power to the plasma inside of a Tokamak reactor, external heating power systems such as an electron cyclotron resonance heating system, ion-cyclotron resonance heating system, lower hybrid current drive system, or neutral beam injection system (NBI system) are required. Among these, the NBI system is known to be the most powerful plasma heating system.

The power supply system for the NBI system at KAERI consists of a filament power supply, an arc power supply, an acceleration power supply, a deceleration power supply, and so on. Among these, the acceleration power supply is the most important, and the output ratings are required to be more than DC 100 kV, 70 A for the ion source [1].

2   Design of the Power Supply

Figure 1 shows the circuit diagram of the acceleration power supply. In figure 1, inputs of 3-phase 22.9 kV ac are connected to the high-voltage power modules (HVTRs and LVTRs) through charging switches (CHSs) and charging resistors or main switches (MSs). The initial charging currents flow through the charging switches and charging resistors in order to prevent the initial surge currents, and then through the main switches.

T.-h. Kim et al. (Eds.): CA/CES³ 2011, CCIS 256, pp. 387–390, 2011.
© Springer-Verlag Berlin Heidelberg 2011

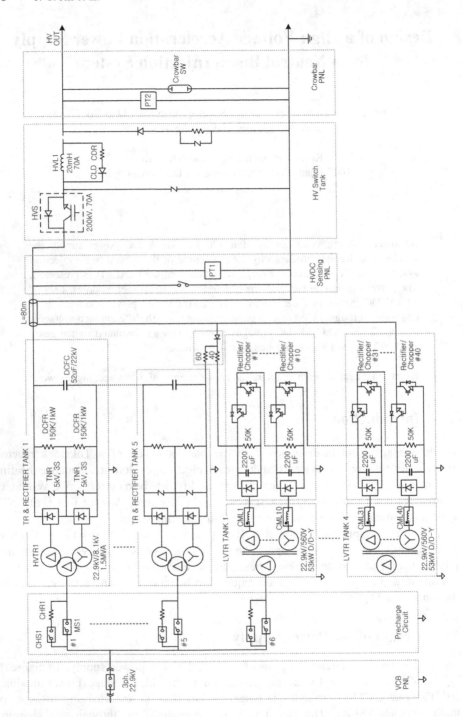

Fig. 1. Circuit diagram of the acceleration power supply

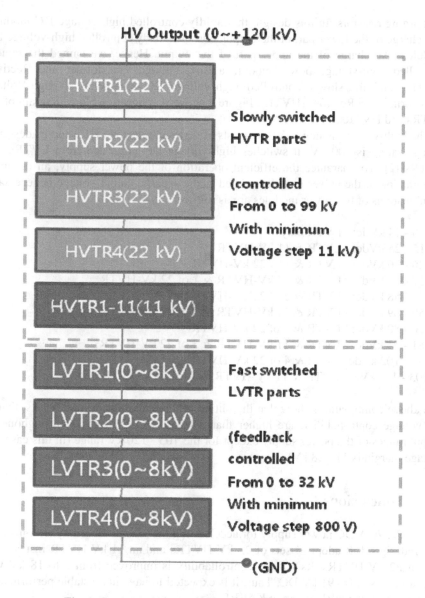

Fig. 2. Connection block diagram of the LVTRs and HVTRs

The rapidly controlled high-voltage DC modules (LVTR1~LVTR4) consist of 40 sets of 800 V DC power modules, and each of them consists of a transformer, protective inductor, diodes, capacitors, and IGBTs controlled by optical control commands.

The slowly controlled high-voltage DC modules (HVTR's) consist of 4 sets of 22 kV DC power modules (HVTR1~HVTR4) and a set of 11 kV DC power module (HVTR1-11). Each of the modules consists of a transformer, diodes, a capacitor, and discharging resistors. In this design, the rapidly controlled high voltage DC modules take charge of the lower part of the output, and the slowly controlled high-voltage DC modules take charge of the upper part of the output. Hence, we named the rapidly controlled high-voltage power module a Low-Voltage Transformer and Rectifier (LVTR), and the slowly controlled high-voltage DC module as a High-Voltage Transformer and Rectifier (HVTR). Figure 2 shows a connection block diagram of the LVTRs and HVTRs.

The high-voltage switch (HVS) consists of series-connected FETs, and its designed voltage rating is 200 kV. It switches high-voltage DC generated from LVTRs and HVTRs [2]. To guarantee the efficient operation of the power supply, an optimum combination of the power modules related to the specific output voltage is necessary. Combinations of the power modules are as follows:

```
  0 - 14 kVdc:  LVTR only
 15 - 25 kVdc:  LVTR & 11 kV-HVTR
 26 - 36 kVdc:  LVTR & 1 of 22 kV-HVTR
 37 - 47 kVdc:  LVTR & 11 kV-HVTR & 1 of 22 kV-HVTR
 48 - 58 kVdc:  LVTR & 2 of 22 kV-HVTR
 59 - 69 kVdc:  LVTR & 11 kV-HVTR & 2 of 22 kV-HVTR
 70 - 80 kVdc:  LVTR & 3 of 22 kV-HVTR
 81 - 91 kVdc:  LVTR & 11 kV-HVTR & 3 of 22 kV-HVTR
 92 - 102 kVdc: LVTR & 4 of 22 kV-HVTR
103 - 120 kVdc: LVTR & 11 kV-HVTR & 4 of 22kV-HVTR.
```

The above combinations show that the output voltage margins of the LVTRs, that is, the voltage controllability, are higher than 18 kV (18 - 28 kV) all throughout the output ranges of the power supply except for the 103 - 120 kV range (in this case, the voltage margin is 11 - 28 kV).

3   Conclusions

A 120 kV, 70 A DC power supply for accelerating the ions produced by an ion source was redesigned. It adopts 4 sets of 22 kV HVTRs and an 11 kV HVTR instead of 5 sets of 22 kV HVTRs. Its voltage controllability is improved from 7 to 18 kV with output ranges of 0 - 91 kV DC. Thus, it is expected to have more stable performances when used for the NBI system at KAERI.

References

1. Oh, B.H., et al.: Development of KSTAR Neutral Beam Heating System. KAERI Research Report KAERI/RR-2853 (2006)
2. Song, I.H., Ahn, H.S., Kim, Y.K., Shin, H.S., Choi, C.H., Cho, M.-H.: Development of the 120kV/70A High Voltage Switching System with MOSFETs Operated by Simple Gate Control Unit. In: Power Electronics Specialists Conference (2002)

Retraction Note to: Control and Automation, and Energy System Engineering

Tai-hoon Kim[1], Hojjat Adeli[2], Adrian Stoica[3], and Byeong-Ho Kang[4]

[1] Hannam University, Daejeon, Korea
taihoonn@empas.com
[2] The Ohio State University, Columbus, OH, USA
adeli.1@osu.edu.
[3] Jet Propulsion Laboratory, Pasadena, CA, USA
adrian.stoica@jpl.nasa.gov
[4] University of Tasmania, Hobart, TAS, Australia
byeong.kang@utas.edu.au

Retraction Note to:
Chapter 8
Characteristics Analysis of the Motor Block Lattice Resistor of a High Speed Train by Structure Improvement
DOI: 10.1007/978-3-642-26010-0_8

The chapter starting on page 65 of this publication has been retracted due to multiple publication

Retraction Note to:
Chapter 38
Characteristics Analysis of the Motor Block Lattice Resistor of a High Speed Train by Structure Improvement
DOI: 10.1007/978-3-642-26010-0_38

The chapter starting on page 302 of this publication has been retracted due to multiple publication.

The updated original online version for these chapters can be found at
DOI: 10.1007/978-3-642-26010-0_8
DOI: 10.1007/978-3-642-26010-0_38
DOI: 10.1007/978-3-642-26010-0_39
DOI: 10.1007/978-3-642-26010-0_40

T.-h. Kim et al. (Eds.): CA/CES³ 2011, CCIS 256, pp. E1–E2, 2011.
© Springer-Verlag Berlin Heidelberg 2017
DOI: 10.1007/978-3-642-26010-0_48

Retraction Note to:
Chapter 39
Estimation of Deterioration Degree in Overhead Transmission
Lines by Tension Load Analysis
DOI: 10.1007/978-3-642-26010-0_39

The chapter starting on page 312 of this publication has been retracted as it is a duplicate of the paper starting on page 86

Retraction Note to:
Chapter 40
Structure Vibration Analysis and Active Noise Control of a Power
Transformer by Mobility Measurement
DOI: 10.1007/978-3-642-26010-0_40

The chapter starting on page 322 of this volume has been retracted due to multiple publication.

Author Index

Printed in the United States
By Bookmasters